THE DARK HUNTERS

VOLUME ONE

SHERRILYN KENYON

ADAPTED BY
JOSHUA HALE FIALKOV

ART BY
CLAUDIA CAMPOS WITH
GLASS HOUSE GRAPHICS AND
GROUNDBREAKERS STUDIOS

ADAPTED BY
BILL TORTOLINI

ST. MARTIN'S GRIFFIN   NEW YORK

This is a work of fiction. All of the characters, organizations, and events portrayed in this novel are either products of the author's imagination or are used fictitiously.

THE DARK-HUNTERS VOLUME I. Copyright © 2009 by Sherrilyn Kenyon. Illustrations copyright © 2009 by Dabel Brothers Productions, LLC. All rights reserved. Printed in the United States of America. For information, address St. Martin's Press, 175 Fifth Avenue, New York, N.Y. 10010.

Art by Claudia Campos with Glass House Graphics and Groundbreakers, Inc.
Adaptation by Joshua Hale Fialkov.
Lettering by Zach Matherney.
Additional design by Bill Tortolini.

www.stmartins.com

ISBN-13: 978-0-312-37687-1
ISBN-10: 0-312-37687-1

First Edition: July 2009

10 9 8 7 6 5 4 3 2 1

the DARK HUNTERS

VOLUME ONE

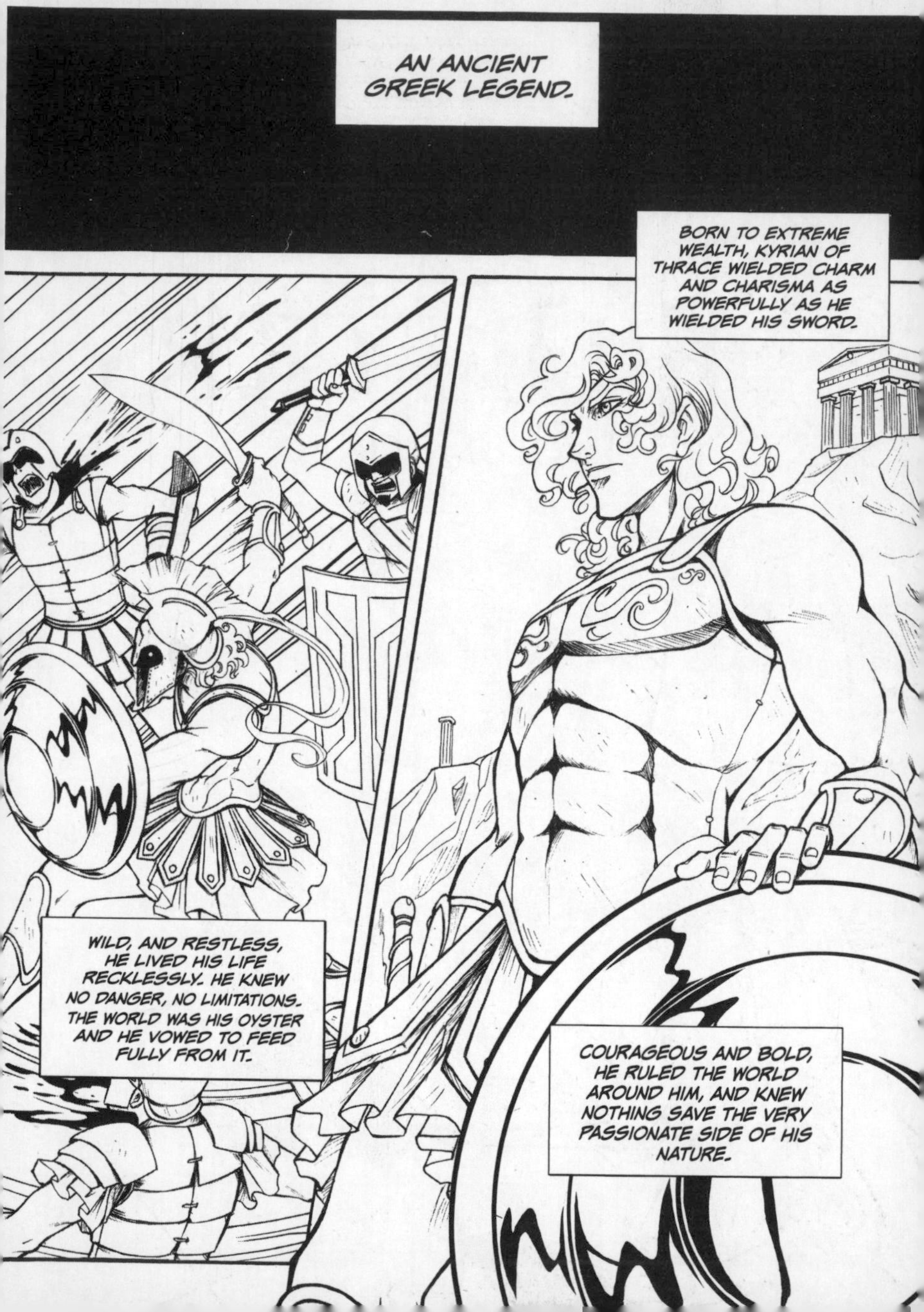
AN ANCIENT GREEK LEGEND.
BORN TO EXTREME WEALTH, KYRIAN OF THRACE WIELDED CHARM AND CHARISMA AS POWERFULLY AS HE WIELDED HIS SWORD.
COURAGEOUS AND BOLD, HE RULED THE WORLD AROUND HIM, AND KNEW NOTHING SAVE THE VERY PASSIONATE SIDE OF HIS NATURE.
WILD, AND RESTLESS, HE LIVED HIS LIFE RECKLESSLY. HE KNEW NO DANGER, NO LIMITATIONS. THE WORLD WAS HIS OYSTER AND HE VOWED TO FEED FULLY FROM IT.

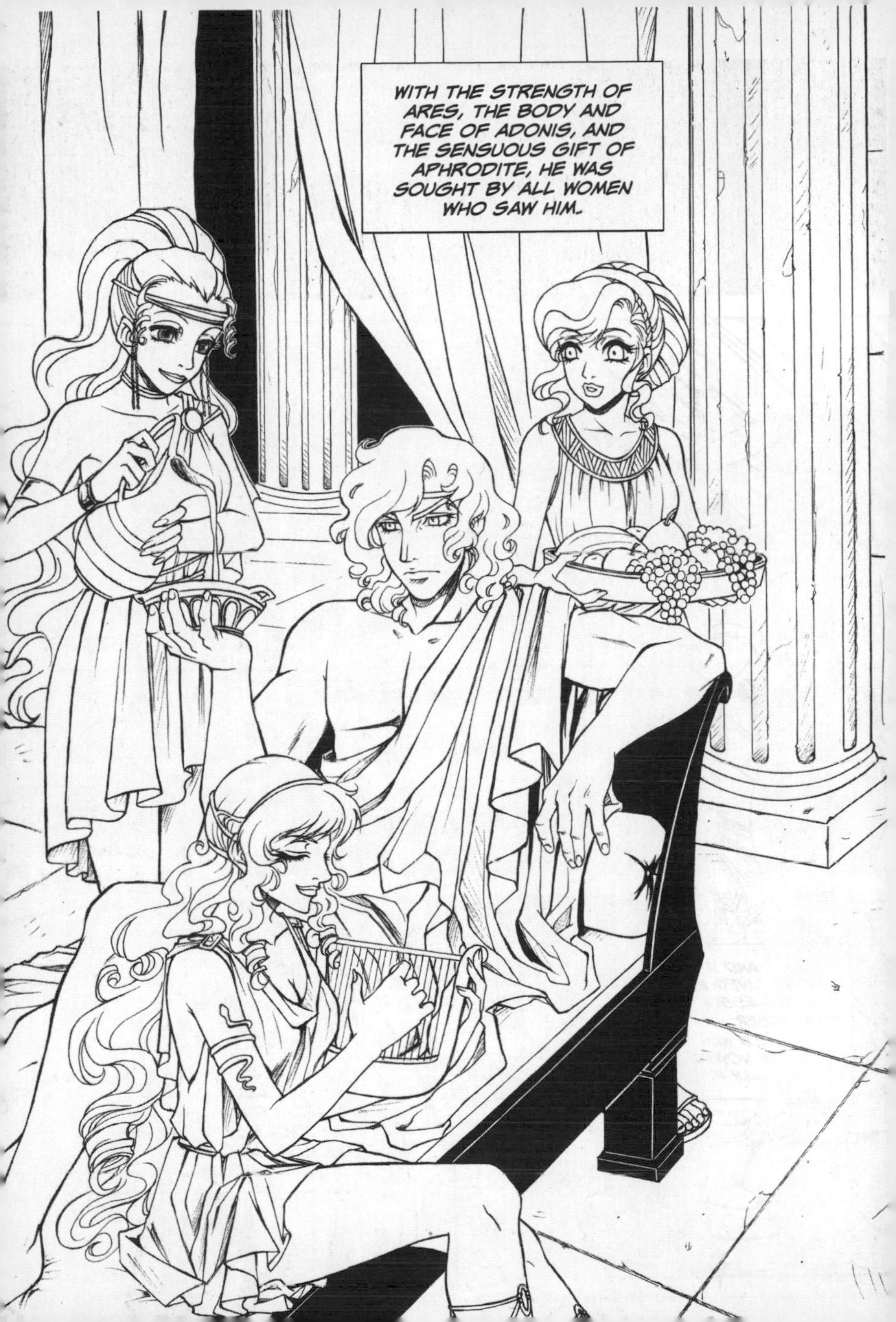
WITH THE STRENGTH OF ARES, THE BODY AND FACE OF ADONIS, AND THE SENSUOUS GIFT OF APHRODITE, HE WAS SOUGHT BY ALL WOMEN WHO SAW HIM.

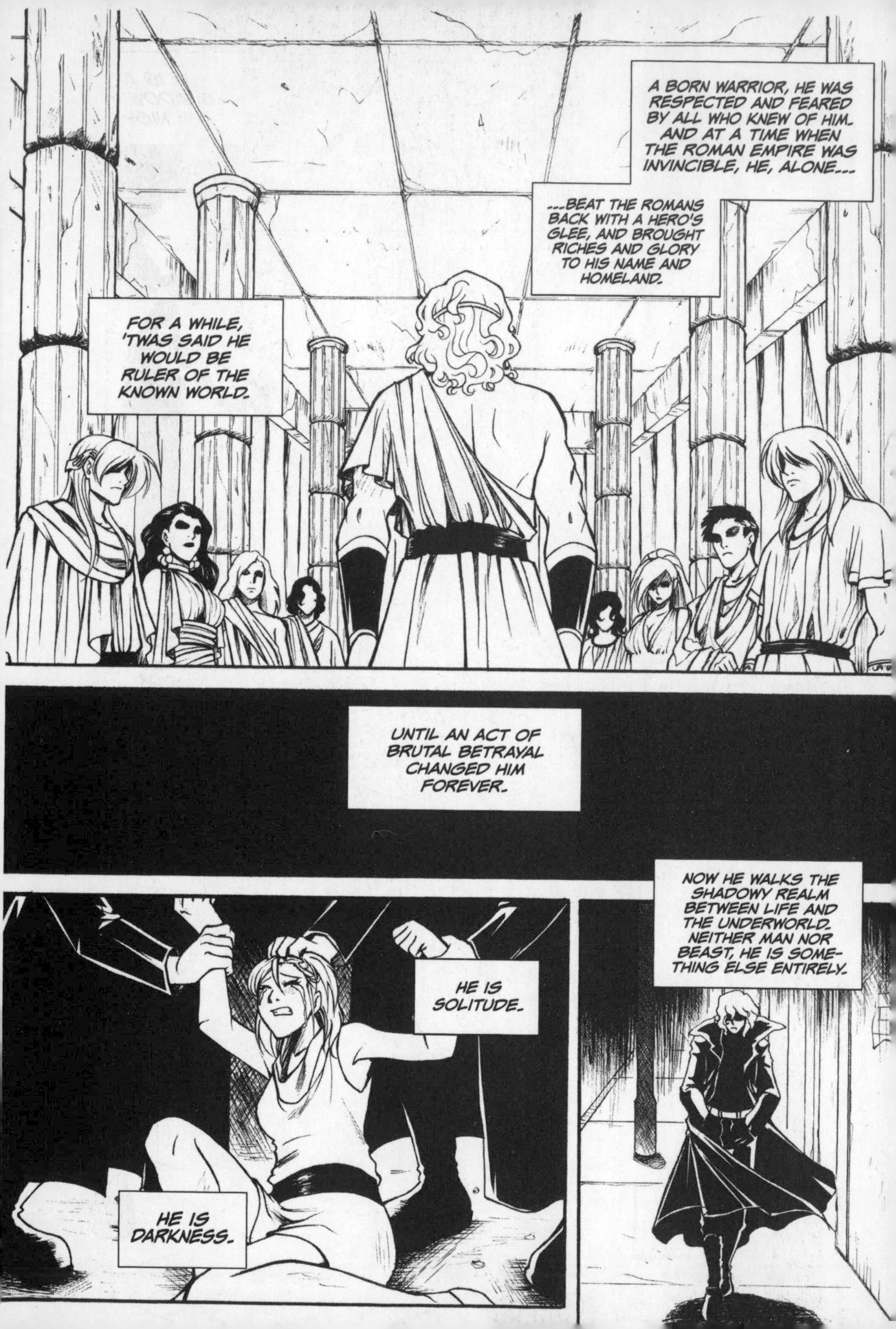
A BORN WARRIOR, HE WAS RESPECTED AND FEARED BY ALL WHO KNEW OF HIM. AND AT A TIME WHEN THE ROMAN EMPIRE WAS INVINCIBLE, HE, ALONE...
...BEAT THE ROMANS BACK WITH A HERO'S GLEE, AND BROUGHT RICHES AND GLORY TO HIS NAME AND HOMELAND.
FOR A WHILE, 'TWAS SAID HE WOULD BE RULER OF THE KNOWN WORLD.
UNTIL AN ACT OF BRUTAL BETRAYAL CHANGED HIM FOREVER.
NOW HE WALKS THE SHADOWY REALM BETWEEN LIFE AND THE UNDERWORLD. NEITHER MAN NOR BEAST, HE IS SOMETHING ELSE ENTIRELY.
HE IS SOLITUDE.
HE IS DARKNESS.

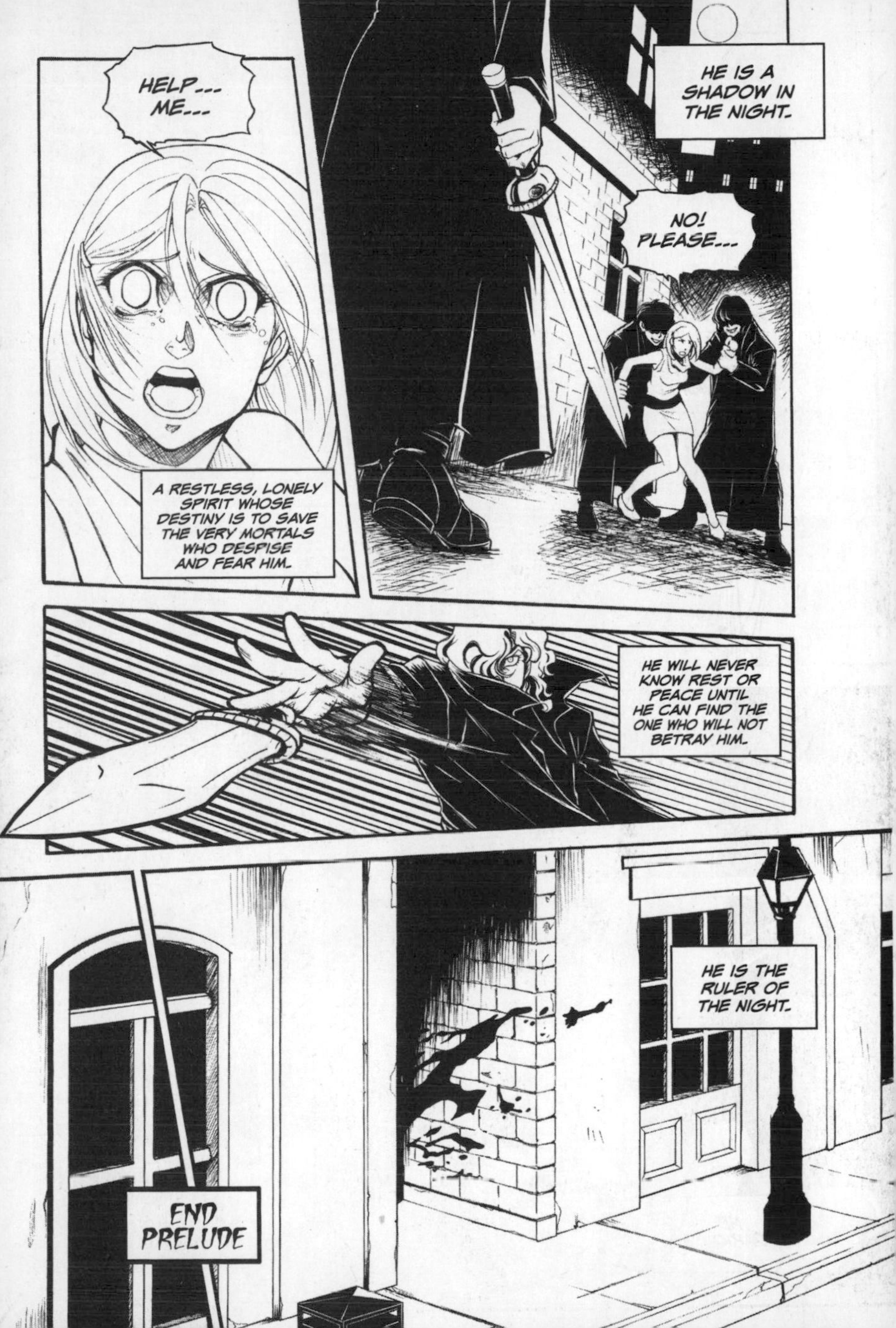
HE IS A SHADOW IN THE NIGHT.
NO! PLEASE...
HELP... ME...
A RESTLESS, LONELY SPIRIT WHOSE DESTINY IS TO SAVE THE VERY MORTALS WHO DESPISE AND FEAR HIM.
HE WILL NEVER KNOW REST OR PEACE UNTIL HE CAN FIND THE ONE WHO WILL NOT BETRAY HIM.
HE IS THE RULER OF THE NIGHT.
END PRELUDE

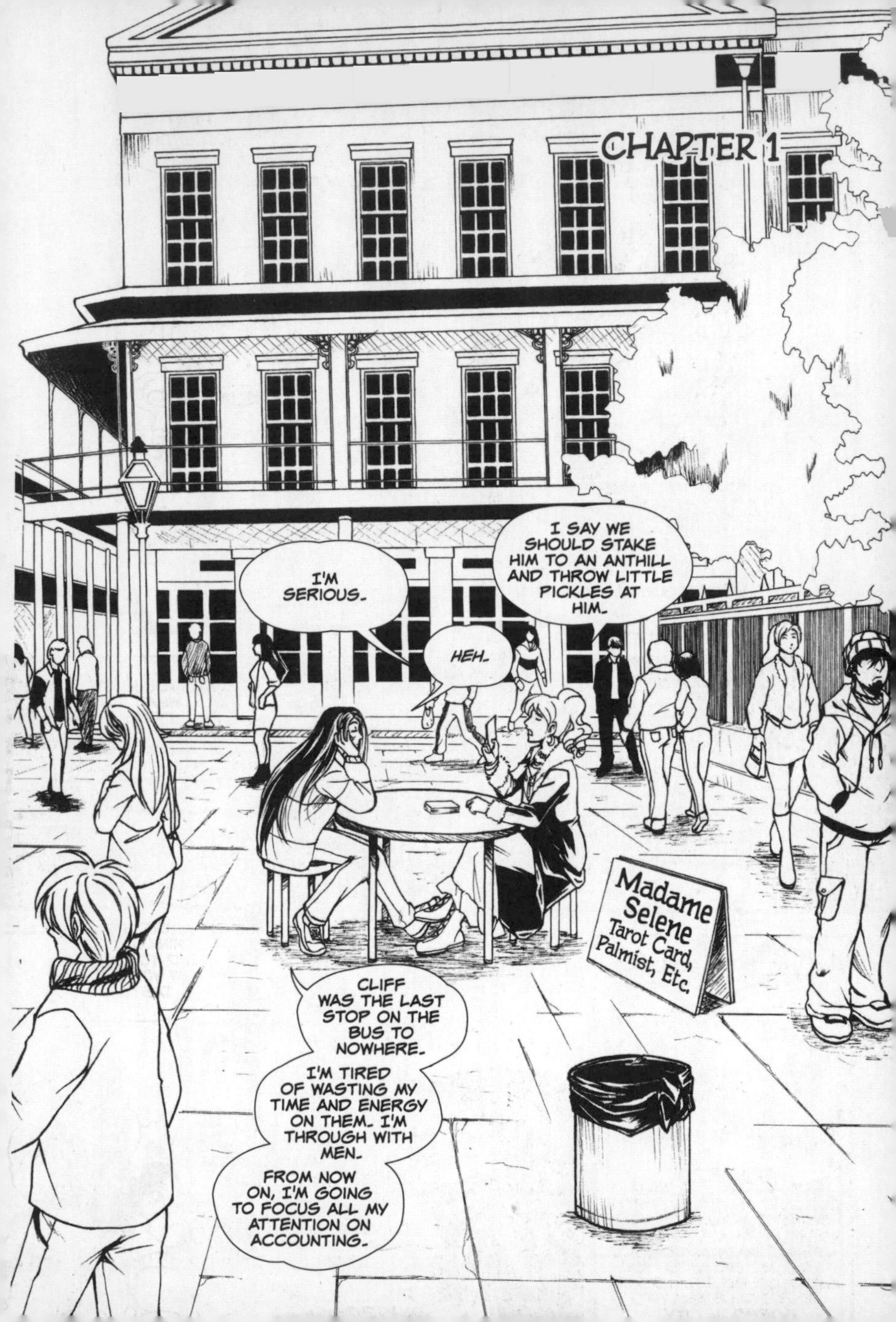
CHAPTER 1
I SAY WE SHOULD STAKE HIM TO AN ANTHILL AND THROW LITTLE PICKLES AT HIM.
I'M SERIOUS.
HEH.
Madame Selene Tarot Card, Palmist, Etc.
CLIFF WAS THE LAST STOP ON THE BUS TO NOWHERE.
I'M TIRED OF WASTING MY TIME AND ENERGY ON THEM. I'M THROUGH WITH MEN.
FROM NOW ON, I'M GOING TO FOCUS ALL MY ATTENTION ON ACCOUNTING.

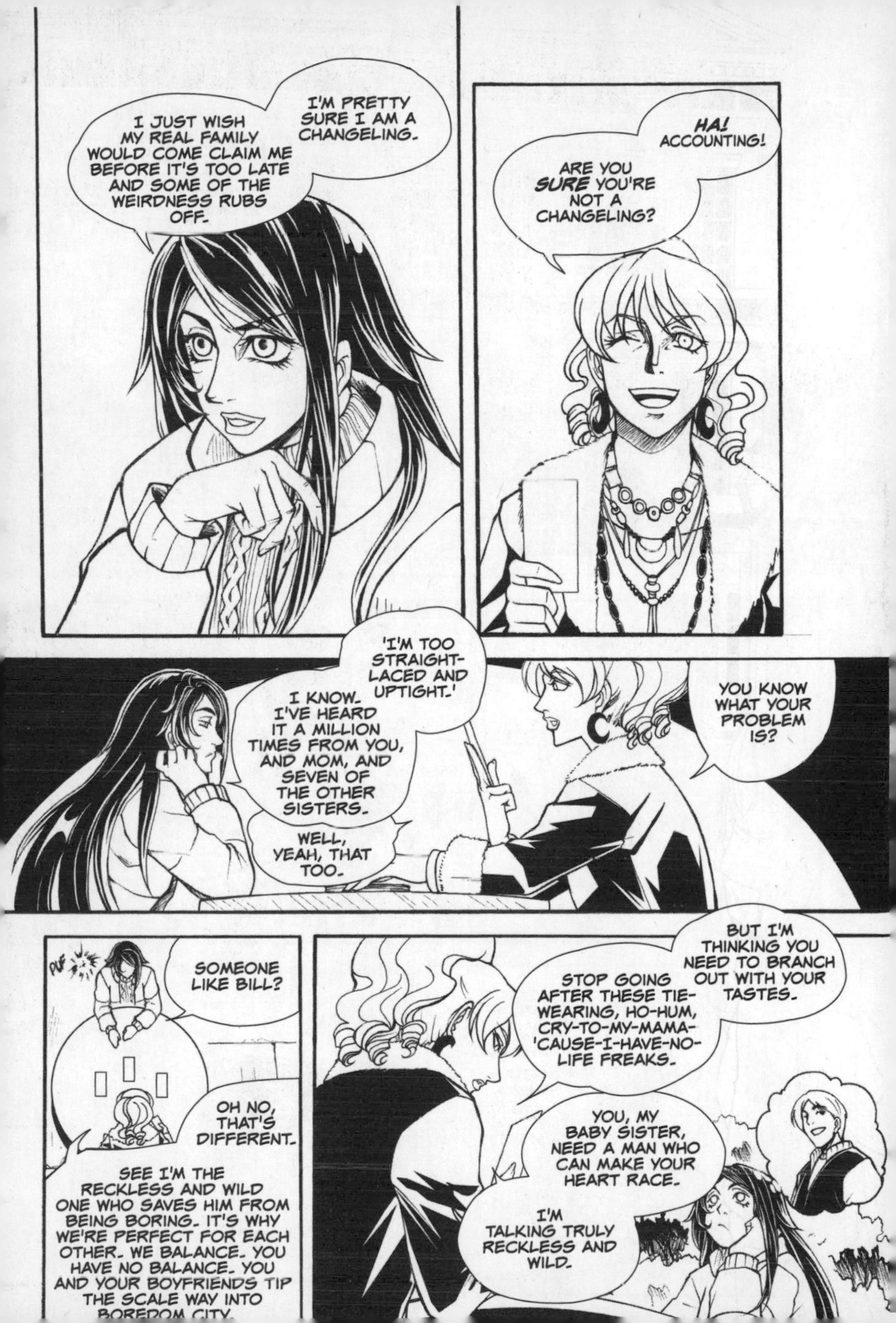
HA! ACCOUNTING!
ARE YOU *SURE* YOU'RE NOT A CHANGELING?
I'M PRETTY SURE I AM A CHANGELING.
I JUST WISH MY REAL FAMILY WOULD COME CLAIM ME BEFORE IT'S TOO LATE AND SOME OF THE WEIRDNESS RUBS OFF.
YOU KNOW WHAT YOUR PROBLEM IS?
'I'M TOO STRAIGHT-LACED AND UPTIGHT.'
I KNOW. I'VE HEARD IT A MILLION TIMES FROM YOU, AND MOM, AND SEVEN OF THE OTHER SISTERS.
WELL, YEAH, THAT TOO.
BUT I'M THINKING YOU NEED TO BRANCH OUT WITH YOUR TASTES.
STOP GOING AFTER THESE TIE-WEARING, HO-HUM, CRY-TO-MY-MAMA-'CAUSE-I-HAVE-NO-LIFE FREAKS.
YOU, MY BABY SISTER, NEED A MAN WHO CAN MAKE YOUR HEART RACE.
I'M TALKING TRULY RECKLESS AND WILD.
PUF
SOMEONE LIKE BILL?
OH NO, THAT'S DIFFERENT.
SEE I'M THE RECKLESS AND WILD ONE WHO SAVES HIM FROM BEING BORING. IT'S WHY WE'RE PERFECT FOR EACH OTHER. WE BALANCE. YOU HAVE NO BALANCE. YOU AND YOUR BOYFRIENDS TIP THE SCALE WAY INTO BOREDOM CITY.

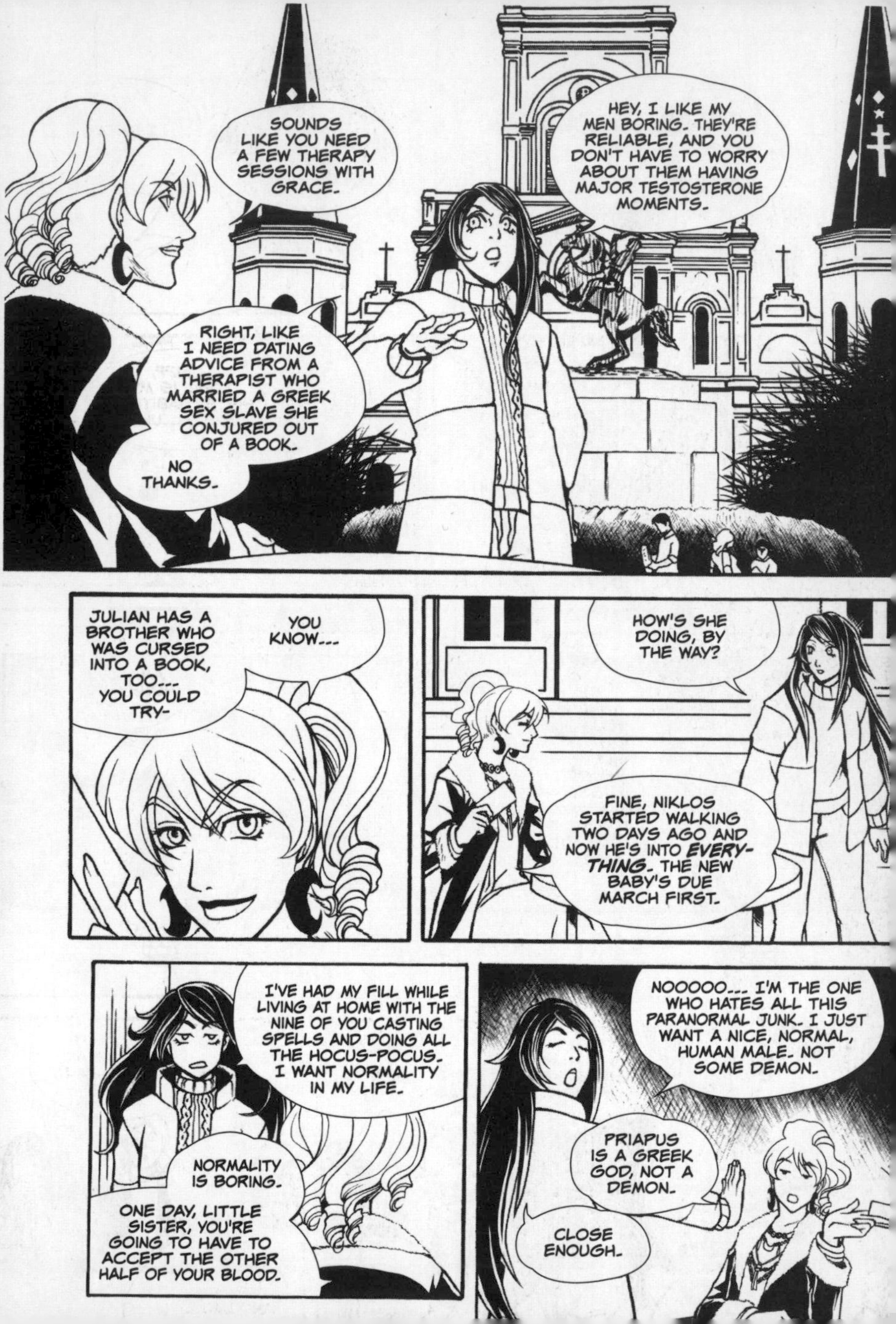
HEY, I LIKE MY MEN BORING. THEY'RE RELIABLE, AND YOU DON'T HAVE TO WORRY ABOUT THEM HAVING MAJOR TESTOSTERONE MOMENTS.
SOUNDS LIKE YOU NEED A FEW THERAPY SESSIONS WITH GRACE.
RIGHT, LIKE I NEED DATING ADVICE FROM A THERAPIST WHO MARRIED A GREEK SEX SLAVE SHE CONJURED OUT OF A BOOK.
NO THANKS.
HOW'S SHE DOING, BY THE WAY?
FINE, NIKLOS STARTED WALKING TWO DAYS AGO AND NOW HE'S INTO ***EVERY-THING***. THE NEW BABY'S DUE MARCH FIRST.
YOU KNOW...
JULIAN HAS A BROTHER WHO WAS CURSED INTO A BOOK, TOO... YOU COULD TRY-
NOOOOO... I'M THE ONE WHO HATES ALL THIS PARANORMAL JUNK. I JUST WANT A NICE, NORMAL, HUMAN MALE. NOT SOME DEMON.
PRIAPUS IS A GREEK GOD, NOT A DEMON.
CLOSE ENOUGH.
I'VE HAD MY FILL WHILE LIVING AT HOME WITH THE NINE OF YOU CASTING SPELLS AND DOING ALL THE HOCUS-POCUS. I WANT NORMALITY IN MY LIFE.
NORMALITY IS BORING.
ONE DAY, LITTLE SISTER, YOU'RE GOING TO HAVE TO ACCEPT THE OTHER HALF OF YOUR BLOOD.

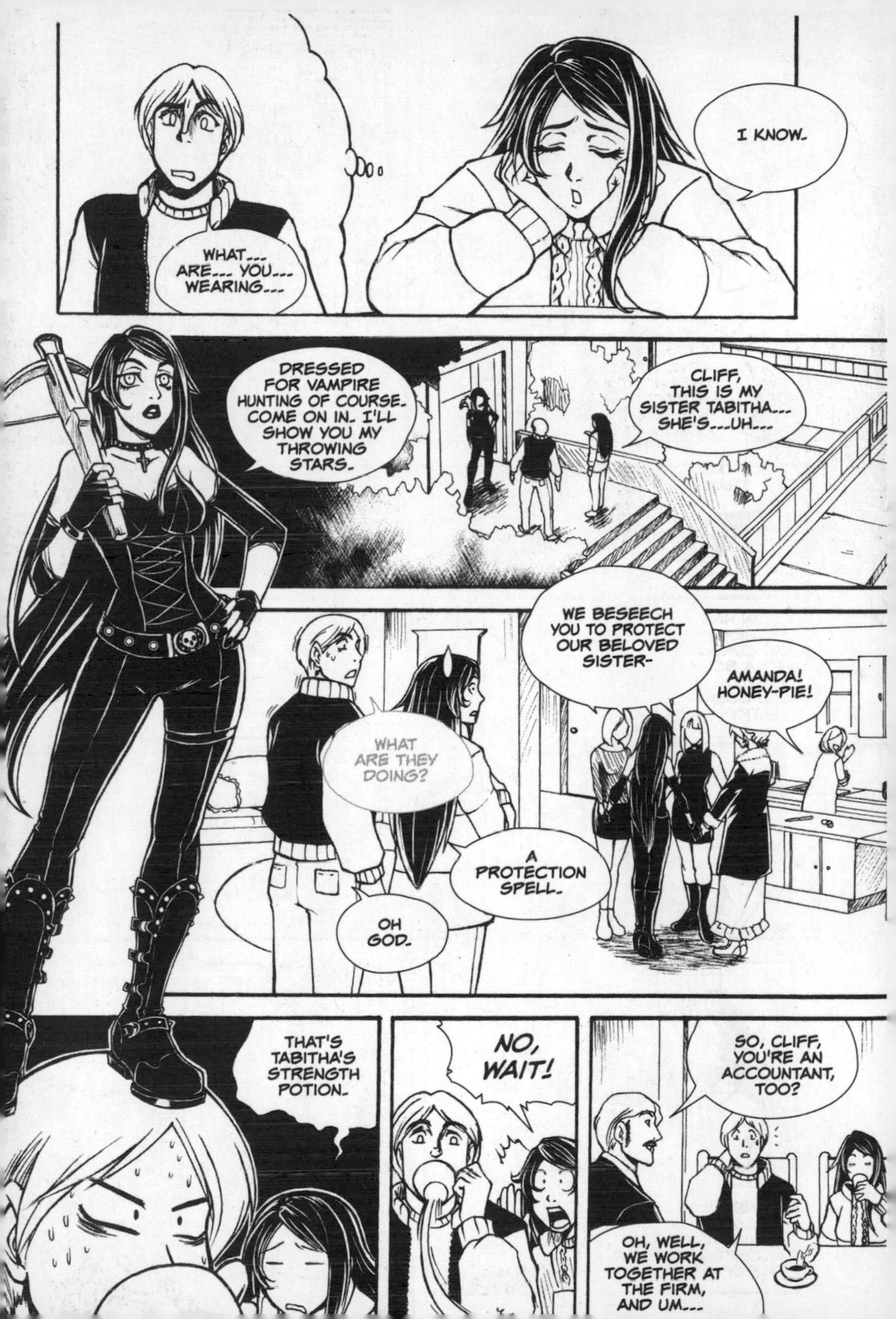
I KNOW.
WHAT... ARE... YOU... WEARING...
CLIFF, THIS IS MY SISTER TABITHA... SHE'S...UH...
WE BESEECH YOU TO PROTECT OUR BELOVED SISTER-
AMANDA! HONEY-PIE!
WHAT ARE THEY DOING?
A PROTECTION SPELL.
OH GOD.
DRESSED FOR VAMPIRE HUNTING OF COURSE. COME ON IN. I'LL SHOW YOU MY THROWING STARS.
SO, CLIFF, YOU'RE AN ACCOUNTANT, TOO?
OH, WELL, WE WORK TOGETHER AT THE FIRM, AND UM...
NO, WAIT!
THAT'S TABITHA'S STRENGTH POTION.

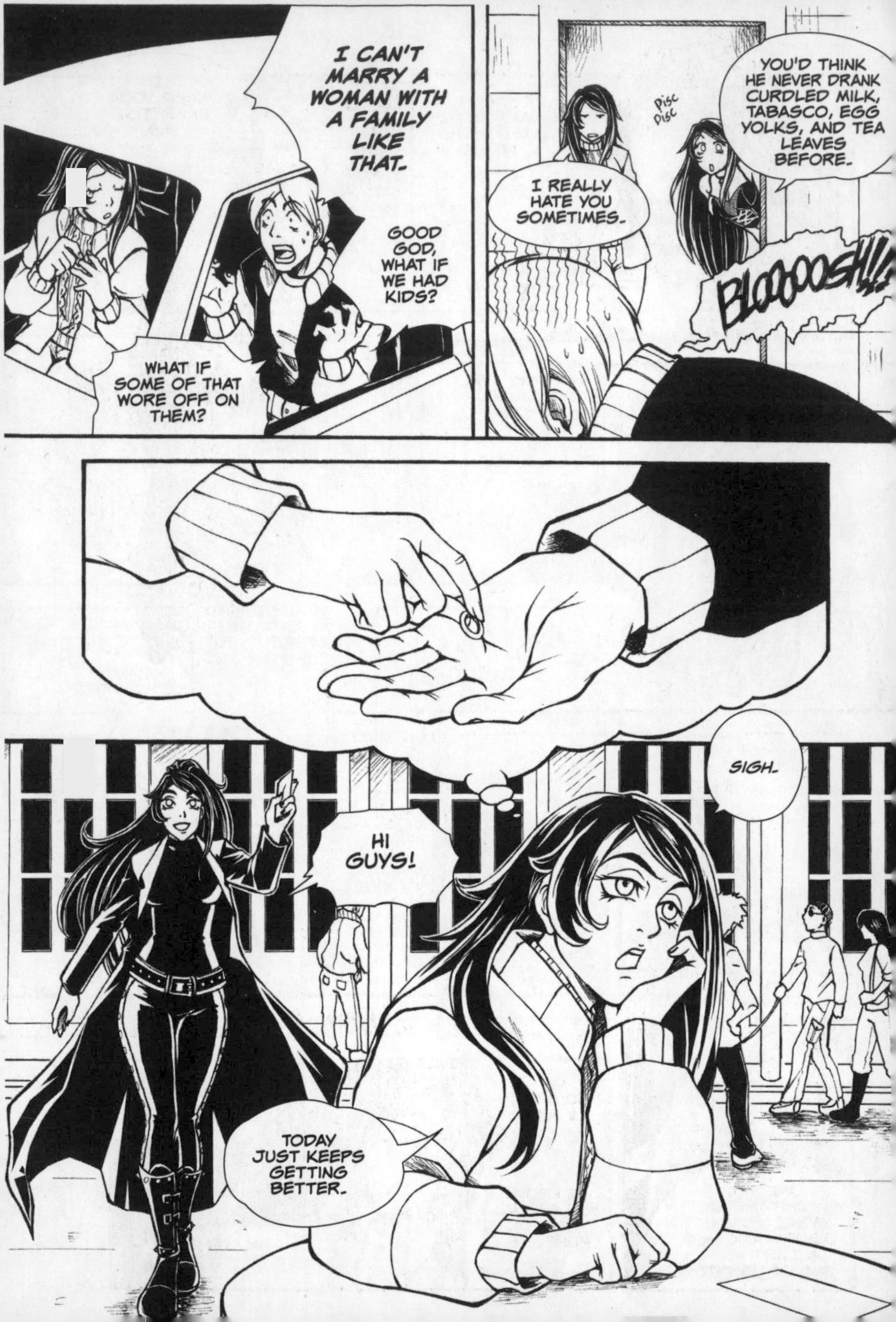
YOU'D THINK HE NEVER DRANK CURDLED MILK, TABASCO, EGG YOLKS, AND TEA LEAVES BEFORE.
Pisc Pisc
I REALLY HATE YOU SOMETIMES.
BLOOOOOSH!!!
I CAN'T MARRY A WOMAN WITH A FAMILY LIKE THAT.
GOOD GOD, WHAT IF WE HAD KIDS?
WHAT IF SOME OF THAT WORE OFF ON THEM?
SIGH.
HI GUYS!
TODAY JUST KEEPS GETTING BETTER.

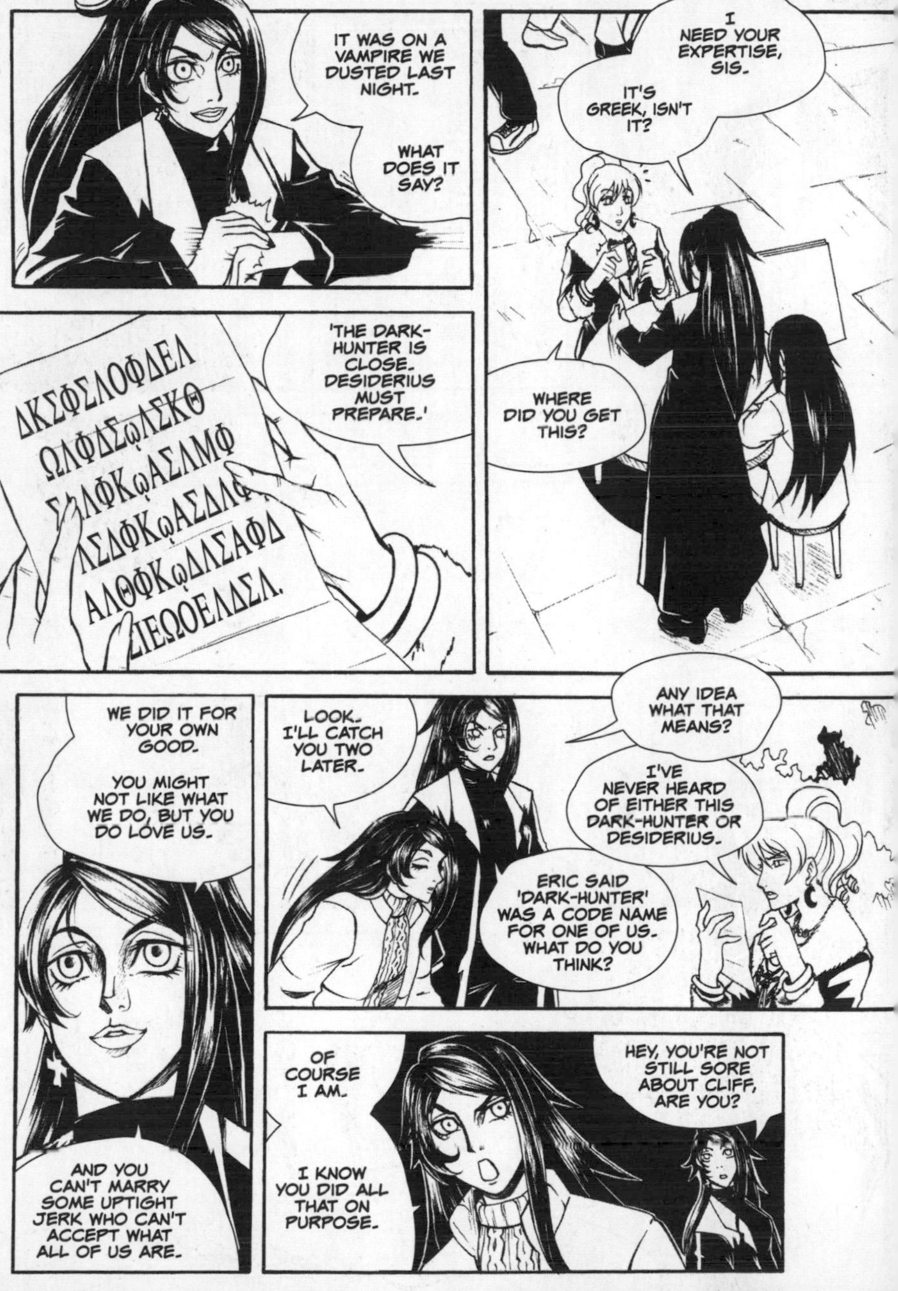
I NEED YOUR EXPERTISE, SIS.
IT'S GREEK, ISN'T IT?
WHERE DID YOU GET THIS?
IT WAS ON A VAMPIRE WE DUSTED LAST NIGHT.
WHAT DOES IT SAY?
'THE DARK-HUNTER IS CLOSE. DESIDERIUS MUST PREPARE.'
ΔΚΣΦΣΛΟΦΔΕΛ
ΩΛΦΔΣωΛΣΚΘ
ΣΛΦΚωΑΣΛΜΦ
ΛΣΔΦΚωΑΣΔΛΦ
ΑΛΘΦΚωΔΛΣΑΦΔ
ΣΙΕΩΟΕΛΔΣΛ.
ANY IDEA WHAT THAT MEANS?
I'VE NEVER HEARD OF EITHER THIS DARK-HUNTER OR DESIDERIUS.
ERIC SAID 'DARK-HUNTER' WAS A CODE NAME FOR ONE OF US. WHAT DO YOU THINK?
LOOK. I'LL CATCH YOU TWO LATER.
HEY, YOU'RE NOT STILL SORE ABOUT CLIFF, ARE YOU?
OF COURSE I AM.
I KNOW YOU DID ALL THAT ON PURPOSE.
WE DID IT FOR YOUR OWN GOOD.
YOU MIGHT NOT LIKE WHAT WE DO, BUT YOU DO LOVE US.
AND YOU CAN'T MARRY SOME UPTIGHT JERK WHO CAN'T ACCEPT WHAT ALL OF US ARE.

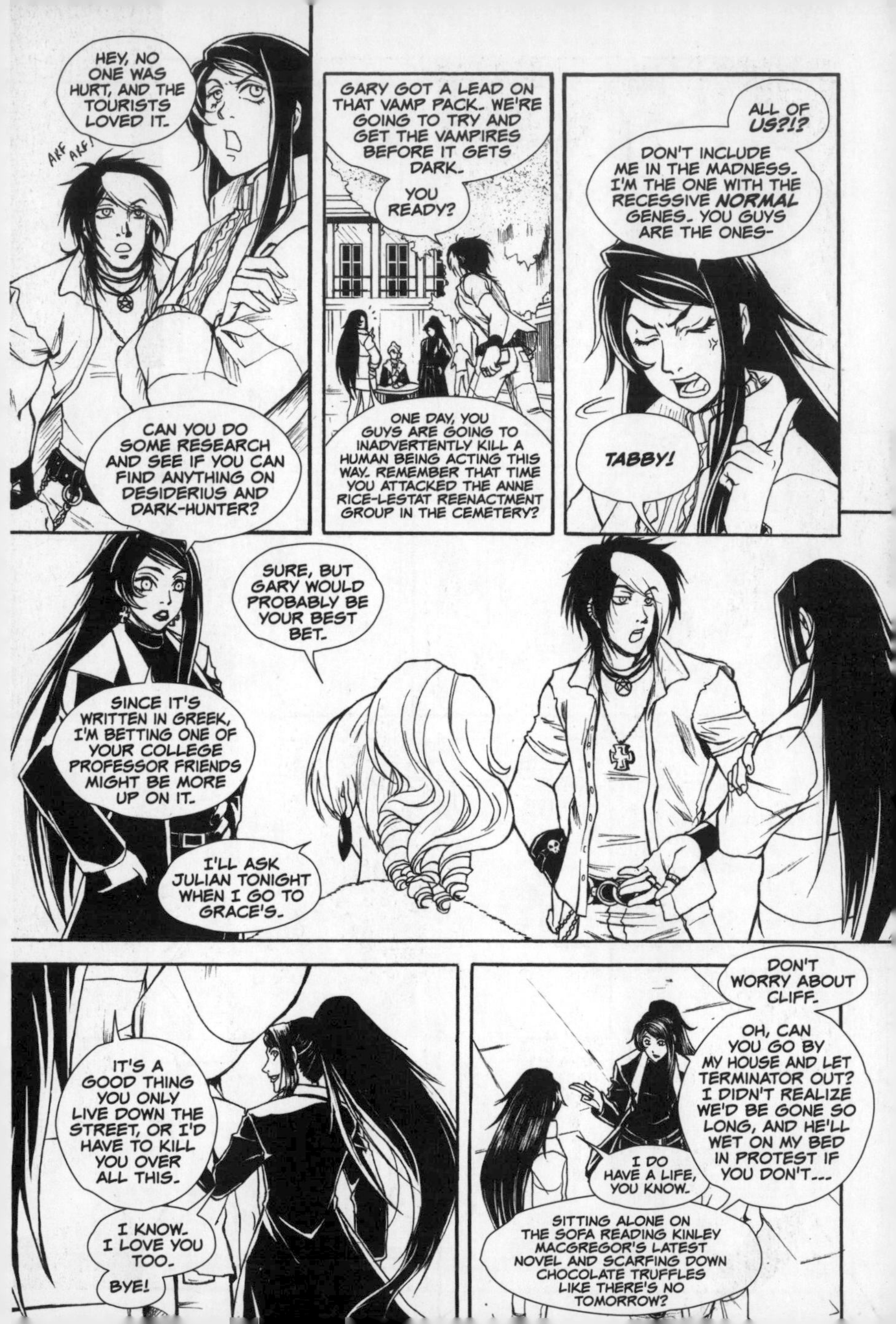
HEY, NO ONE WAS HURT, AND THE TOURISTS LOVED IT.
ARF ARF!
CAN YOU DO SOME RESEARCH AND SEE IF YOU CAN FIND ANYTHING ON DESIDERIUS AND DARK-HUNTER?
GARY GOT A LEAD ON THAT VAMP PACK. WE'RE GOING TO TRY AND GET THE VAMPIRES BEFORE IT GETS DARK.
YOU READY?
ONE DAY, YOU GUYS ARE GOING TO INADVERTENTLY KILL A HUMAN BEING ACTING THIS WAY. REMEMBER THAT TIME YOU ATTACKED THE ANNE RICE-LESTAT REENACTMENT GROUP IN THE CEMETERY?
ALL OF US?!?
DON'T INCLUDE ME IN THE MADNESS. I'M THE ONE WITH THE RECESSIVE NORMAL GENES. YOU GUYS ARE THE ONES-
TABBY!
SURE, BUT GARY WOULD PROBABLY BE YOUR BEST BET.
SINCE IT'S WRITTEN IN GREEK, I'M BETTING ONE OF YOUR COLLEGE PROFESSOR FRIENDS MIGHT BE MORE UP ON IT.
I'LL ASK JULIAN TONIGHT WHEN I GO TO GRACE'S.
IT'S A GOOD THING YOU ONLY LIVE DOWN THE STREET, OR I'D HAVE TO KILL YOU OVER ALL THIS.
I KNOW. I LOVE YOU TOO.
BYE!
DON'T WORRY ABOUT CLIFF.
OH, CAN YOU GO BY MY HOUSE AND LET TERMINATOR OUT? I DIDN'T REALIZE WE'D BE GONE SO LONG, AND HE'LL WET ON MY BED IN PROTEST IF YOU DON'T...
I DO HAVE A LIFE, YOU KNOW.
SITTING ALONE ON THE SOFA READING KINLEY MACGREGOR'S LATEST NOVEL AND SCARFING DOWN CHOCOLATE TRUFFLES LIKE THERE'S NO TOMORROW?

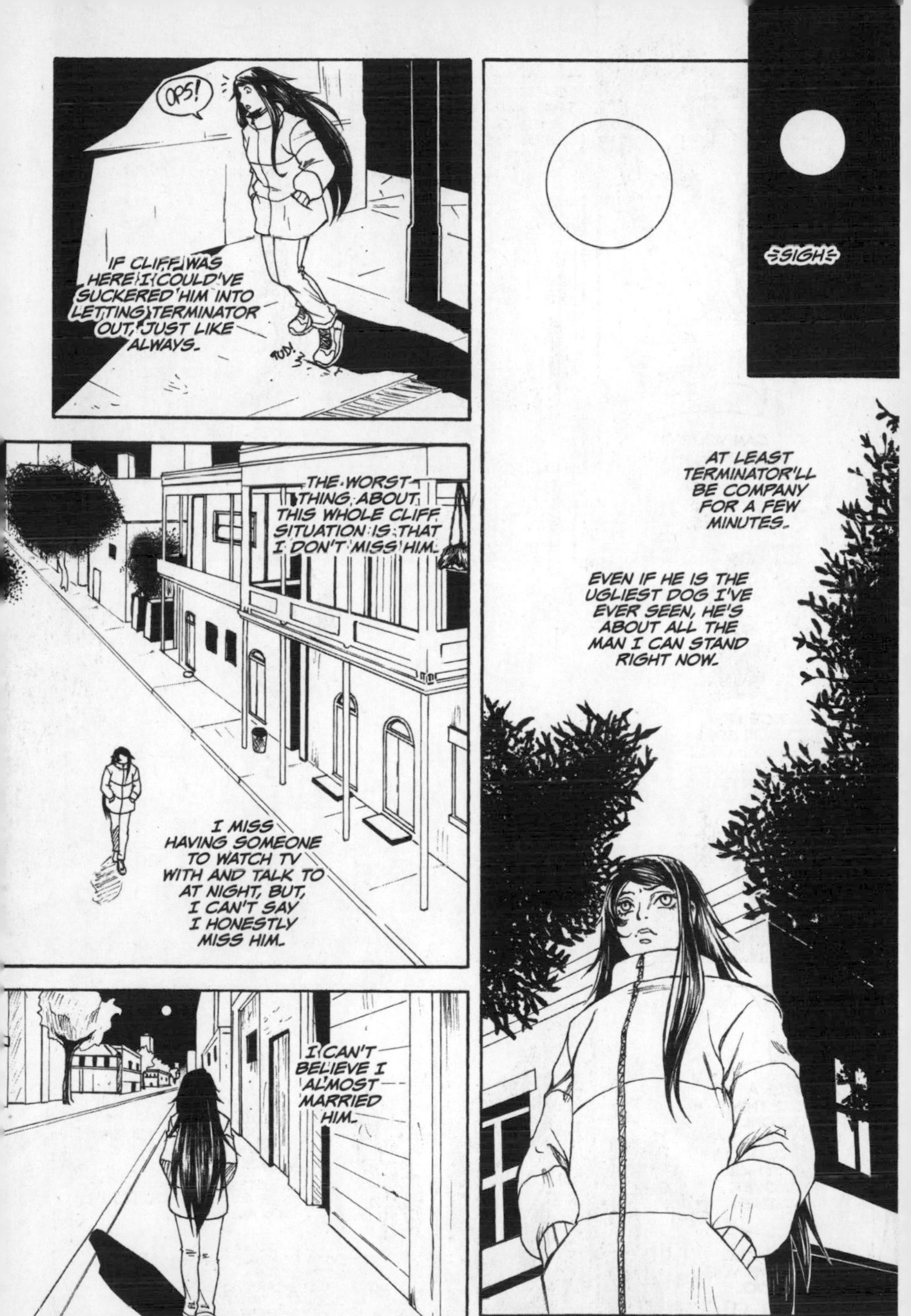
SIGH
AT LEAST TERMINATOR'LL BE COMPANY FOR A FEW MINUTES.
EVEN IF HE IS THE UGLIEST DOG I'VE EVER SEEN, HE'S ABOUT ALL THE MAN I CAN STAND RIGHT NOW.
OPS!
IF CLIFF WAS HERE I COULD'VE SUCKERED HIM INTO LETTING TERMINATOR OUT, JUST LIKE ALWAYS.
TUD!
THE WORST THING ABOUT THIS WHOLE CLIFF SITUATION IS THAT I DON'T MISS HIM.
I MISS HAVING SOMEONE TO WATCH TV WITH AND TALK TO AT NIGHT, BUT, I CAN'T SAY I HONESTLY MISS HIM.
I CAN'T BELIEVE I ALMOST MARRIED HIM.

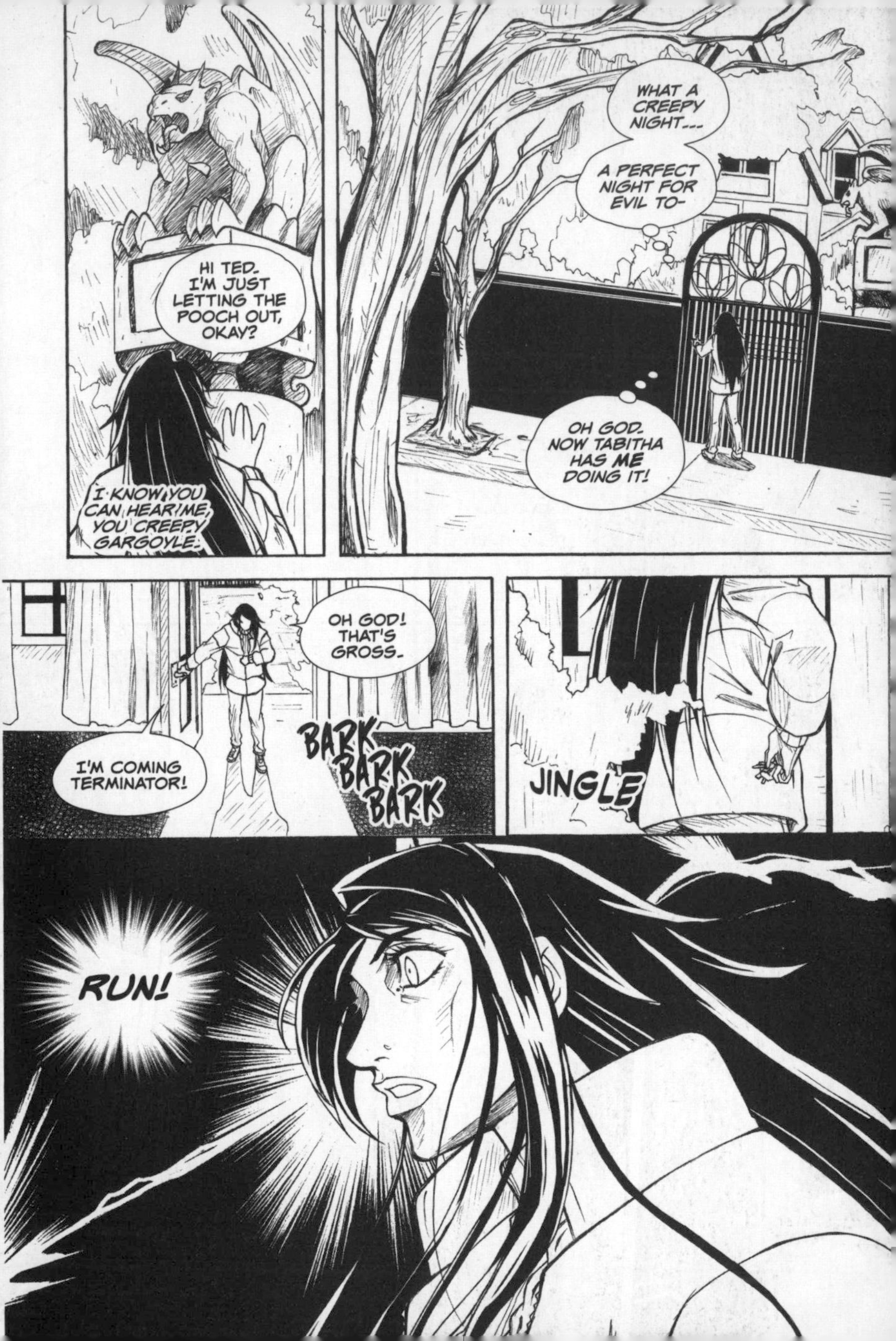
WHAT A CREEPY NIGHT...
A PERFECT NIGHT FOR EVIL TO-
OH GOD. NOW TABITHA HAS ME DOING IT!
HI TED. I'M JUST LETTING THE POOCH OUT, OKAY?
I KNOW YOU CAN HEAR ME, YOU CREEPY GARGOYLE.
JINGLE
OH GOD! THAT'S GROSS.
I'M COMING TERMINATOR!
BARK BARK BARK
RUN!

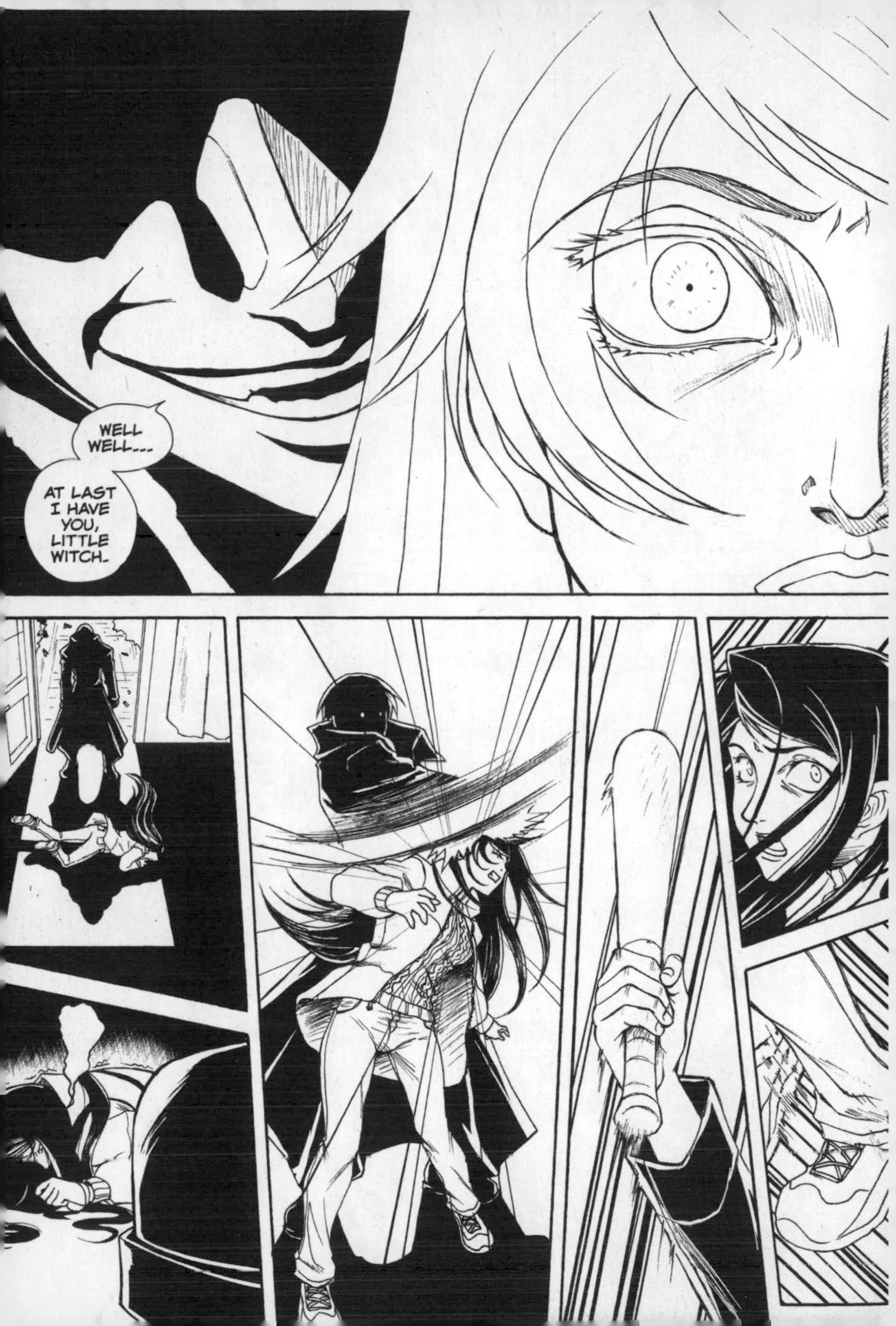
WELL WELL...
AT LAST I HAVE YOU, LITTLE WITCH.

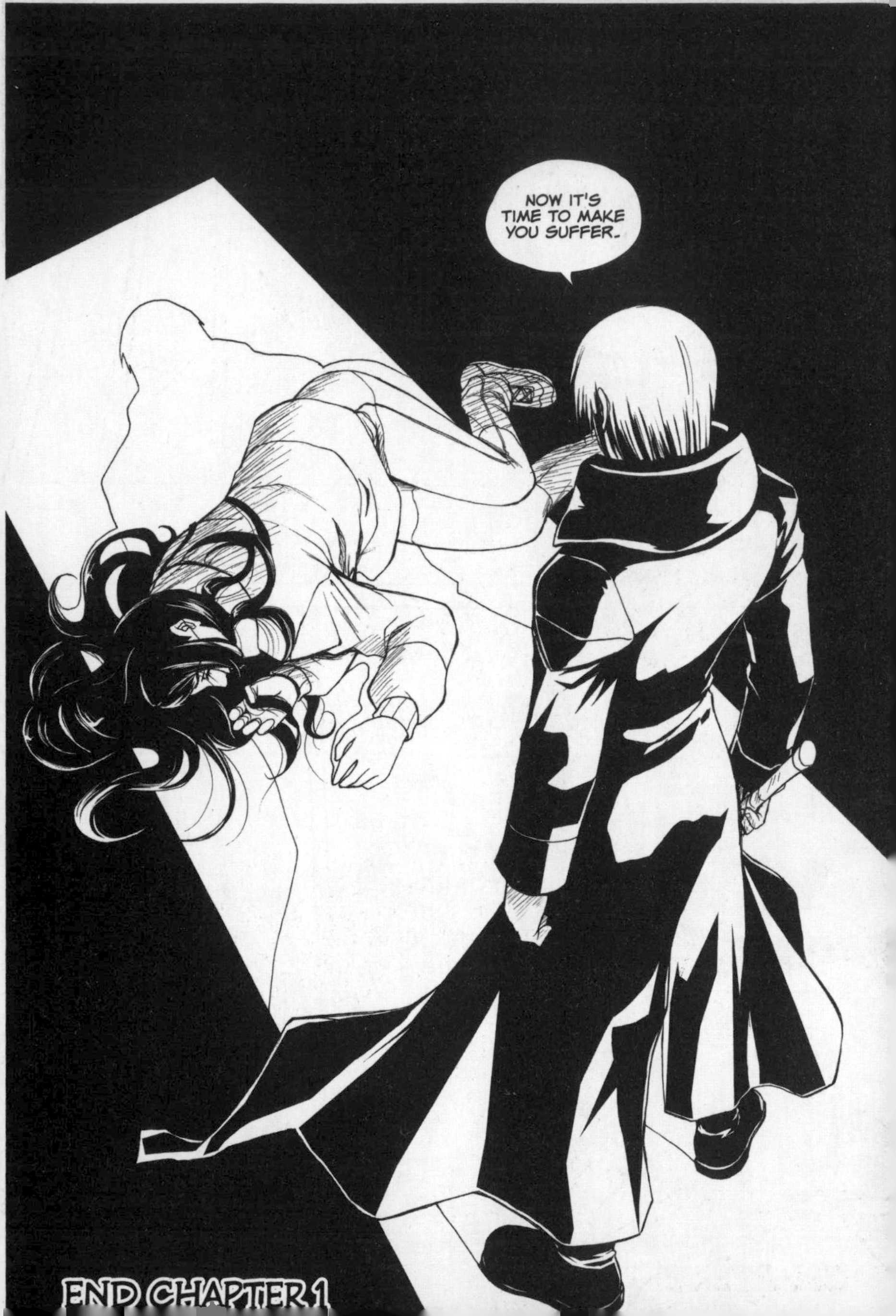
NOW IT'S TIME TO MAKE YOU SUFFER...
END CHAPTER 1

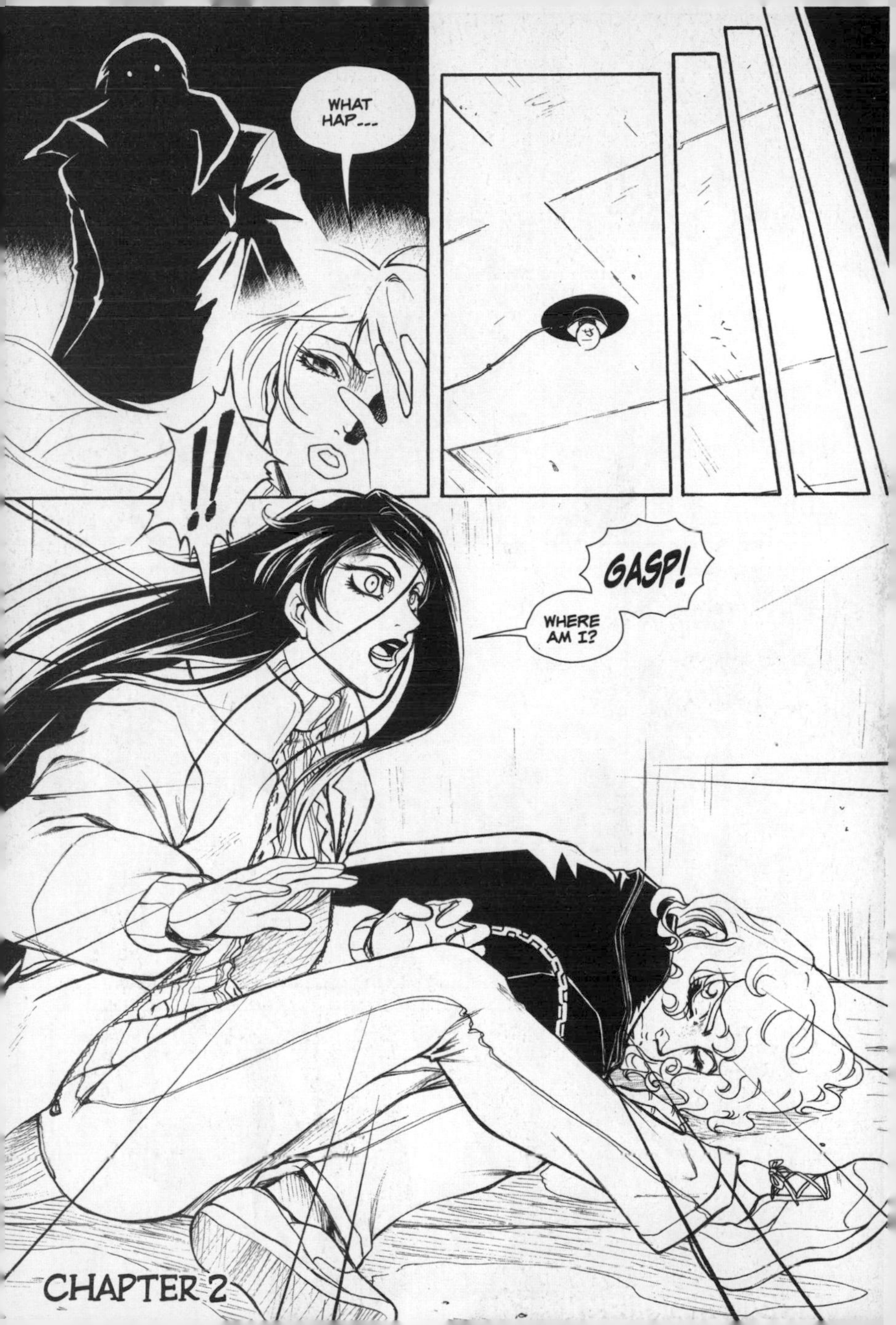
WHAT HAP---
GASP!
WHERE AM I?
CHAPTER 2

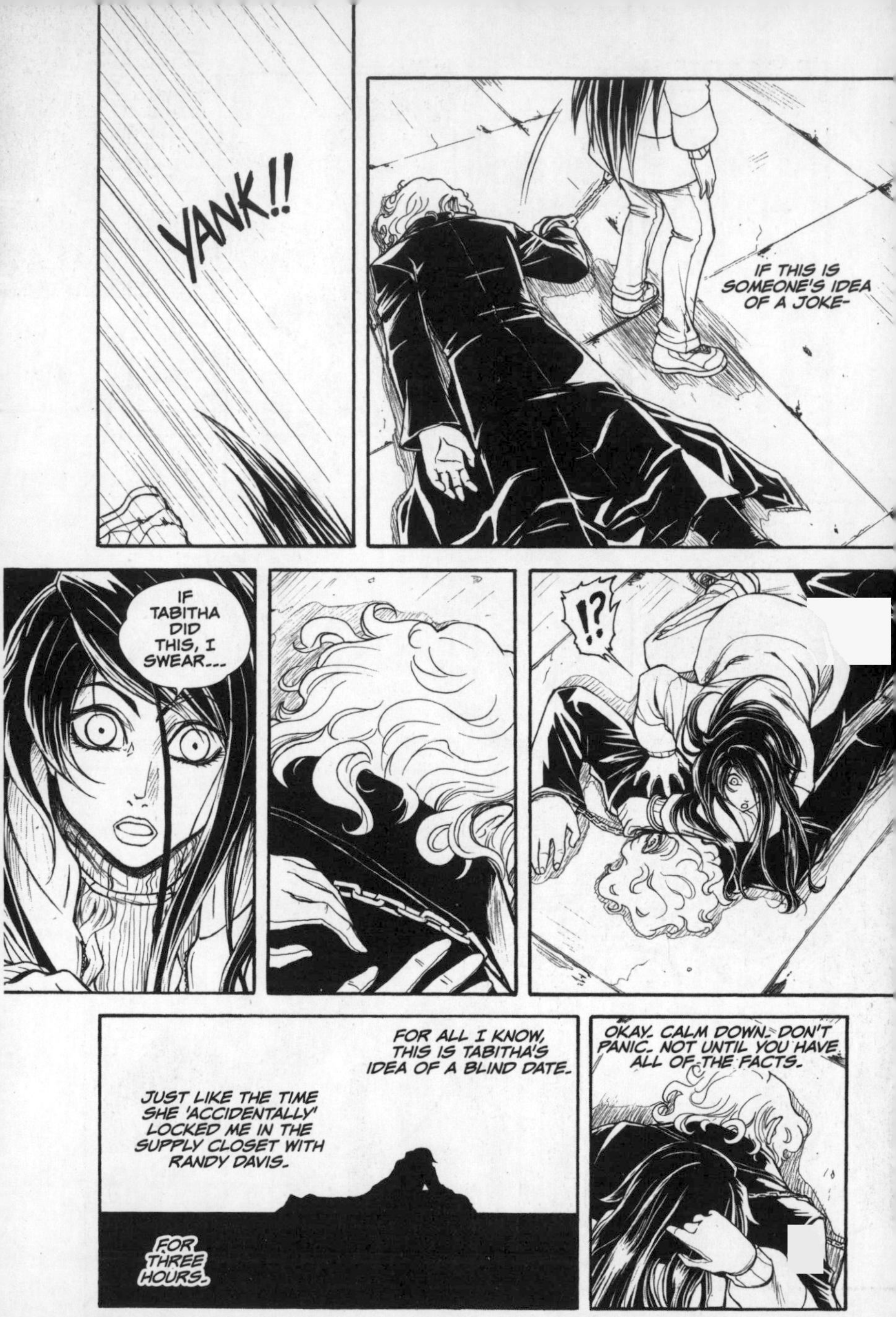
IF THIS IS SOMEONE'S IDEA OF A JOKE-
YANK!!
!?
IF TABITHA DID THIS, I SWEAR...
OKAY. CALM DOWN. DON'T PANIC. NOT UNTIL YOU HAVE ALL OF THE FACTS.
FOR ALL I KNOW, THIS IS TABITHA'S IDEA OF A BLIND DATE.
JUST LIKE THE TIME SHE 'ACCIDENTALLY' LOCKED ME IN THE SUPPLY CLOSET WITH RANDY DAVIS.
FOR THREE HOURS.

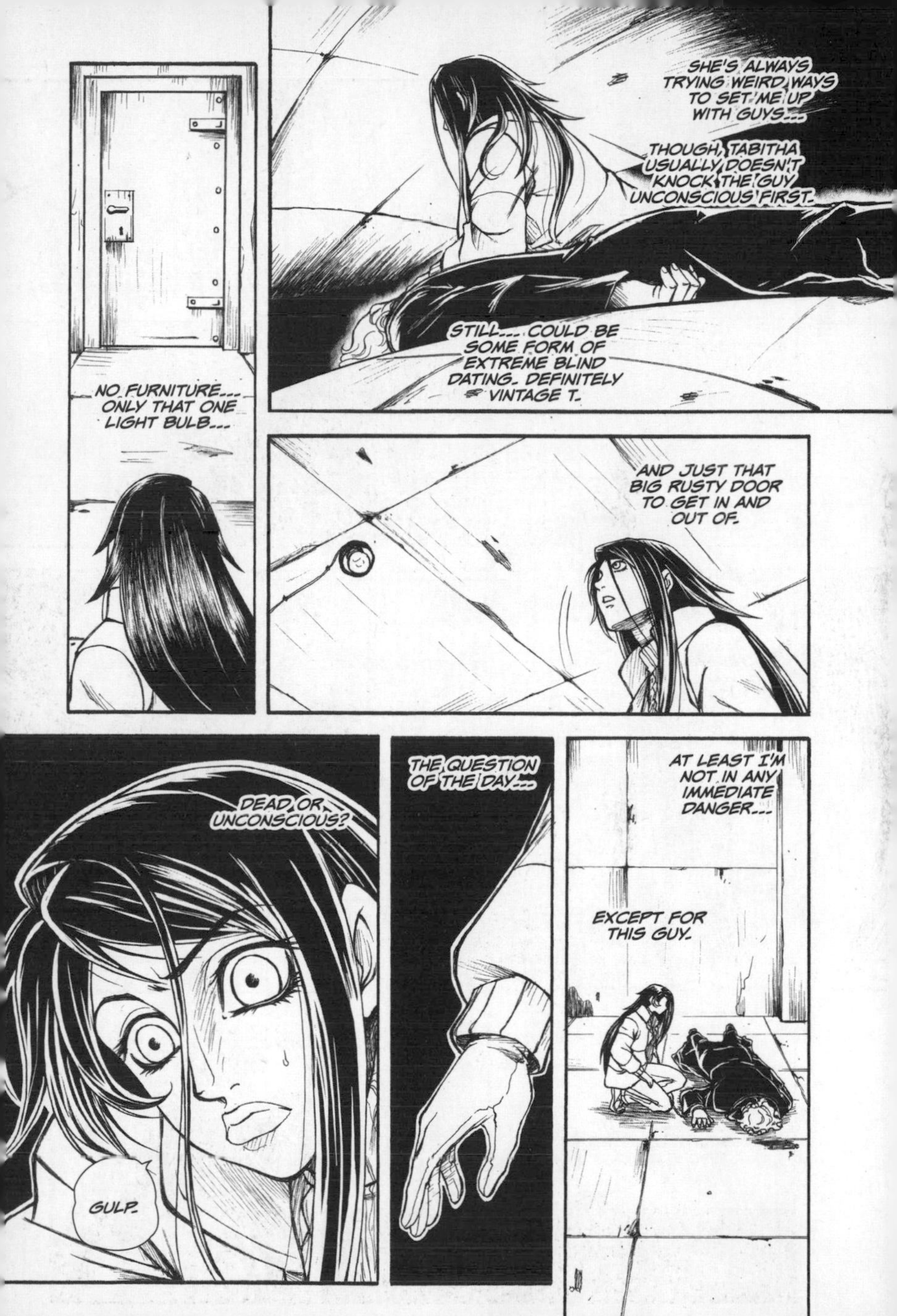
SHE'S ALWAYS TRYING WEIRD WAYS TO SET ME UP WITH GUYS...
THOUGH, TABITHA USUALLY DOESN'T KNOCK THE GUY UNCONSCIOUS FIRST.
STILL... COULD BE SOME FORM OF EXTREME BLIND DATING. DEFINITELY VINTAGE T.
AND JUST THAT BIG RUSTY DOOR TO GET IN AND OUT OF.
NO FURNITURE... ONLY THAT ONE LIGHT BULB...
AT LEAST I'M NOT IN ANY IMMEDIATE DANGER...
EXCEPT FOR THIS GUY.
THE QUESTION OF THE DAY...
DEAD OR UNCONSCIOUS?
GULP.

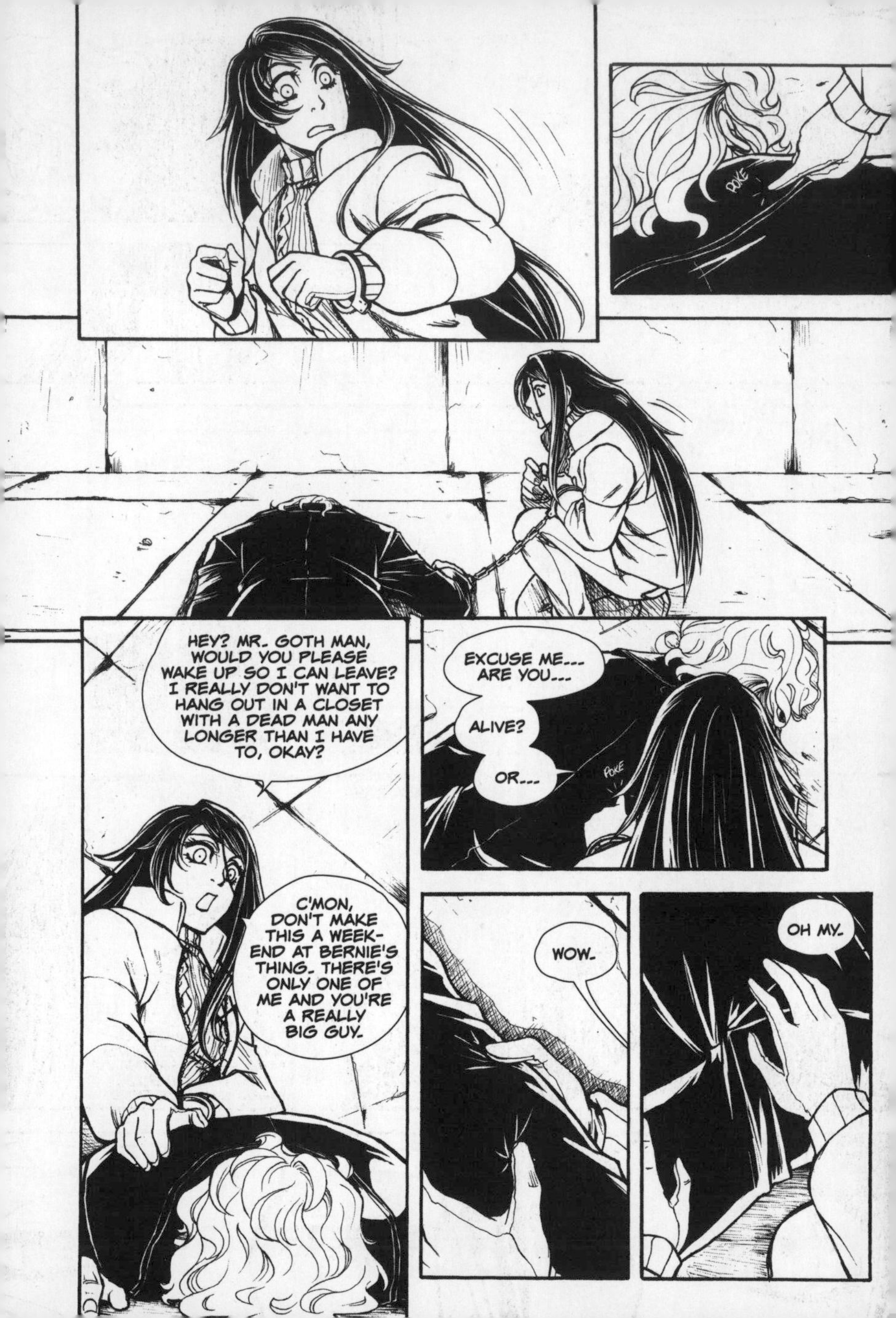
POKE
EXCUSE ME... ARE YOU...
ALIVE?
OR...
POKE
OH MY.
WOW.
HEY? MR. GOTH MAN, WOULD YOU PLEASE WAKE UP SO I CAN LEAVE? I REALLY DON'T WANT TO HANG OUT IN A CLOSET WITH A DEAD MAN ANY LONGER THAN I HAVE TO, OKAY?
C'MON, DON'T MAKE THIS A WEEK-END AT BERNIE'S THING. THERE'S ONLY ONE OF ME AND YOU'RE A REALLY BIG GUY.

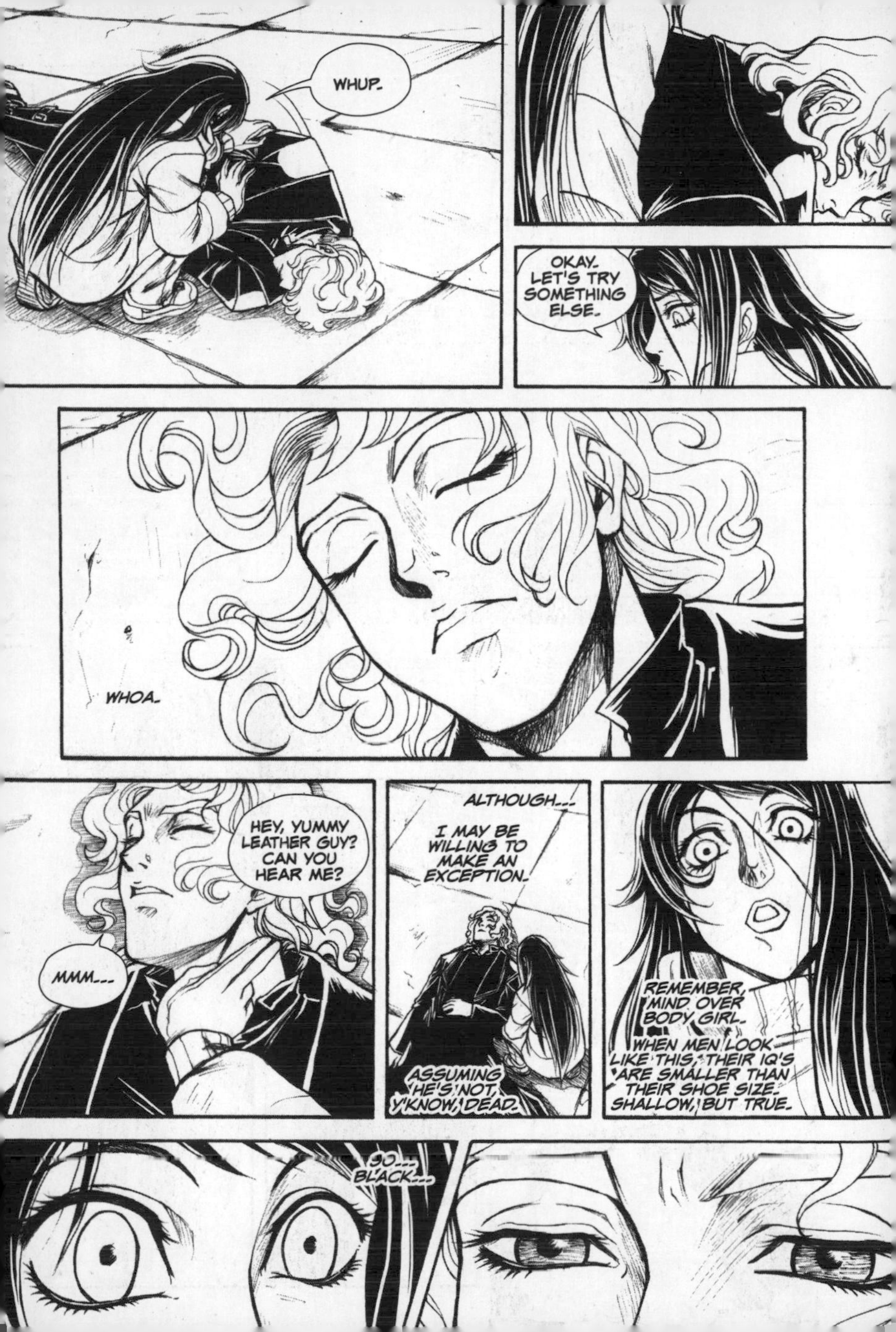
OKAY. LET'S TRY SOMETHING ELSE.
WHUP.
WHOA.
REMEMBER, MIND OVER BODY GIRL.
WHEN MEN LOOK LIKE THIS, THEIR IQ'S ARE SMALLER THAN THEIR SHOE SIZE. SHALLOW, BUT TRUE.
ALTHOUGH...
I MAY BE WILLING TO MAKE AN EXCEPTION.
ASSUMING HE'S NOT, Y'KNOW, DEAD.
HEY, YUMMY LEATHER GUY? CAN YOU HEAR ME?
MMM...
SO... BLACK...

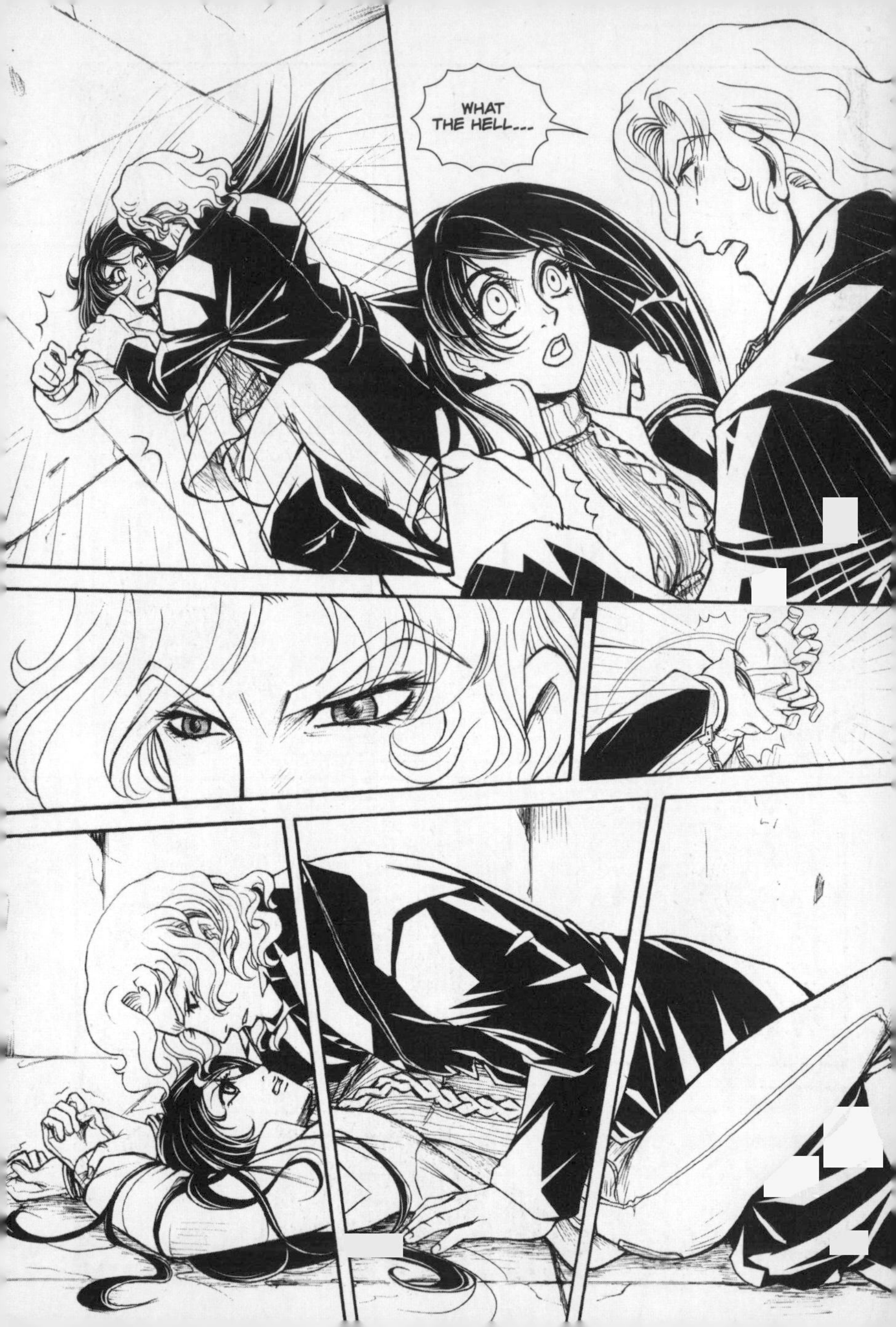
WHAT THE HELL...

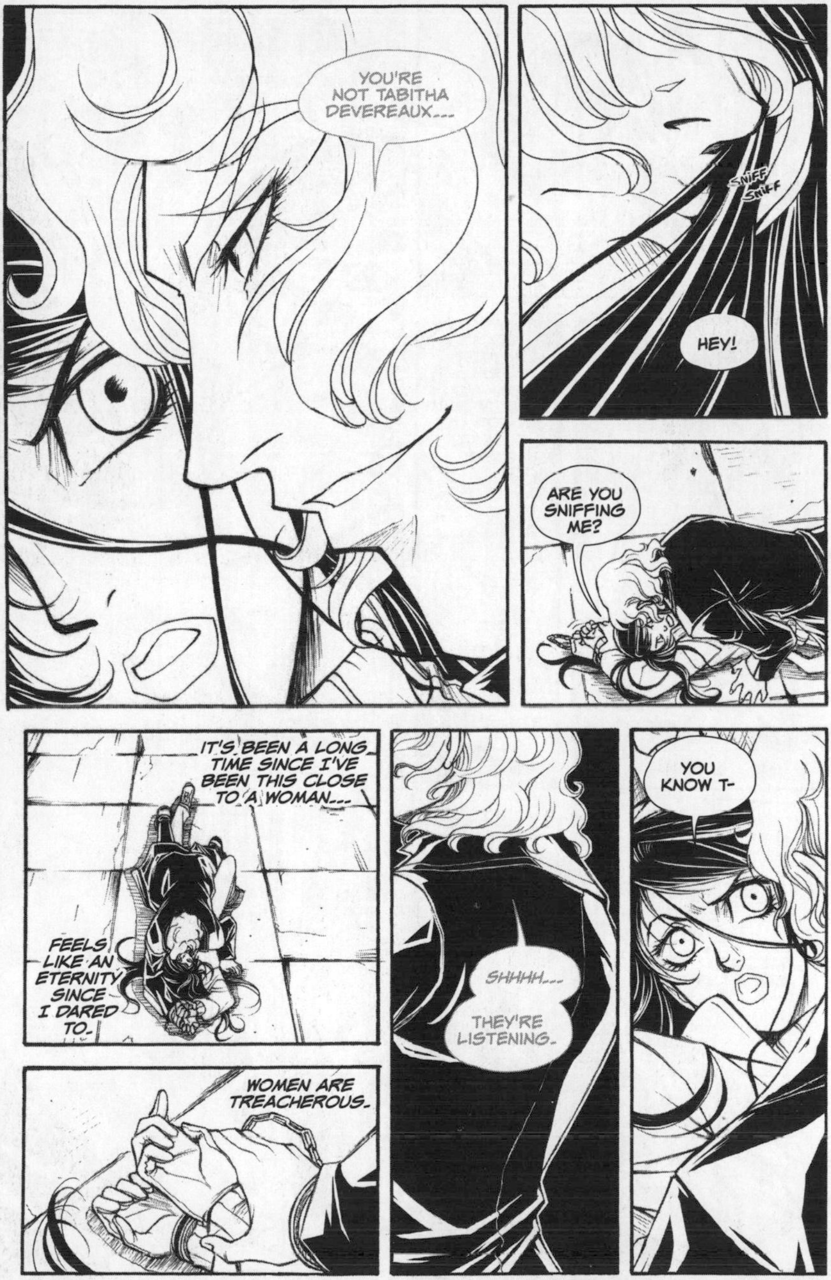
SNIFF SNIFF
HEY!
ARE YOU SNIFFING ME?
YOU'RE NOT TABITHA DEVEREAUX...
YOU KNOW T-
SHHHH...
THEY'RE LISTENING.
IT'S BEEN A LONG TIME SINCE I'VE BEEN THIS CLOSE TO A WOMAN...
FEELS LIKE AN ETERNITY SINCE I DARED TO.
WOMEN ARE TREACHEROUS.

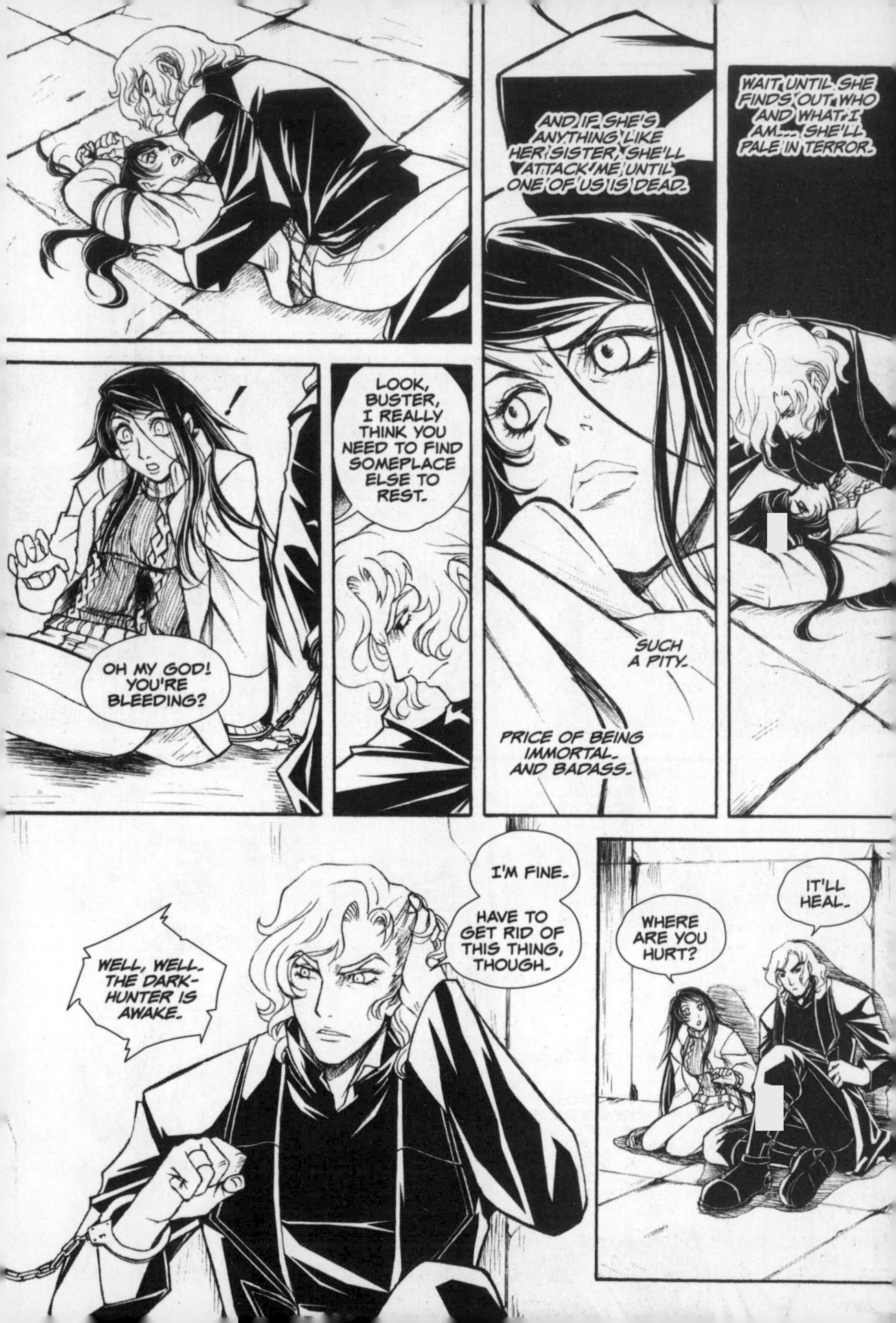
WAIT UNTIL SHE FINDS OUT WHO AND WHAT I AM... SHE'LL PALE IN TERROR.
AND IF SHE'S ANYTHING LIKE HER SISTER, SHE'LL ATTACK ME UNTIL ONE OF US IS DEAD.
SUCH A PITY.
PRICE OF BEING IMMORTAL. AND BADASS.
LOOK, BUSTER, I REALLY THINK YOU NEED TO FIND SOMEPLACE ELSE TO REST.
!
OH MY GOD! YOU'RE BLEEDING?
IT'LL HEAL.
WHERE ARE YOU HURT?
I'M FINE.
HAVE TO GET RID OF THIS THING, THOUGH.
WELL, WELL. THE DARK-HUNTER IS AWAKE.

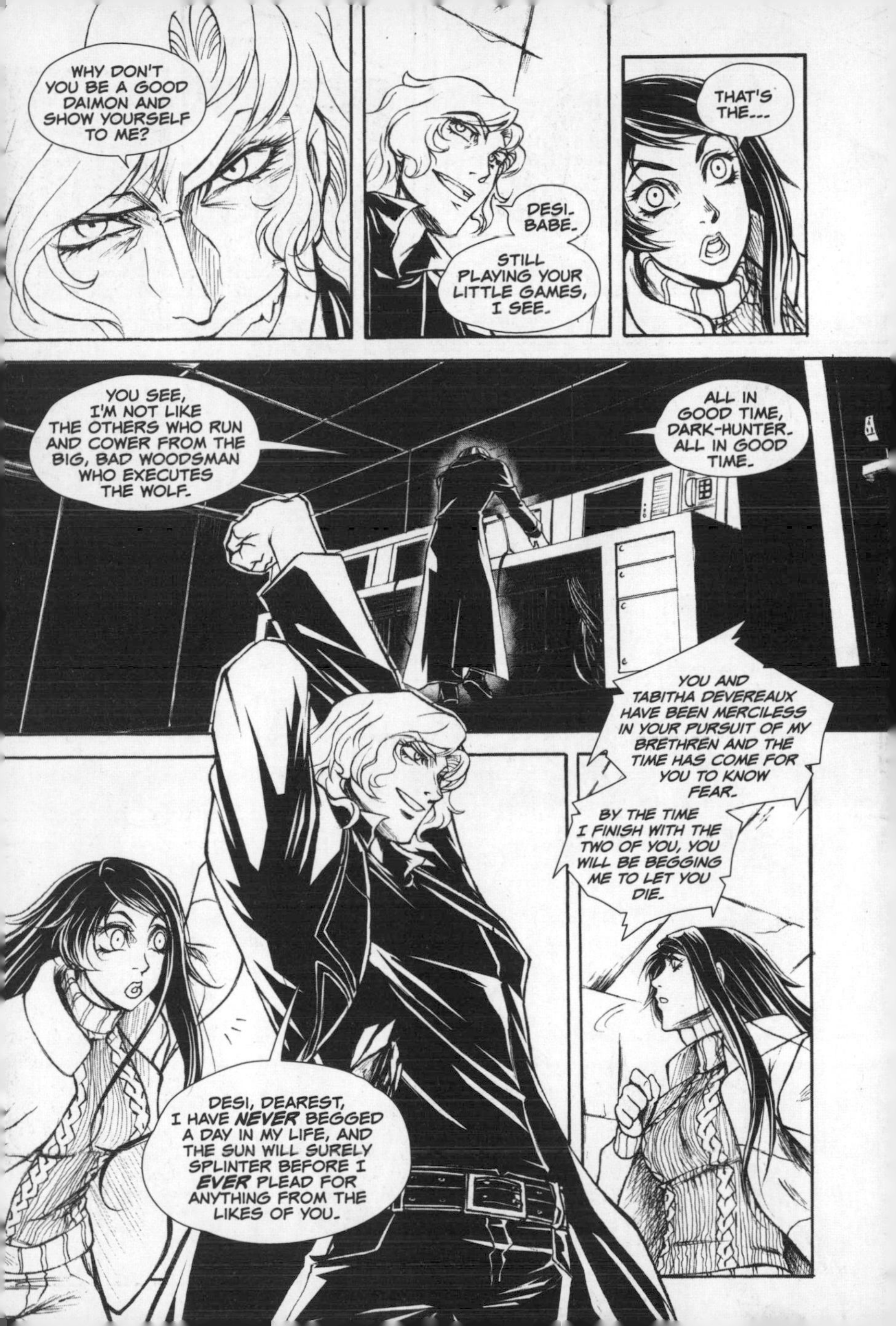
THAT'S THE...
DESI. BABE.
STILL PLAYING YOUR LITTLE GAMES, I SEE.
WHY DON'T YOU BE A GOOD DAIMON AND SHOW YOURSELF TO ME?
ALL IN GOOD TIME, DARK-HUNTER. ALL IN GOOD TIME.
YOU SEE, I'M NOT LIKE THE OTHERS WHO RUN AND COWER FROM THE BIG, BAD WOODSMAN WHO EXECUTES THE WOLF.
YOU AND TABITHA DEVEREAUX HAVE BEEN MERCILESS IN YOUR PURSUIT OF MY BRETHREN AND THE TIME HAS COME FOR YOU TO KNOW FEAR.
BY THE TIME I FINISH WITH THE TWO OF YOU, YOU WILL BE BEGGING ME TO LET YOU DIE.
DESI, DEAREST, I HAVE NEVER BEGGED A DAY IN MY LIFE, AND THE SUN WILL SURELY SPLINTER BEFORE I EVER PLEAD FOR ANYTHING FROM THE LIKES OF YOU.

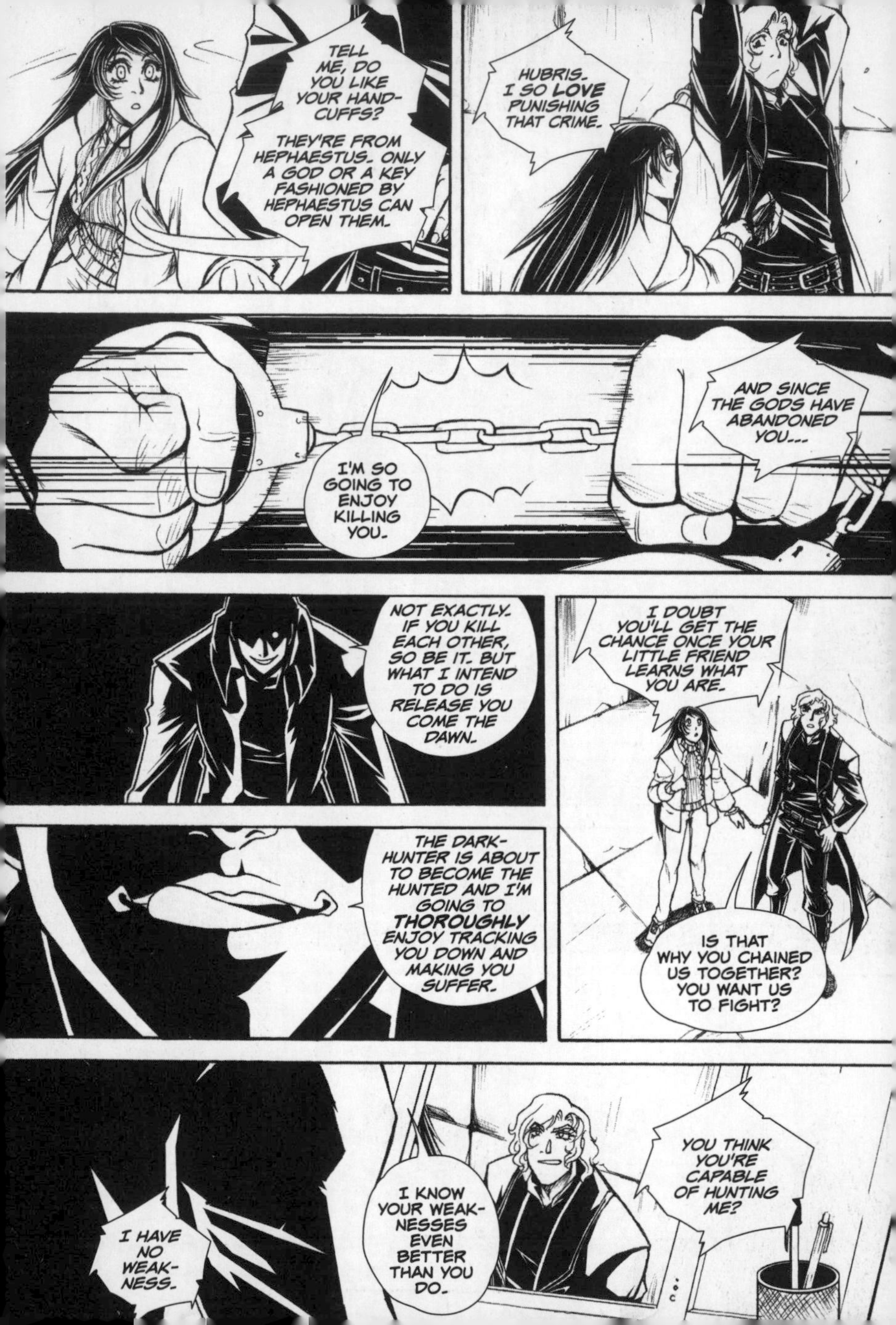
HUBRIS. I SO LOVE PUNISHING THAT CRIME.
TELL ME, DO YOU LIKE YOUR HAND-CUFFS?
THEY'RE FROM HEPHAESTUS. ONLY A GOD OR A KEY FASHIONED BY HEPHAESTUS CAN OPEN THEM.
AND SINCE THE GODS HAVE ABANDONED YOU...
I'M SO GOING TO ENJOY KILLING YOU.
I DOUBT YOU'LL GET THE CHANCE ONCE YOUR LITTLE FRIEND LEARNS WHAT YOU ARE.
IS THAT WHY YOU CHAINED US TOGETHER? YOU WANT US TO FIGHT?
NOT EXACTLY. IF YOU KILL EACH OTHER, SO BE IT. BUT WHAT I INTEND TO DO IS RELEASE YOU COME THE DAWN.
THE DARK-HUNTER IS ABOUT TO BECOME THE HUNTED AND I'M GOING TO THOROUGHLY ENJOY TRACKING YOU DOWN AND MAKING YOU SUFFER.
YOU THINK YOU'RE CAPABLE OF HUNTING ME?
I KNOW YOUR WEAK-NESSES EVEN BETTER THAN YOU DO.
I HAVE NO WEAK-NESS.

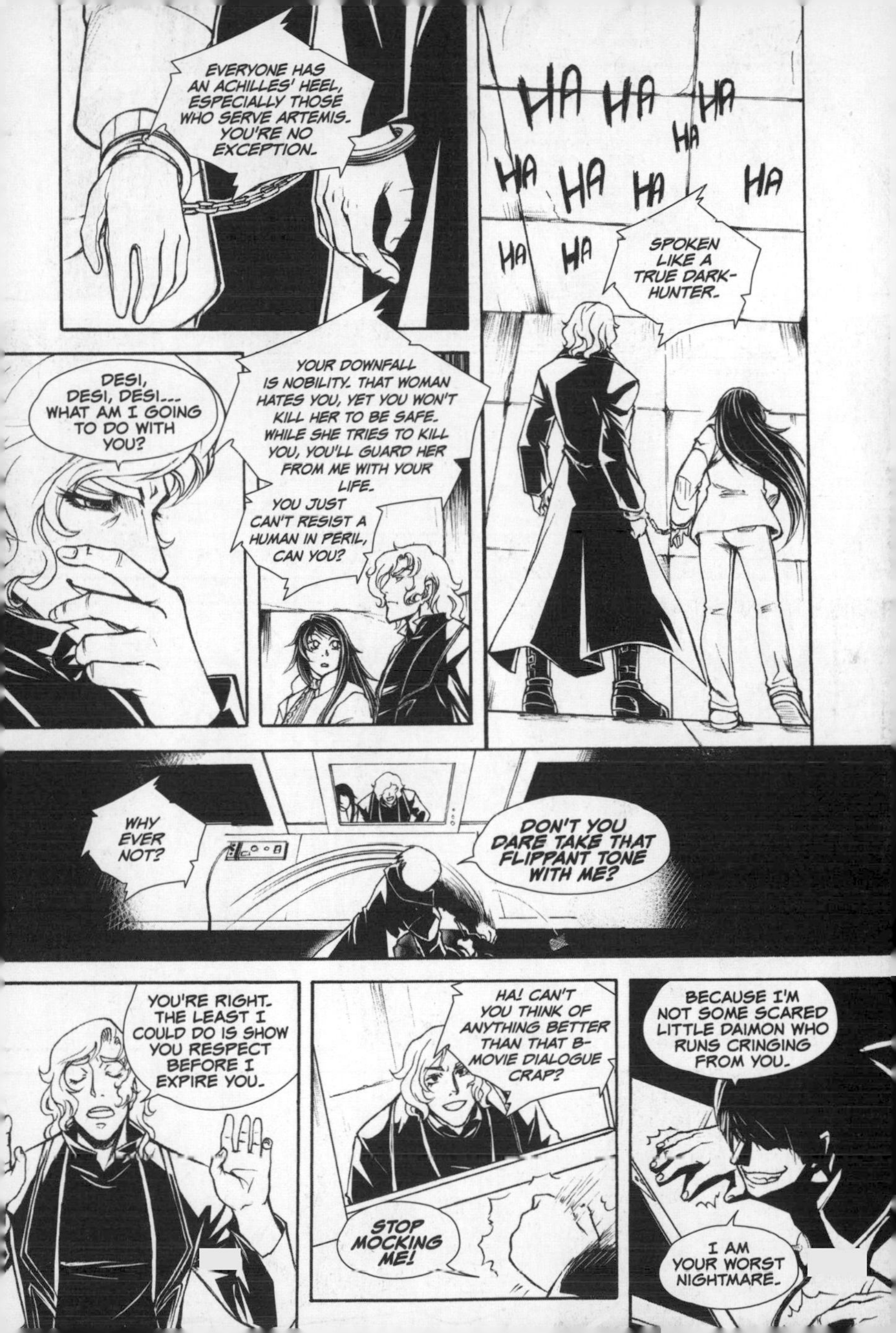
HA HA HA HA HA HA HA HA HA HA HA
SPOKEN LIKE A TRUE DARK-HUNTER.
EVERYONE HAS AN ACHILLES' HEEL, ESPECIALLY THOSE WHO SERVE ARTEMIS. YOU'RE NO EXCEPTION.
YOUR DOWNFALL IS NOBILITY. THAT WOMAN HATES YOU, YET YOU WON'T KILL HER TO BE SAFE. WHILE SHE TRIES TO KILL YOU, YOU'LL GUARD HER FROM ME WITH YOUR LIFE.
YOU JUST CAN'T RESIST A HUMAN IN PERIL, CAN YOU?
DESI, DESI, DESI... WHAT AM I GOING TO DO WITH YOU?
DON'T YOU DARE TAKE THAT FLIPPANT TONE WITH ME?
WHY EVER NOT?
BECAUSE I'M NOT SOME SCARED LITTLE DAIMON WHO RUNS CRINGING FROM YOU.
I AM YOUR WORST NIGHTMARE.
HA! CAN'T YOU THINK OF ANYTHING BETTER THAN THAT B-MOVIE DIALOGUE CRAP?
STOP MOCKING ME!
YOU'RE RIGHT. THE LEAST I COULD DO IS SHOW YOU RESPECT BEFORE I EXPIRE YOU.

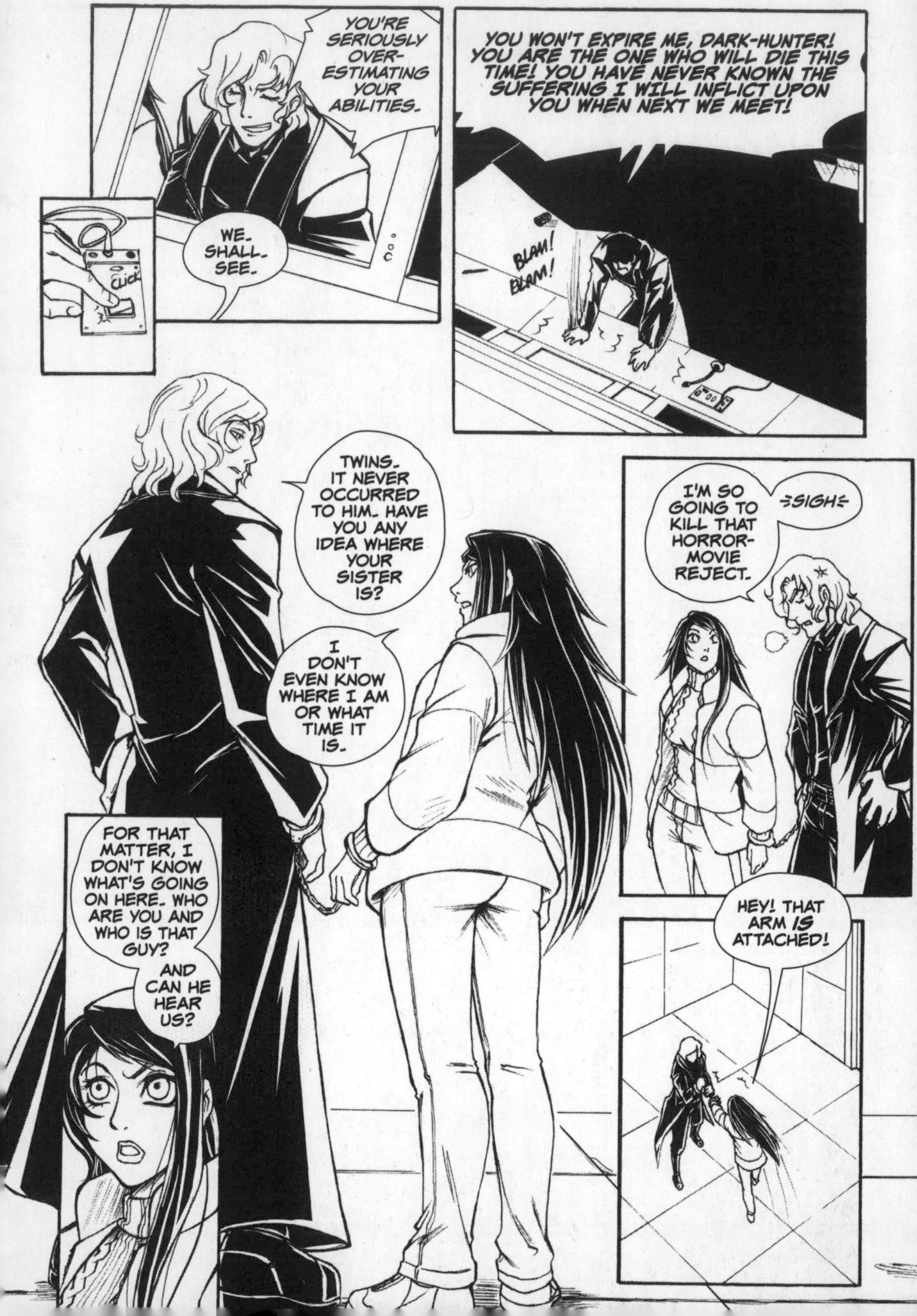
YOU WON'T EXPIRE ME, DARK-HUNTER! YOU ARE THE ONE WHO WILL DIE THIS TIME! YOU HAVE NEVER KNOWN THE SUFFERING I WILL INFLICT UPON YOU WHEN NEXT WE MEET!
BLAM! BLAM!
YOU'RE SERIOUSLY OVER-ESTIMATING YOUR ABILITIES.
WE. SHALL. SEE.
CLICK
I'M SO GOING TO KILL THAT HORROR-MOVIE REJECT.
=SIGH=
HEY! THAT ARM IS ATTACHED!
TWINS. IT NEVER OCCURRED TO HIM. HAVE YOU ANY IDEA WHERE YOUR SISTER IS?
I DON'T EVEN KNOW WHERE I AM OR WHAT TIME IT IS.
FOR THAT MATTER, I DON'T KNOW WHAT'S GOING ON HERE. WHO ARE YOU AND WHO IS THAT GUY?
AND CAN HE HEAR US?

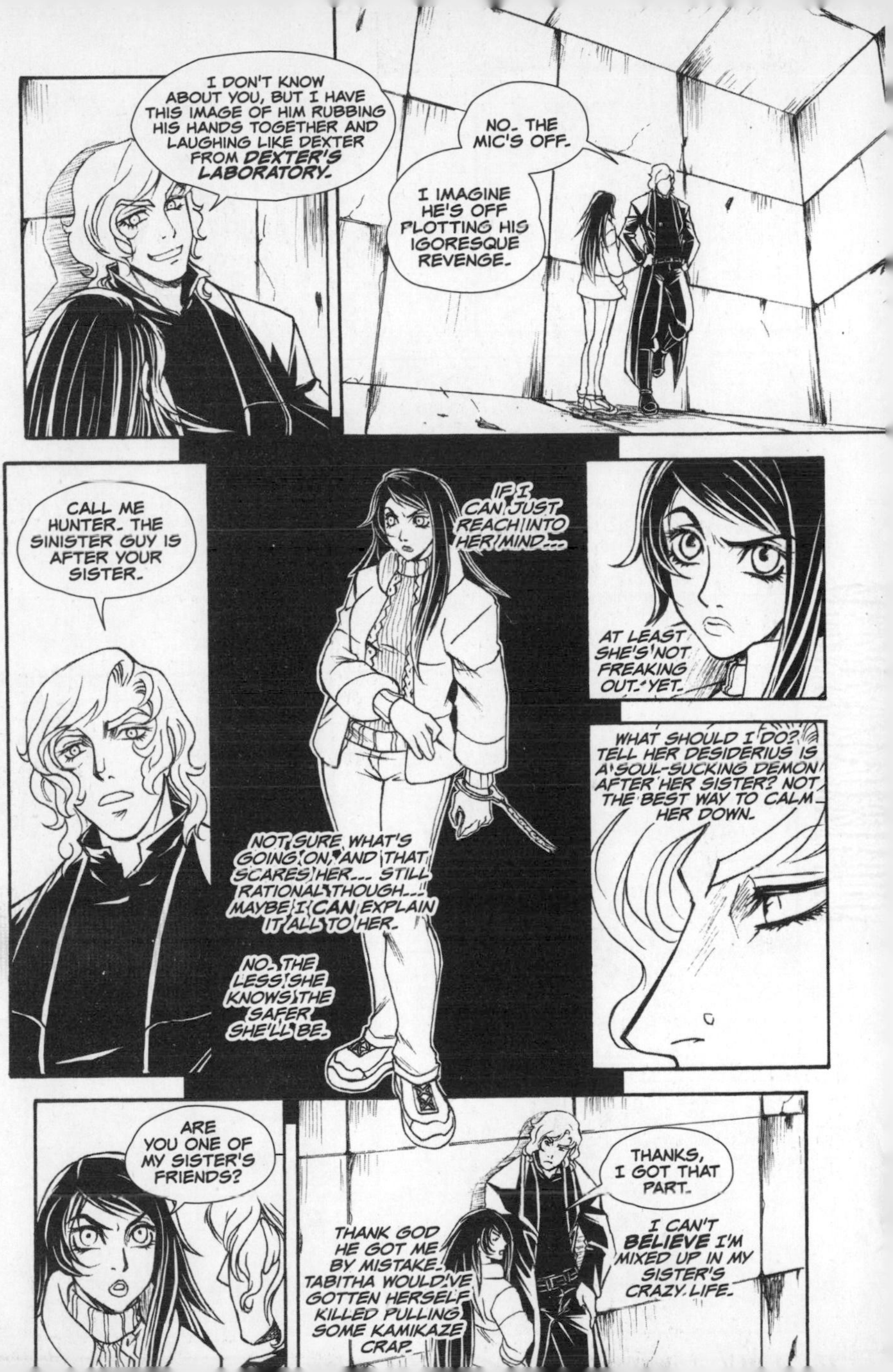
NO. THE MIC'S OFF.
I IMAGINE HE'S OFF PLOTTING HIS IGORESQUE REVENGE.
I DON'T KNOW ABOUT YOU, BUT I HAVE THIS IMAGE OF HIM RUBBING HIS HANDS TOGETHER AND LAUGHING LIKE DEXTER FROM ***DEXTER'S LABORATORY***.
AT LEAST SHE'S NOT FREAKING OUT. YET.
WHAT SHOULD I DO? TELL HER DESIDERIUS IS A SOUL-SUCKING DEMON AFTER HER SISTER? NOT THE BEST WAY TO CALM HER DOWN.
IF I CAN JUST REACH INTO HER MIND...
NOT SURE WHAT'S GOING ON, AND THAT SCARES HER... STILL RATIONAL THOUGH... MAYBE I **CAN** EXPLAIN IT ALL TO HER.
NO. THE LESS SHE KNOWS THE SAFER SHE'LL BE.
CALL ME HUNTER. THE SINISTER GUY IS AFTER YOUR SISTER.
THANKS, I GOT THAT PART.
I CAN'T **BELIEVE** I'M MIXED UP IN MY SISTER'S CRAZY LIFE.
THANK GOD HE GOT ME BY MISTAKE. TABITHA WOULD'VE GOTTEN HERSELF KILLED PULLING SOME KAMIKAZE CRAP.
ARE YOU ONE OF MY SISTER'S FRIENDS?

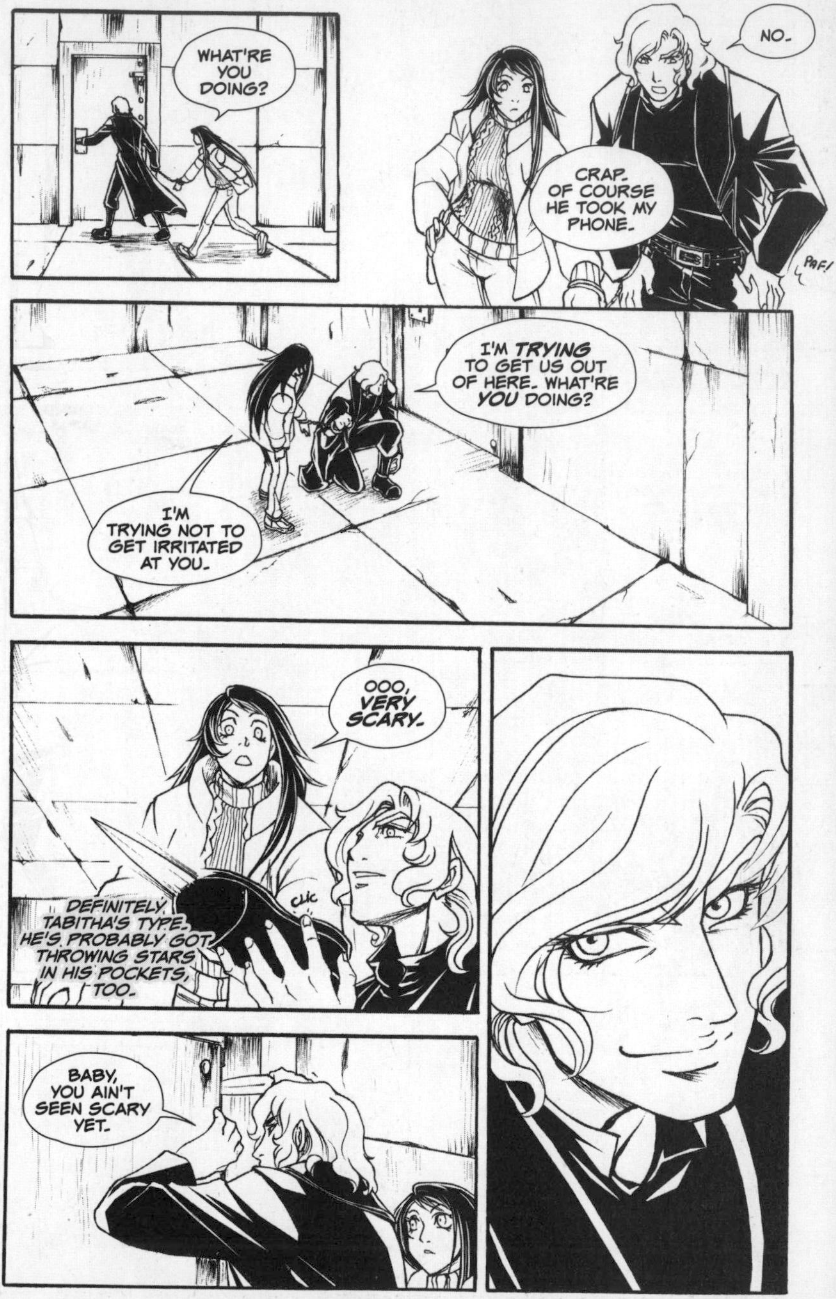
NO.
CRAP. OF COURSE HE TOOK MY PHONE.
PAF!
WHAT'RE YOU DOING?
I'M *TRYING* TO GET US OUT OF HERE. WHAT'RE *YOU* DOING?
I'M TRYING NOT TO GET IRRITATED AT YOU.
OOO, *VERY SCARY.*
CLIC
DEFINITELY TABITHA'S TYPE. HE'S PROBABLY GOT THROWING STARS IN HIS POCKETS, TOO.
BABY, YOU AIN'T SEEN SCARY YET.

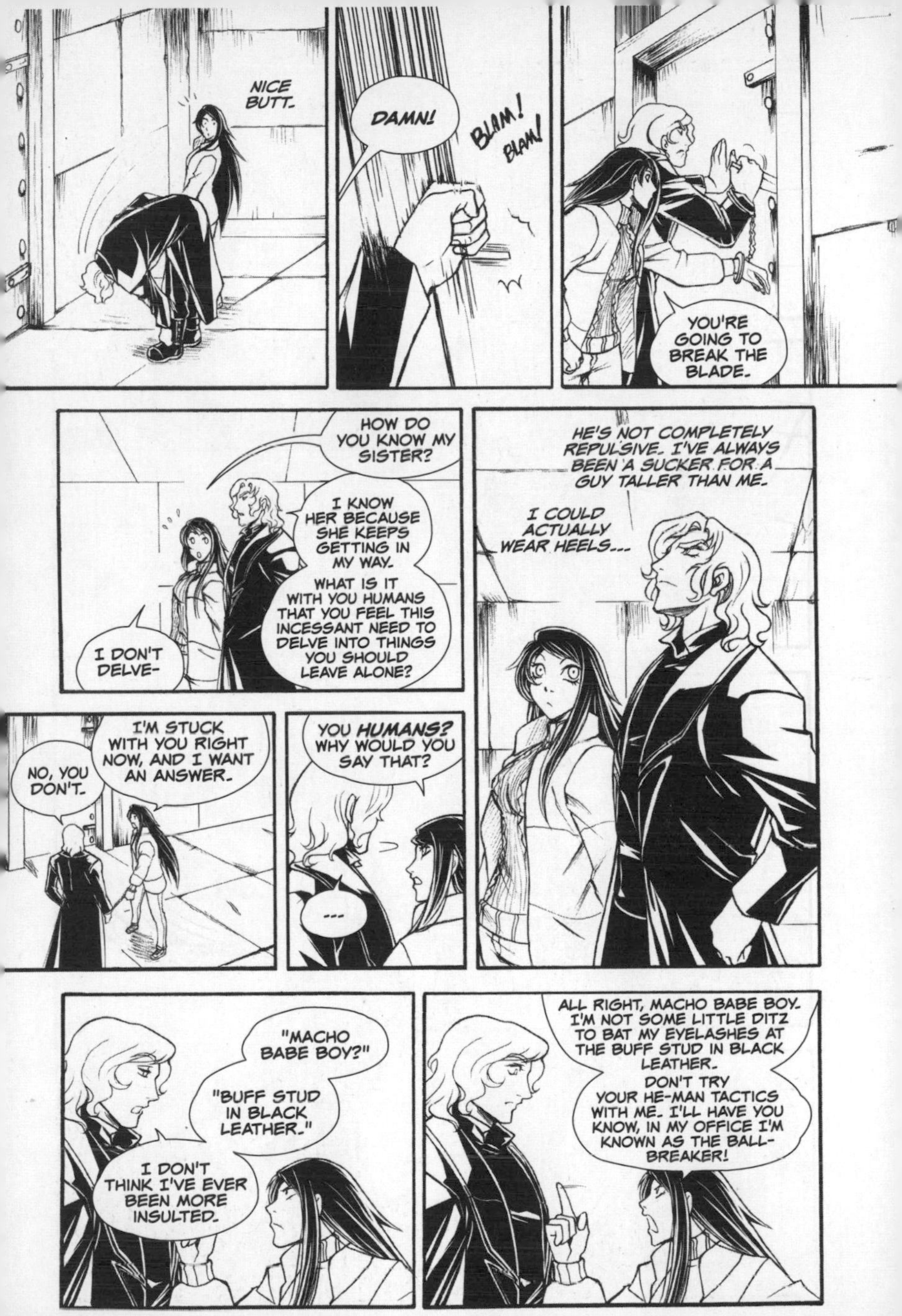
YOU'RE GOING TO BREAK THE BLADE.
DAMN!
BLAM! BLAM!
NICE BUTT.
HE'S NOT COMPLETELY REPULSIVE. I'VE ALWAYS BEEN A SUCKER FOR A GUY TALLER THAN ME.
I COULD ACTUALLY WEAR HEELS...
HOW DO YOU KNOW MY SISTER?
I KNOW HER BECAUSE SHE KEEPS GETTING IN MY WAY.
WHAT IS IT WITH YOU HUMANS THAT YOU FEEL THIS INCESSANT NEED TO DELVE INTO THINGS YOU SHOULD LEAVE ALONE?
I DON'T DELVE-
YOU *HUMANS?* WHY WOULD YOU SAY THAT?
...
I'M STUCK WITH YOU RIGHT NOW, AND I WANT AN ANSWER.
NO, YOU DON'T.
ALL RIGHT, MACHO BABE BOY. I'M NOT SOME LITTLE DITZ TO BAT MY EYELASHES AT THE BUFF STUD IN BLACK LEATHER.
DON'T TRY YOUR HE-MAN TACTICS WITH ME. I'LL HAVE YOU KNOW, IN MY OFFICE I'M KNOWN AS THE BALL-BREAKER!
"MACHO BABE BOY?"
"BUFF STUD IN BLACK LEATHER."
I DON'T THINK I'VE EVER BEEN MORE INSULTED.

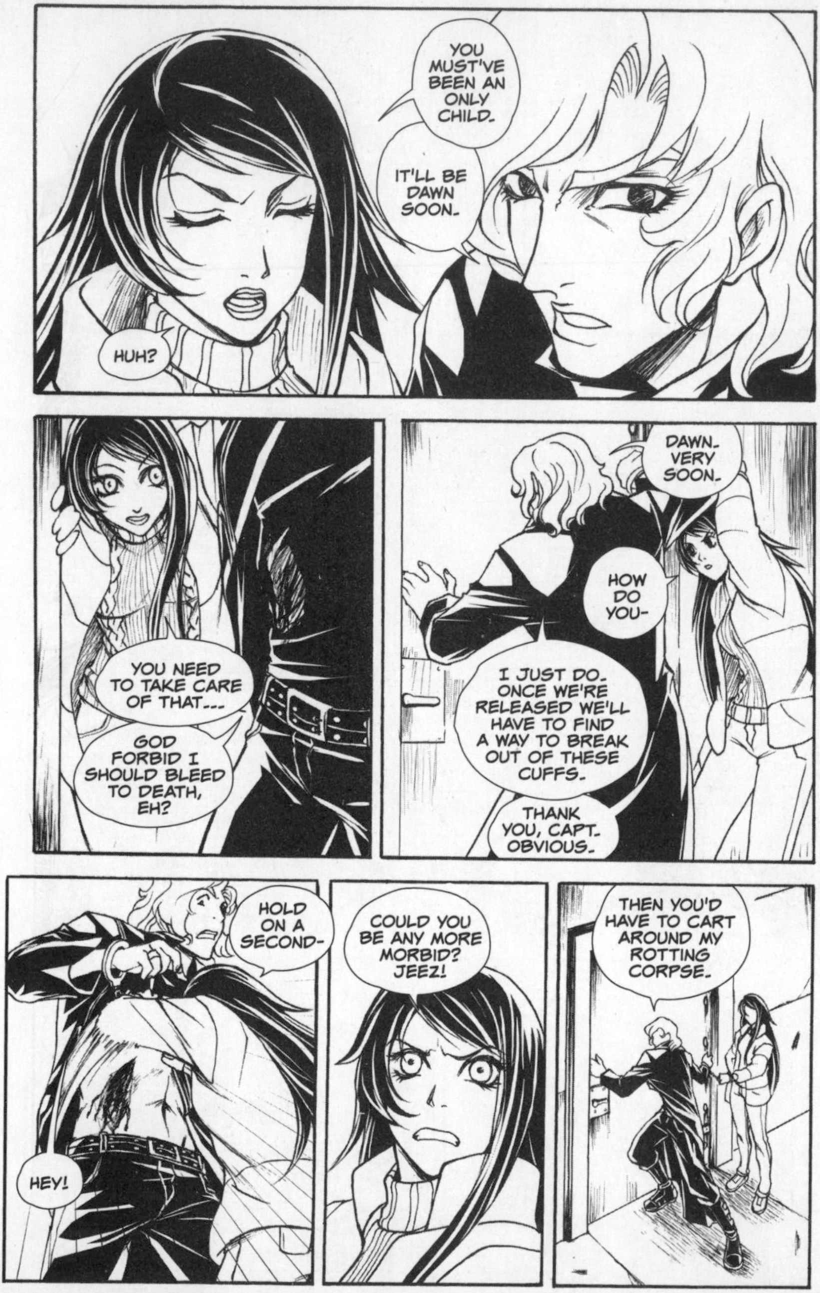
YOU MUST'VE BEEN AN ONLY CHILD.
IT'LL BE DAWN SOON.
HUH?
DAWN. VERY SOON.
HOW DO YOU-
I JUST DO. ONCE WE'RE RELEASED WE'LL HAVE TO FIND A WAY TO BREAK OUT OF THESE CUFFS.
THANK YOU, CAPT. OBVIOUS.
YOU NEED TO TAKE CARE OF THAT...
GOD FORBID I SHOULD BLEED TO DEATH, EH?
THEN YOU'D HAVE TO CART AROUND MY ROTTING CORPSE.
COULD YOU BE ANY MORE MORBID? JEEZ!
HOLD ON A SECOND-
HEY!

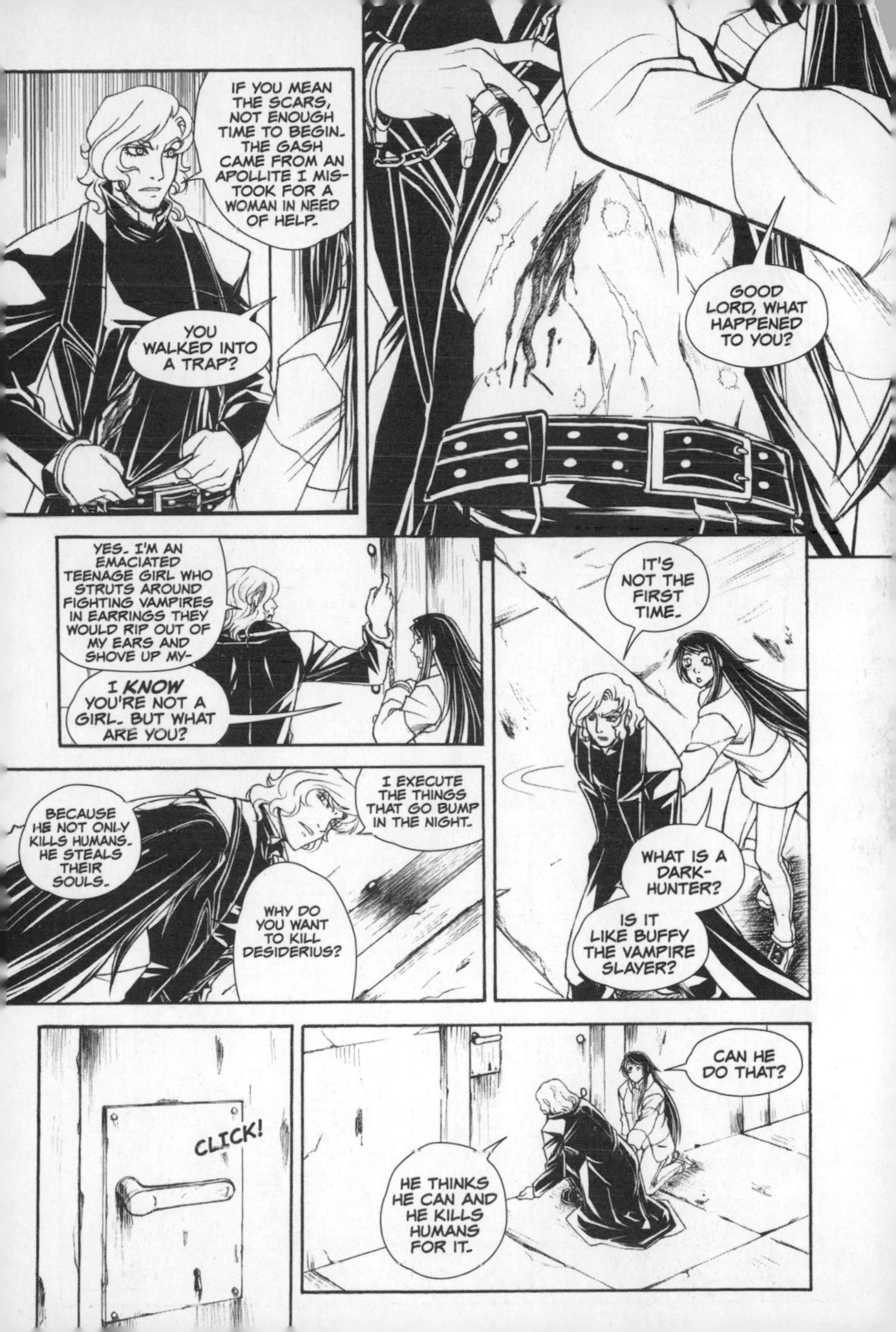
GOOD LORD, WHAT HAPPENED TO YOU?
IF YOU MEAN THE SCARS, NOT ENOUGH TIME TO BEGIN. THE GASH CAME FROM AN APOLLITE I MISTOOK FOR A WOMAN IN NEED OF HELP.
YOU WALKED INTO A TRAP?
IT'S NOT THE FIRST TIME.
WHAT IS A DARK-HUNTER?
IS IT LIKE BUFFY THE VAMPIRE SLAYER?
YES. I'M AN EMACIATED TEENAGE GIRL WHO STRUTS AROUND FIGHTING VAMPIRES IN EARRINGS THEY WOULD RIP OUT OF MY EARS AND SHOVE UP MY-
I ***KNOW*** YOU'RE NOT A GIRL. BUT WHAT ARE YOU?
I EXECUTE THE THINGS THAT GO BUMP IN THE NIGHT.
WHY DO YOU WANT TO KILL DESIDERIUS?
BECAUSE HE NOT ONLY KILLS HUMANS. HE STEALS THEIR SOULS.
CAN HE DO THAT?
HE THINKS HE CAN AND HE KILLS HUMANS FOR IT.
CLICK!

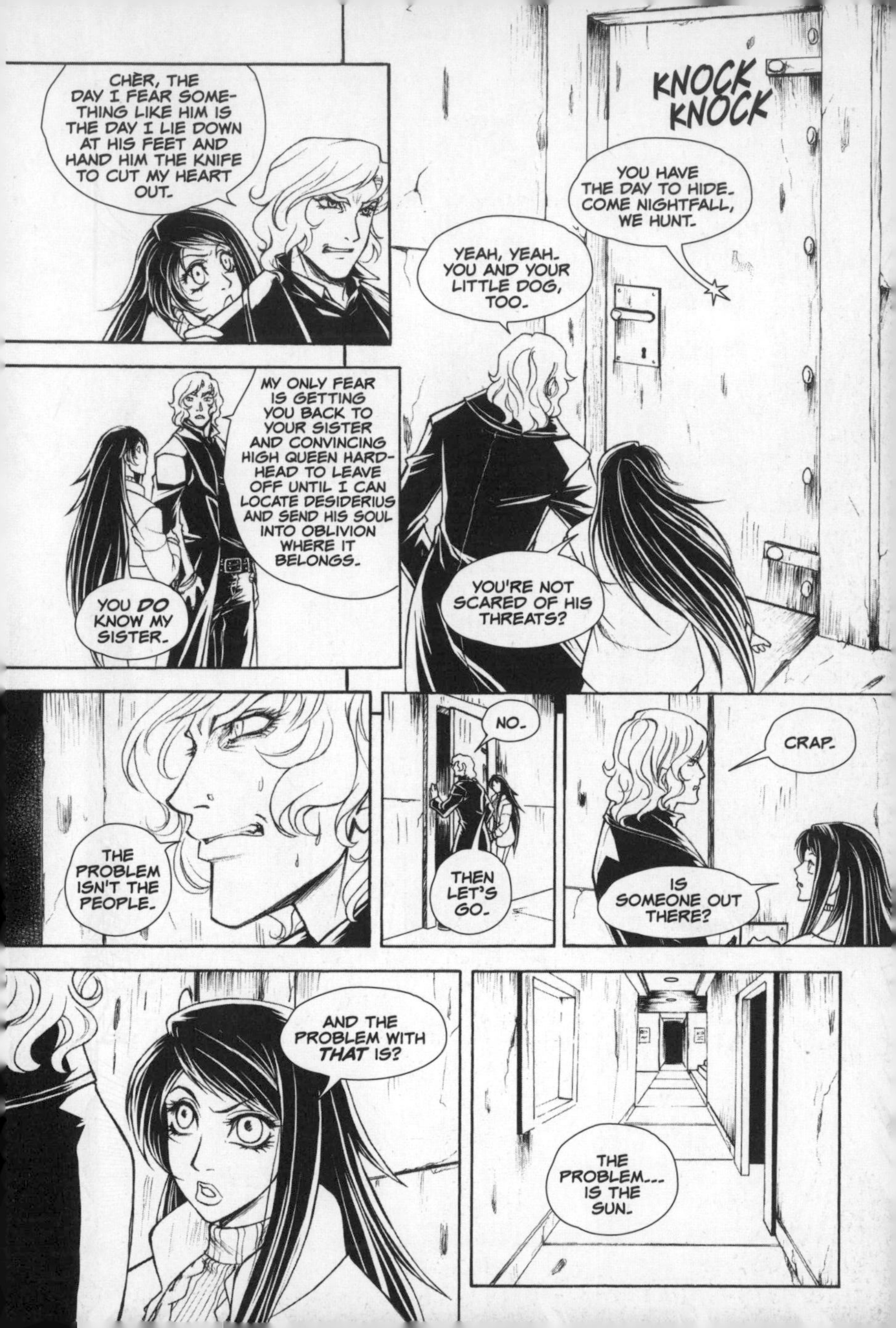
KNOCK KNOCK
YOU HAVE THE DAY TO HIDE. COME NIGHTFALL, WE HUNT.
YEAH, YEAH. YOU AND YOUR LITTLE DOG, TOO.
YOU'RE NOT SCARED OF HIS THREATS?
CHÈR, THE DAY I FEAR SOMETHING LIKE HIM IS THE DAY I LIE DOWN AT HIS FEET AND HAND HIM THE KNIFE TO CUT MY HEART OUT.
MY ONLY FEAR IS GETTING YOU BACK TO YOUR SISTER AND CONVINCING HIGH QUEEN HARDHEAD TO LEAVE OFF UNTIL I CAN LOCATE DESIDERIUS AND SEND HIS SOUL INTO OBLIVION WHERE IT BELONGS.
YOU *DO* KNOW MY SISTER.
CRAP.
IS SOMEONE OUT THERE?
NO.
THEN LET'S GO.
THE PROBLEM ISN'T THE PEOPLE.
THE PROBLEM... IS THE SUN.
AND THE PROBLEM WITH *THAT* IS?

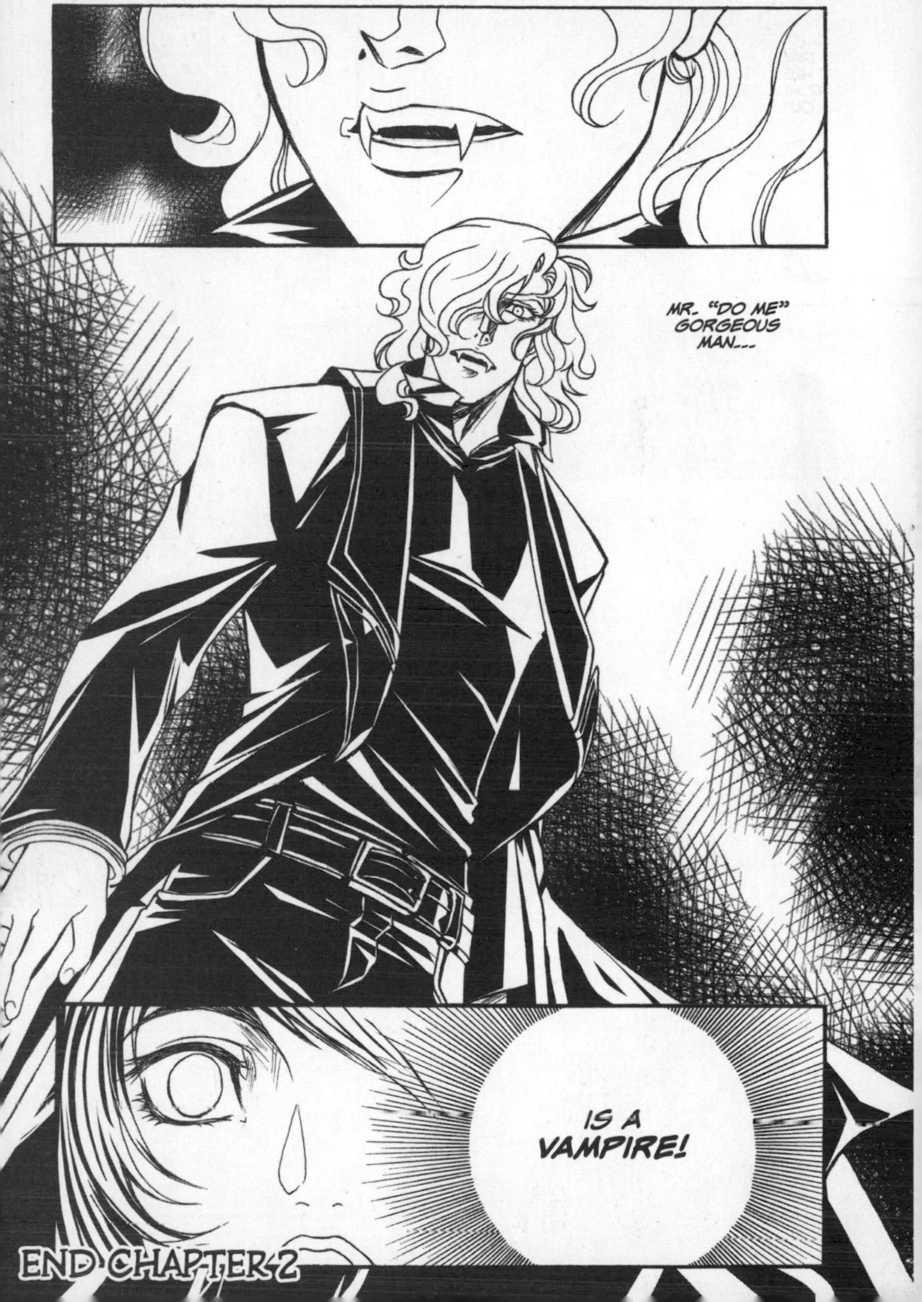
MR. "DO ME" GORGEOUS MAN...
IS A VAMPIRE!
END CHAPTER 2

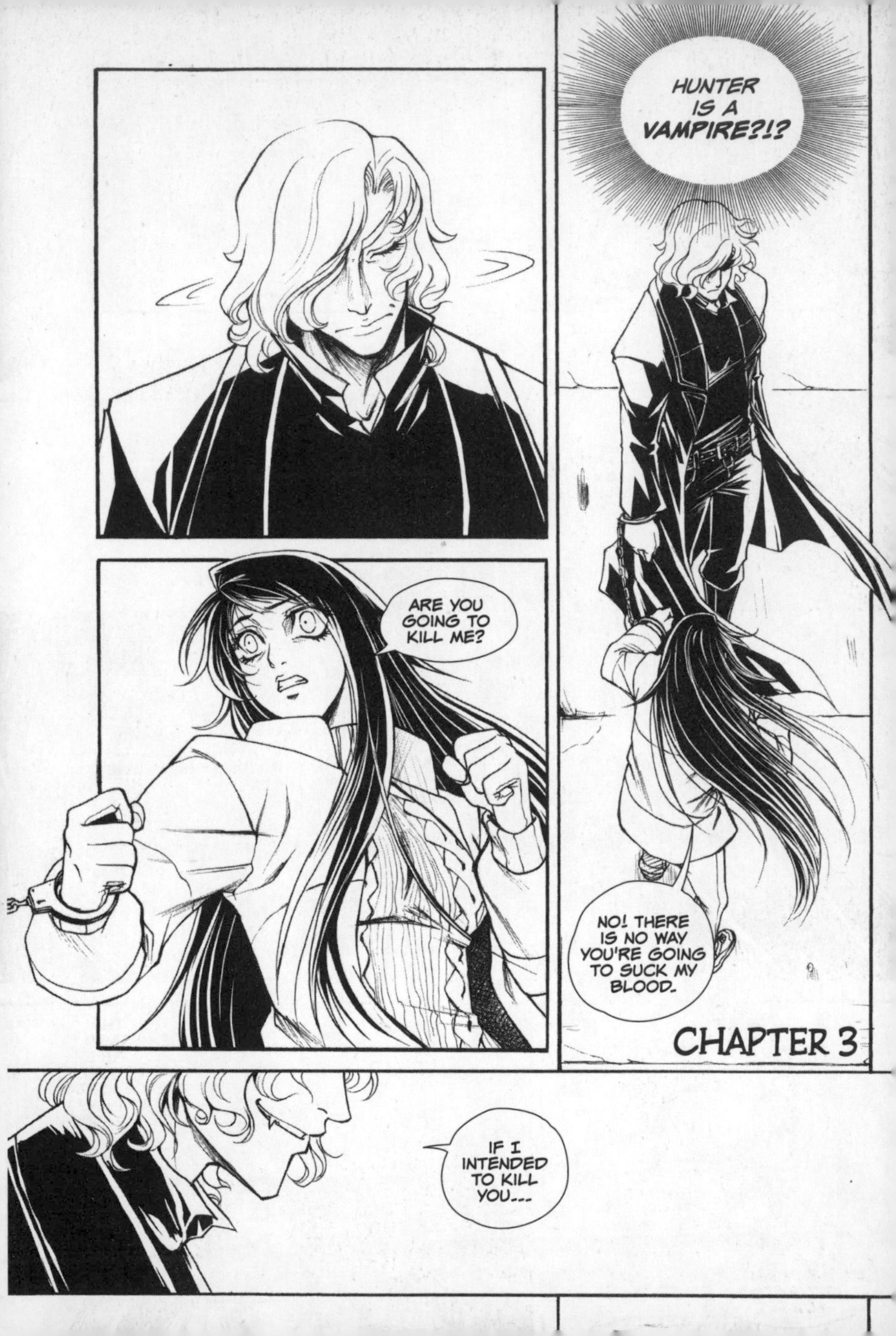
HUNTER IS A VAMPIRE?!?
NO! THERE IS NO WAY YOU'RE GOING TO SUCK MY BLOOD.
CHAPTER 3
ARE YOU GOING TO KILL ME?
IF I INTENDED TO KILL YOU...

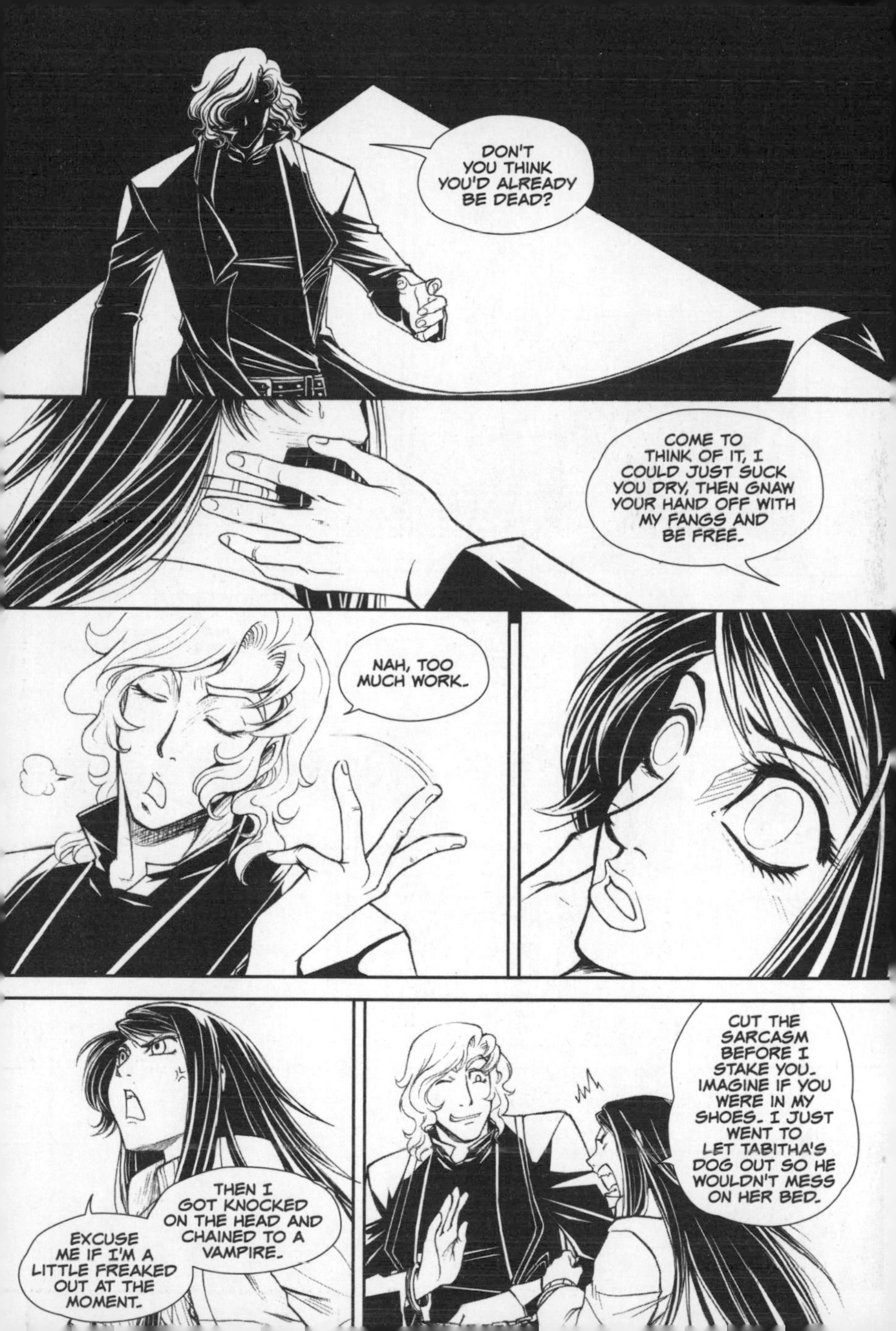
DON'T YOU THINK YOU'D ALREADY BE DEAD?
COME TO THINK OF IT, I COULD JUST SUCK YOU DRY, THEN GNAW YOUR HAND OFF WITH MY FANGS AND BE FREE.
NAH, TOO MUCH WORK.
CUT THE SARCASM BEFORE I STAKE YOU. IMAGINE IF YOU WERE IN MY SHOES. I JUST WENT TO LET TABITHA'S DOG OUT SO HE WOULDN'T MESS ON HER BED.
THEN I GOT KNOCKED ON THE HEAD AND CHAINED TO A VAMPIRE.
EXCUSE ME IF I'M A LITTLE FREAKED OUT AT THE MOMENT.

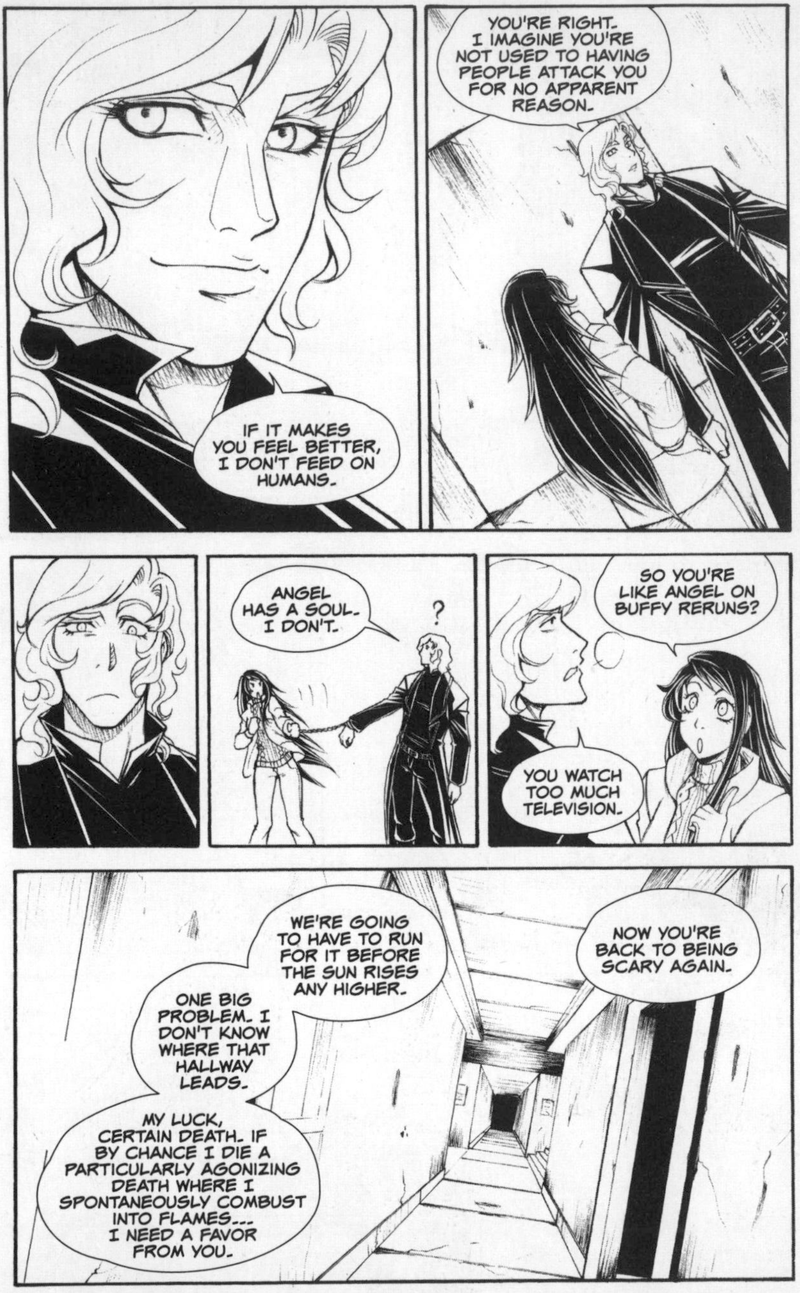
YOU'RE RIGHT. I IMAGINE YOU'RE NOT USED TO HAVING PEOPLE ATTACK YOU FOR NO APPARENT REASON.
IF IT MAKES YOU FEEL BETTER, I DON'T FEED ON HUMANS.
SO YOU'RE LIKE ANGEL ON BUFFY RERUNS?
YOU WATCH TOO MUCH TELEVISION.
?
ANGEL HAS A SOUL. I DON'T.
NOW YOU'RE BACK TO BEING SCARY AGAIN.
WE'RE GOING TO HAVE TO RUN FOR IT BEFORE THE SUN RISES ANY HIGHER.
ONE BIG PROBLEM. I DON'T KNOW WHERE THAT HALLWAY LEADS.
MY LUCK, CERTAIN DEATH. IF BY CHANCE I DIE A PARTICULARLY AGONIZING DEATH WHERE I SPONTANEOUSLY COMBUST INTO FLAMES... I NEED A FAVOR FROM YOU.

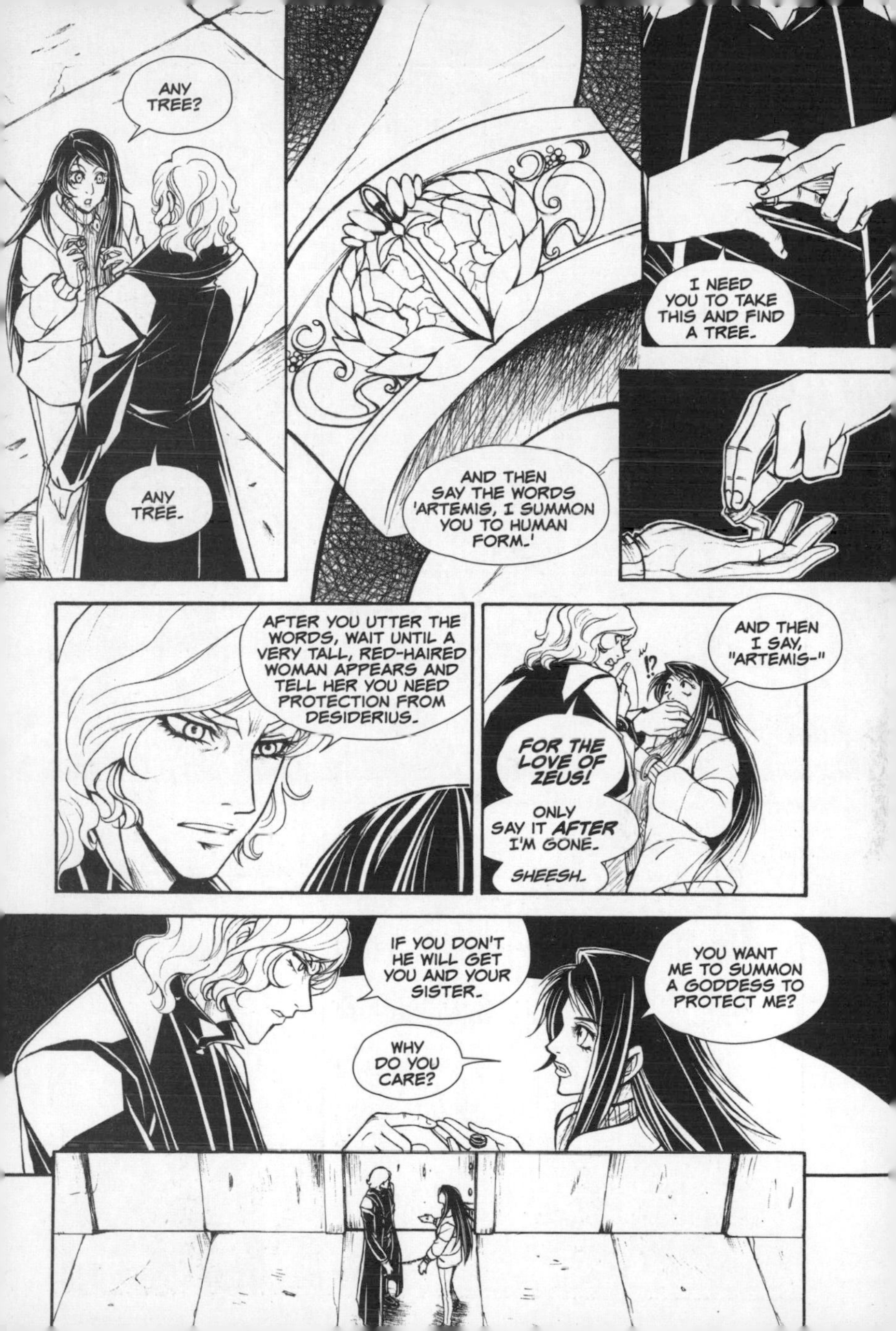
I NEED YOU TO TAKE THIS AND FIND A TREE.
AND THEN SAY THE WORDS 'ARTEMIS, I SUMMON YOU TO HUMAN FORM.'
ANY TREE?
ANY TREE.
AND THEN I SAY, "ARTEMIS-"
!?
FOR THE LOVE OF ZEUS!
ONLY SAY IT AFTER I'M GONE.
SHEESH.
AFTER YOU UTTER THE WORDS, WAIT UNTIL A VERY TALL, RED-HAIRED WOMAN APPEARS AND TELL HER YOU NEED PROTECTION FROM DESIDERIUS.
YOU WANT ME TO SUMMON A GODDESS TO PROTECT ME?
IF YOU DON'T HE WILL GET YOU AND YOUR SISTER.
WHY DO YOU CARE?

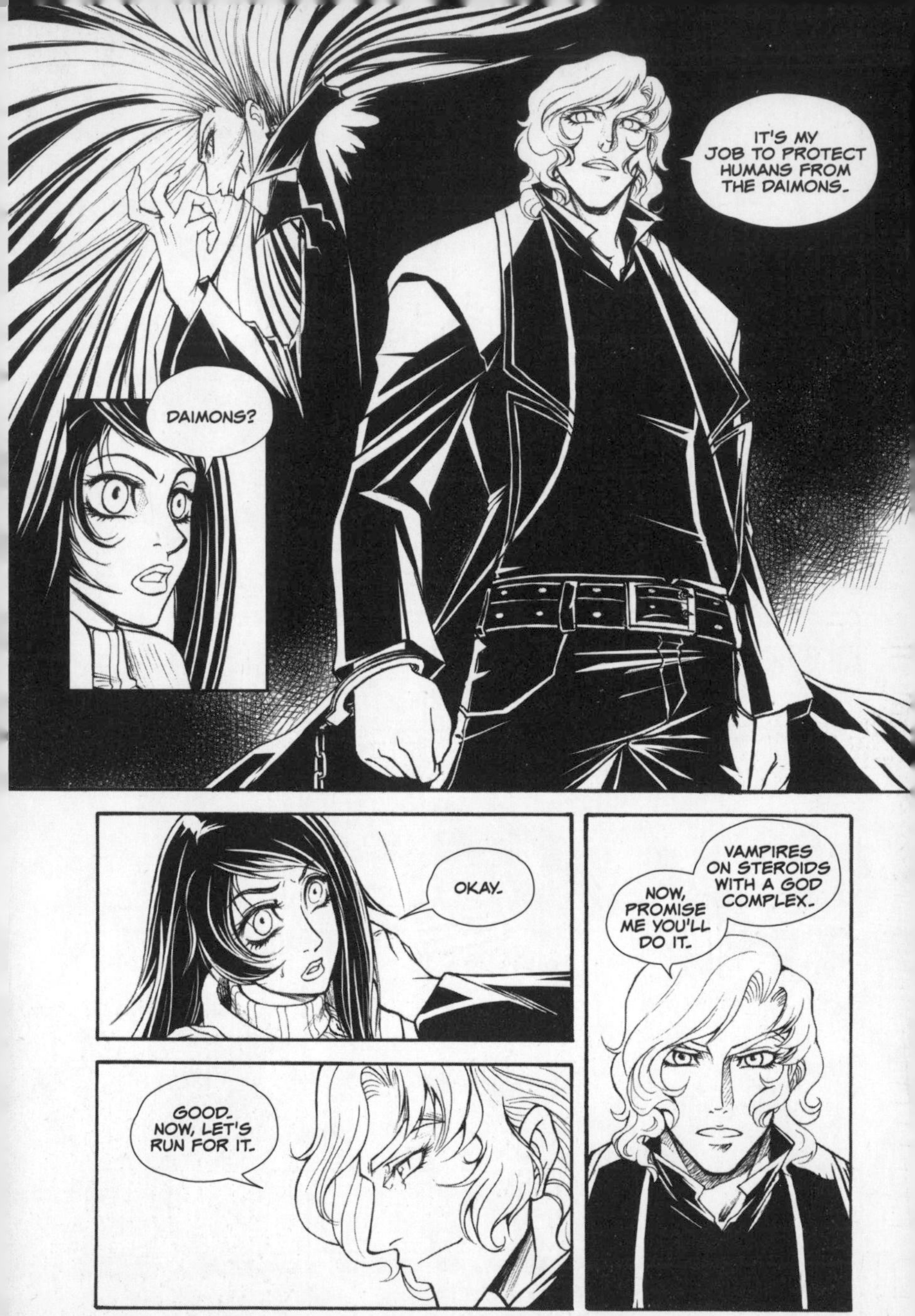
IT'S MY JOB TO PROTECT HUMANS FROM THE DAIMONS.
DAIMONS?
VAMPIRES ON STEROIDS WITH A GOD COMPLEX.
NOW, PROMISE ME YOU'LL DO IT.
OKAY.
GOOD. NOW, LET'S RUN FOR IT.

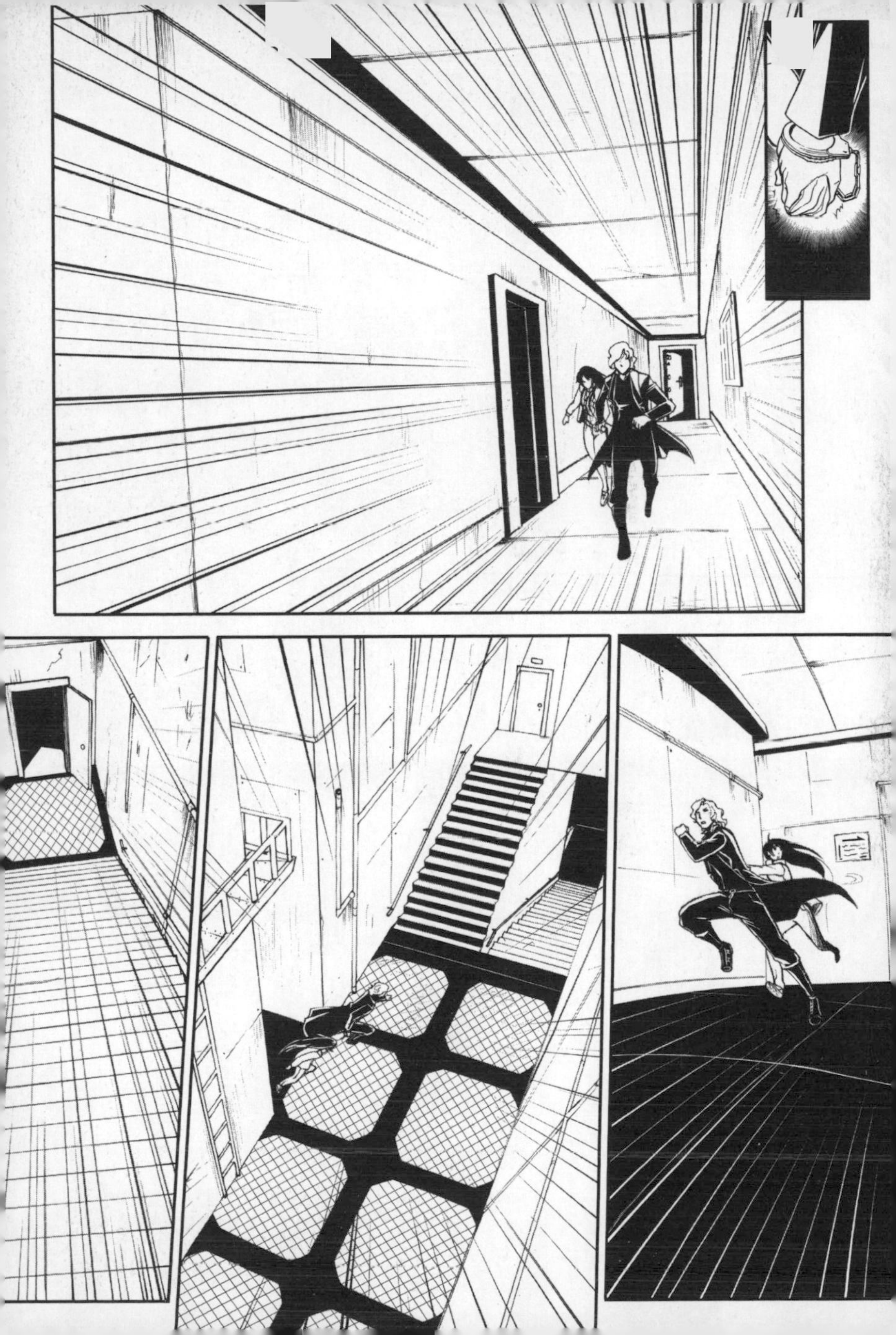

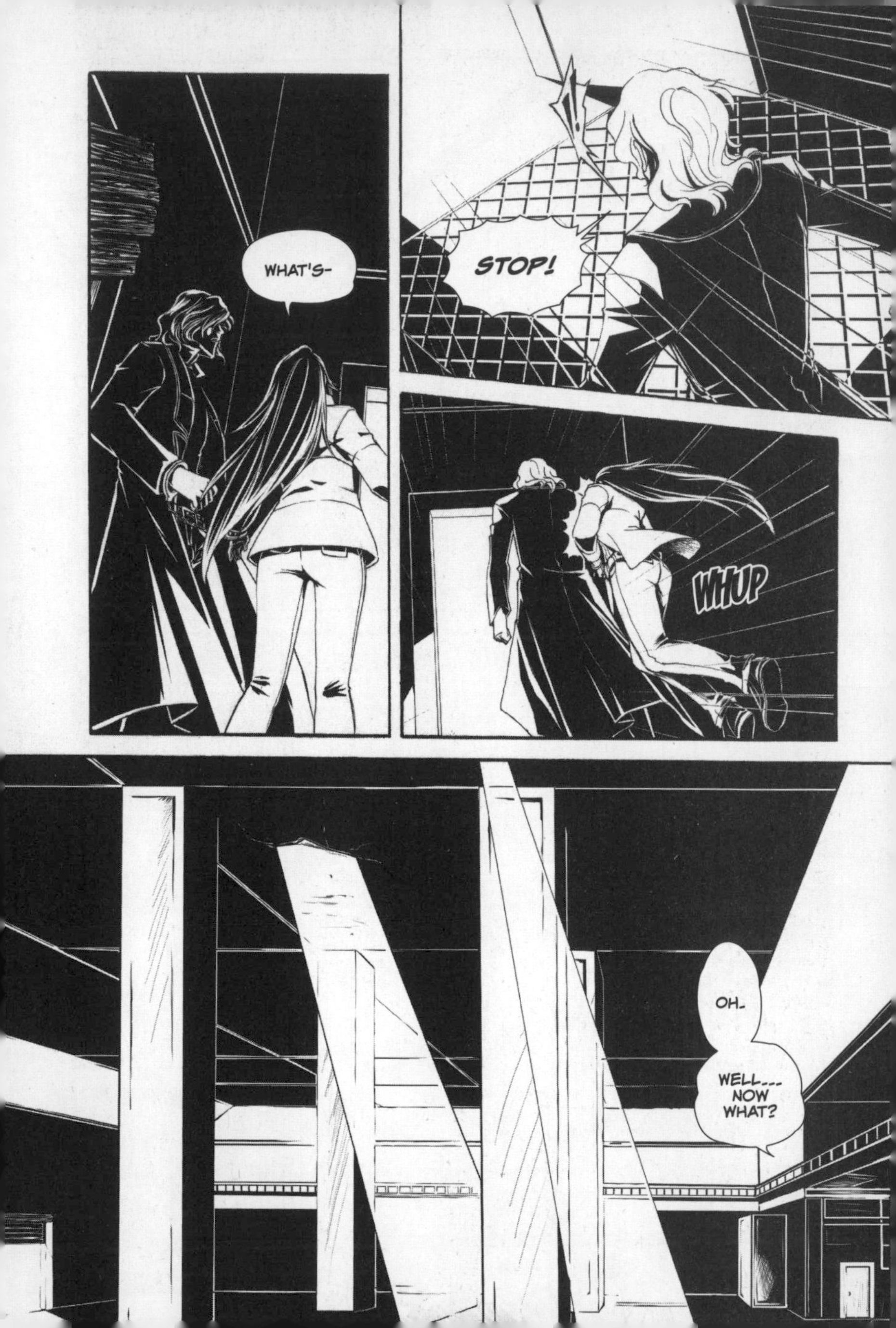
STOP!
WHUP
WHAT'S-
OH-
WELL... NOW WHAT?

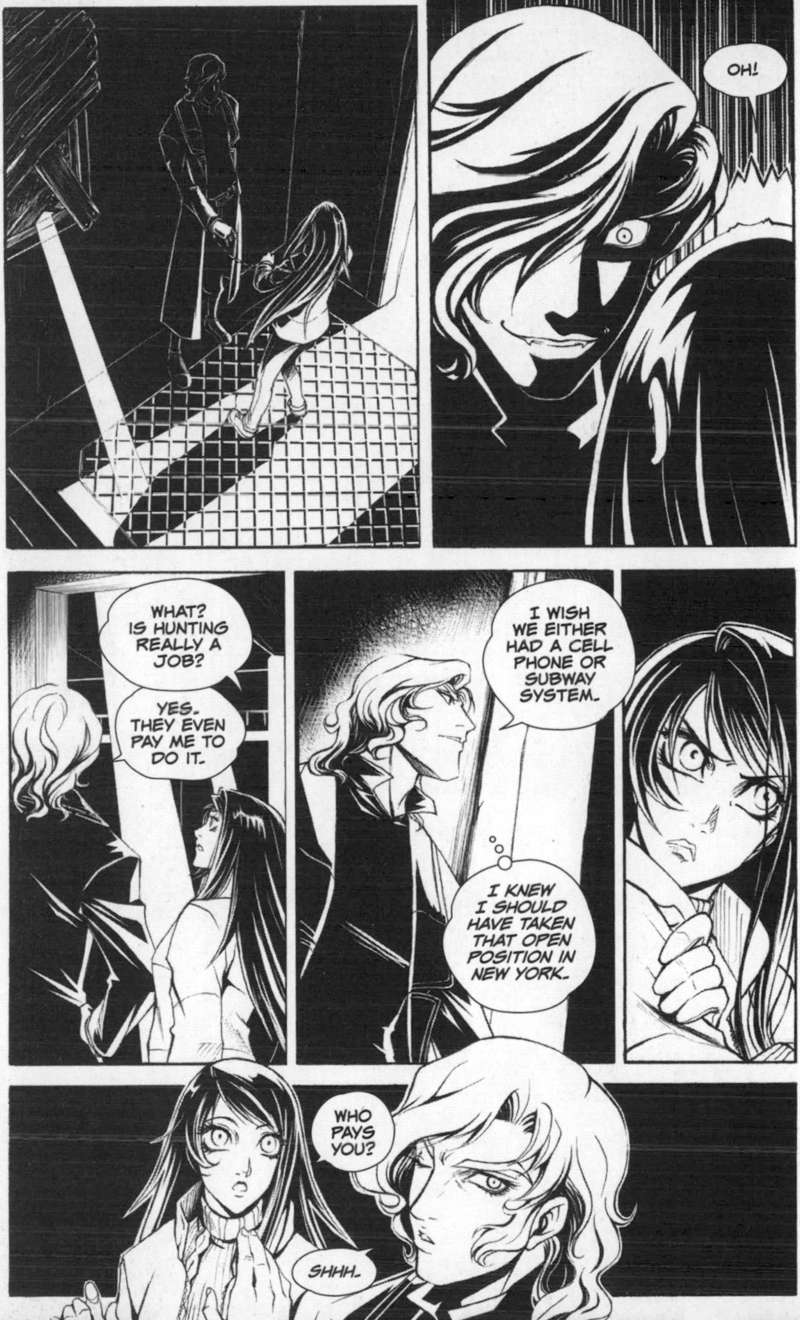
OH!
I WISH WE EITHER HAD A CELL PHONE OR SUBWAY SYSTEM.
I KNEW I SHOULD HAVE TAKEN THAT OPEN POSITION IN NEW YORK.
WHAT? IS HUNTING REALLY A JOB?
YES. THEY EVEN PAY ME TO DO IT.
WHO PAYS YOU?
SHHH.

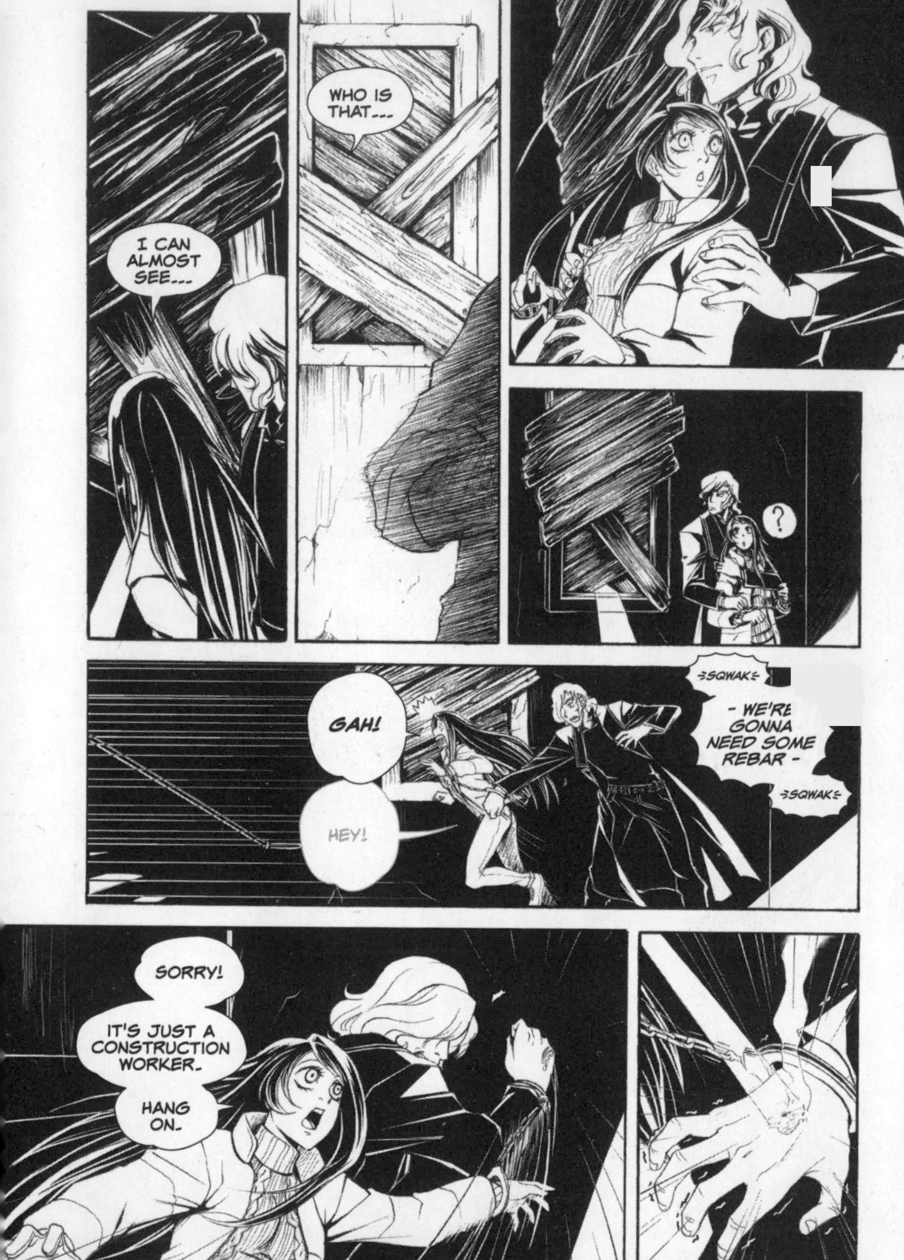
?
WHO IS THAT...
I CAN ALMOST SEE...
-SQWAK-
- WE'RE GONNA NEED SOME REBAR -
-SQWAK-
GAH!
HEY!
SORRY!
IT'S JUST A CONSTRUCTION WORKER.
HANG ON.

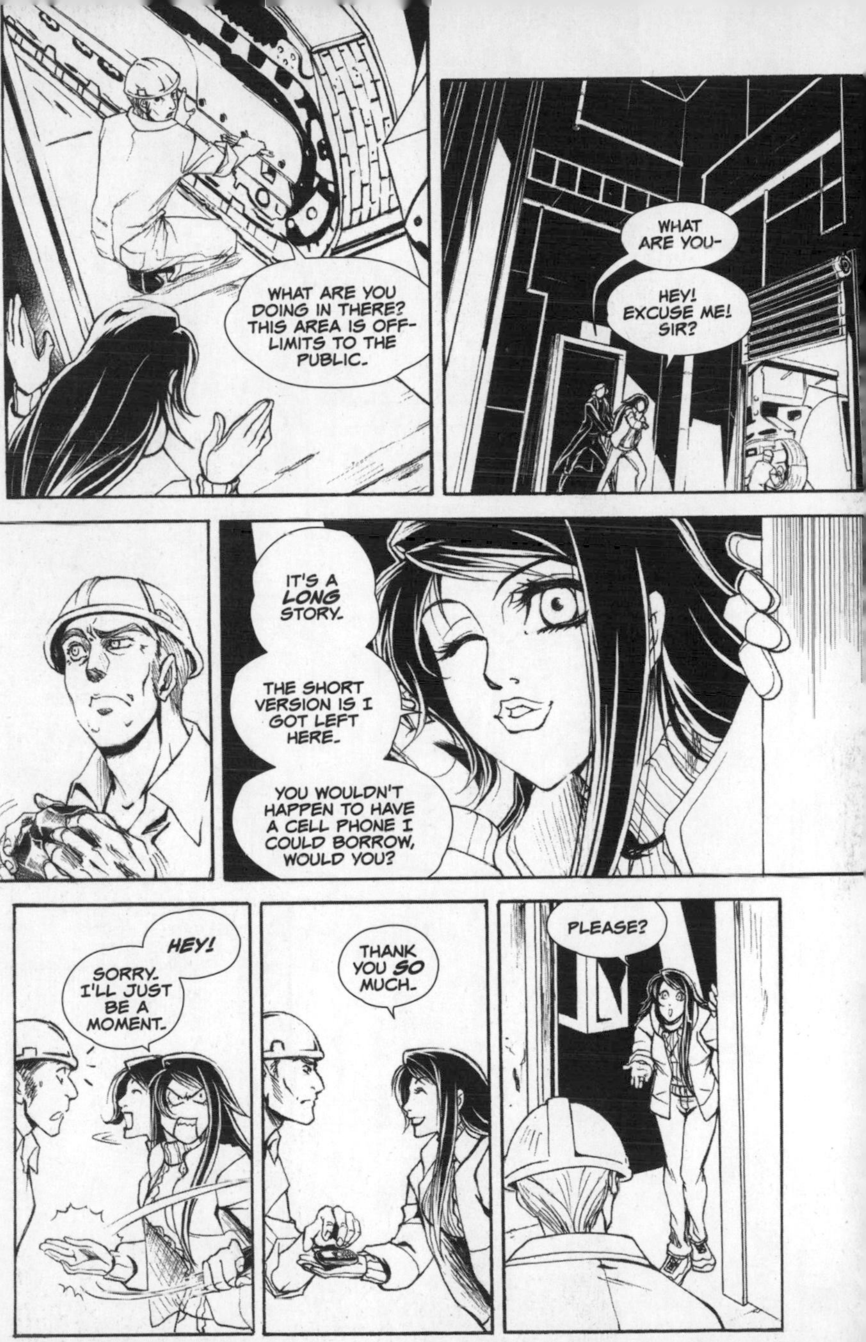
WHAT ARE YOU-
HEY! EXCUSE ME! SIR?
WHAT ARE YOU DOING IN THERE? THIS AREA IS OFF-LIMITS TO THE PUBLIC.
IT'S A LONG STORY.
THE SHORT VERSION IS I GOT LEFT HERE.
YOU WOULDN'T HAPPEN TO HAVE A CELL PHONE I COULD BORROW, WOULD YOU?
PLEASE?
THANK YOU SO MUCH.
HEY!
SORRY. I'LL JUST BE A MOMENT.

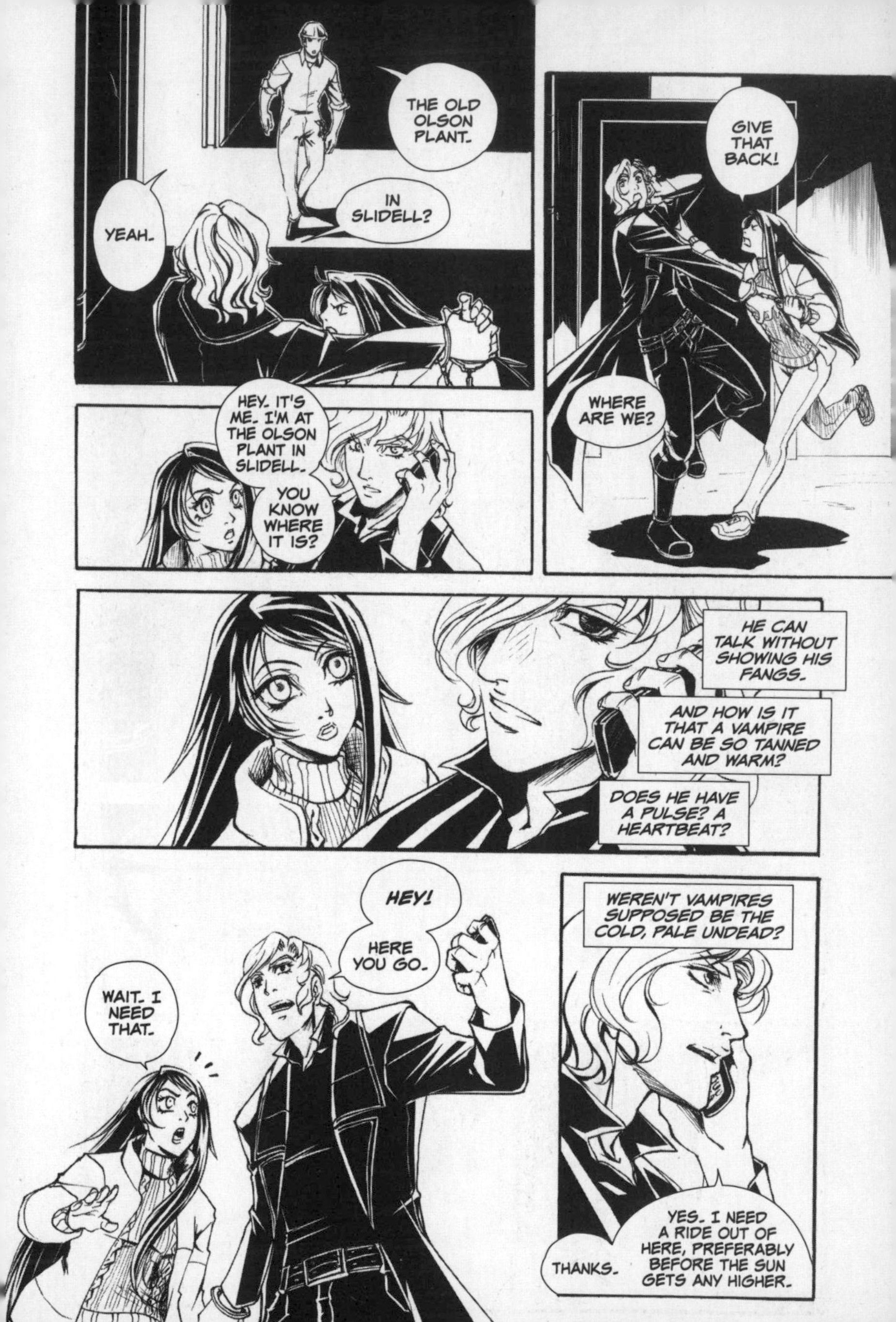

THE OLD OLSON PLANT.
IN SLIDELL?
YEAH.
HEY. IT'S ME. I'M AT THE OLSON PLANT IN SLIDELL.
YOU KNOW WHERE IT IS?
GIVE THAT BACK!
WHERE ARE WE?
HE CAN TALK WITHOUT SHOWING HIS FANGS.
AND HOW IS IT THAT A VAMPIRE CAN BE SO TANNED AND WARM?
DOES HE HAVE A PULSE? A HEARTBEAT?
HEY!
HERE YOU GO.
WAIT. I NEED THAT.
WEREN'T VAMPIRES SUPPOSED BE THE COLD, PALE UNDEAD?
YES. I NEED A RIDE OUT OF HERE, PREFERABLY BEFORE THE SUN GETS ANY HIGHER.
THANKS.

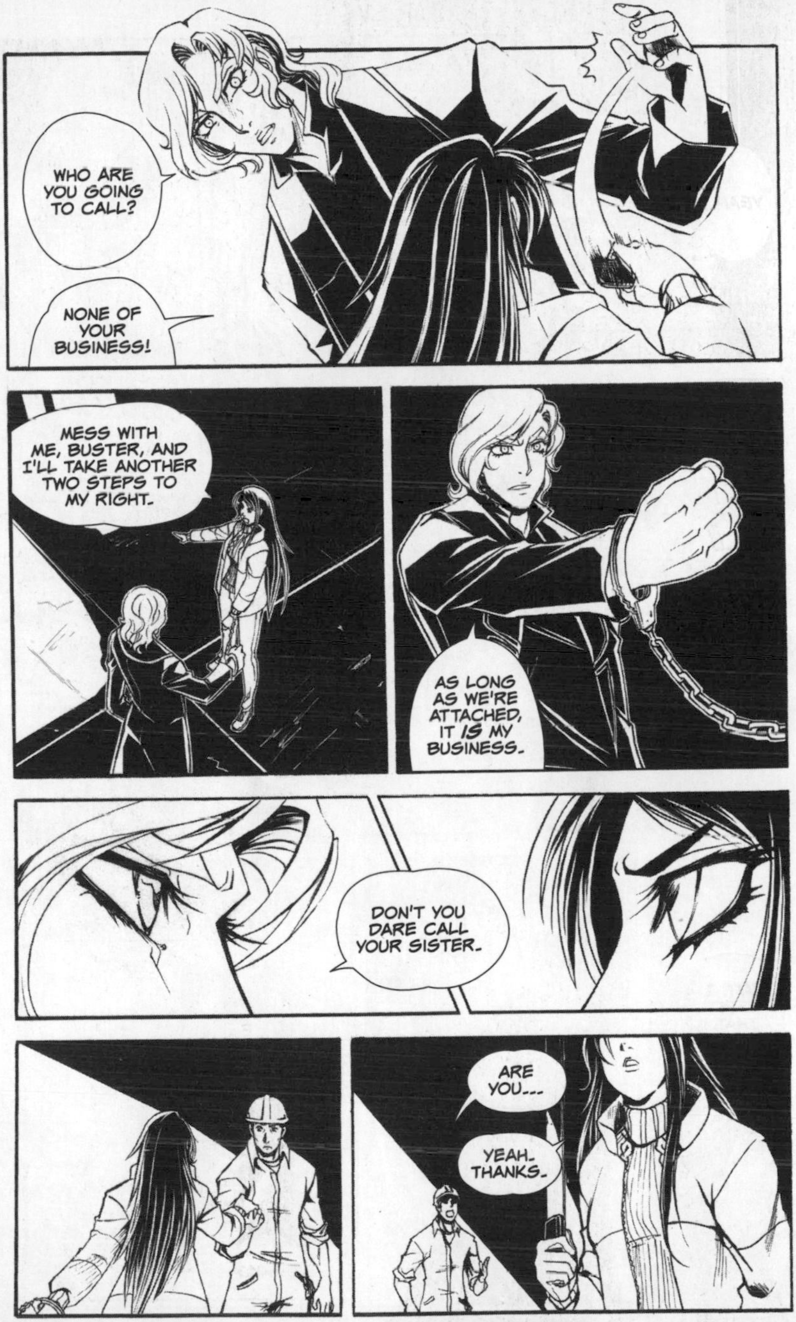
WHO ARE YOU GOING TO CALL?
NONE OF YOUR BUSINESS!
AS LONG AS WE'RE ATTACHED, IT *IS* MY BUSINESS.
MESS WITH ME, BUSTER, AND I'LL TAKE ANOTHER TWO STEPS TO MY RIGHT.
DON'T YOU DARE CALL YOUR SISTER.
ARE YOU...
YEAH. THANKS.

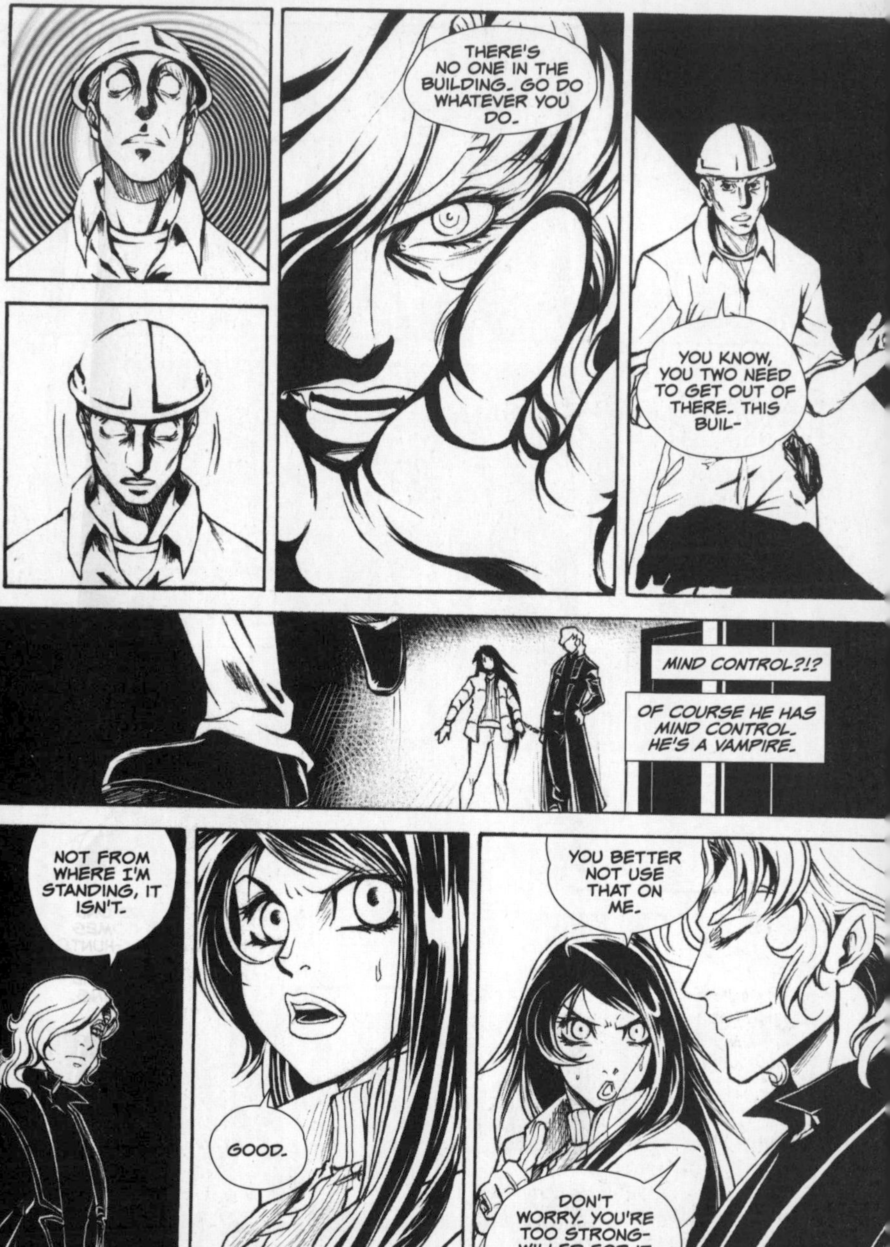
YOU KNOW, YOU TWO NEED TO GET OUT OF THERE. THIS BUIL-
THERE'S NO ONE IN THE BUILDING. GO DO WHATEVER YOU DO.
MIND CONTROL?!?
OF COURSE HE HAS MIND CONTROL. HE'S A VAMPIRE.
YOU BETTER NOT USE THAT ON ME.
DON'T WORRY. YOU'RE TOO STRONG-WILLED FOR IT TO WORK.
GOOD.
NOT FROM WHERE I'M STANDING, IT ISN'T.

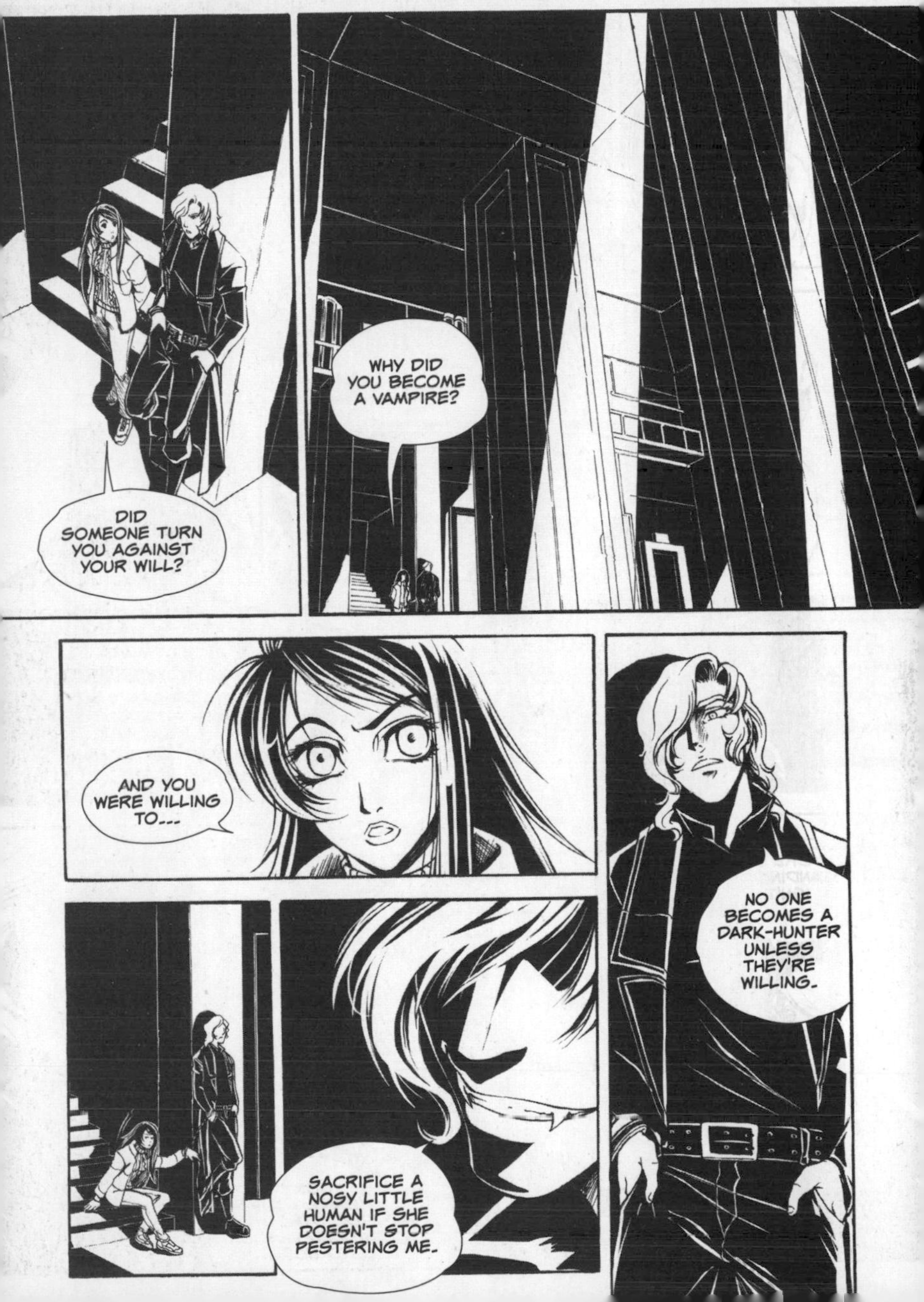
WHY DID YOU BECOME A VAMPIRE?
DID SOMEONE TURN YOU AGAINST YOUR WILL?
NO ONE BECOMES A DARK-HUNTER UNLESS THEY'RE WILLING.
AND YOU WERE WILLING TO...
SACRIFICE A NOSY LITTLE HUMAN IF SHE DOESN'T STOP PESTERING ME.

HOW LONG
DO YOU THINK
WE'LL HAVE TO
WAIT?

SO...

I DON'T
KNOW...

WHO
DID YOU
CALL?

NO ONE...

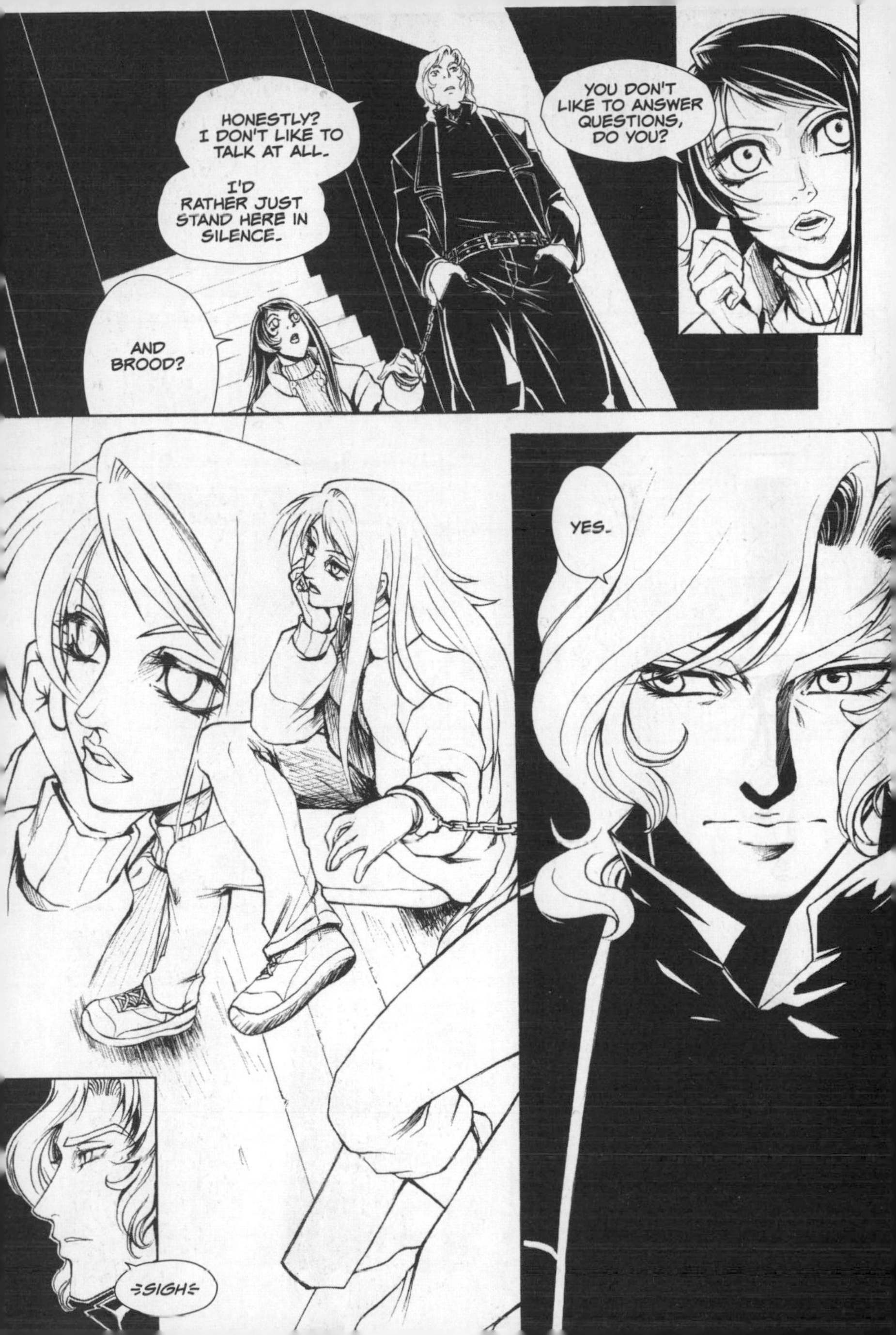
YOU DON'T LIKE TO ANSWER QUESTIONS, DO YOU?
HONESTLY? I DON'T LIKE TO TALK AT ALL.
I'D RATHER JUST STAND HERE IN SILENCE.
AND BROOD?
YES.
=SIGH=

WE-OOO-
WE-OOO-
WE-OOO-

WE-OOO-WE-OOO-WE-OOO.

YOUR
RIDE?

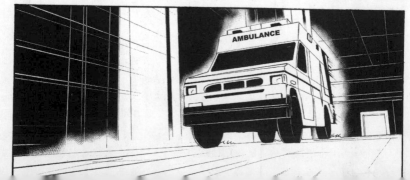

AMBULANCE

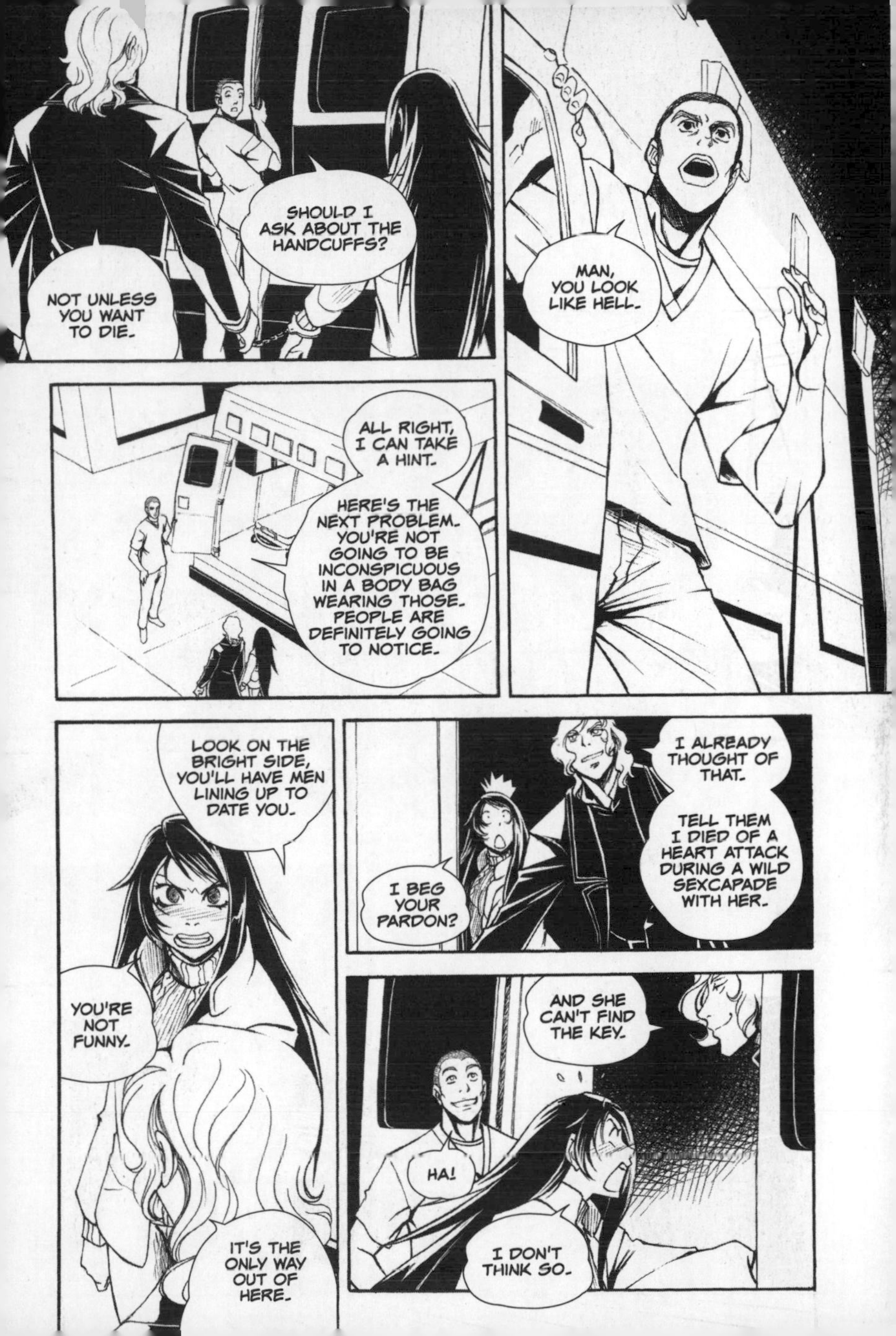
MAN, YOU LOOK LIKE HELL.
SHOULD I ASK ABOUT THE HANDCUFFS?
NOT UNLESS YOU WANT TO DIE.
ALL RIGHT, I CAN TAKE A HINT.
HERE'S THE NEXT PROBLEM. YOU'RE NOT GOING TO BE INCONSPICUOUS IN A BODY BAG WEARING THOSE. PEOPLE ARE DEFINITELY GOING TO NOTICE.
I ALREADY THOUGHT OF THAT.
TELL THEM I DIED OF A HEART ATTACK DURING A WILD SEXCAPADE WITH HER.
I BEG YOUR PARDON?
AND SHE CAN'T FIND THE KEY.
HA!
I DON'T THINK SO.
LOOK ON THE BRIGHT SIDE, YOU'LL HAVE MEN LINING UP TO DATE YOU.
YOU'RE NOT FUNNY.
IT'S THE ONLY WAY OUT OF HERE.

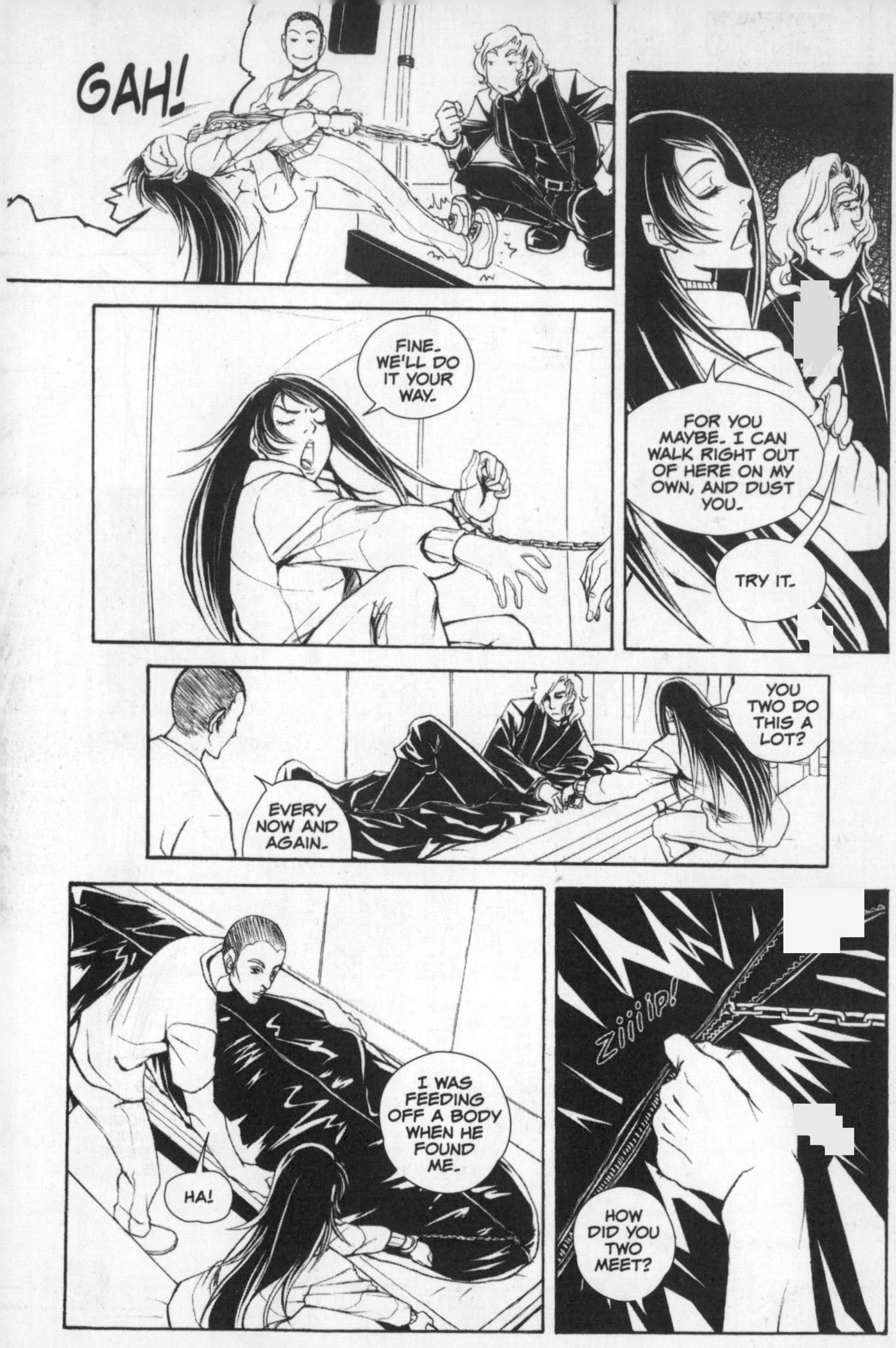
GAH!
FINE. WE'LL DO IT YOUR WAY.
FOR YOU MAYBE. I CAN WALK RIGHT OUT OF HERE ON MY OWN, AND DUST YOU.
TRY IT.
YOU TWO DO THIS A LOT?
EVERY NOW AND AGAIN.
I WAS FEEDING OFF A BODY WHEN HE FOUND ME.
HA!
ZIIIIP!
HOW DID YOU TWO MEET?

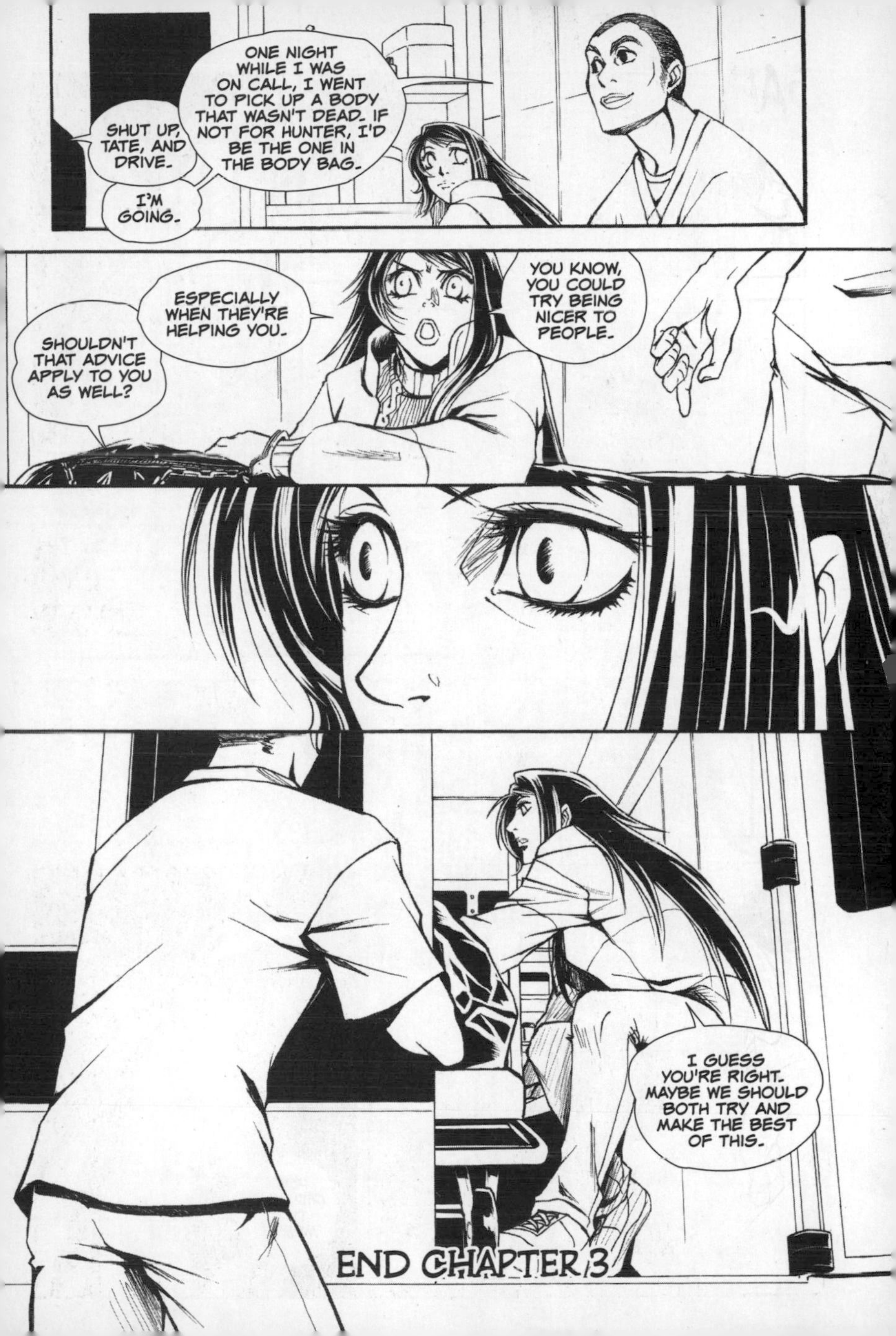
ONE NIGHT WHILE I WAS ON CALL, I WENT TO PICK UP A BODY THAT WASN'T DEAD. IF NOT FOR HUNTER, I'D BE THE ONE IN THE BODY BAG.
SHUT UP, TATE, AND DRIVE.
I'M GOING.
YOU KNOW, YOU COULD TRY BEING NICER TO PEOPLE.
ESPECIALLY WHEN THEY'RE HELPING YOU.
SHOULDN'T THAT ADVICE APPLY TO YOU AS WELL?
I GUESS YOU'RE RIGHT. MAYBE WE SHOULD BOTH TRY AND MAKE THE BEST OF THIS.
END CHAPTER 3

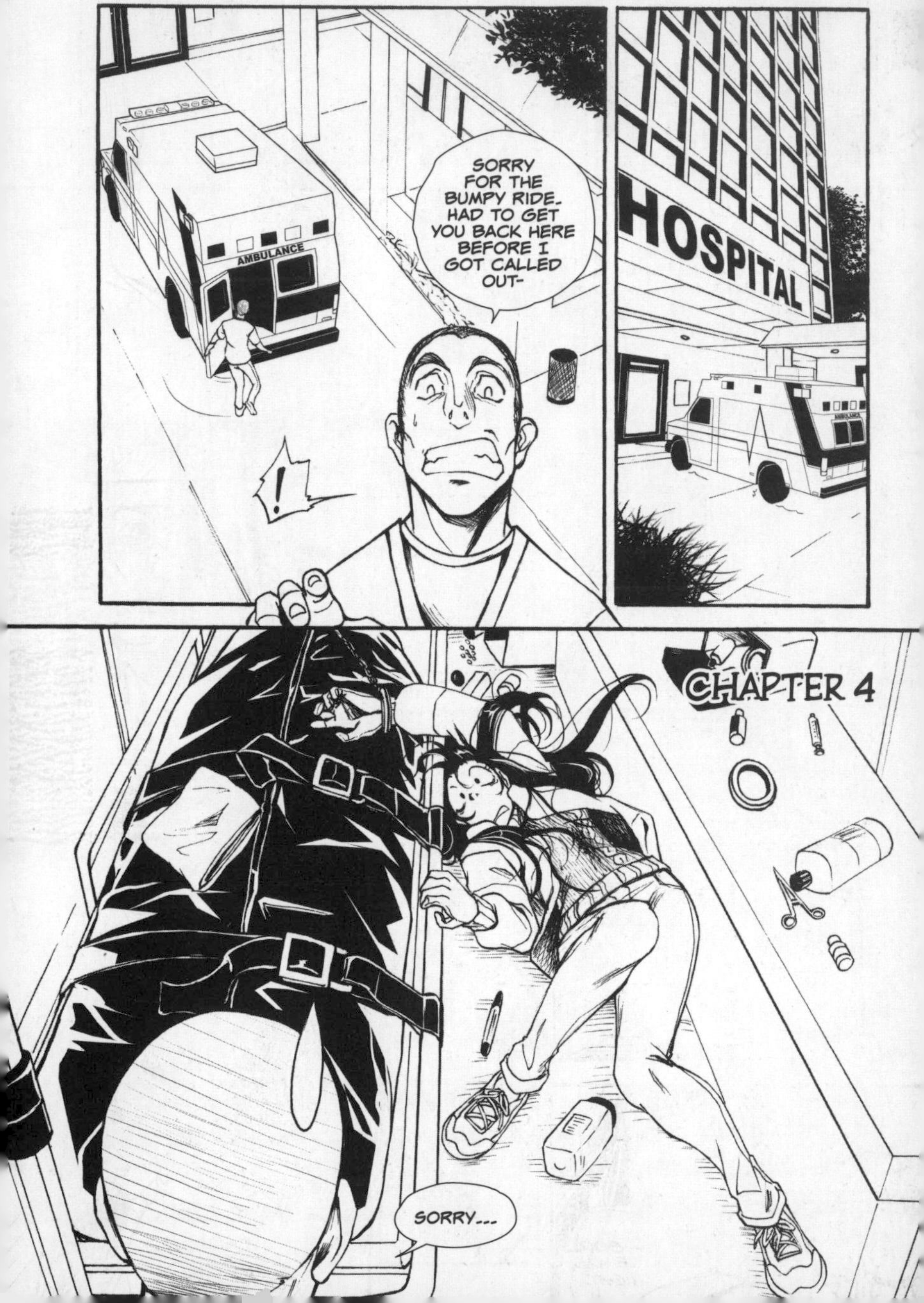
HOSPITAL
AMBULANCE
AMBULANCE
SORRY FOR THE BUMPY RIDE. HAD TO GET YOU BACK HERE BEFORE I GOT CALLED OUT-
!
CHAPTER 4
SORRY...

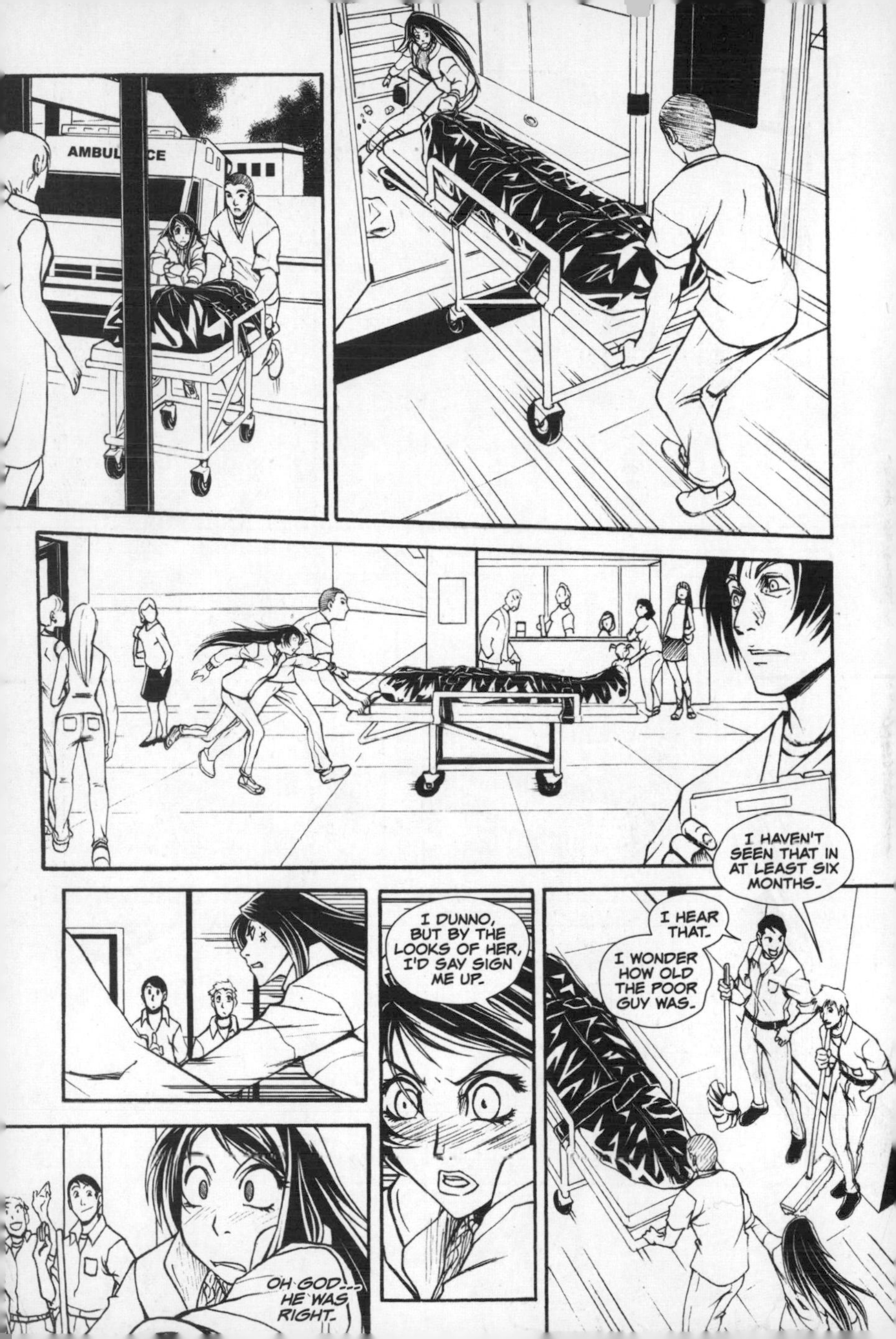
AMBUL CE
I HAVEN'T SEEN THAT IN AT LEAST SIX MONTHS.
I HEAR THAT.
I WONDER HOW OLD THE POOR GUY WAS.
I DUNNO, BUT BY THE LOOKS OF HER, I'D SAY SIGN ME UP.
OH GOD... HE WAS RIGHT.

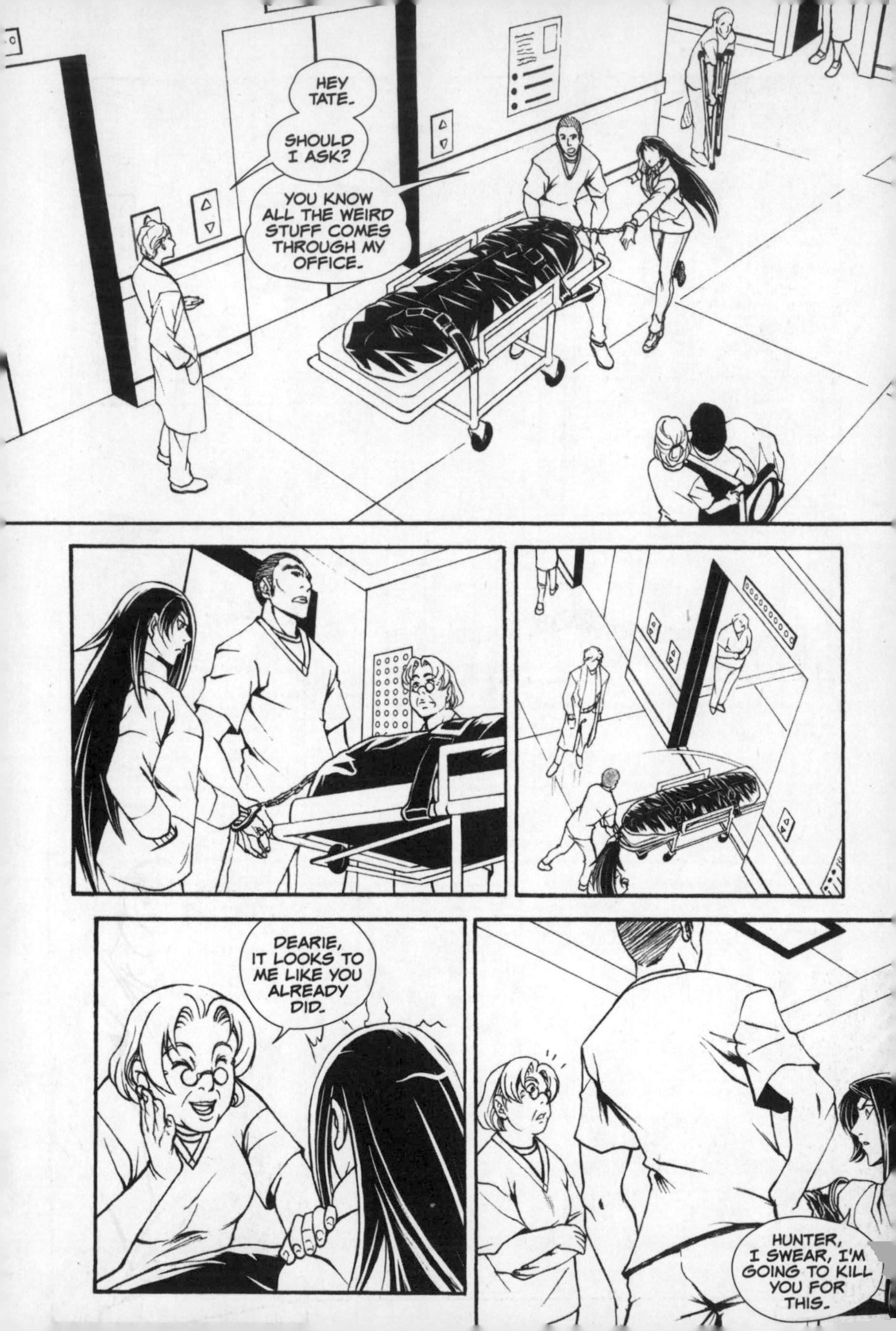
HEY TATE.
SHOULD I ASK?
YOU KNOW ALL THE WEIRD STUFF COMES THROUGH MY OFFICE.
HUNTER, I SWEAR, I'M GOING TO KILL YOU FOR THIS.
DEARIE, IT LOOKS TO ME LIKE YOU ALREADY DID.

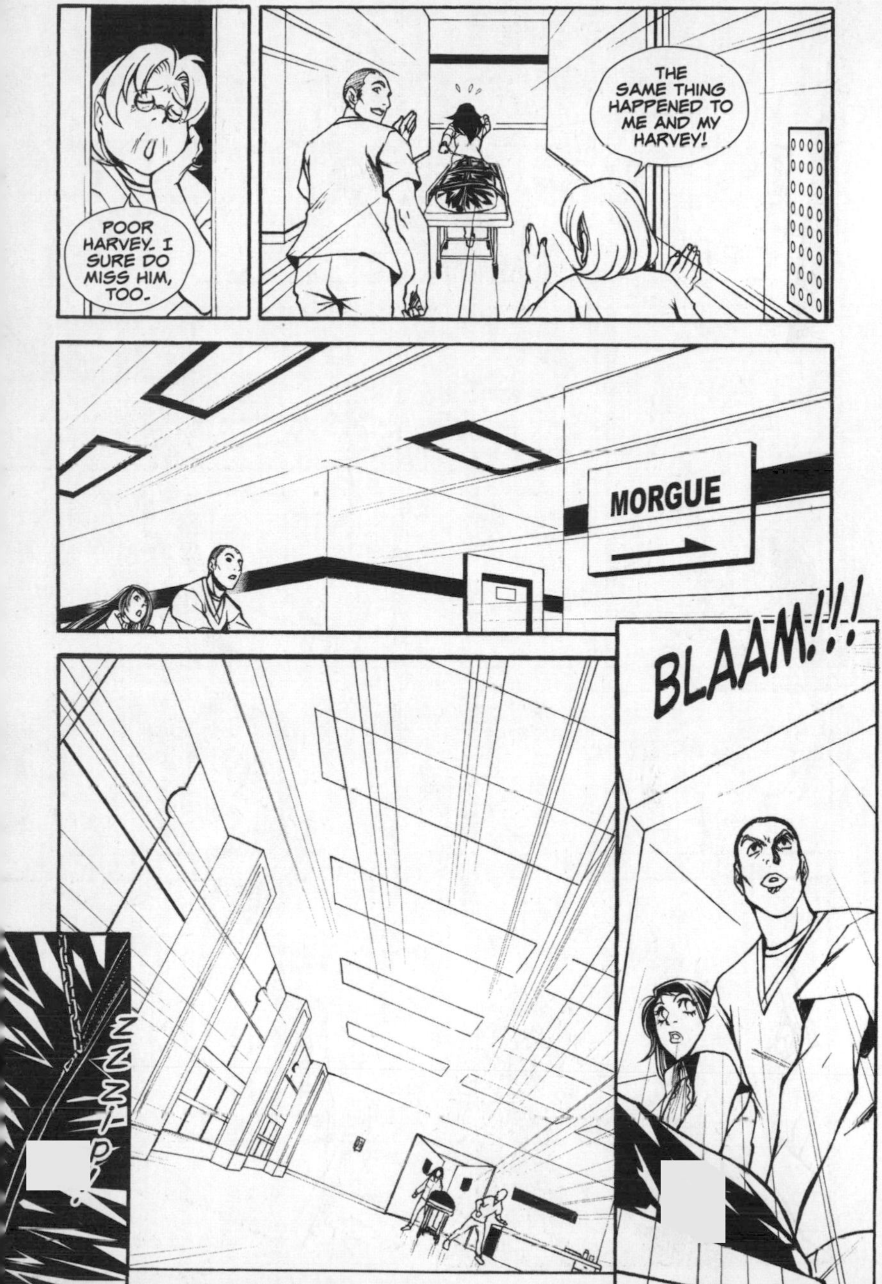
THE SAME THING HAPPENED TO ME AND MY HARVEY!
POOR HARVEY. I SURE DO MISS HIM, TOO.
MORGUE
BLAAM!!!
ZZZIP!

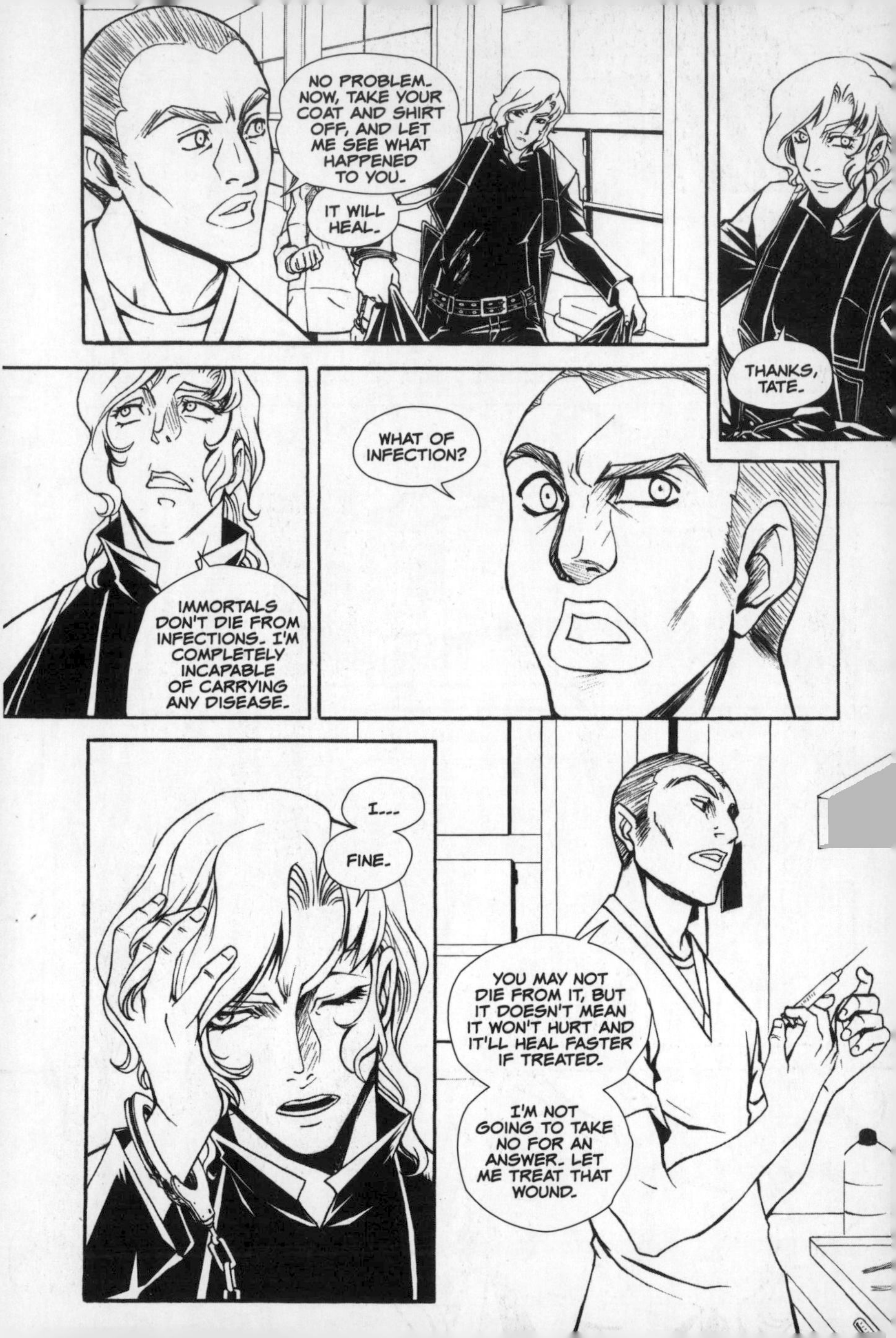
THANKS, TATE.
NO PROBLEM. NOW, TAKE YOUR COAT AND SHIRT OFF, AND LET ME SEE WHAT HAPPENED TO YOU.
IT WILL HEAL.
WHAT OF INFECTION?
IMMORTALS DON'T DIE FROM INFECTIONS. I'M COMPLETELY INCAPABLE OF CARRYING ANY DISEASE.
YOU MAY NOT DIE FROM IT, BUT IT DOESN'T MEAN IT WON'T HURT AND IT'LL HEAL FASTER IF TREATED.
I'M NOT GOING TO TAKE NO FOR AN ANSWER. LET ME TREAT THAT WOUND.
I...
FINE.

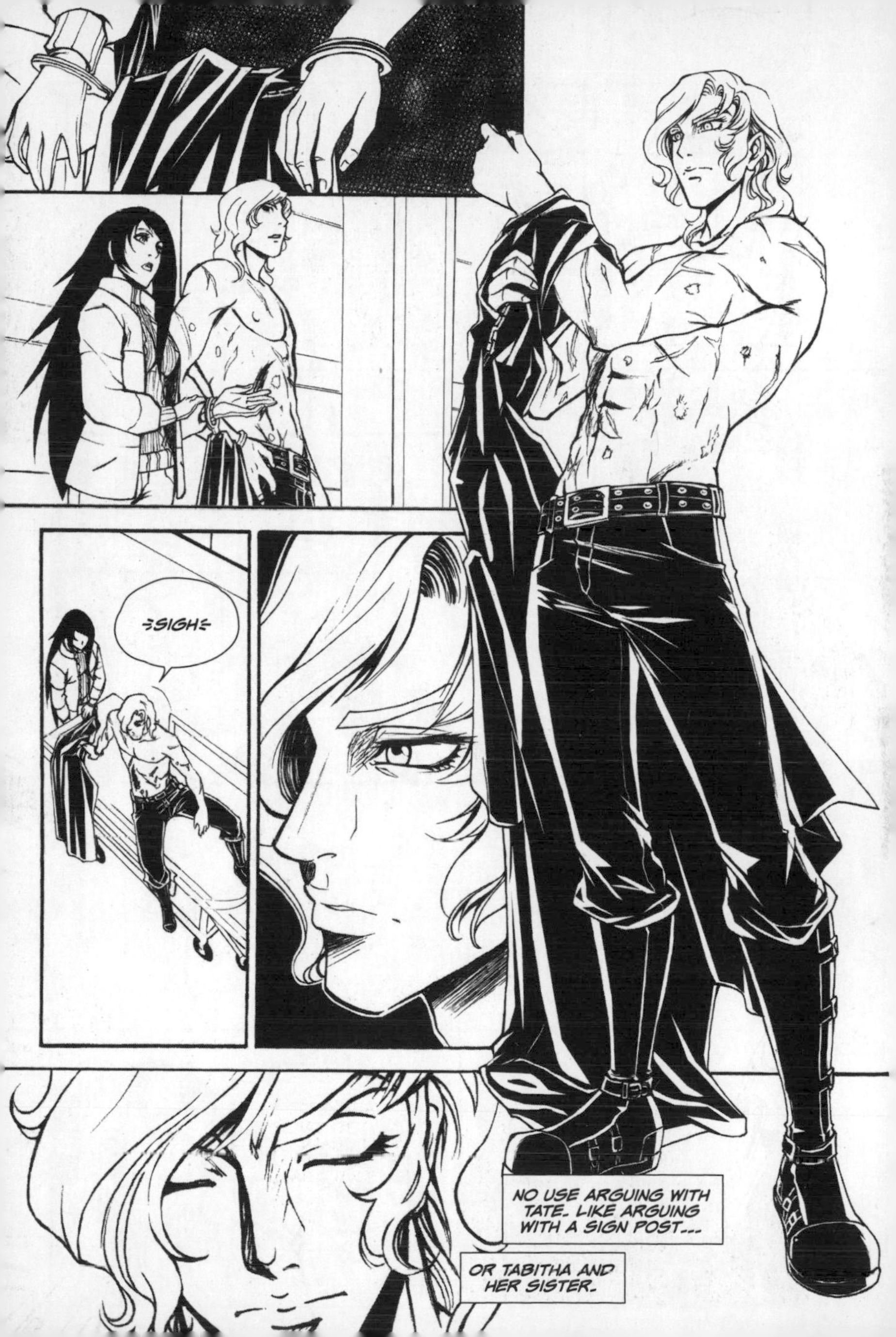
-SIGH-
NO USE ARGUING WITH TATE. LIKE ARGUING WITH A SIGN POST...
OR TABITHA AND HER SISTER.

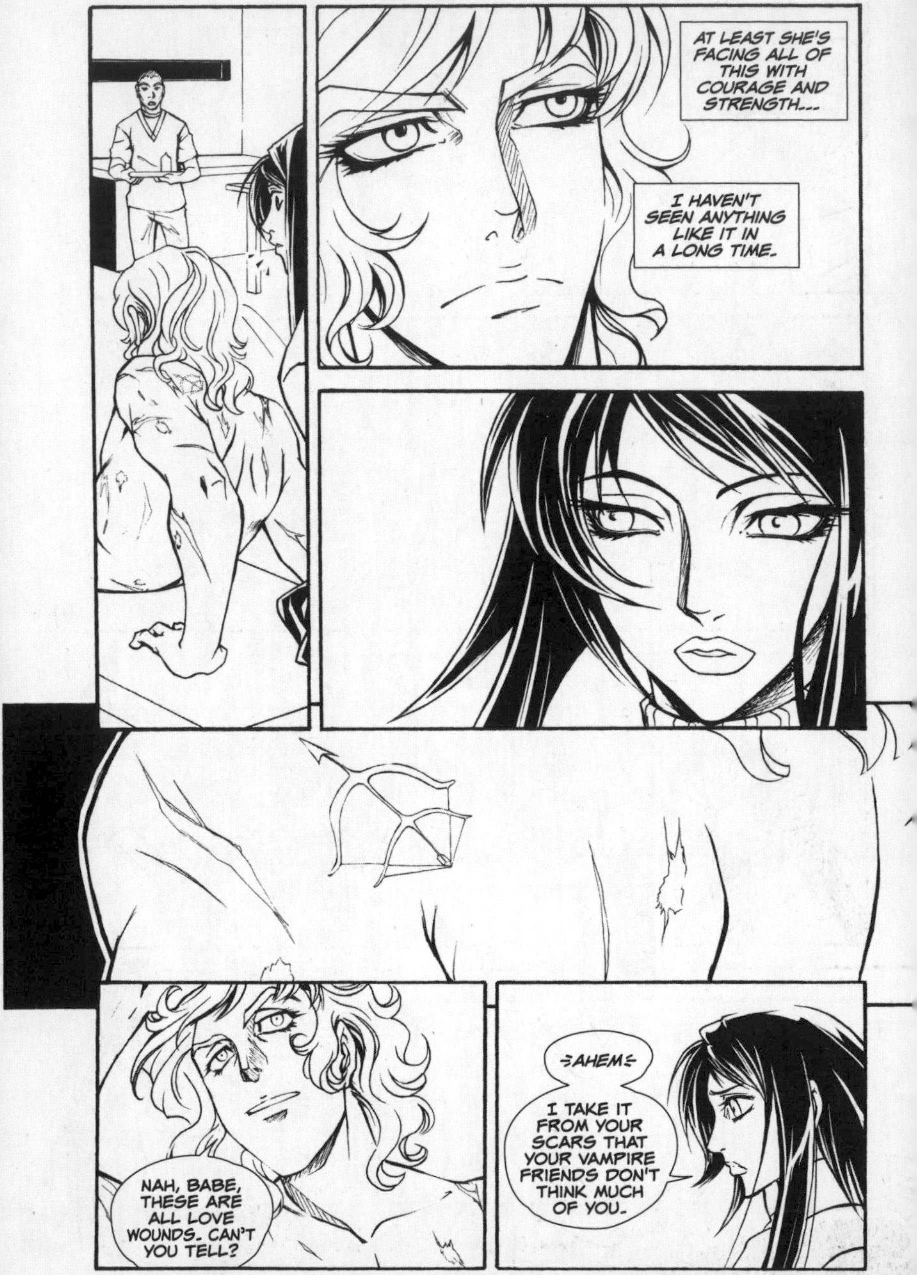
AT LEAST SHE'S FACING ALL OF THIS WITH COURAGE AND STRENGTH...
I HAVEN'T SEEN ANYTHING LIKE IT IN A LONG TIME.
=AHEM=
I TAKE IT FROM YOUR SCARS THAT YOUR VAMPIRE FRIENDS DON'T THINK MUCH OF YOU.
NAH, BABE, THESE ARE ALL LOVE WOUNDS. CAN'T YOU TELL?

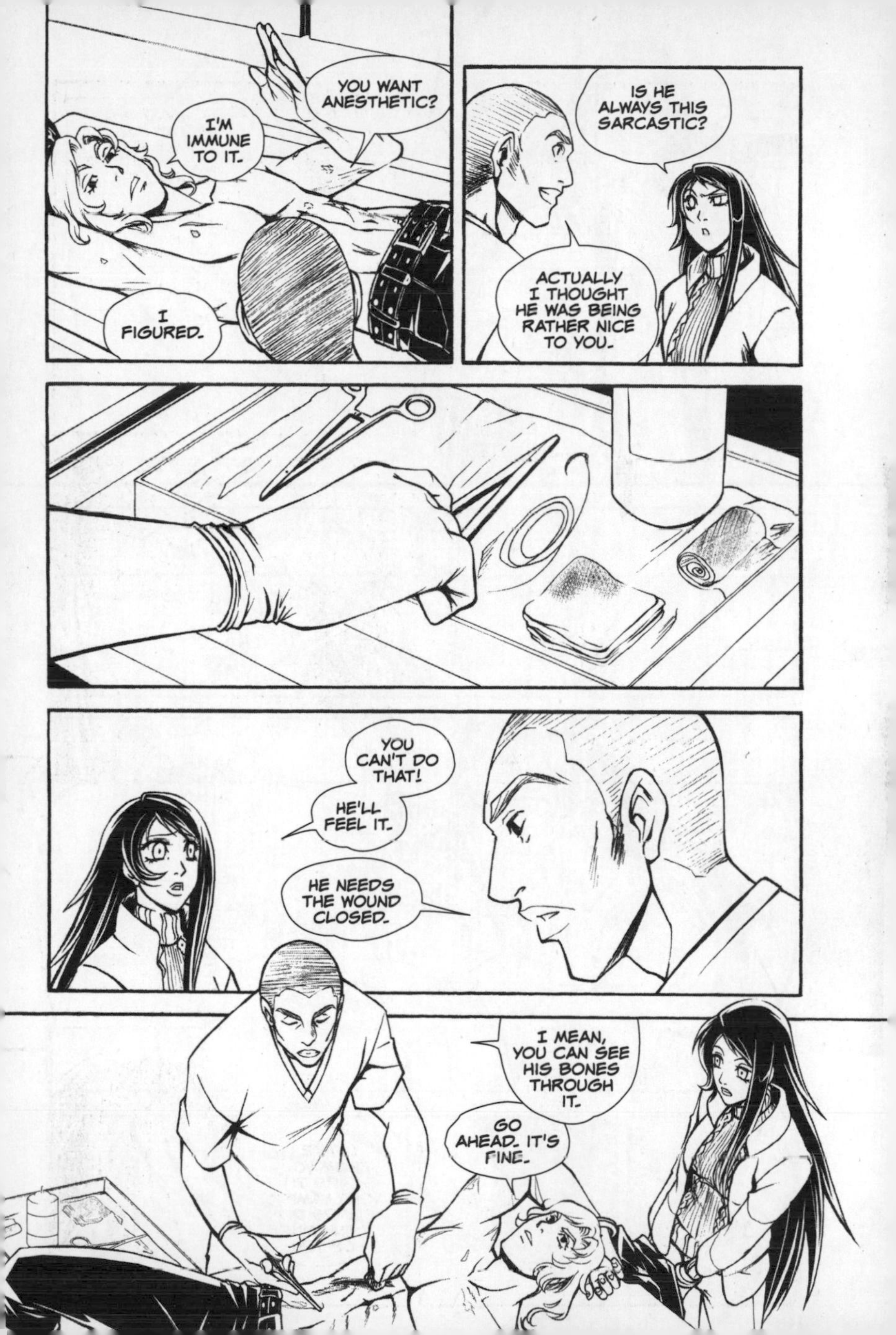
IS HE ALWAYS THIS SARCASTIC?
ACTUALLY I THOUGHT HE WAS BEING RATHER NICE TO YOU.
YOU WANT ANESTHETIC?
I'M IMMUNE TO IT.
I FIGURED.
YOU CAN'T DO THAT!
HE'LL FEEL IT.
HE NEEDS THE WOUND CLOSED.
I MEAN, YOU CAN SEE HIS BONES THROUGH IT.
GO AHEAD. IT'S FINE.

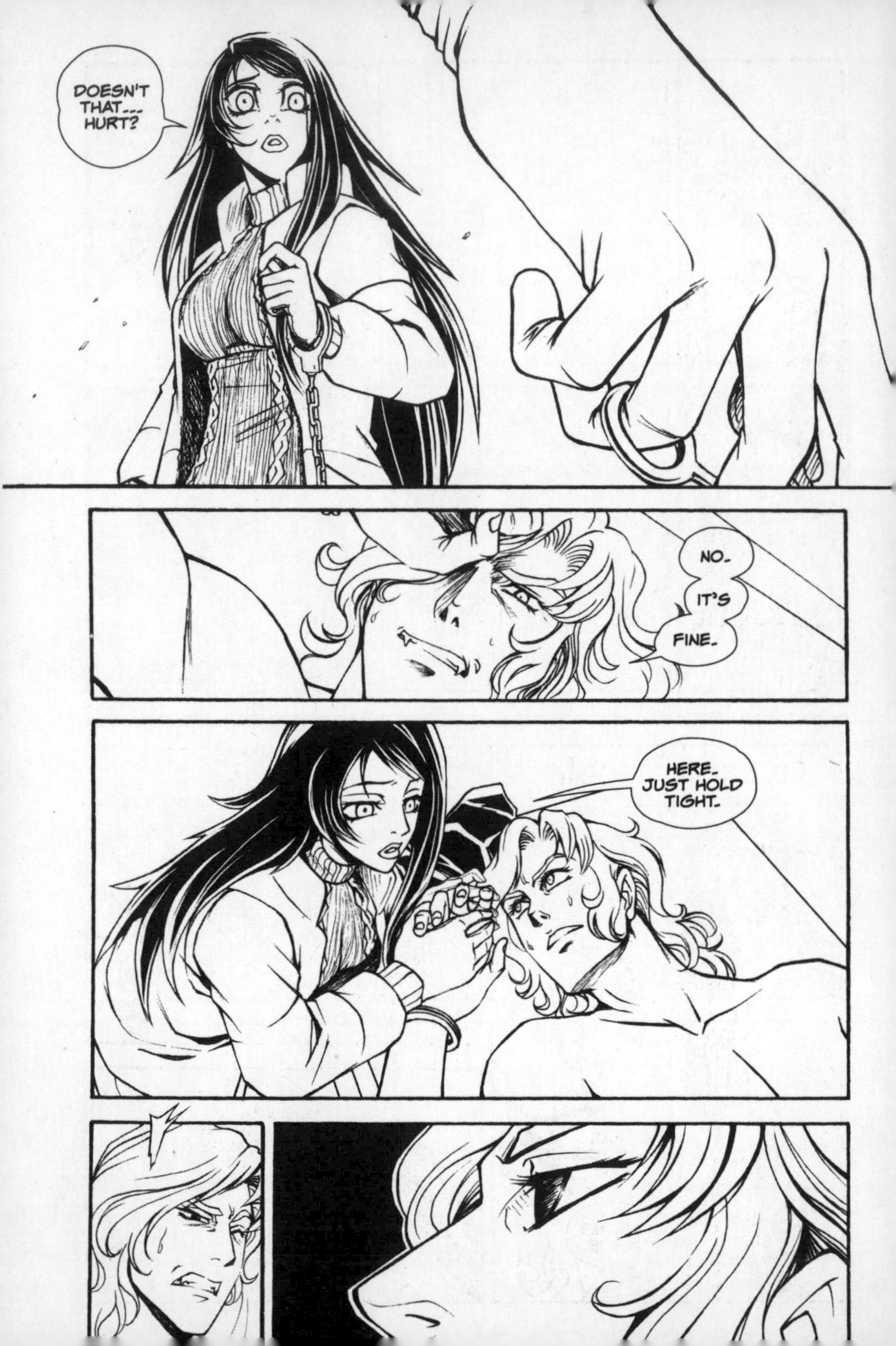
DOESN'T THAT... HURT?
NO.
IT'S
FINE.
HERE. JUST HOLD TIGHT.

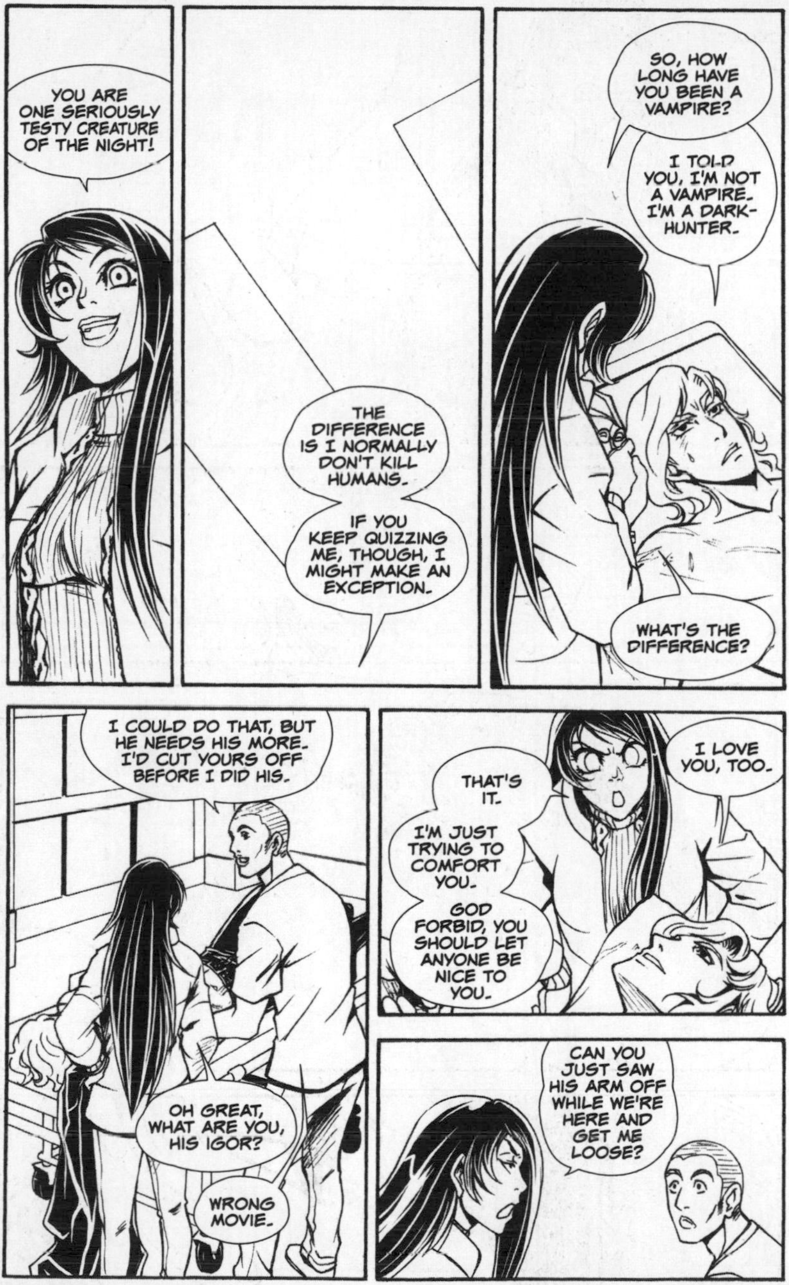
SO, HOW LONG HAVE YOU BEEN A VAMPIRE?
I TOLD YOU, I'M NOT A VAMPIRE. I'M A DARK-HUNTER.
WHAT'S THE DIFFERENCE?
THE DIFFERENCE IS I NORMALLY DON'T KILL HUMANS.
IF YOU KEEP QUIZZING ME, THOUGH, I MIGHT MAKE AN EXCEPTION.
YOU ARE ONE SERIOUSLY TESTY CREATURE OF THE NIGHT!
I LOVE YOU, TOO.
THAT'S IT.
I'M JUST TRYING TO COMFORT YOU.
GOD FORBID, YOU SHOULD LET ANYONE BE NICE TO YOU.
CAN YOU JUST SAW HIS ARM OFF WHILE WE'RE HERE AND GET ME LOOSE?
I COULD DO THAT, BUT HE NEEDS HIS MORE. I'D CUT YOURS OFF BEFORE I DID HIS.
OH GREAT, WHAT ARE YOU, HIS IGOR?
WRONG MOVIE.

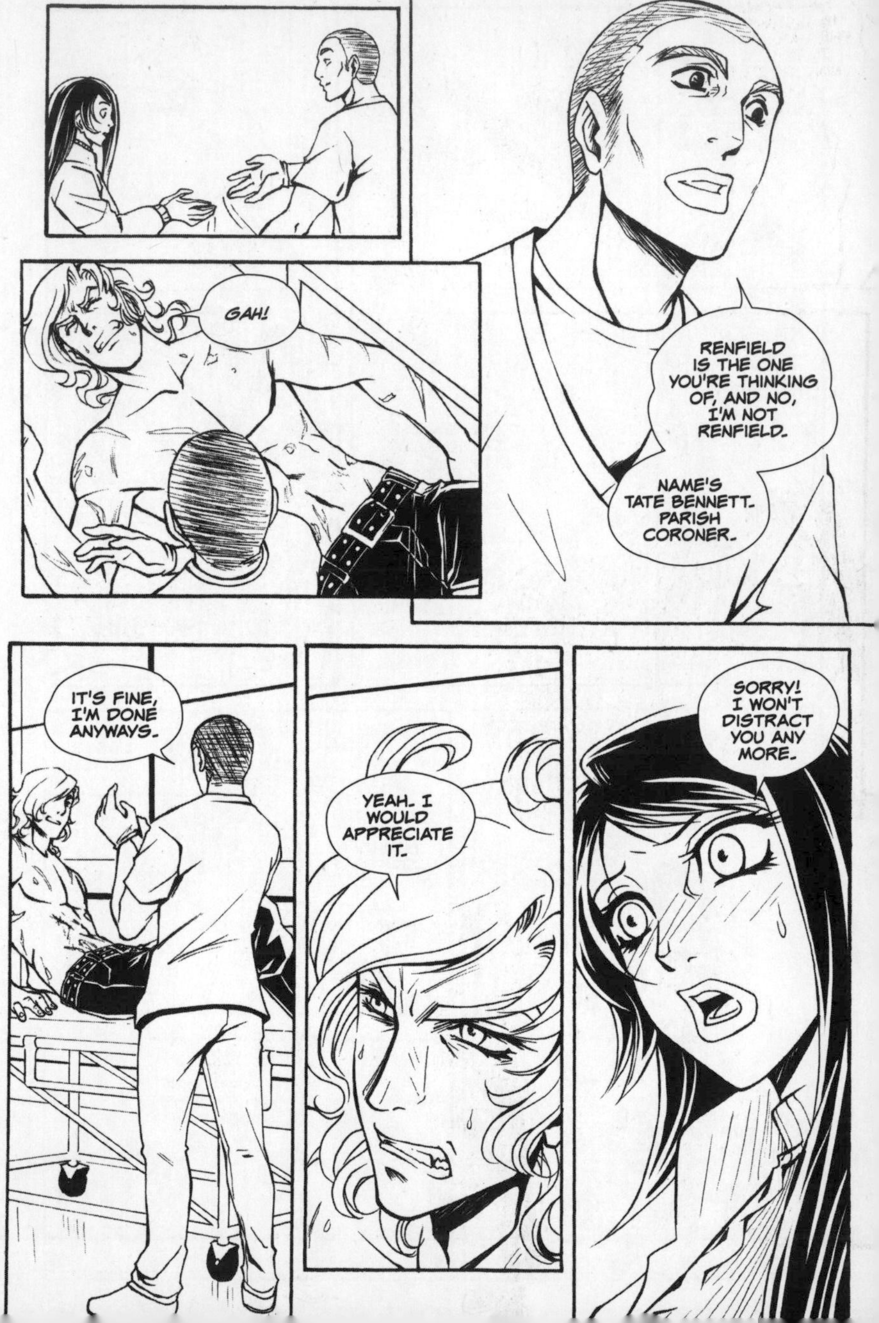
RENFIELD IS THE ONE YOU'RE THINKING OF, AND NO, I'M NOT RENFIELD.
NAME'S TATE BENNETT. PARISH CORONER.
GAH!
SORRY! I WON'T DISTRACT YOU ANY MORE.
YEAH. I WOULD APPRECIATE IT.
IT'S FINE, I'M DONE ANYWAYS.

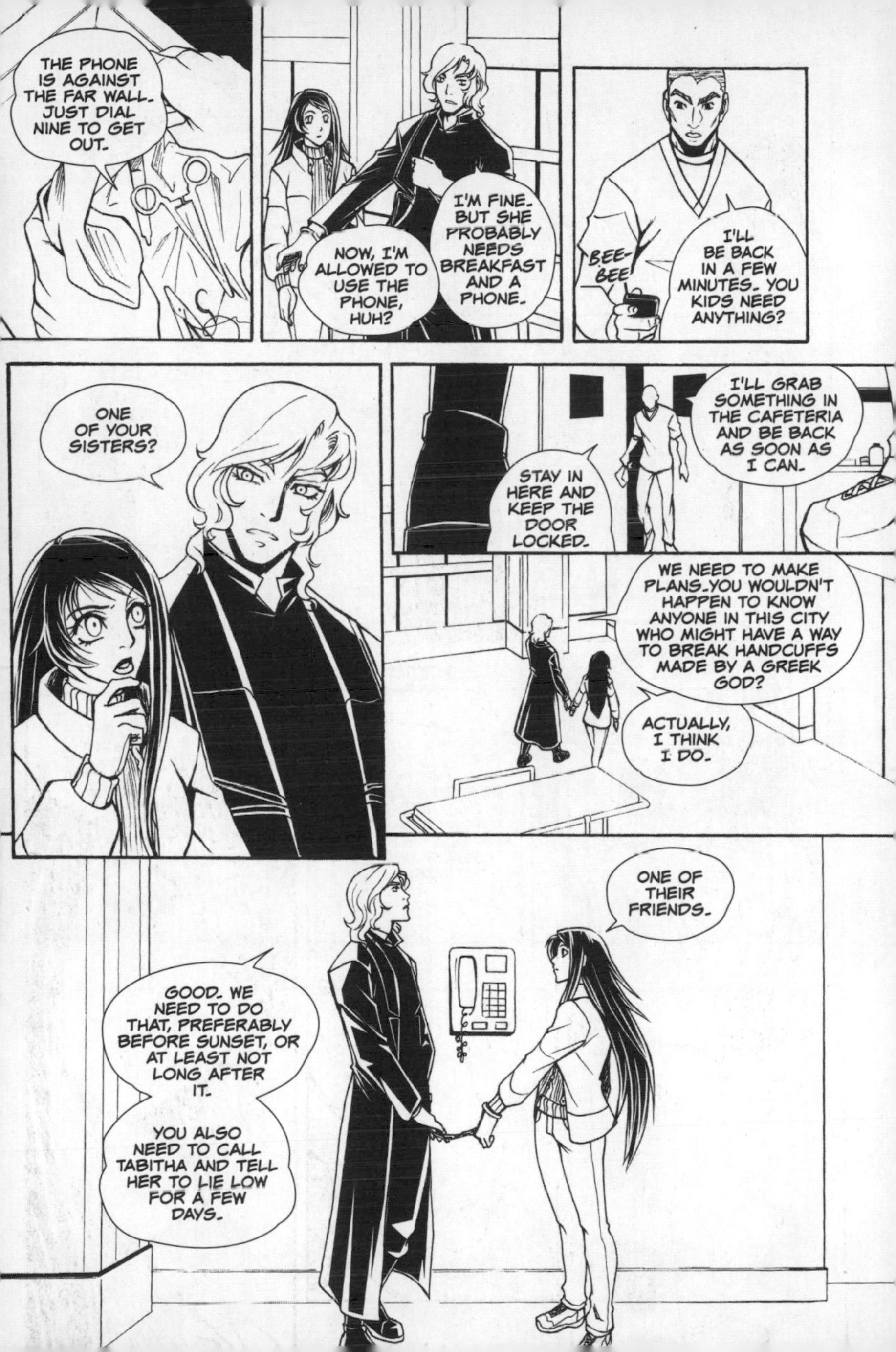

THE PHONE IS AGAINST THE FAR WALL. JUST DIAL NINE TO GET OUT.
NOW, I'M ALLOWED TO USE THE PHONE, HUH?
I'M FINE. BUT SHE PROBABLY NEEDS BREAKFAST AND A PHONE.
BEE-BEE
I'LL BE BACK IN A FEW MINUTES. YOU KIDS NEED ANYTHING?
ONE OF YOUR SISTERS?
STAY IN HERE AND KEEP THE DOOR LOCKED.
I'LL GRAB SOMETHING IN THE CAFETERIA AND BE BACK AS SOON AS I CAN.
WE NEED TO MAKE PLANS. YOU WOULDN'T HAPPEN TO KNOW ANYONE IN THIS CITY WHO MIGHT HAVE A WAY TO BREAK HANDCUFFS MADE BY A GREEK GOD?
ACTUALLY, I THINK I DO.
ONE OF THEIR FRIENDS.
GOOD. WE NEED TO DO THAT, PREFERABLY BEFORE SUNSET, OR AT LEAST NOT LONG AFTER IT.
YOU ALSO NEED TO CALL TABITHA AND TELL HER TO LIE LOW FOR A FEW DAYS.

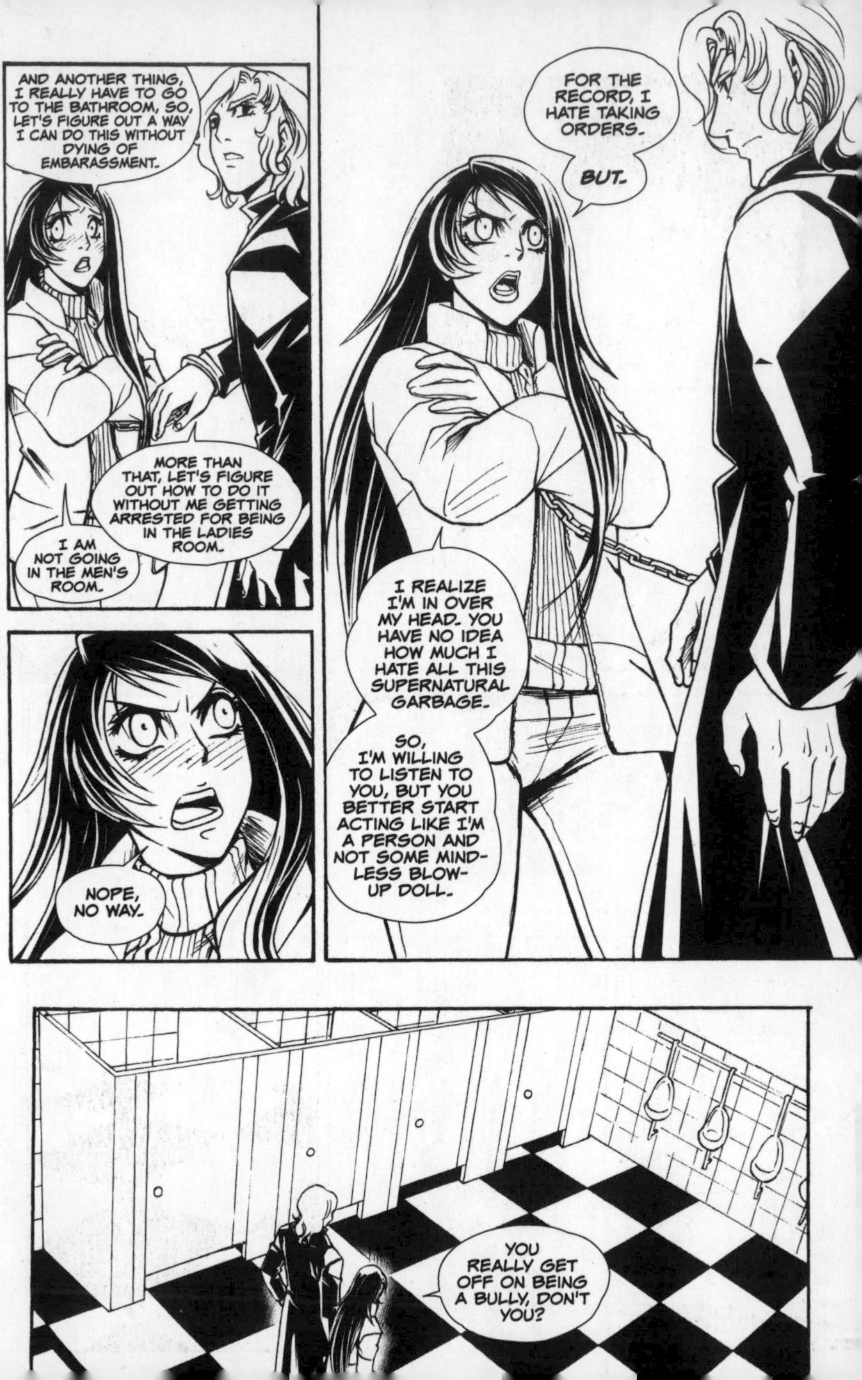
FOR THE RECORD, I HATE TAKING ORDERS.
BUT.
I REALIZE I'M IN OVER MY HEAD. YOU HAVE NO IDEA HOW MUCH I HATE ALL THIS SUPERNATURAL GARBAGE.
SO, I'M WILLING TO LISTEN TO YOU, BUT YOU BETTER START ACTING LIKE I'M A PERSON AND NOT SOME MIND-LESS BLOW-UP DOLL.
AND ANOTHER THING, I REALLY HAVE TO GO TO THE BATHROOM, SO, LET'S FIGURE OUT A WAY I CAN DO THIS WITHOUT DYING OF EMBARASSMENT.
MORE THAN THAT, LET'S FIGURE OUT HOW TO DO IT WITHOUT ME GETTING ARRESTED FOR BEING IN THE LADIES ROOM.
I AM NOT GOING IN THE MEN'S ROOM.
NOPE, NO WAY.
YOU REALLY GET OFF ON BEING A BULLY, DON'T YOU?

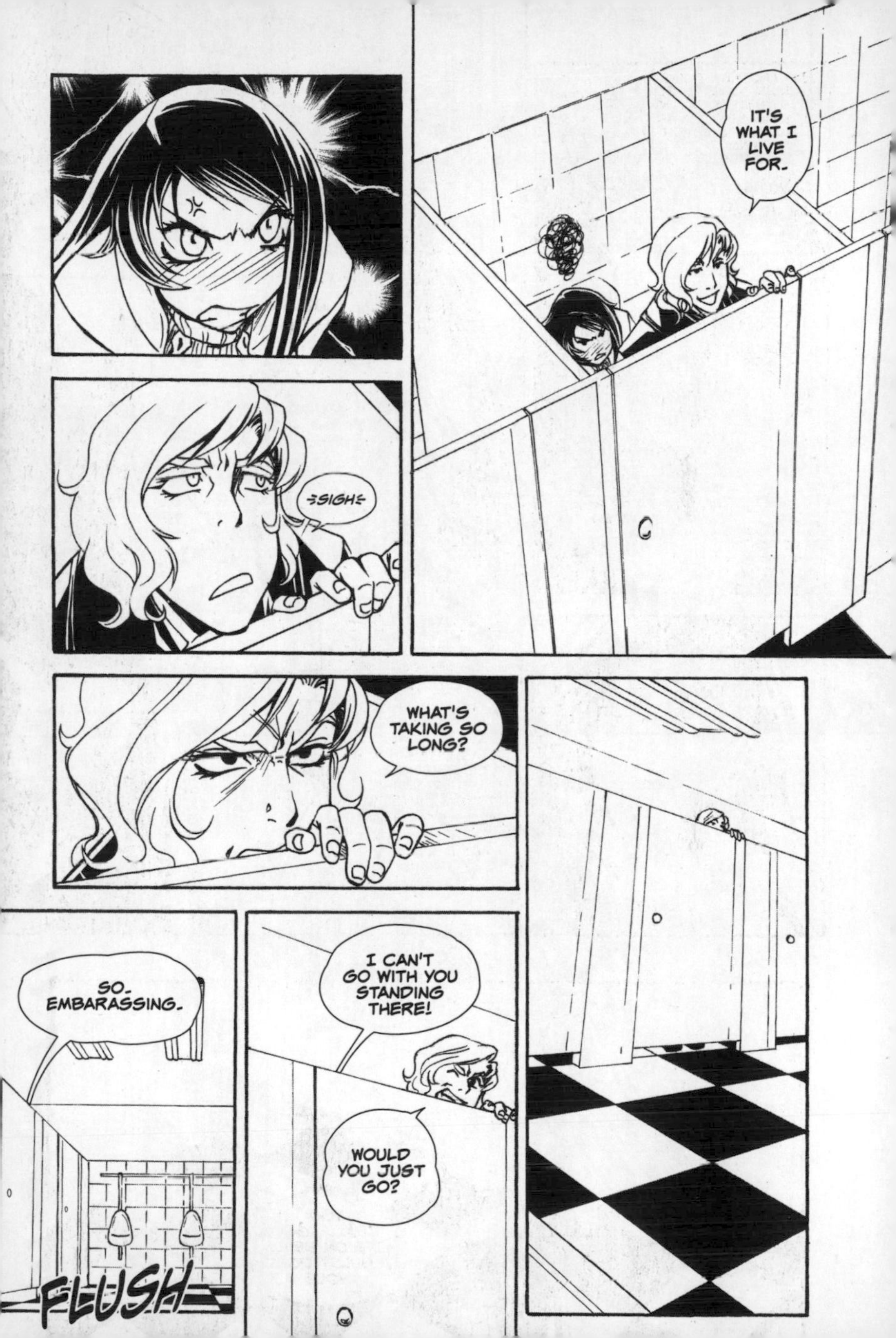

IT'S WHAT I LIVE FOR.
=SIGH=
WHAT'S TAKING SO LONG?
I CAN'T GO WITH YOU STANDING THERE!
WOULD YOU JUST GO?
SO. EMBARASSING.
FLUSH

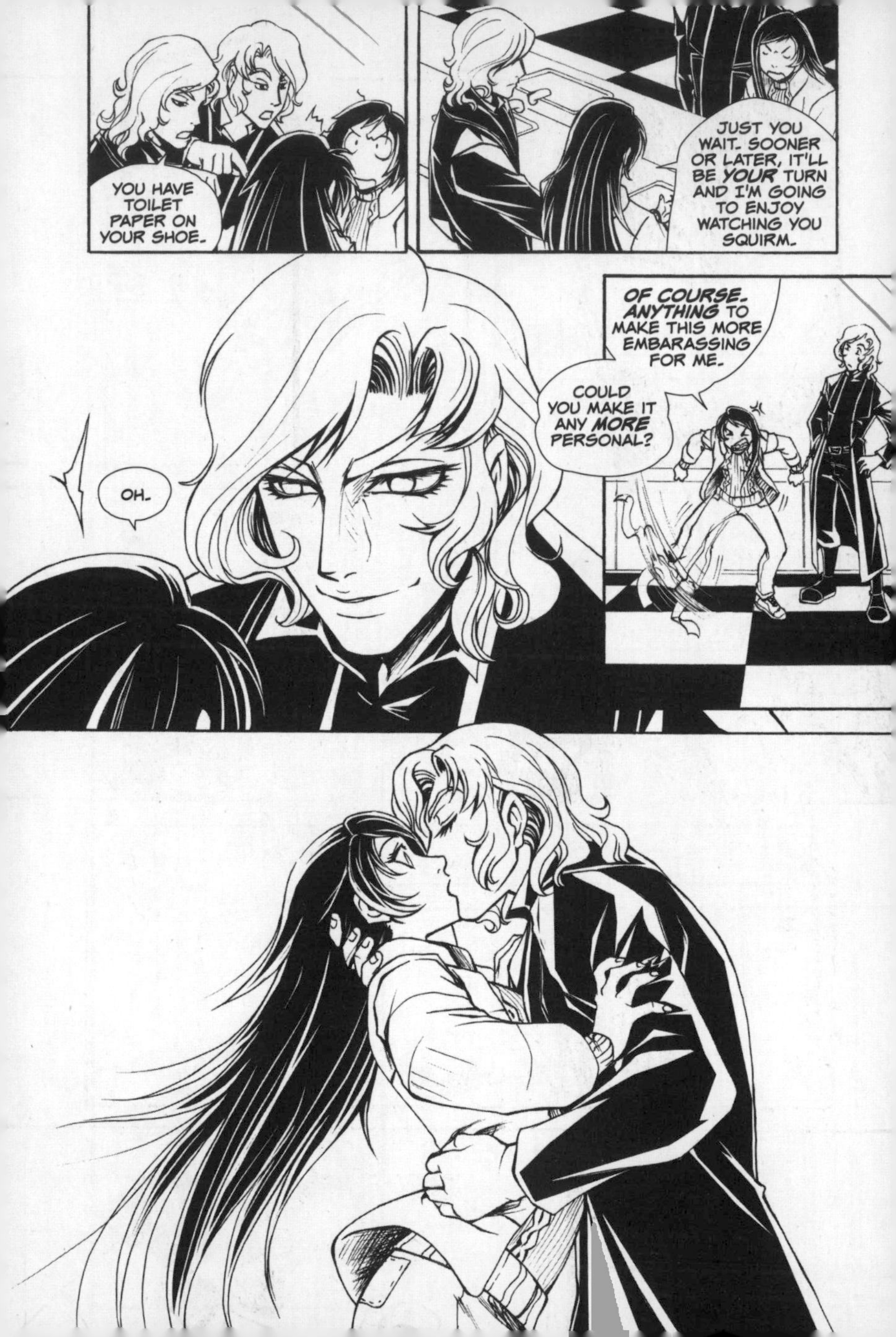
JUST YOU WAIT. SOONER OR LATER, IT'LL BE *YOUR* TURN AND I'M GOING TO ENJOY WATCHING YOU SQUIRM.
YOU HAVE TOILET PAPER ON YOUR SHOE.
OF COURSE. ANYTHING TO MAKE THIS MORE EMBARASSING FOR ME.
COULD YOU MAKE IT ANY *MORE* PERSONAL?
OH.

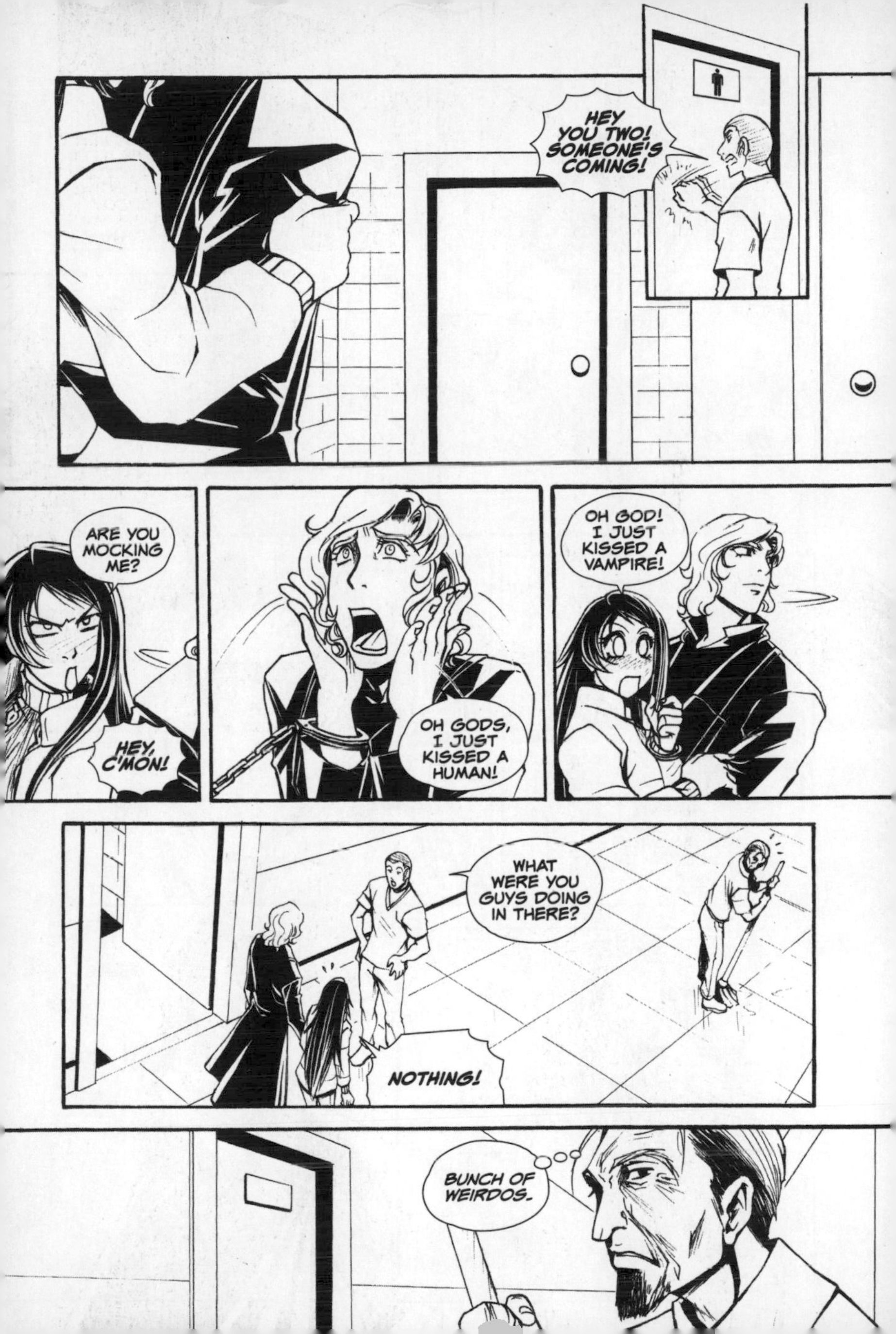
HEY YOU TWO! SOMEONE'S COMING!
OH GOD! I JUST KISSED A VAMPIRE!
OH GODS, I JUST KISSED A HUMAN!
ARE YOU MOCKING ME?
HEY, C'MON!
WHAT WERE YOU GUYS DOING IN THERE?
NOTHING!
BUNCH OF WEIRDOS.

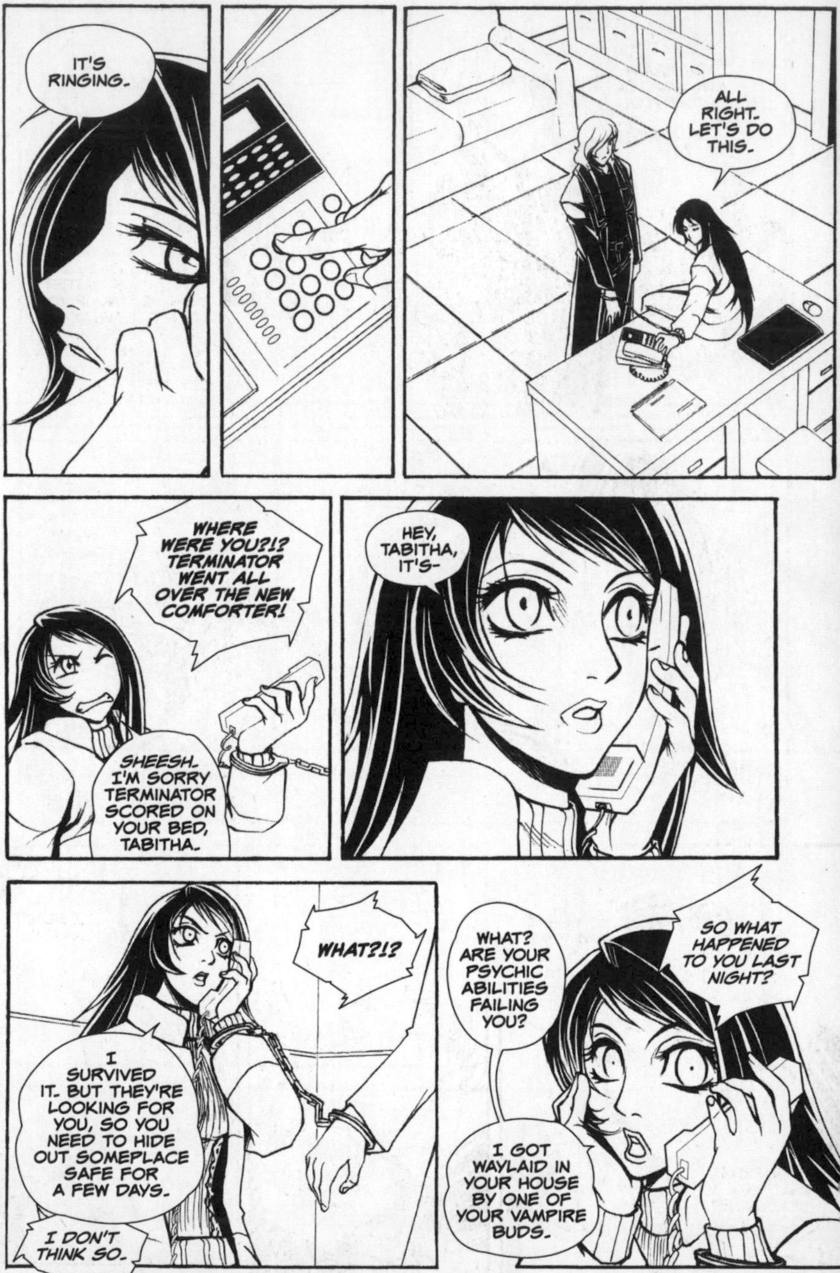
ALL RIGHT. LET'S DO THIS.
IT'S RINGING.
HEY, TABITHA, IT'S-
WHERE WERE YOU?!? TERMINATOR WENT ALL OVER THE NEW COMFORTER!
SHEESH. I'M SORRY TERMINATOR SCORED ON YOUR BED, TABITHA.
SO WHAT HAPPENED TO YOU LAST NIGHT?
WHAT? ARE YOUR PSYCHIC ABILITIES FAILING YOU?
I GOT WAYLAID IN YOUR HOUSE BY ONE OF YOUR VAMPIRE BUDS.
WHAT?!?
I SURVIVED IT. BUT THEY'RE LOOKING FOR YOU, SO YOU NEED TO HIDE OUT SOMEPLACE SAFE FOR A FEW DAYS.
I DON'T THINK SO.

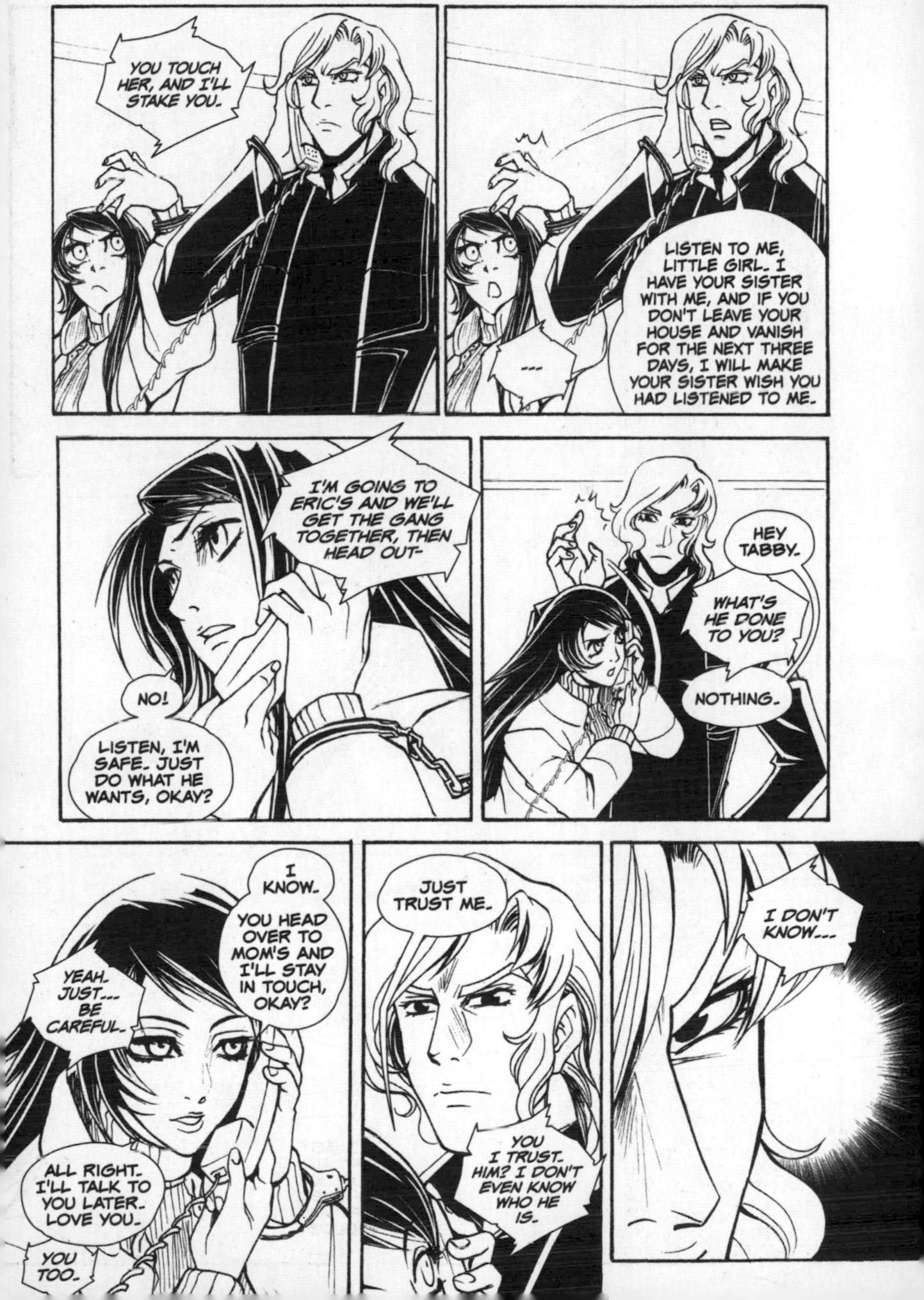
LISTEN TO ME, LITTLE GIRL. I HAVE YOUR SISTER WITH ME, AND IF YOU DON'T LEAVE YOUR HOUSE AND VANISH FOR THE NEXT THREE DAYS, I WILL MAKE YOUR SISTER WISH YOU HAD LISTENED TO ME.
...
YOU TOUCH HER, AND I'LL STAKE YOU.
HEY TABBY.
WHAT'S HE DONE TO YOU?
NOTHING.
I'M GOING TO ERIC'S AND WE'LL GET THE GANG TOGETHER, THEN HEAD OUT-
NO!
LISTEN, I'M SAFE. JUST DO WHAT HE WANTS, OKAY?
I DON'T KNOW...
JUST TRUST ME.
YOU I TRUST. HIM? I DON'T EVEN KNOW WHO HE IS.
I KNOW.
YOU HEAD OVER TO MOM'S AND I'LL STAY IN TOUCH, OKAY?
YEAH. JUST... BE CAREFUL.
ALL RIGHT. I'LL TALK TO YOU LATER. LOVE YOU.
YOU TOO.

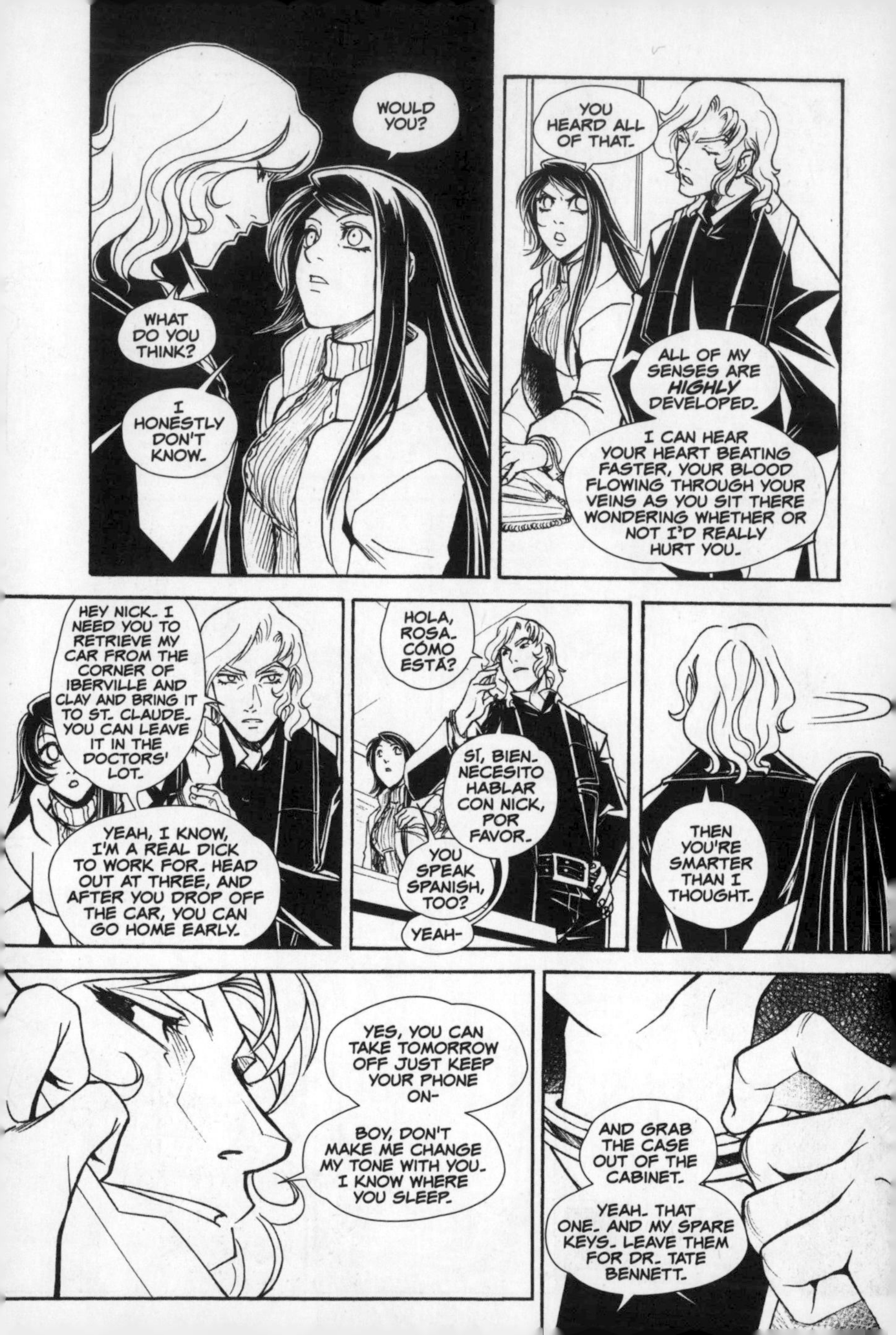
WOULD YOU?
WHAT DO YOU THINK?
I HONESTLY DON'T KNOW.
YOU HEARD ALL OF THAT.
ALL OF MY SENSES ARE HIGHLY DEVELOPED.
I CAN HEAR YOUR HEART BEATING FASTER, YOUR BLOOD FLOWING THROUGH YOUR VEINS AS YOU SIT THERE WONDERING WHETHER OR NOT I'D REALLY HURT YOU.
HEY NICK. I NEED YOU TO RETRIEVE MY CAR FROM THE CORNER OF IBERVILLE AND CLAY AND BRING IT TO ST. CLAUDE. YOU CAN LEAVE IT IN THE DOCTORS' LOT.
YEAH, I KNOW, I'M A REAL DICK TO WORK FOR. HEAD OUT AT THREE, AND AFTER YOU DROP OFF THE CAR, YOU CAN GO HOME EARLY.
HOLA, ROSA. CÓMO ESTÁ?
SÍ, BIEN. NECESITO HABLAR CON NICK, POR FAVOR.
YOU SPEAK SPANISH, TOO?
YEAH-
THEN YOU'RE SMARTER THAN I THOUGHT.
YES, YOU CAN TAKE TOMORROW OFF JUST KEEP YOUR PHONE ON-
BOY, DON'T MAKE ME CHANGE MY TONE WITH YOU. I KNOW WHERE YOU SLEEP.
AND GRAB THE CASE OUT OF THE CABINET.
YEAH. THAT ONE. AND MY SPARE KEYS. LEAVE THEM FOR DR. TATE BENNETT.

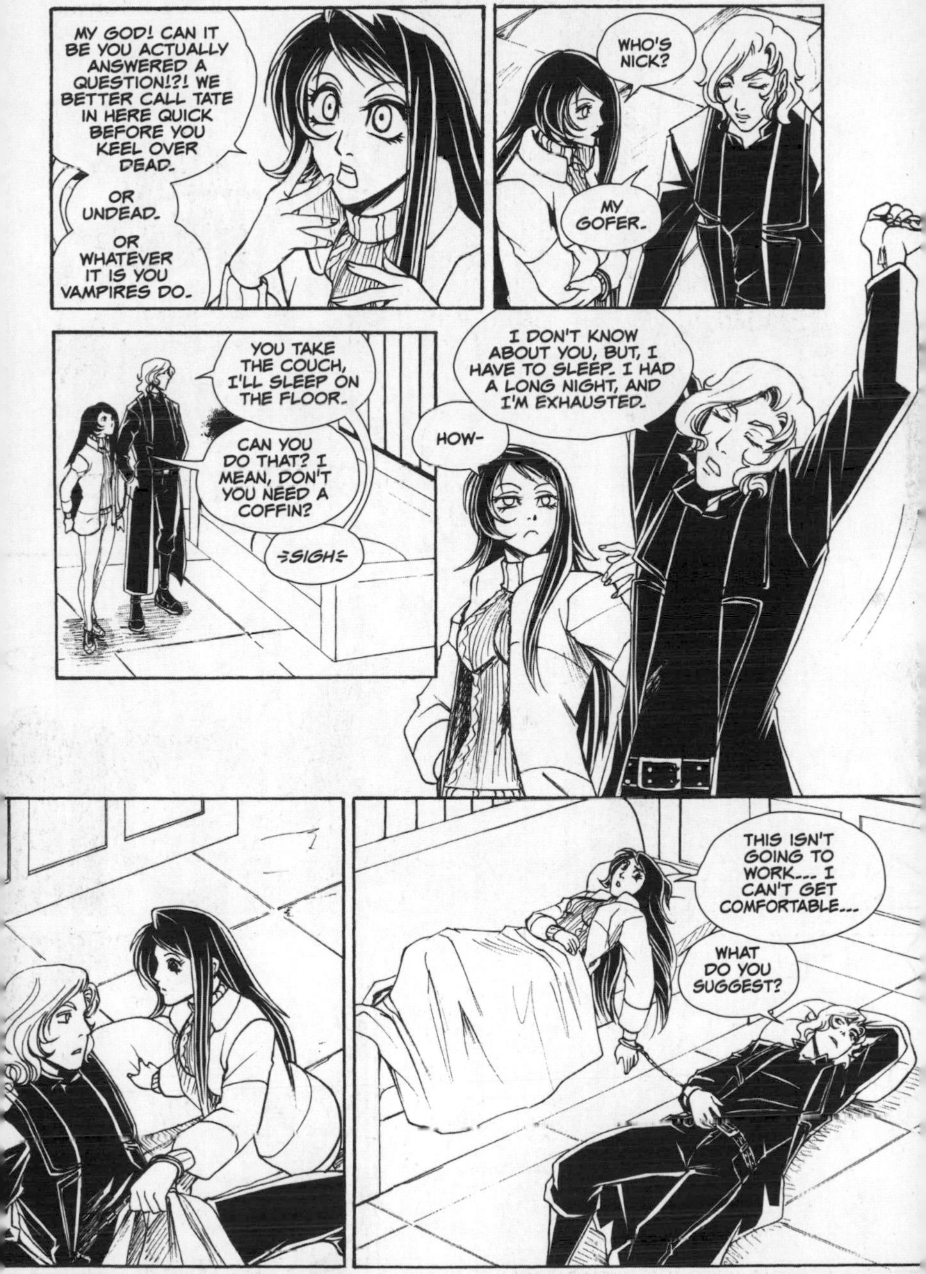
WHO'S NICK?
MY GOFER.
MY GOD! CAN IT BE YOU ACTUALLY ANSWERED A QUESTION!?! WE BETTER CALL TATE IN HERE QUICK BEFORE YOU KEEL OVER DEAD.
OR UNDEAD.
OR WHATEVER IT IS YOU VAMPIRES DO.
I DON'T KNOW ABOUT YOU, BUT, I HAVE TO SLEEP. I HAD A LONG NIGHT, AND I'M EXHAUSTED.
HOW-
YOU TAKE THE COUCH, I'LL SLEEP ON THE FLOOR.
CAN YOU DO THAT? I MEAN, DON'T YOU NEED A COFFIN?
=SIGH=
THIS ISN'T GOING TO WORK... I CAN'T GET COMFORTABLE...
WHAT DO YOU SUGGEST?

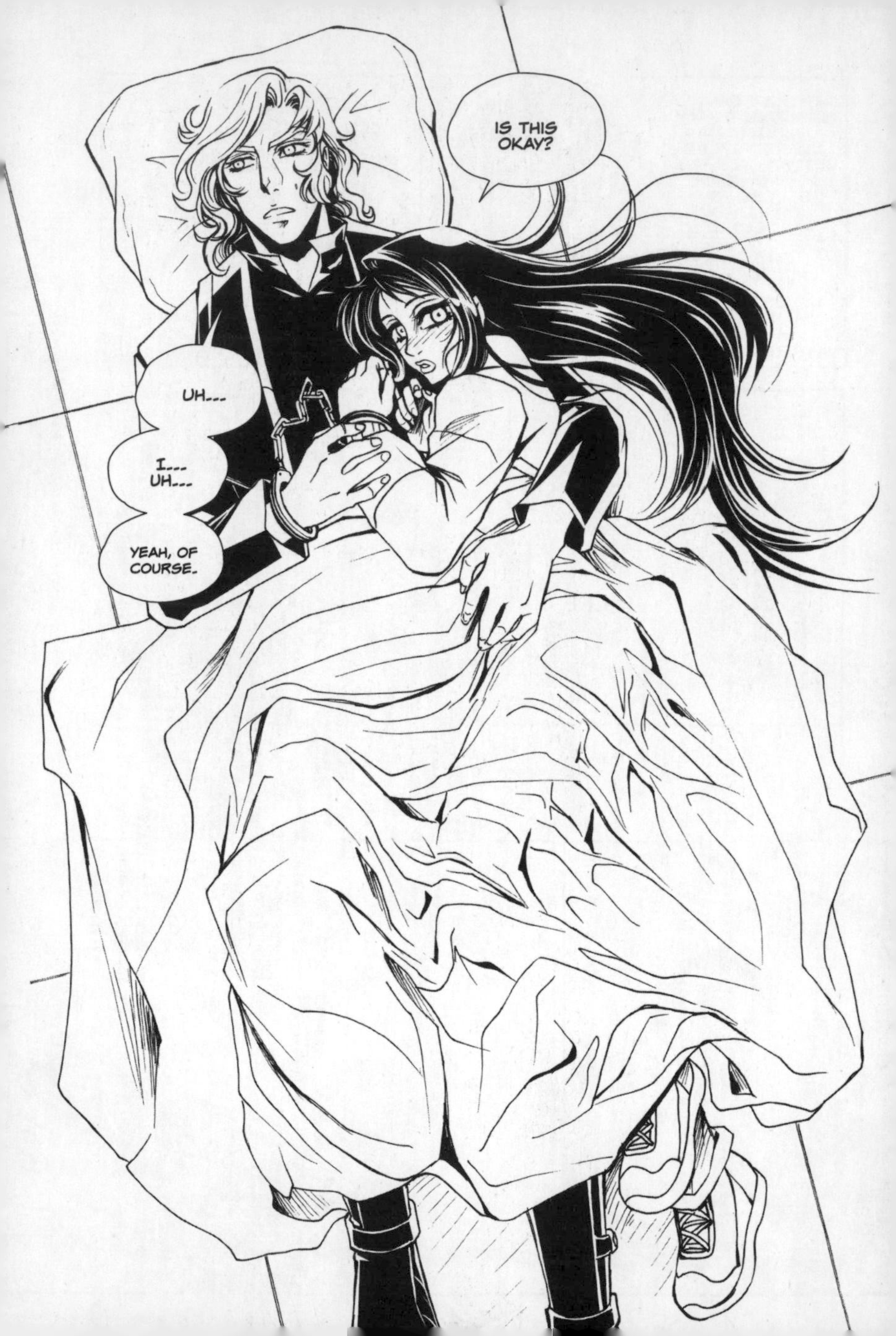
IS THIS OKAY?
UH...
I... UH...
YEAH, OF COURSE.

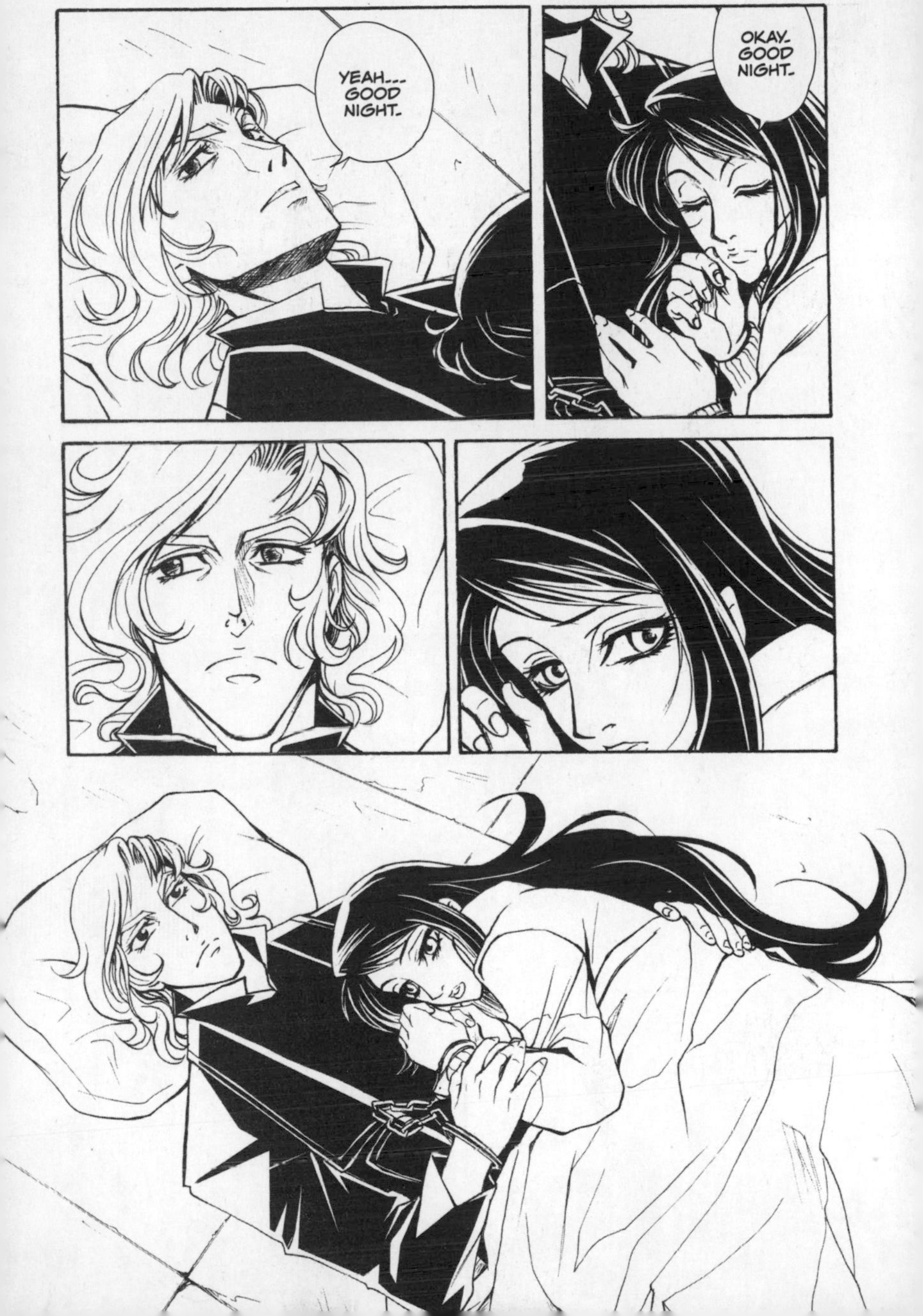
OKAY. GOOD NIGHT.
YEAH... GOOD NIGHT.

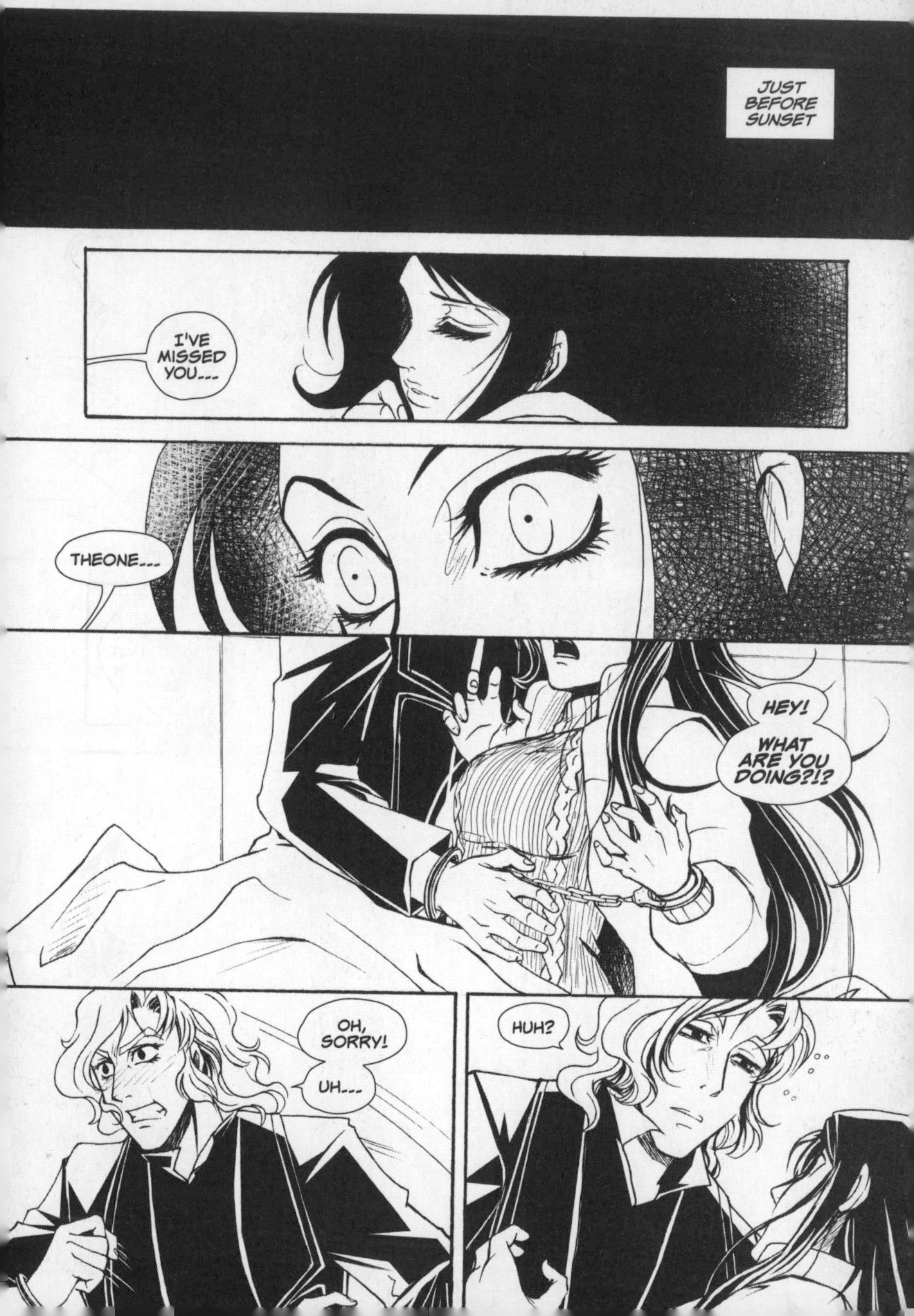
JUST BEFORE SUNSET
I'VE MISSED YOU...
THEONE...
HEY!
WHAT ARE YOU DOING?!?
HUH?
OH, SORRY!
UH...

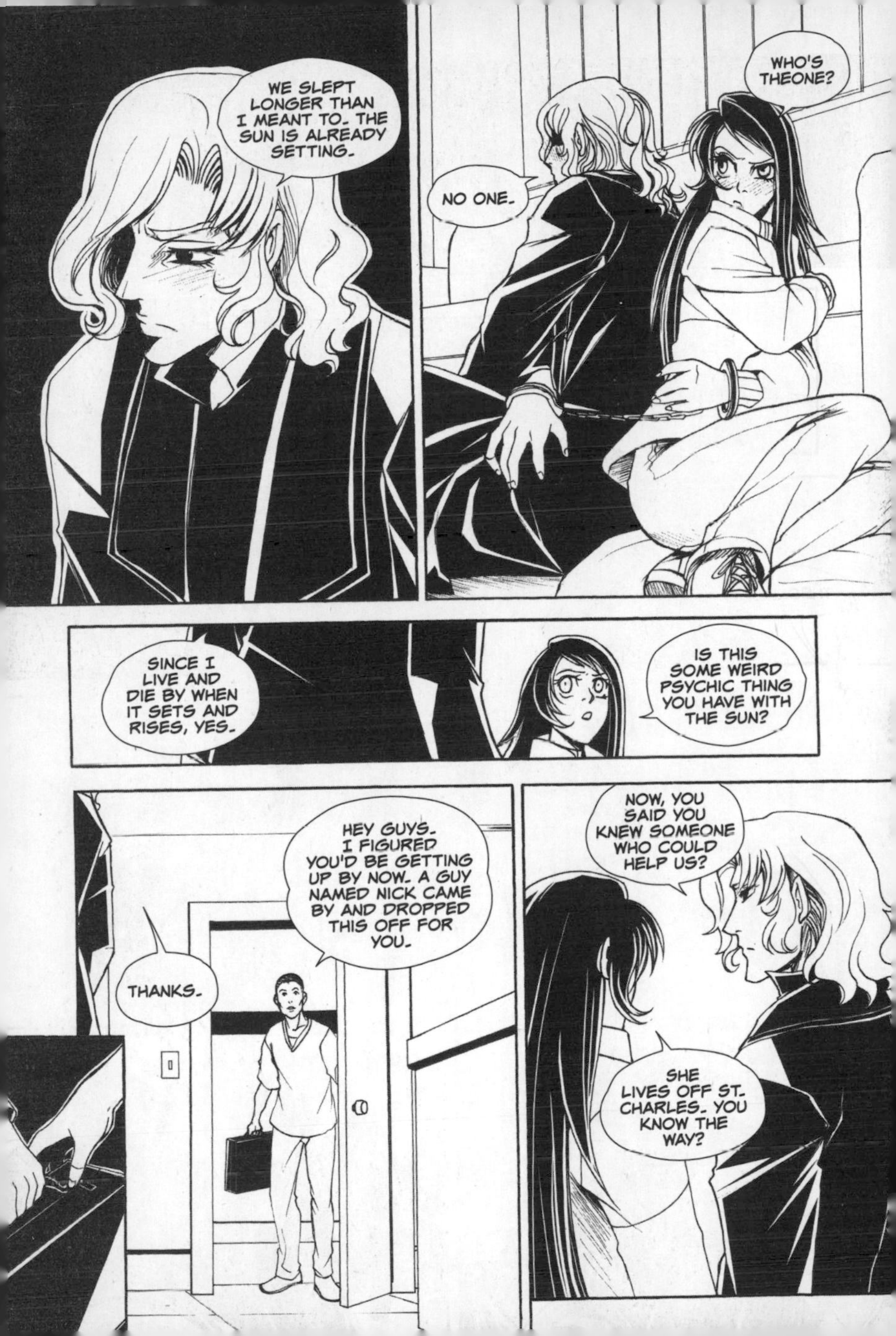
WHO'S THEONE?
NO ONE.
WE SLEPT LONGER THAN I MEANT TO. THE SUN IS ALREADY SETTING.
IS THIS SOME WEIRD PSYCHIC THING YOU HAVE WITH THE SUN?
SINCE I LIVE AND DIE BY WHEN IT SETS AND RISES, YES.
NOW, YOU SAID YOU KNEW SOMEONE WHO COULD HELP US?
SHE LIVES OFF ST. CHARLES. YOU KNOW THE WAY?
HEY GUYS. I FIGURED YOU'D BE GETTING UP BY NOW. A GUY NAMED NICK CAME BY AND DROPPED THIS OFF FOR YOU.
THANKS.

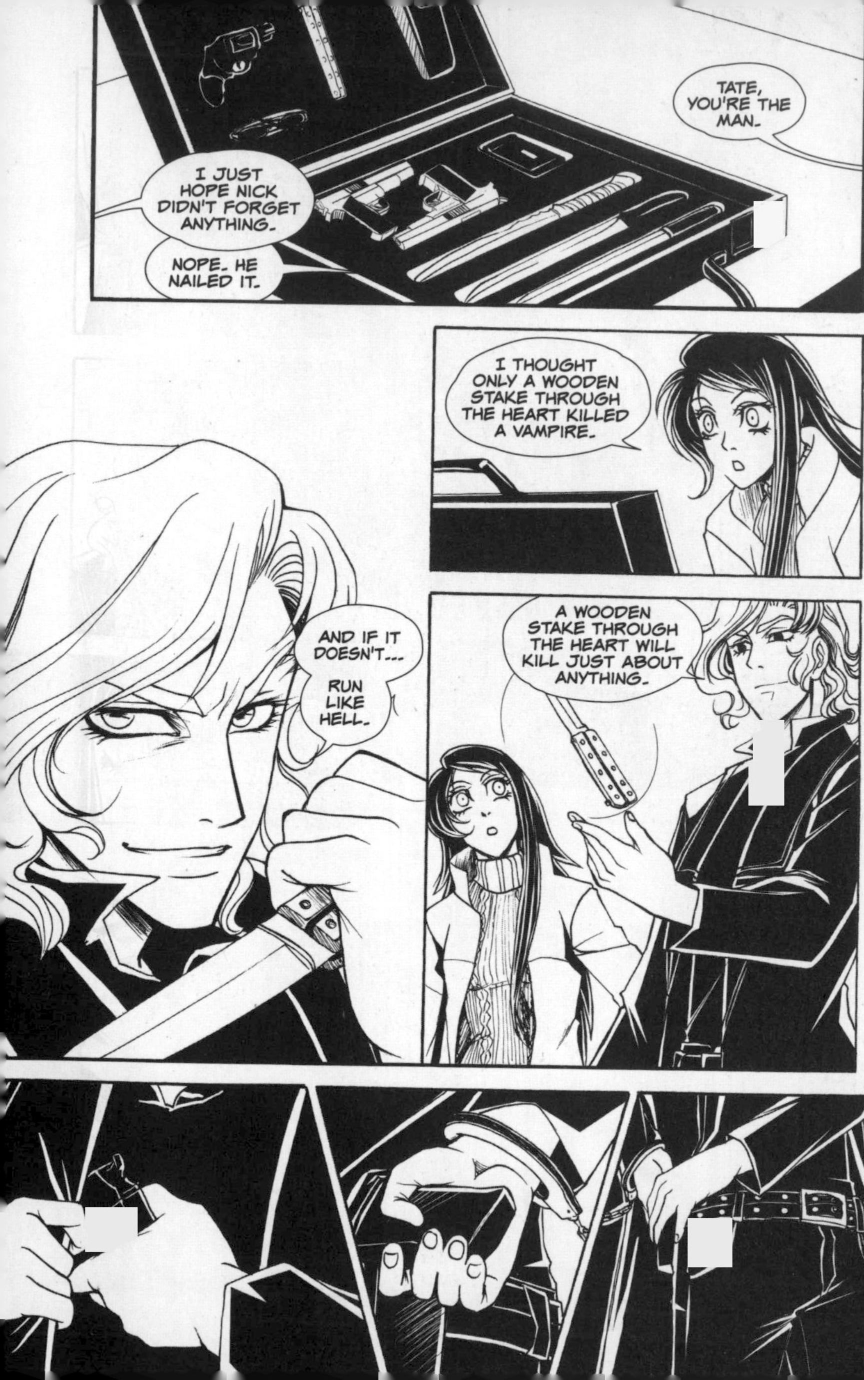
TATE, YOU'RE THE MAN.
I JUST HOPE NICK DIDN'T FORGET ANYTHING.
NOPE. HE NAILED IT.
I THOUGHT ONLY A WOODEN STAKE THROUGH THE HEART KILLED A VAMPIRE.
A WOODEN STAKE THROUGH THE HEART WILL KILL JUST ABOUT ANYTHING.
AND IF IT DOESN'T...
RUN LIKE HELL.

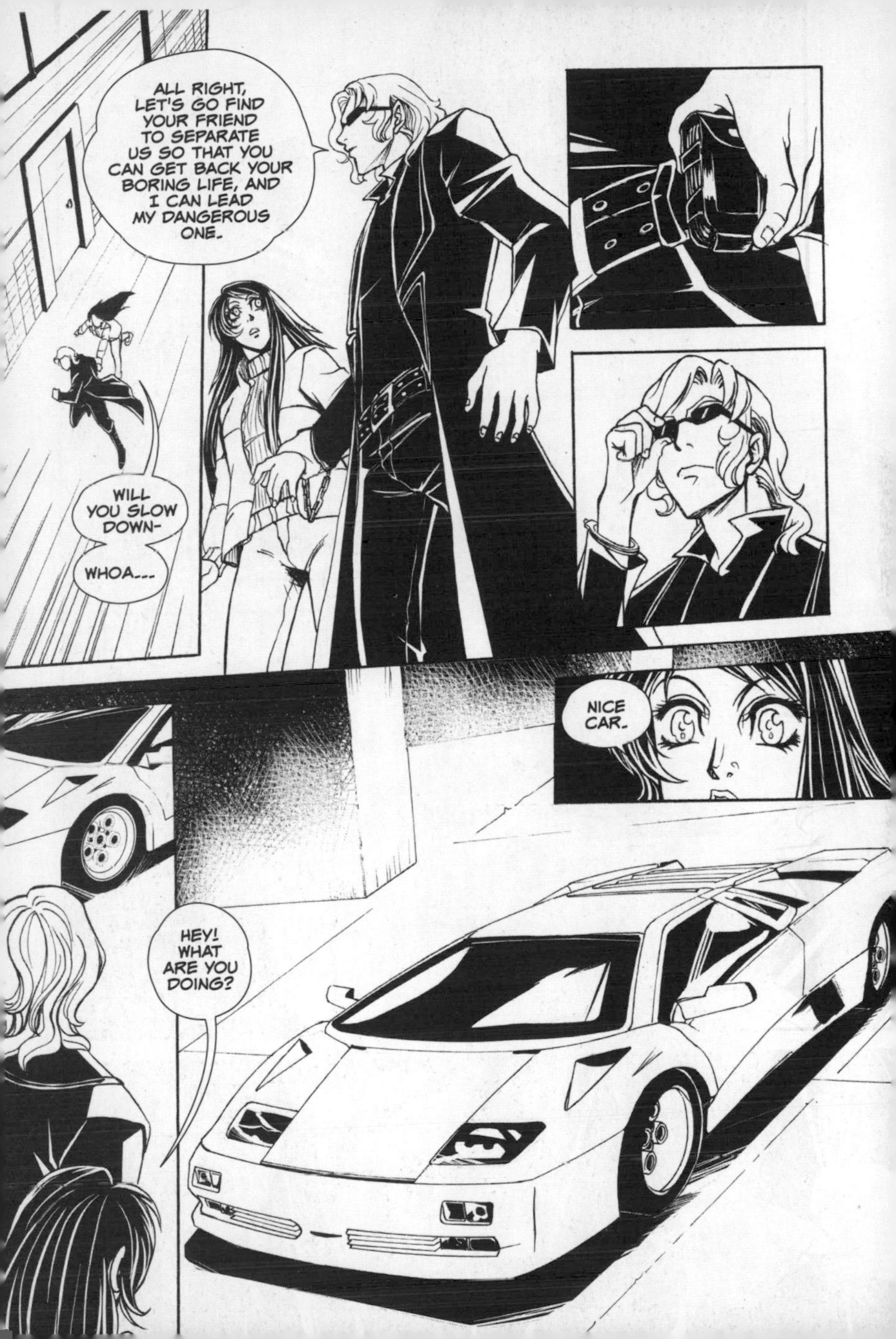
ALL RIGHT, LET'S GO FIND YOUR FRIEND TO SEPARATE US SO THAT YOU CAN GET BACK YOUR BORING LIFE, AND I CAN LEAD MY DANGEROUS ONE.
WILL YOU SLOW DOWN-
WHOA...
NICE CAR.
HEY! WHAT ARE YOU DOING?

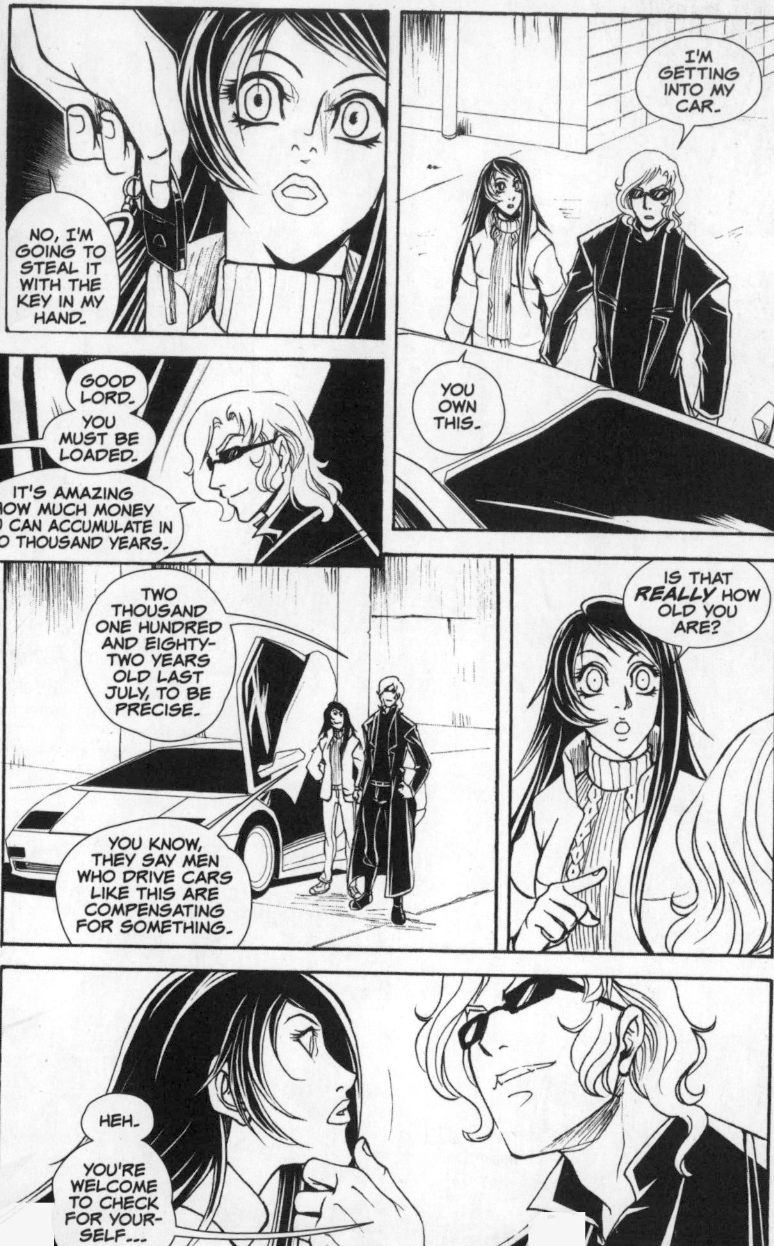
I'M GETTING INTO MY CAR.
YOU OWN THIS.
NO, I'M GOING TO STEAL IT WITH THE KEY IN MY HAND.
GOOD LORD.
YOU MUST BE LOADED.
IT'S AMAZING HOW MUCH MONEY YOU CAN ACCUMULATE IN TWO THOUSAND YEARS.
IS THAT *REALLY* HOW OLD YOU ARE?
TWO THOUSAND ONE HUNDRED AND EIGHTY-TWO YEARS OLD LAST JULY, TO BE PRECISE.
YOU KNOW, THEY SAY MEN WHO DRIVE CARS LIKE THIS ARE COMPENSATING FOR SOMETHING.
HEH.
YOU'RE WELCOME TO CHECK FOR YOURSELF...

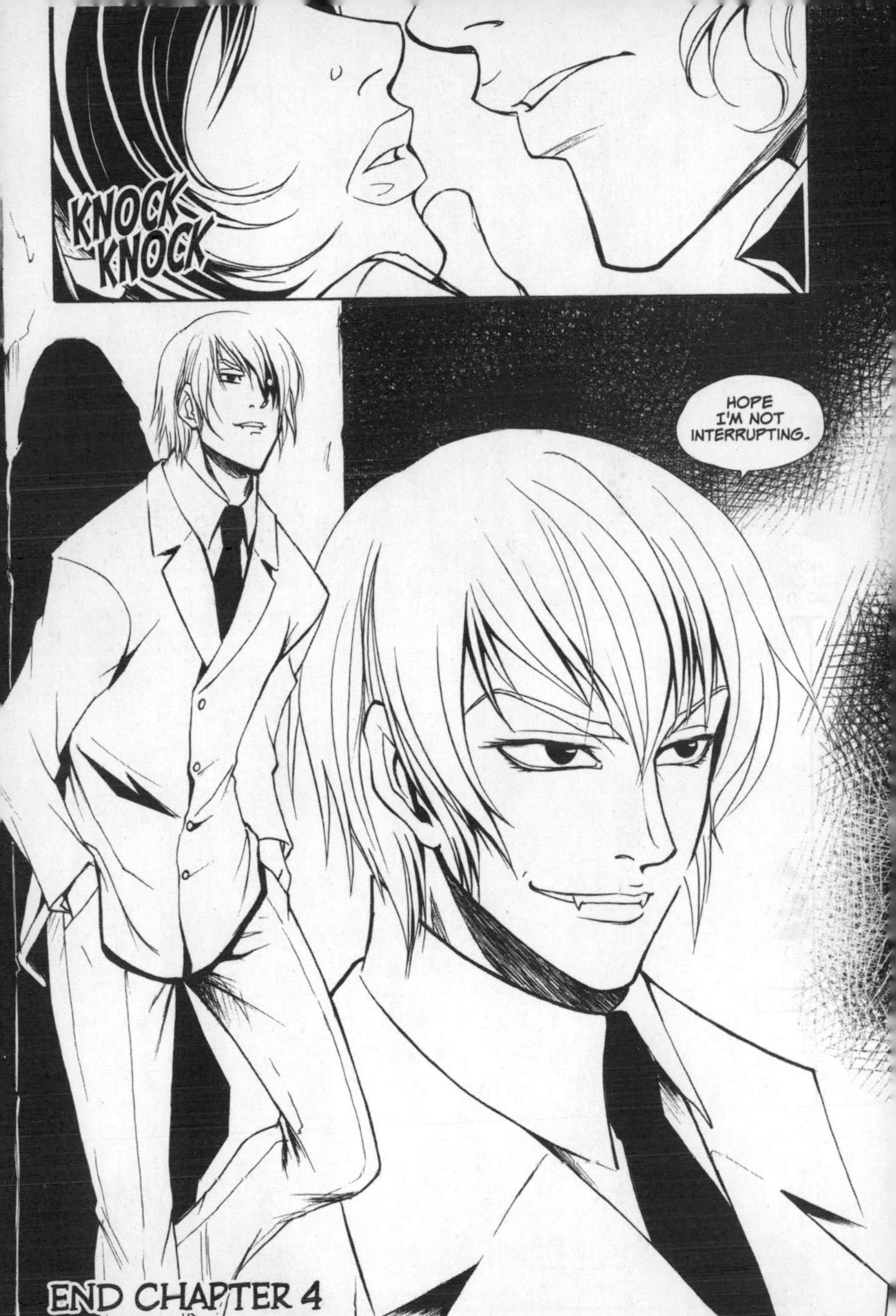
KNOCK KNOCK
HOPE I'M NOT INTERRUPTING.
END CHAPTER 4

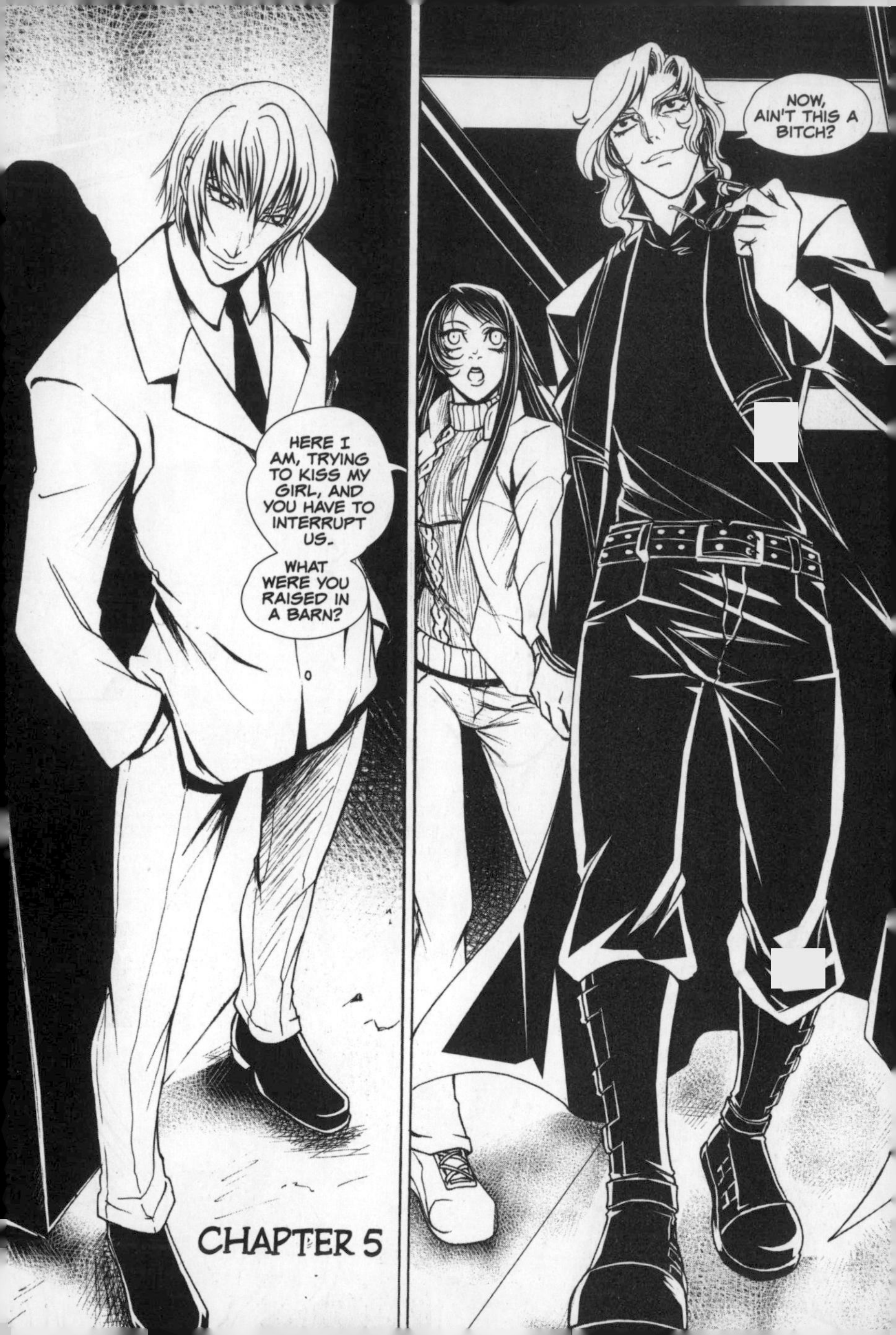
NOW, AIN'T THIS A BITCH?
HERE I AM, TRYING TO KISS MY GIRL, AND YOU HAVE TO INTERRUPT US.
WHAT WERE YOU RAISED IN A BARN?
CHAPTER 5

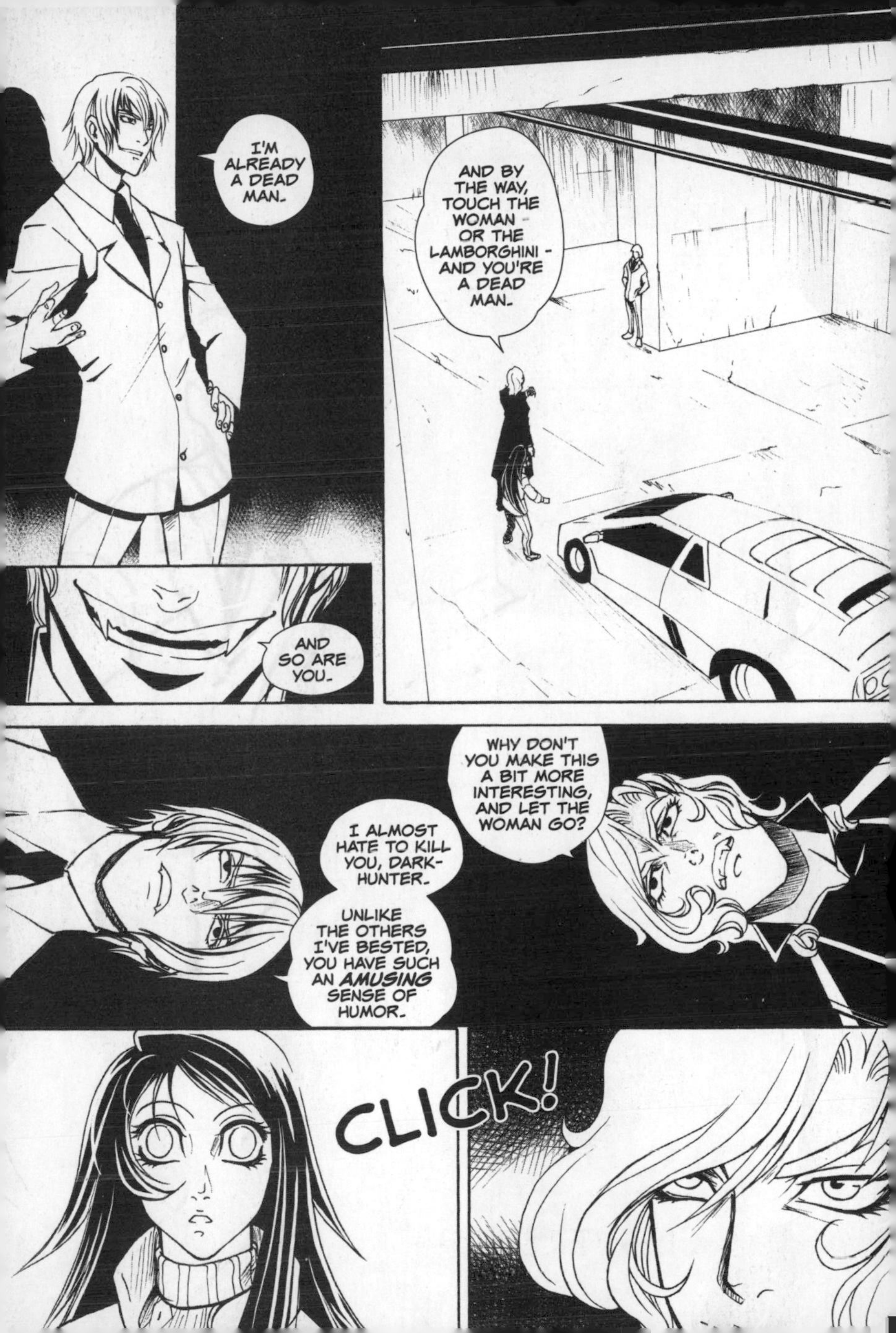
AND BY THE WAY, TOUCH THE WOMAN - OR THE LAMBORGHINI - AND YOU'RE A DEAD MAN.
I'M ALREADY A DEAD MAN.
AND SO ARE YOU.
WHY DON'T YOU MAKE THIS A BIT MORE INTERESTING, AND LET THE WOMAN GO?
I ALMOST HATE TO KILL YOU, DARK-HUNTER.
UNLIKE THE OTHERS I'VE BESTED, YOU HAVE SUCH AN *AMUSING* SENSE OF HUMOR.
CLICK!

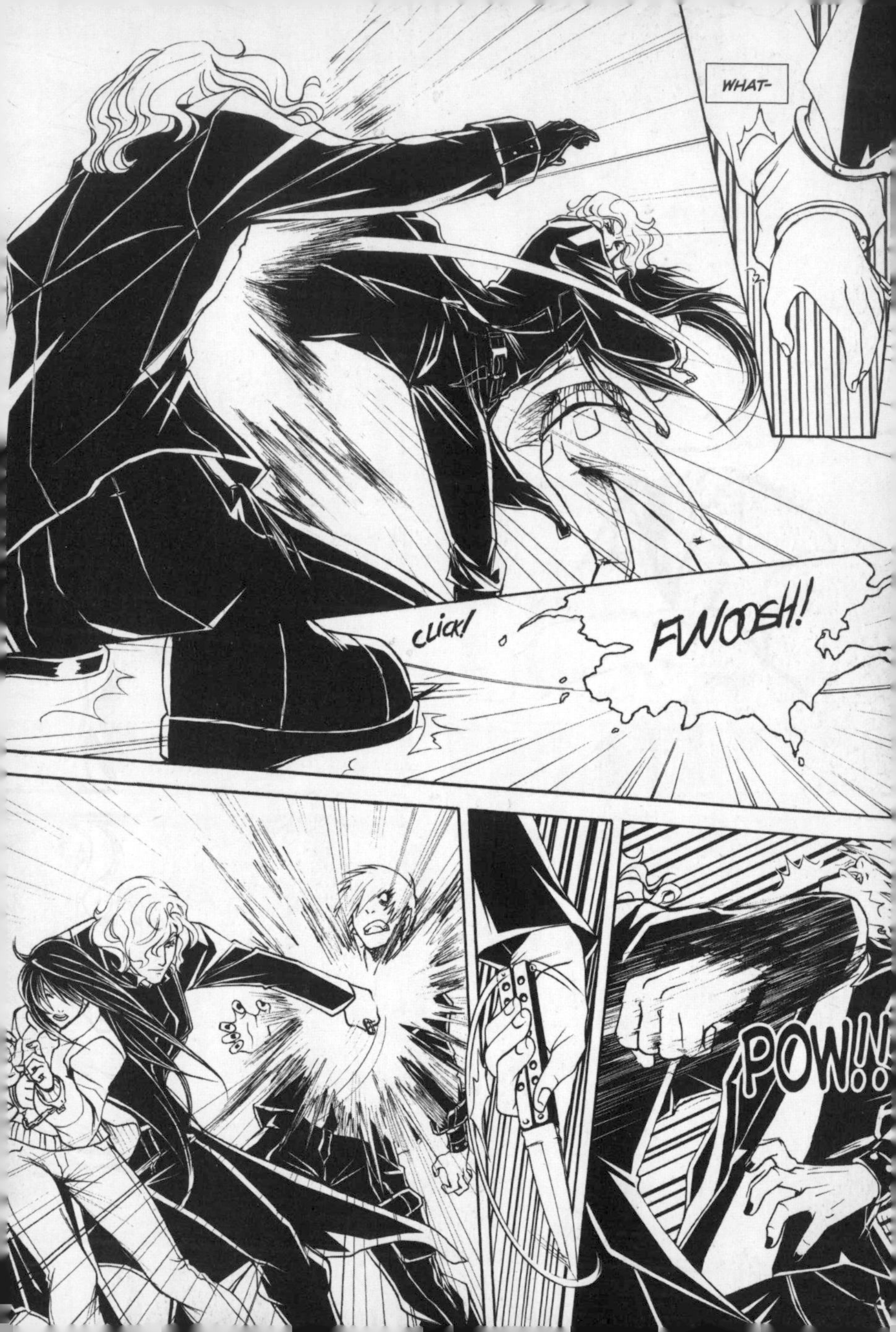
WHAT-
CLICK!
FWOOSH!
POW!!

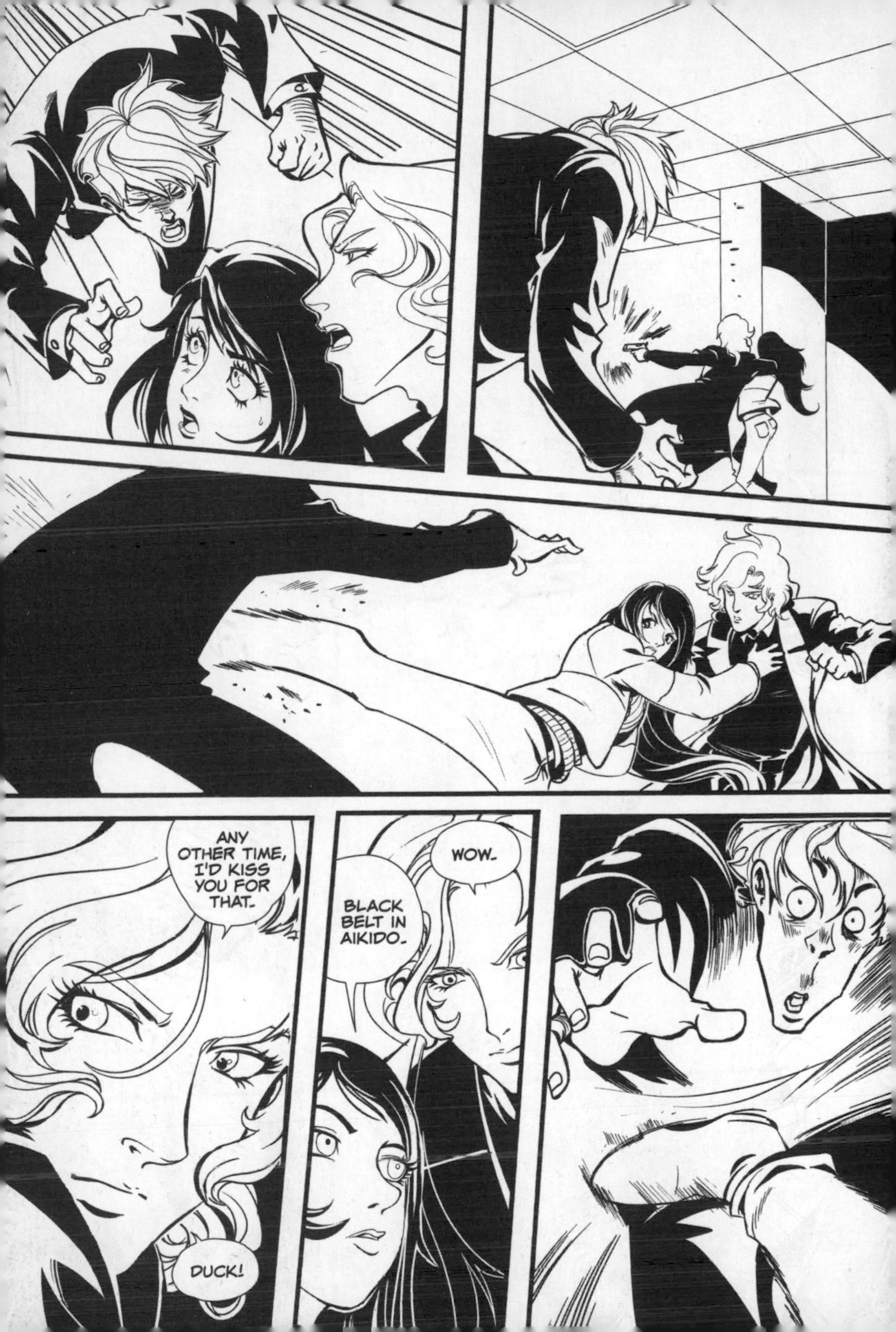
WOW.
BLACK BELT IN AIKIDO.
ANY OTHER TIME, I'D KISS YOU FOR THAT.
DUCK!

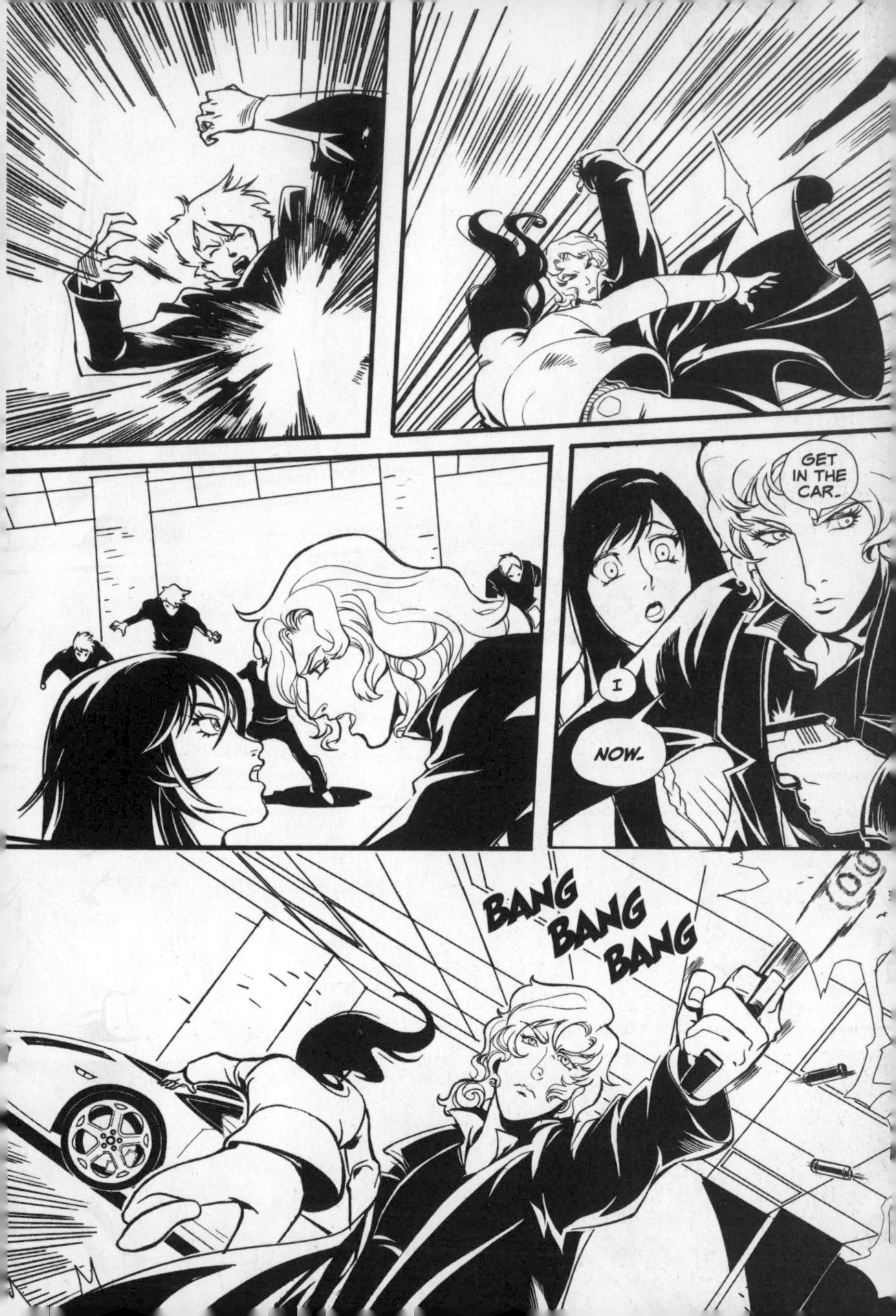
GET IN THE CAR.
I
NOW.
BANG
BANG
BANG

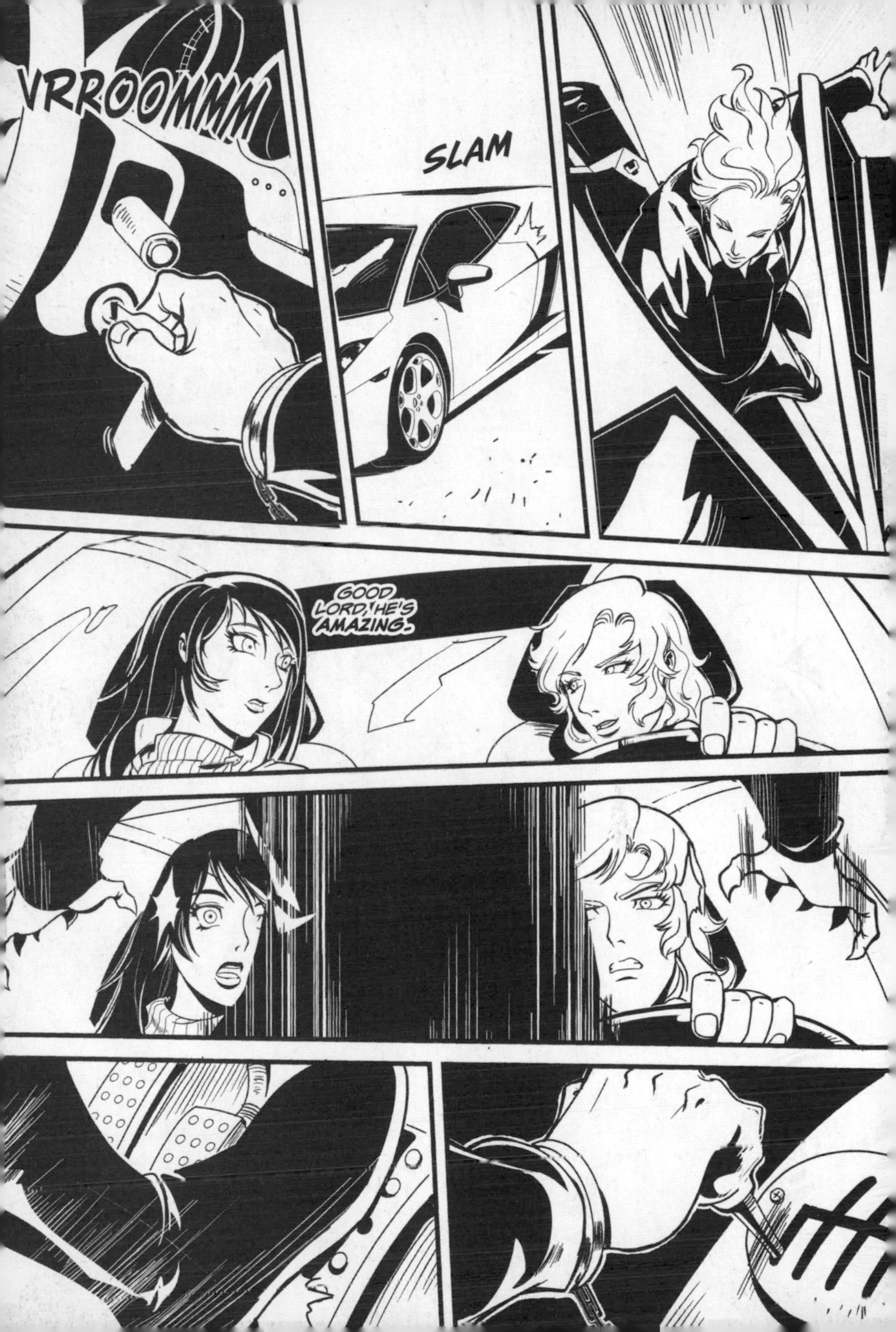
SLAM
VRROOMMM
GOOD LORD, HE'S AMAZING.

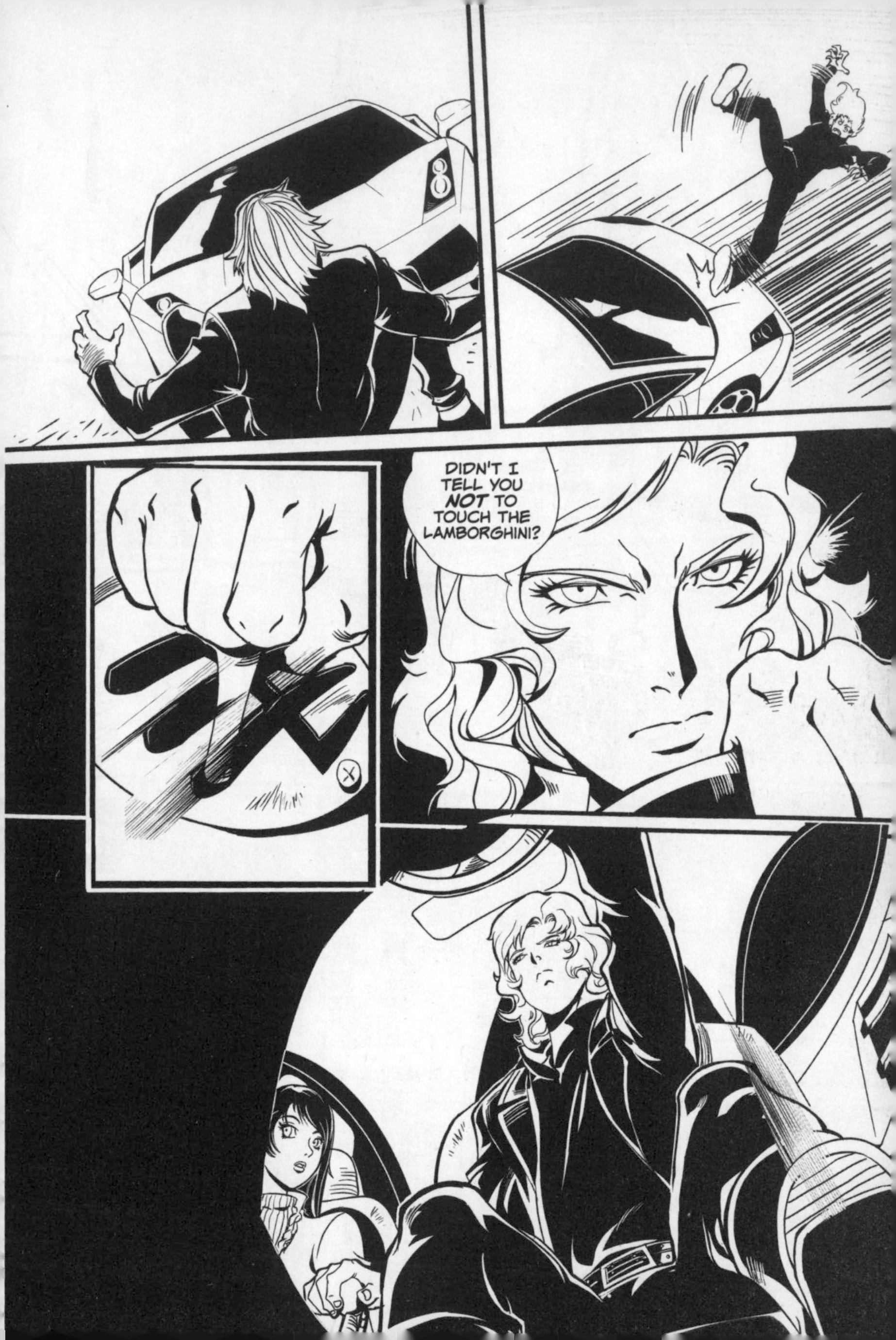
DIDN'T I TELL YOU NOT TO TOUCH THE LAMBORGHINI?

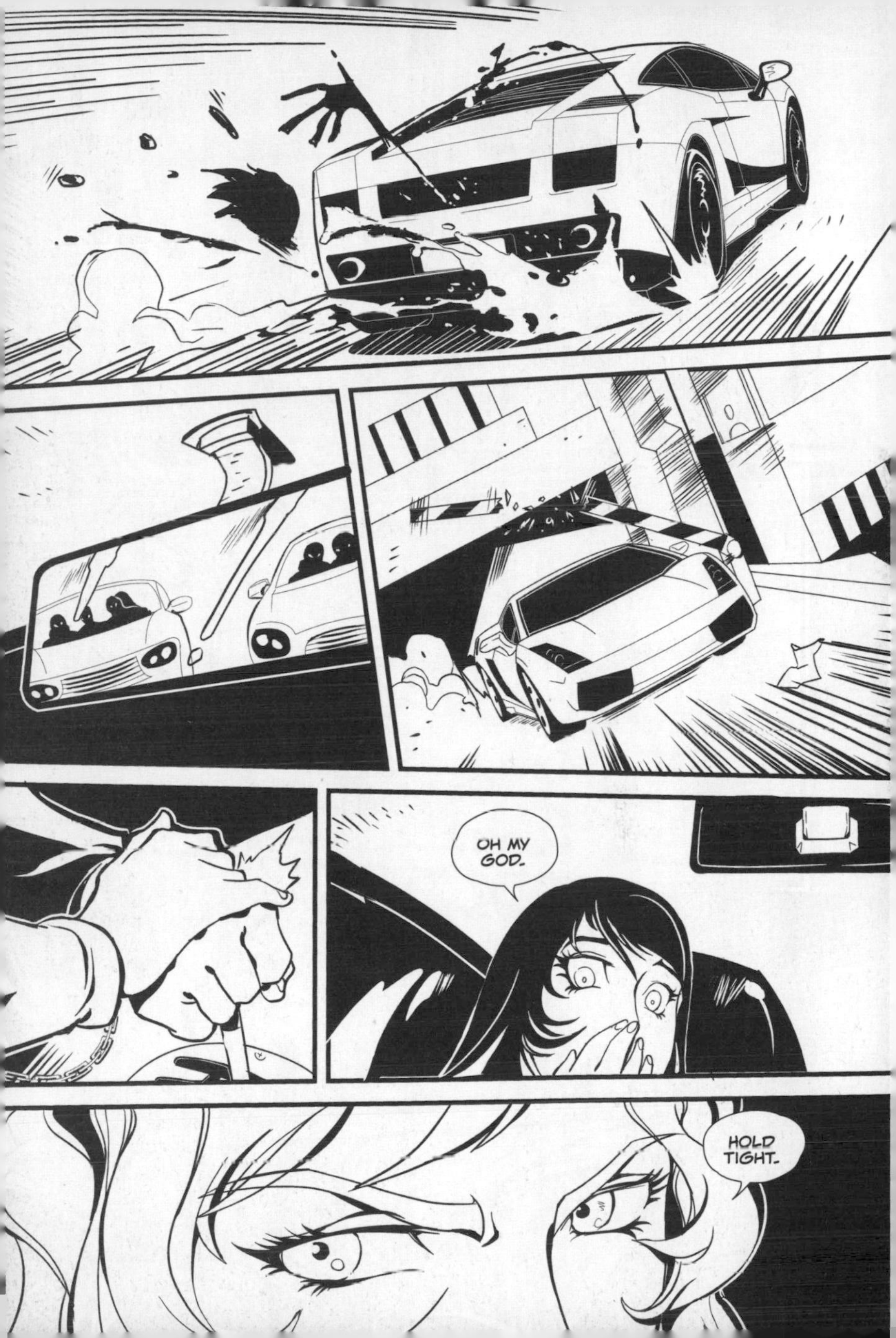
OH MY GOD.
HOLD TIGHT.

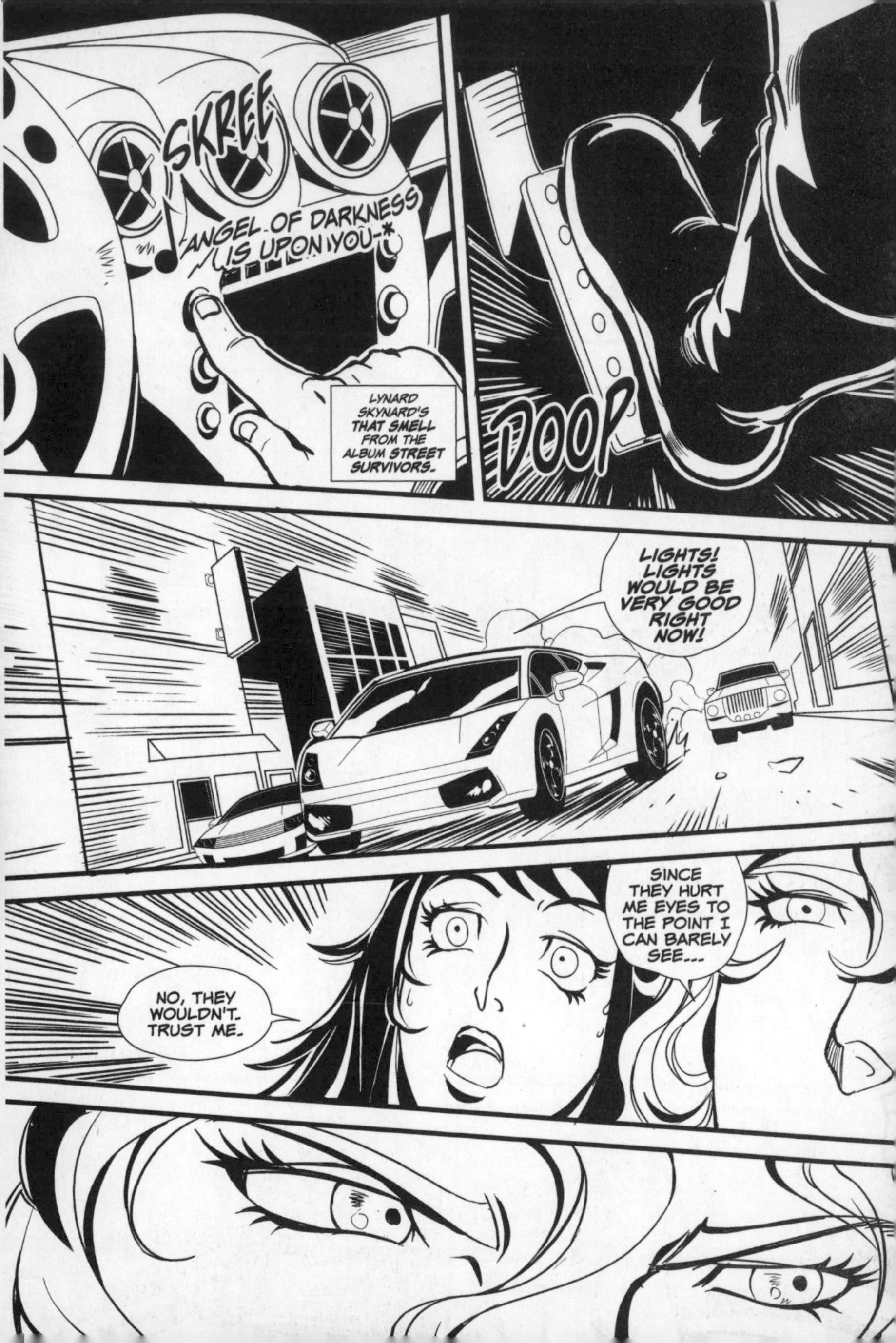
DOOP
SKREE
ANGEL OF DARKNESS IS UPON YOU-*
LYNARD SKYNARD'S THAT SMELL FROM THE ALBUM STREET SURVIVORS.
LIGHTS! LIGHTS WOULD BE VERY GOOD RIGHT NOW!
SINCE THEY HURT ME EYES TO THE POINT I CAN BARELY SEE...
NO, THEY WOULDN'T. TRUST ME.

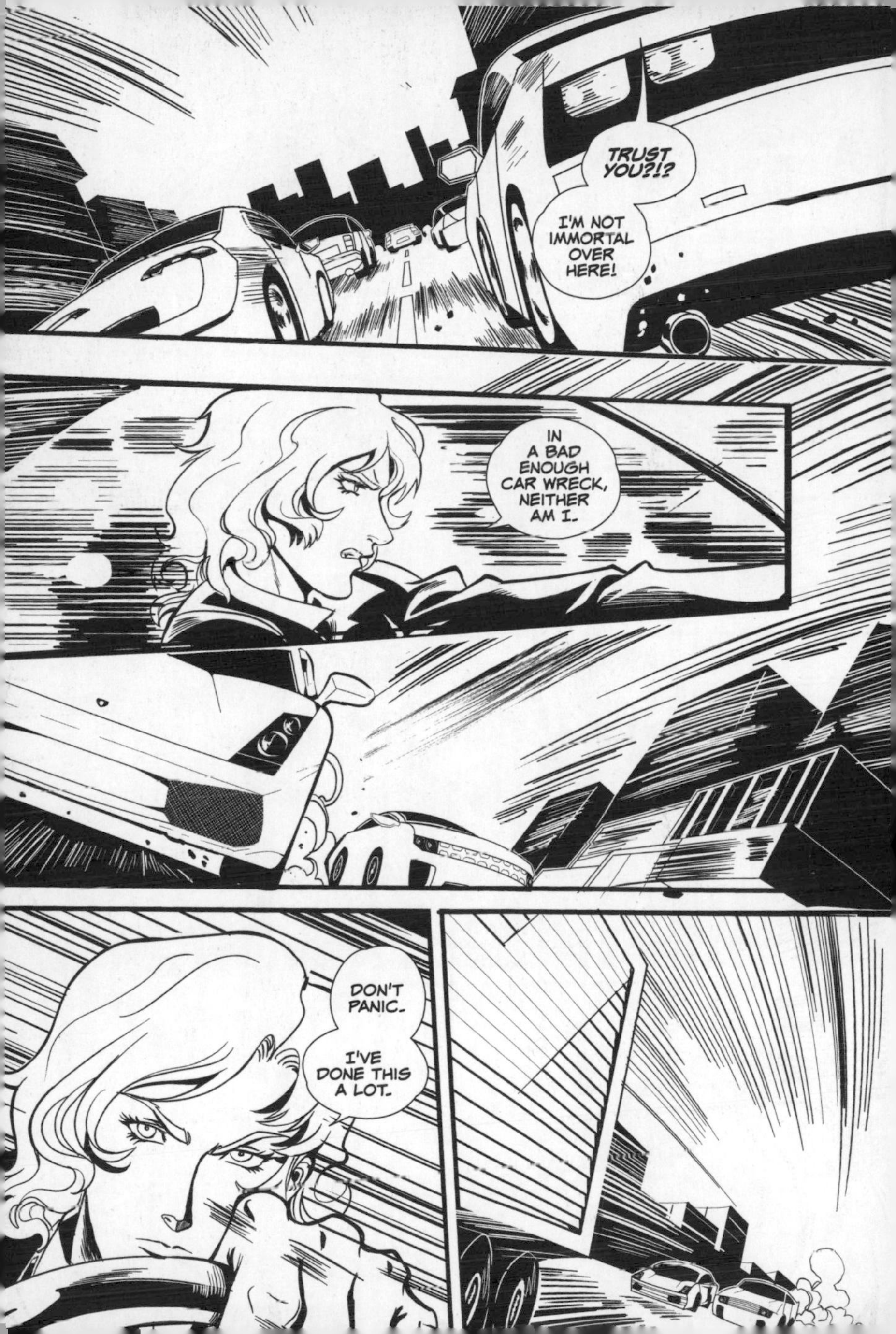
TRUST YOU?!?
I'M NOT IMMORTAL OVER HERE!
IN A BAD ENOUGH CAR WRECK, NEITHER AM I.
DON'T PANIC.
I'VE DONE THIS A LOT.

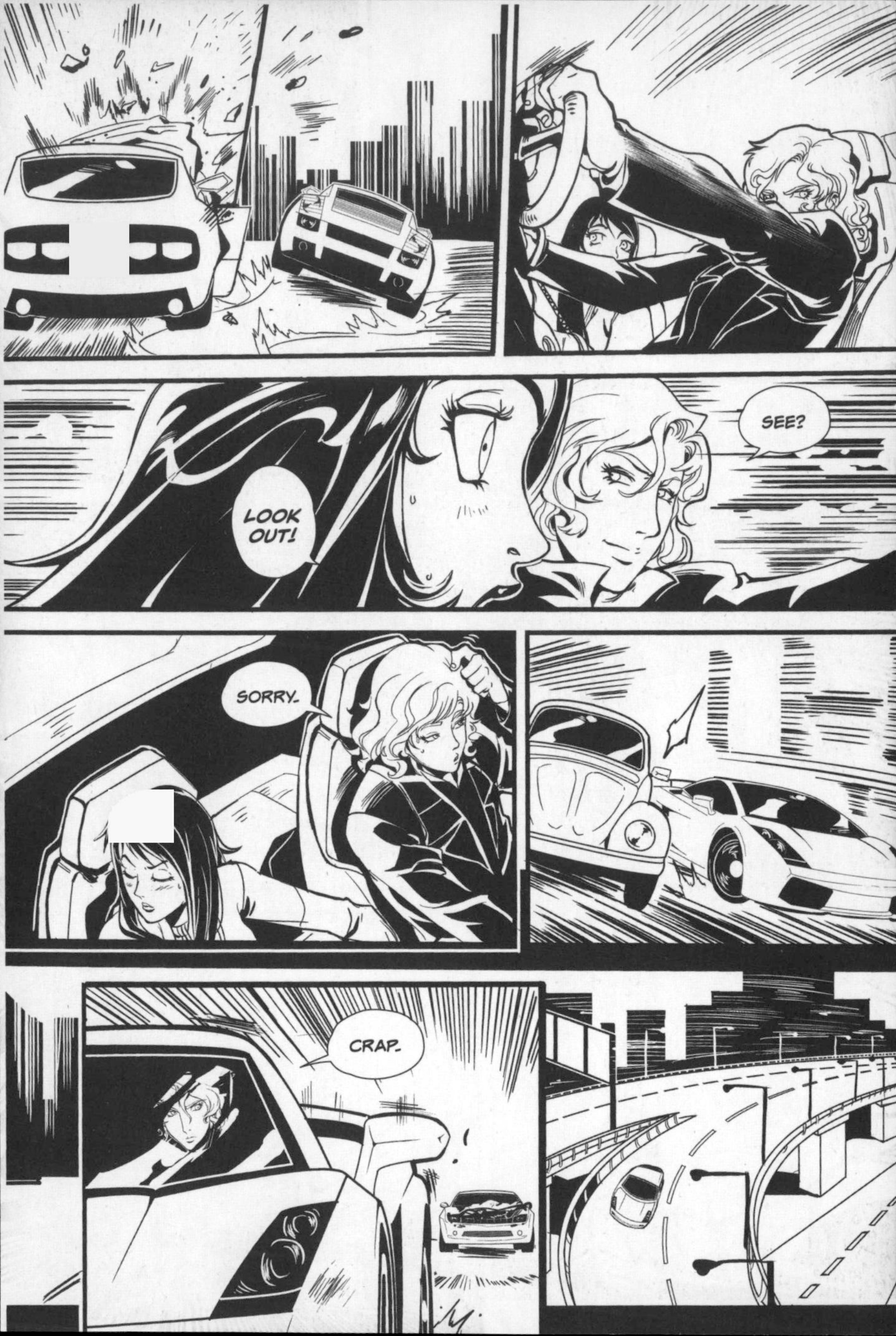
SEE?
LOOK OUT!
SORRY.
CRAP.

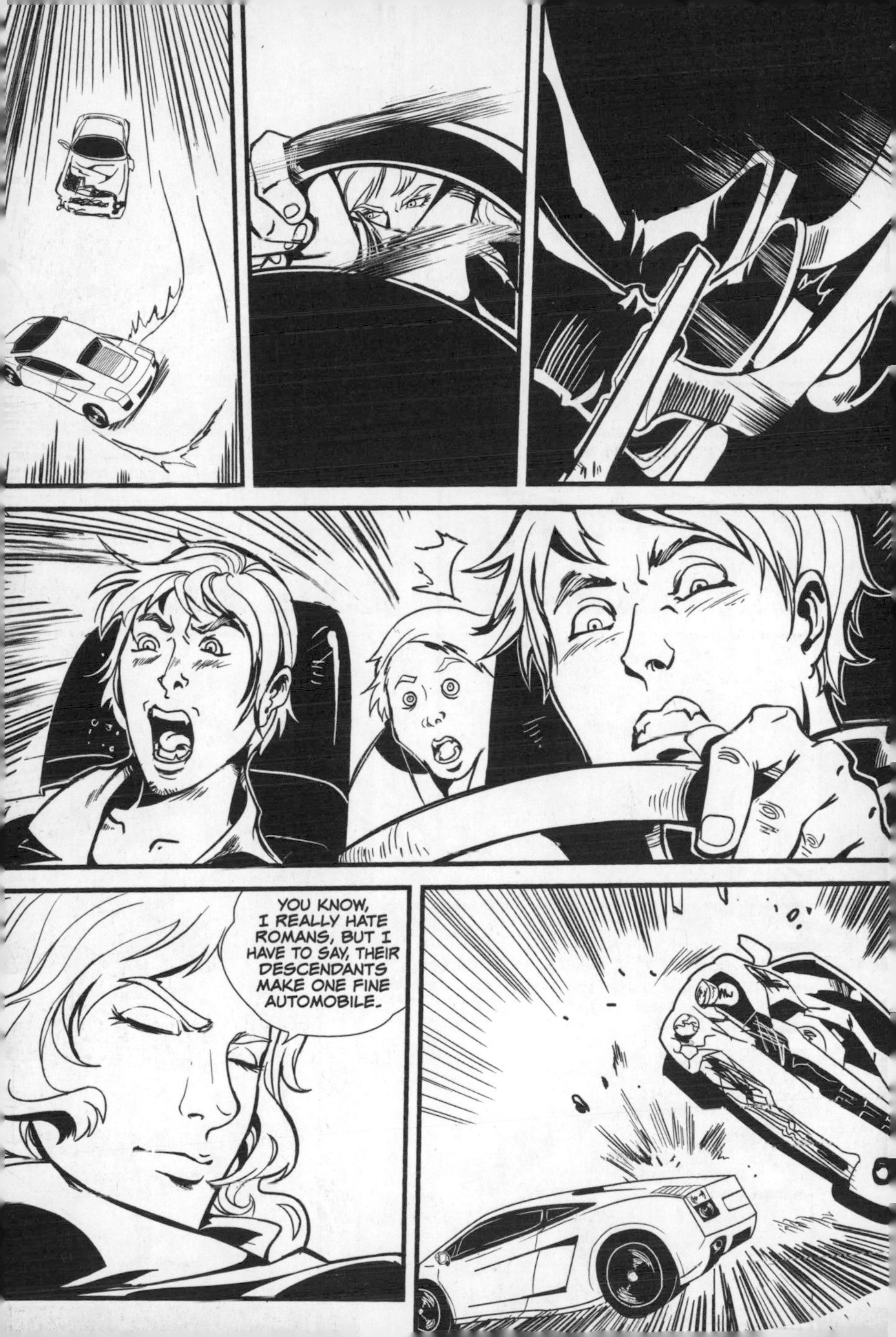
YOU KNOW, I REALLY HATE ROMANS, BUT I HAVE TO SAY, THEIR DESCENDANTS MAKE ONE FINE AUTOMOBILE.

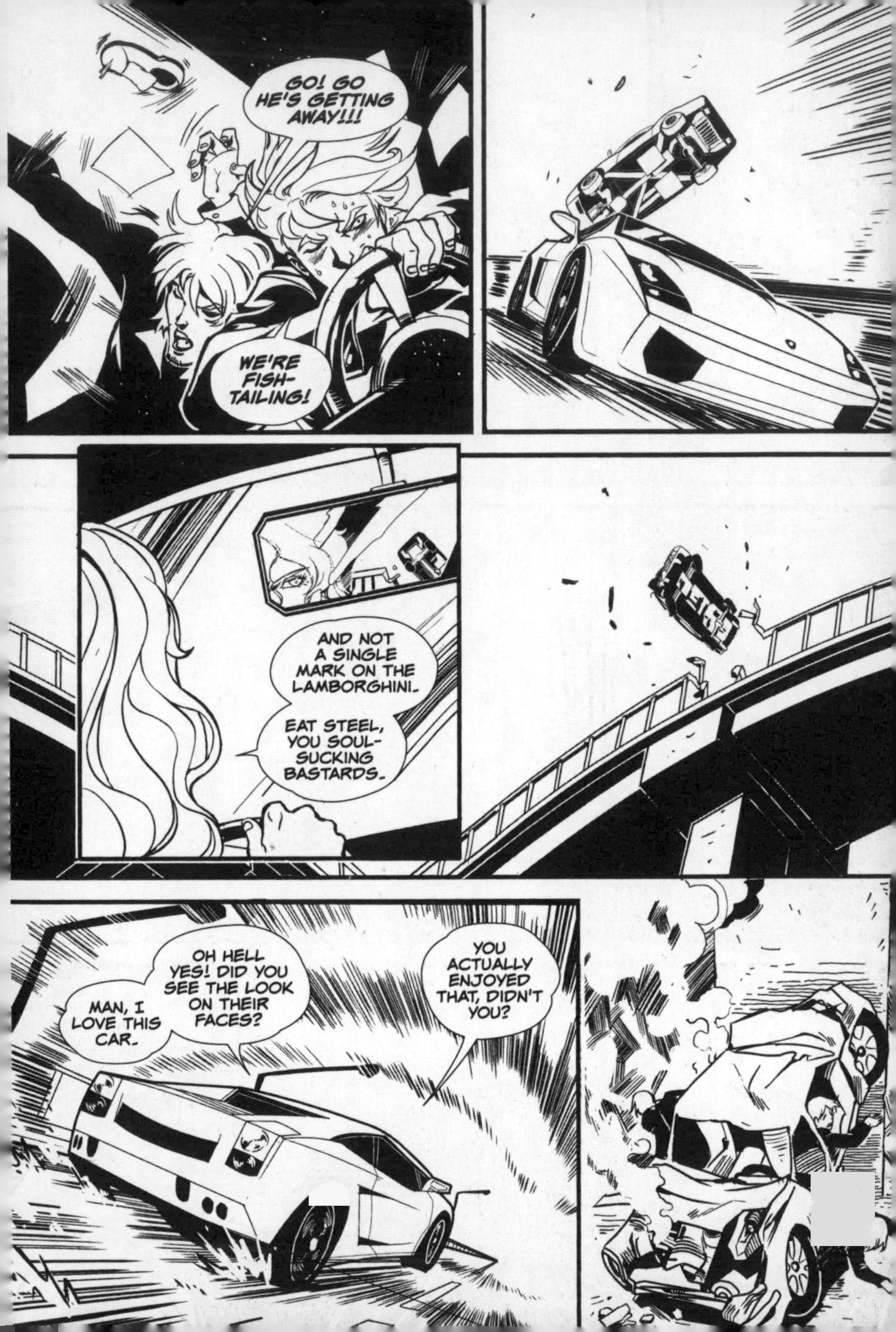
GO! GO HE'S GETTING AWAY!!!
WE'RE FISH-TAILING!
AND NOT A SINGLE MARK ON THE LAMBORGHINI.
EAT STEEL, YOU SOUL-SUCKING BASTARDS.
YOU ACTUALLY ENJOYED THAT, DIDN'T YOU?
OH HELL YES! DID YOU SEE THE LOOK ON THEIR FACES?
MAN, I LOVE THIS CAR.

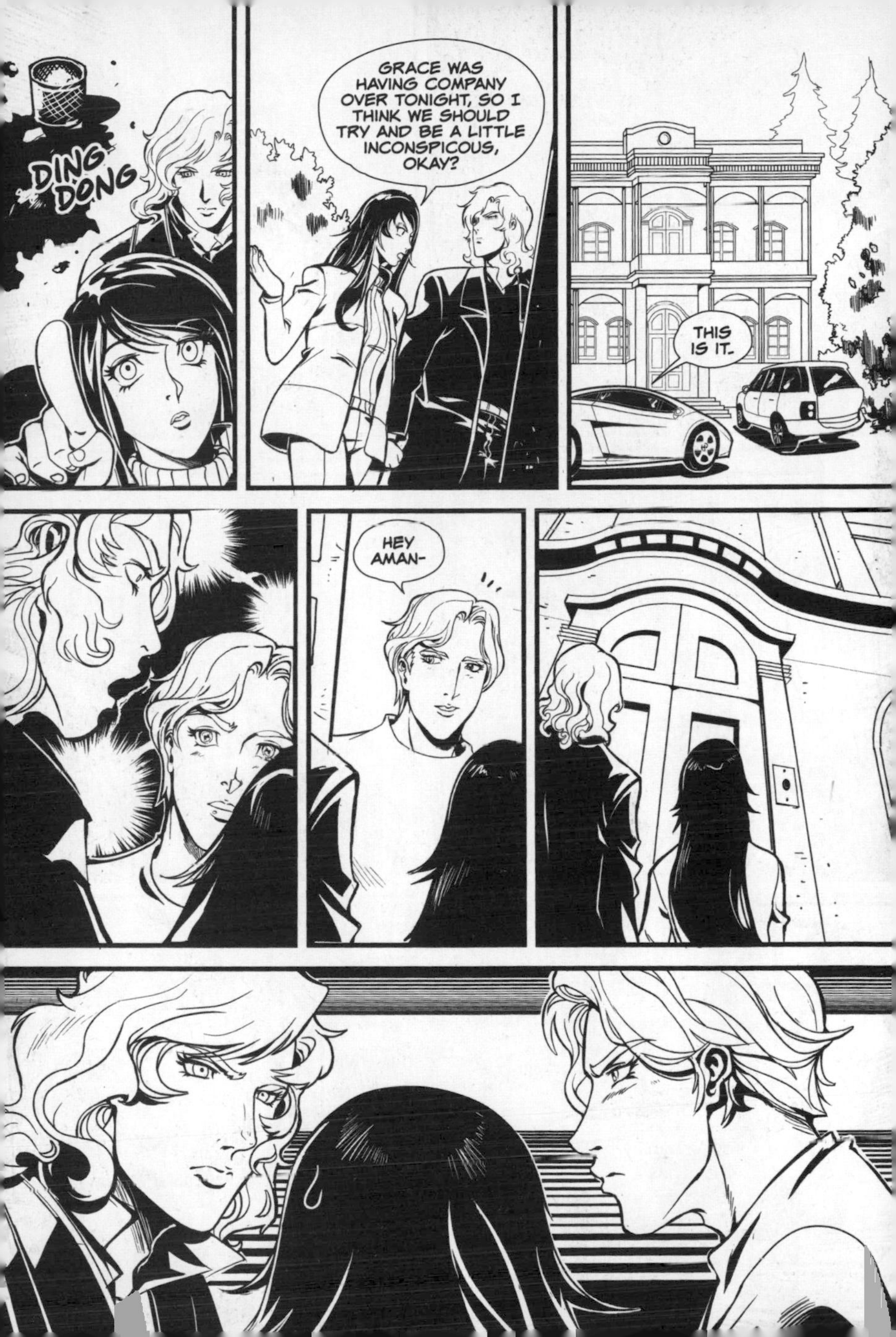
THIS IS IT.
GRACE WAS HAVING COMPANY OVER TONIGHT, SO I THINK WE SHOULD TRY AND BE A LITTLE INCONSPICOUS, OKAY?
DING DONG
HEY AMAN-

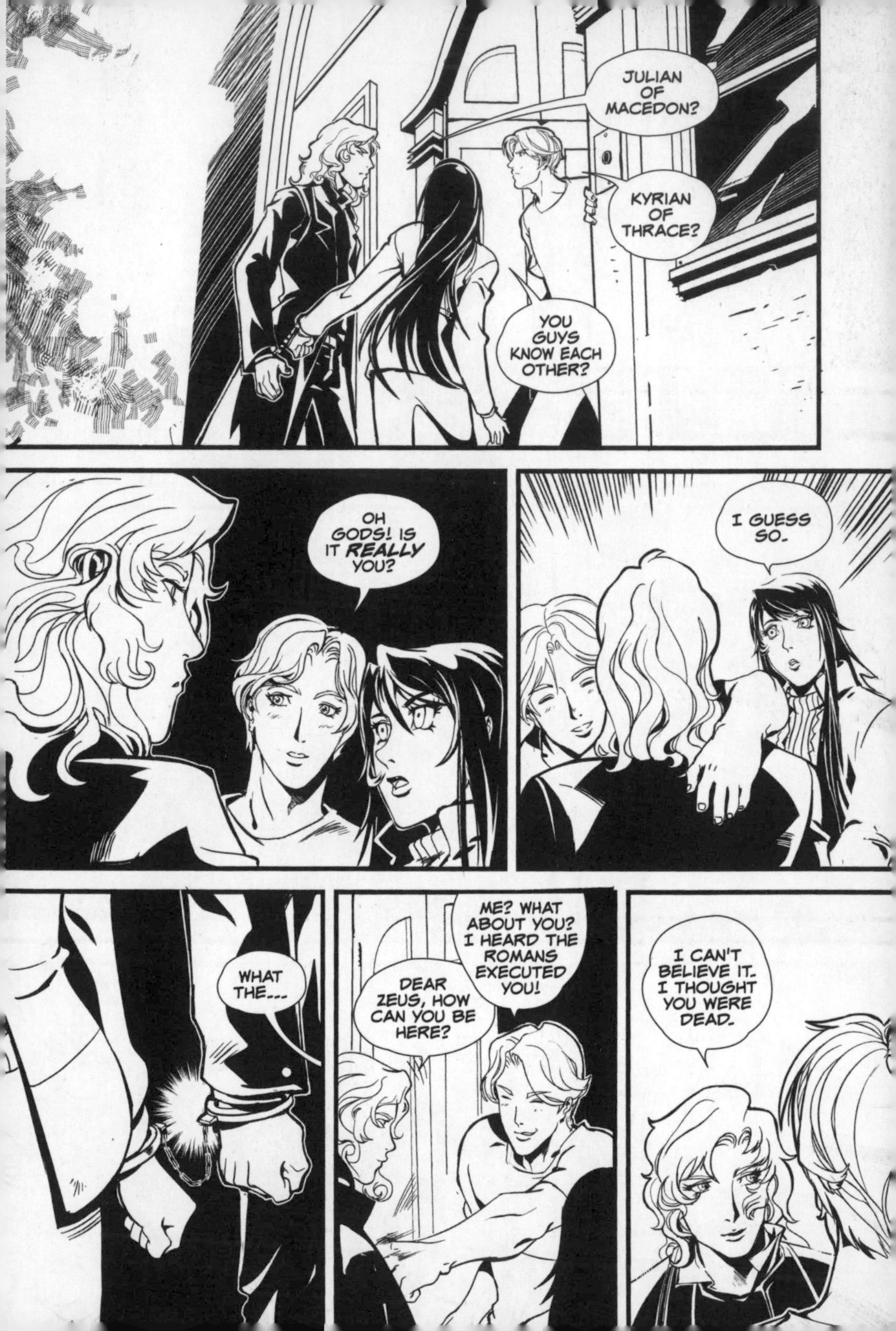
JULIAN OF MACEDON?
KYRIAN OF THRACE?
YOU GUYS KNOW EACH OTHER?
OH GODS! IS IT *REALLY* YOU?
I GUESS SO.
WHAT THE...
DEAR ZEUS, HOW CAN YOU BE HERE?
ME? WHAT ABOUT YOU? I HEARD THE ROMANS EXECUTED YOU!
I CAN'T BELIEVE IT. I THOUGHT YOU WERE DEAD.

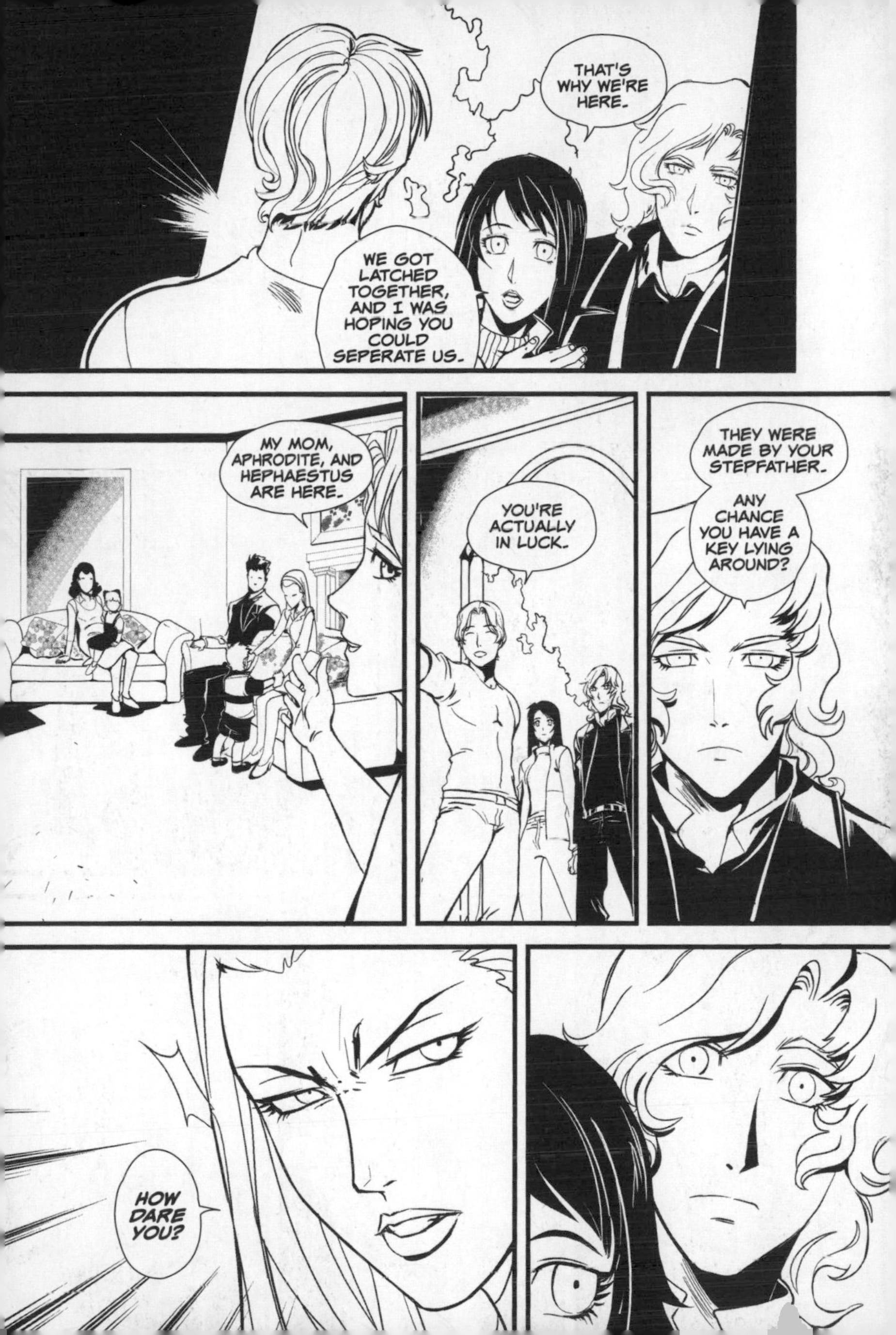
THAT'S WHY WE'RE HERE.
WE GOT LATCHED TOGETHER, AND I WAS HOPING YOU COULD SEPERATE US.
THEY WERE MADE BY YOUR STEPFATHER.
ANY CHANCE YOU HAVE A KEY LYING AROUND?
YOU'RE ACTUALLY IN LUCK.
MY MOM, APHRODITE, AND HEPHAESTUS ARE HERE.
HOW DARE YOU?

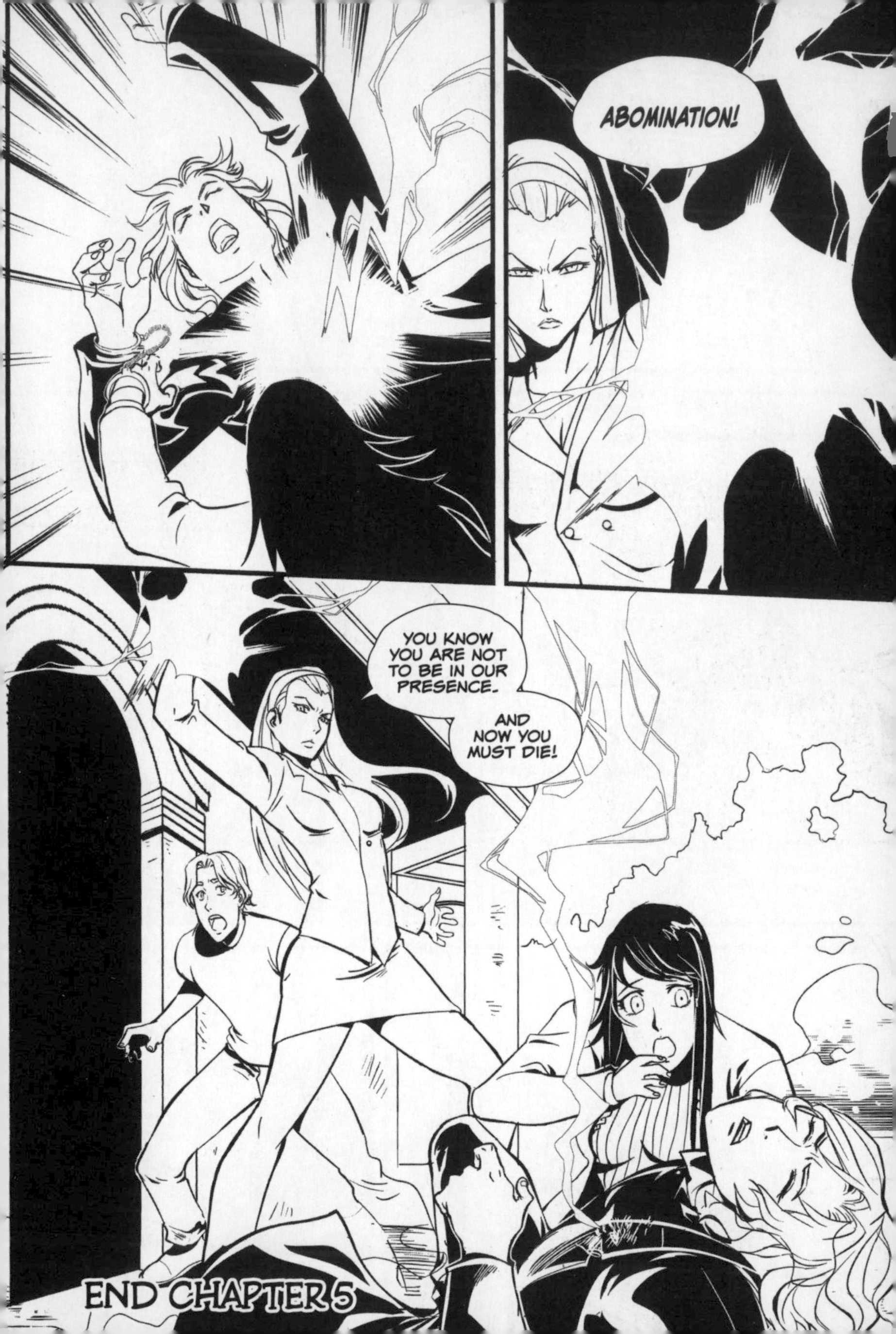
ABOMINATION!
YOU KNOW YOU ARE NOT TO BE IN OUR PRESENCE.
AND NOW YOU MUST DIE!
END CHAPTER 5

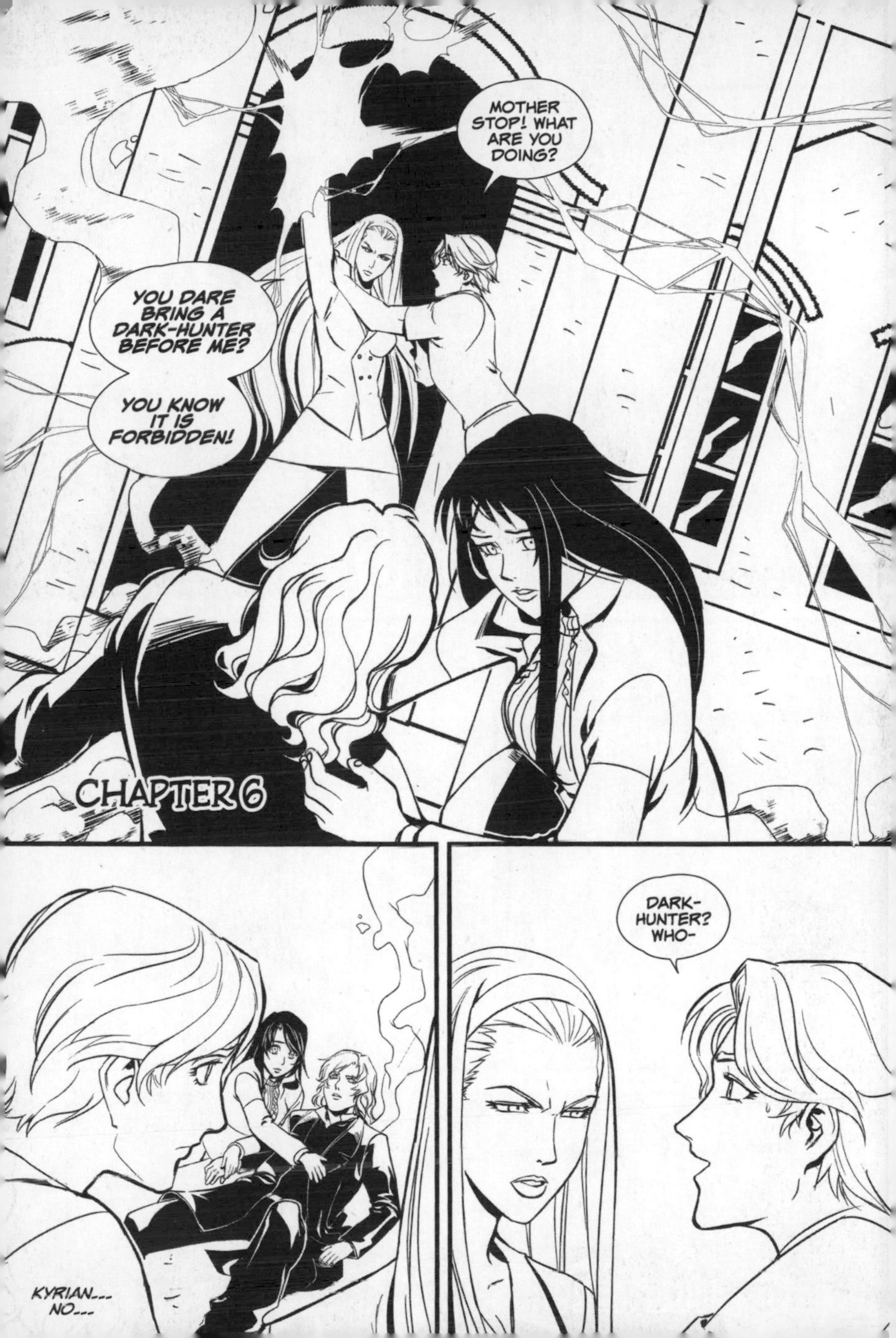
MOTHER STOP! WHAT ARE YOU DOING?
YOU DARE BRING A DARK-HUNTER BEFORE ME?
YOU KNOW IT IS FORBIDDEN!
CHAPTER 6
DARK-HUNTER? WHO-
KYRIAN... NO...

NO!

YOU'RE ABOUT TO BE FREE, LITTLE ONE.

YOU KILL HIM, AND I WILL NEVER FORGIVE YOU FOR IT.

I HAVE NEVER, IN MY ENTIRE LIFE, ASKED YOU FOR ANYTHING.

BUT I'M ASKING YOU NOW, AS YOUR SON, HELP HIM.

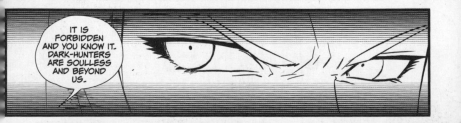

IT IS FORBIDDEN AND YOU KNOW IT. DARK-HUNTERS ARE SOULLESS AND BEYOND US.

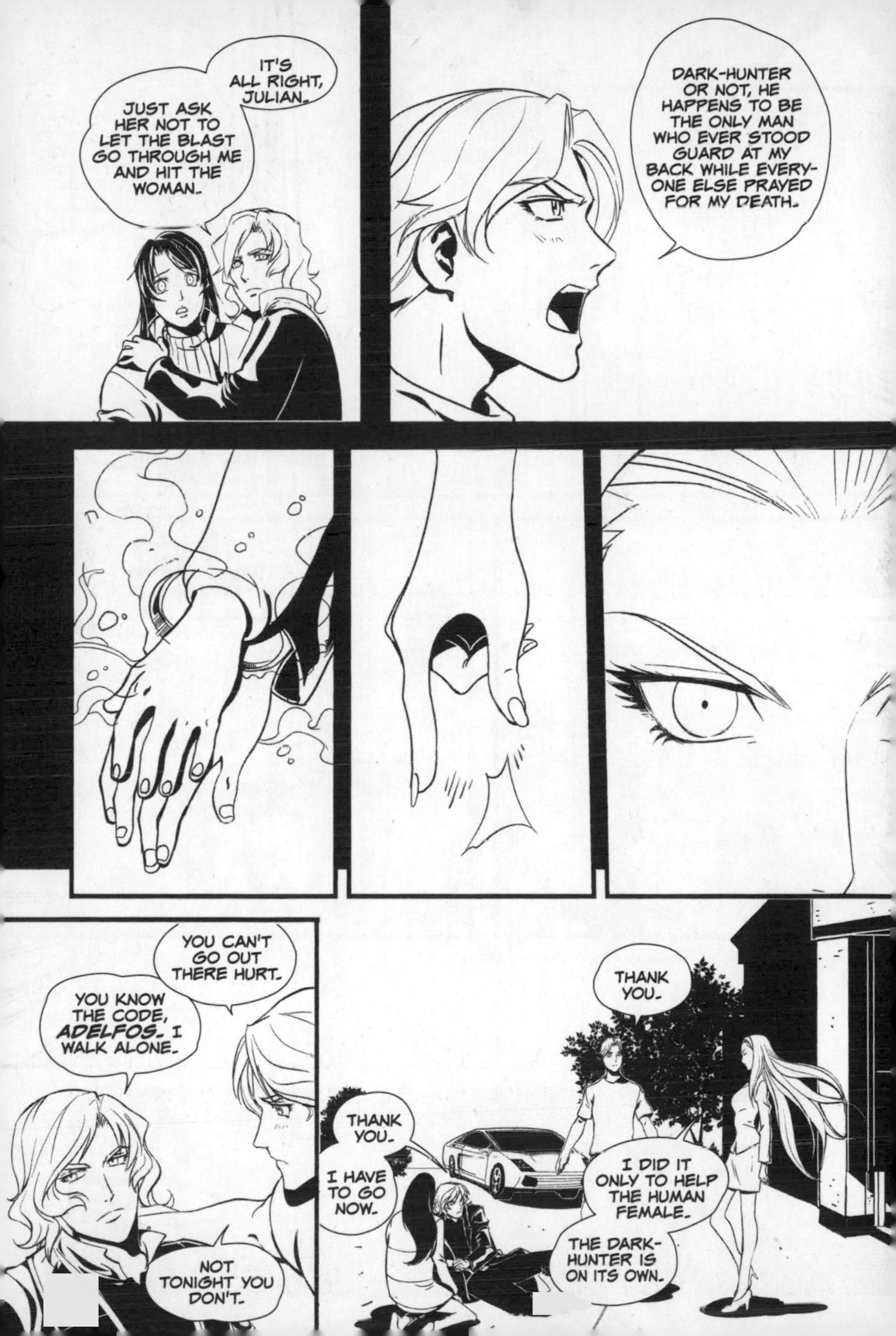
DARK-HUNTER OR NOT, HE HAPPENS TO BE THE ONLY MAN WHO EVER STOOD GUARD AT MY BACK WHILE EVERY-ONE ELSE PRAYED FOR MY DEATH.
IT'S ALL RIGHT, JULIAN.
JUST ASK HER NOT TO LET THE BLAST GO THROUGH ME AND HIT THE WOMAN.
THANK YOU.
I DID IT ONLY TO HELP THE HUMAN FEMALE.
THE DARK-HUNTER IS ON ITS OWN.
THANK YOU.
I HAVE TO GO NOW.
YOU CAN'T GO OUT THERE HURT.
YOU KNOW THE CODE, *ADELFOS*. I WALK ALONE.
NOT TONIGHT YOU DON'T.

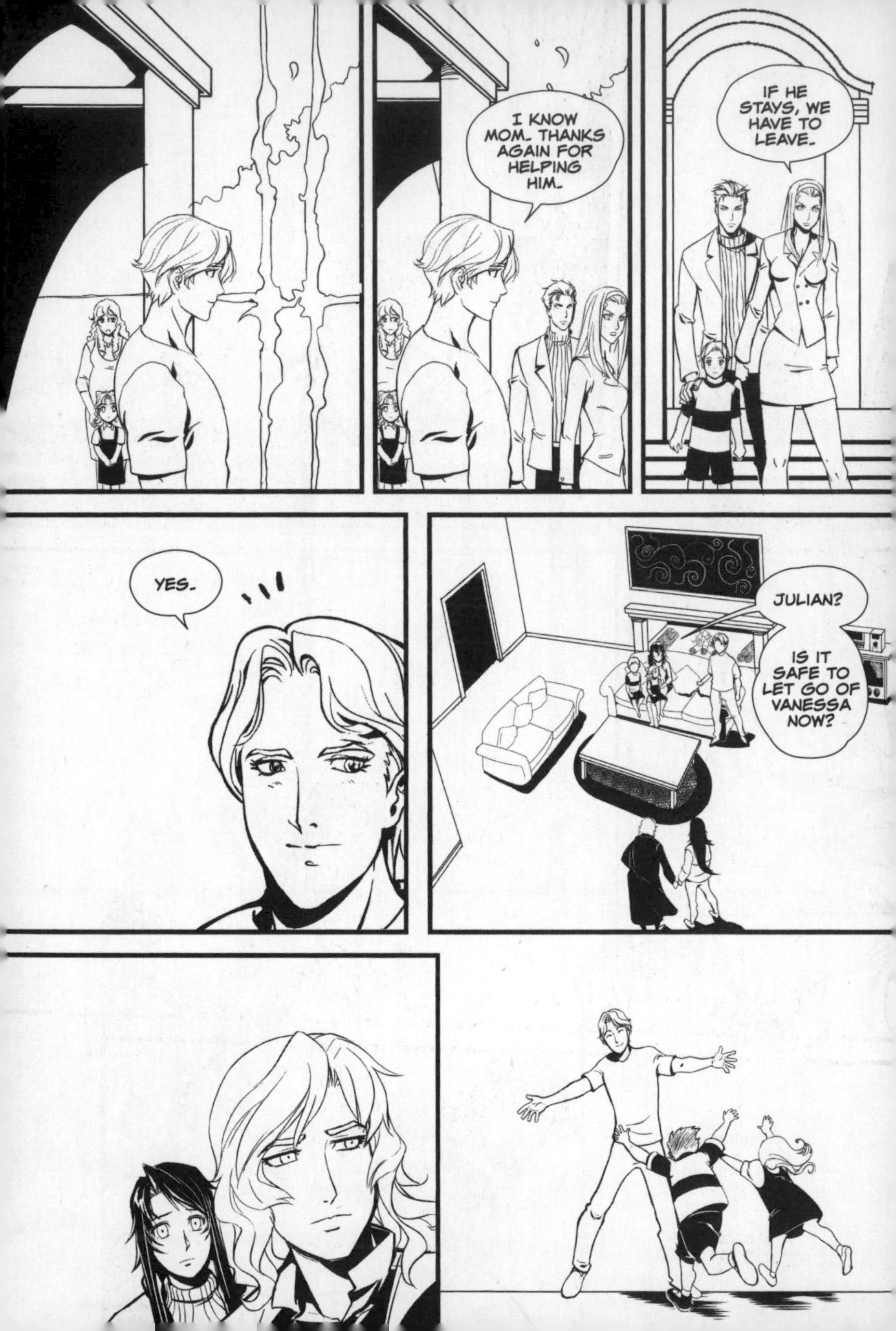
IF HE STAYS, WE HAVE TO LEAVE.
I KNOW MOM. THANKS AGAIN FOR HELPING HIM.
JULIAN?
IS IT SAFE TO LET GO OF VANESSA NOW?
YES.

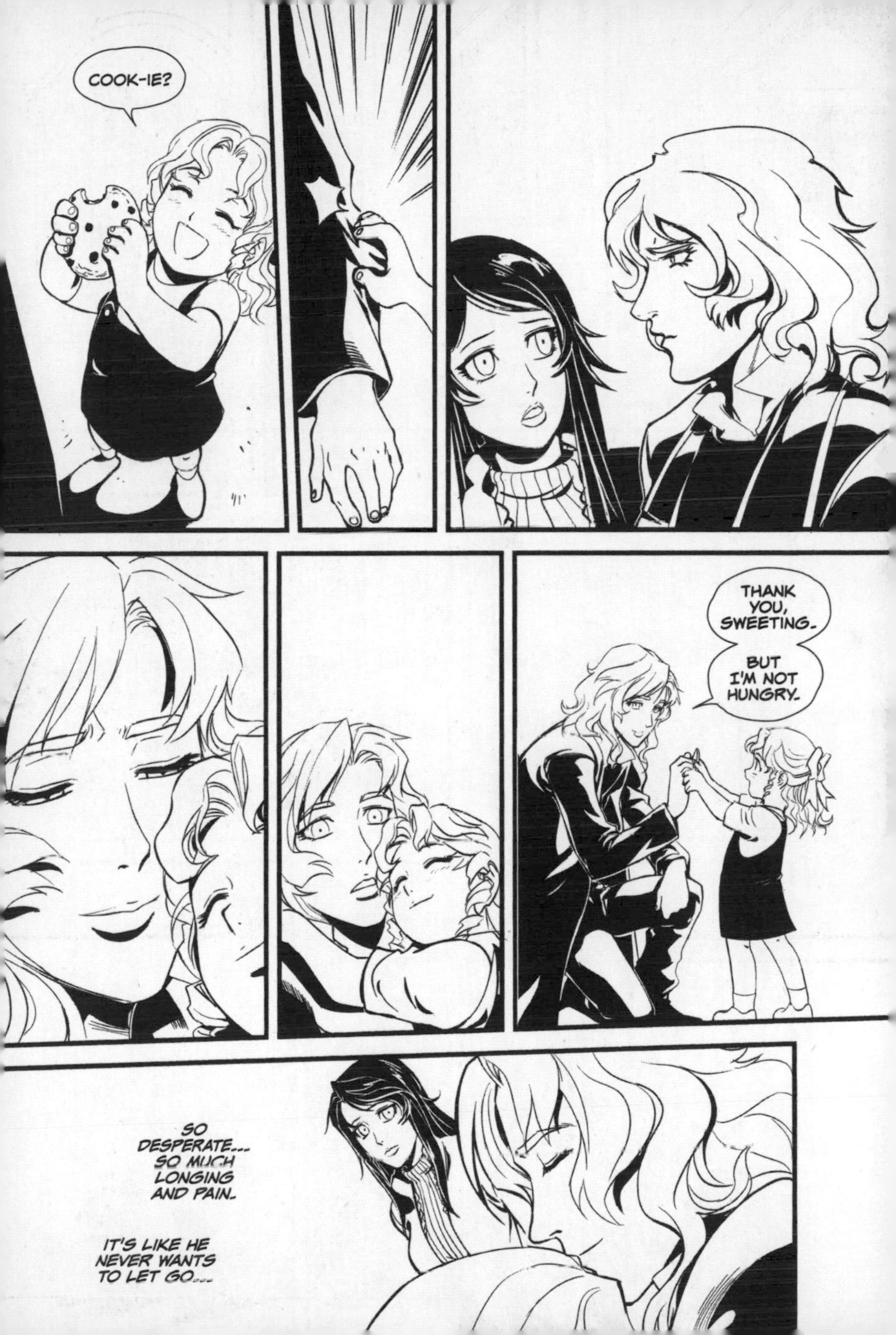
COOK-IE?
THANK YOU, SWEETING.
BUT I'M NOT HUNGRY.
SO DESPERATE... SO MUCH LONGING AND PAIN.
IT'S LIKE HE NEVER WANTS TO LET GO...

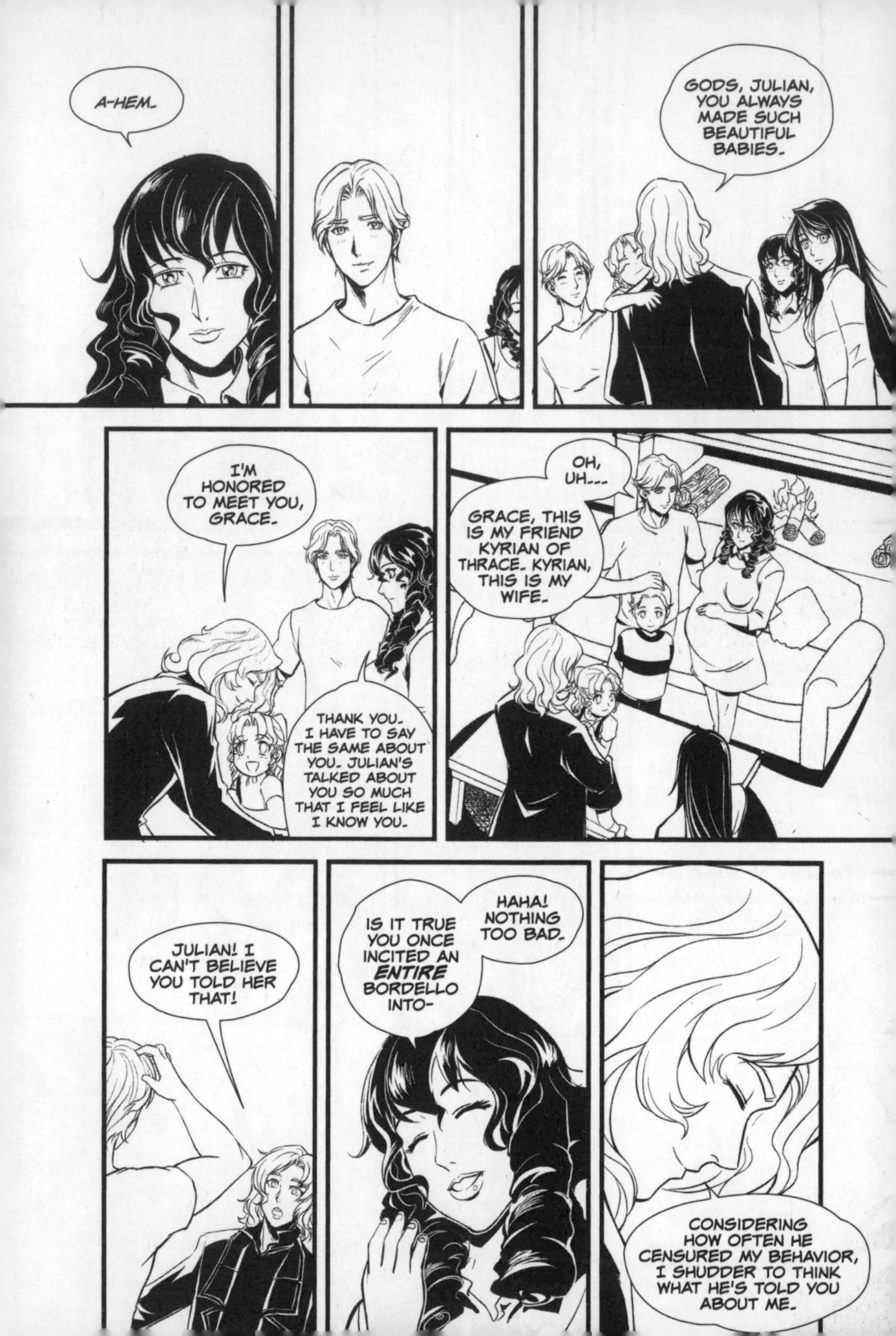
GODS, JULIAN, YOU ALWAYS MADE SUCH BEAUTIFUL BABIES.
A-HEM.
OH, UH...
GRACE, THIS IS MY FRIEND KYRIAN OF THRACE. KYRIAN, THIS IS MY WIFE.
I'M HONORED TO MEET YOU, GRACE.
THANK YOU. I HAVE TO SAY THE SAME ABOUT YOU. JULIAN'S TALKED ABOUT YOU SO MUCH THAT I FEEL LIKE I KNOW YOU.
CONSIDERING HOW OFTEN HE CENSURED MY BEHAVIOR, I SHUDDER TO THINK WHAT HE'S TOLD YOU ABOUT ME.
HAHA! NOTHING TOO BAD.
IS IT TRUE YOU ONCE INCITED AN *ENTIRE* BORDELLO INTO-
JULIAN! I CAN'T BELIEVE YOU TOLD HER THAT!

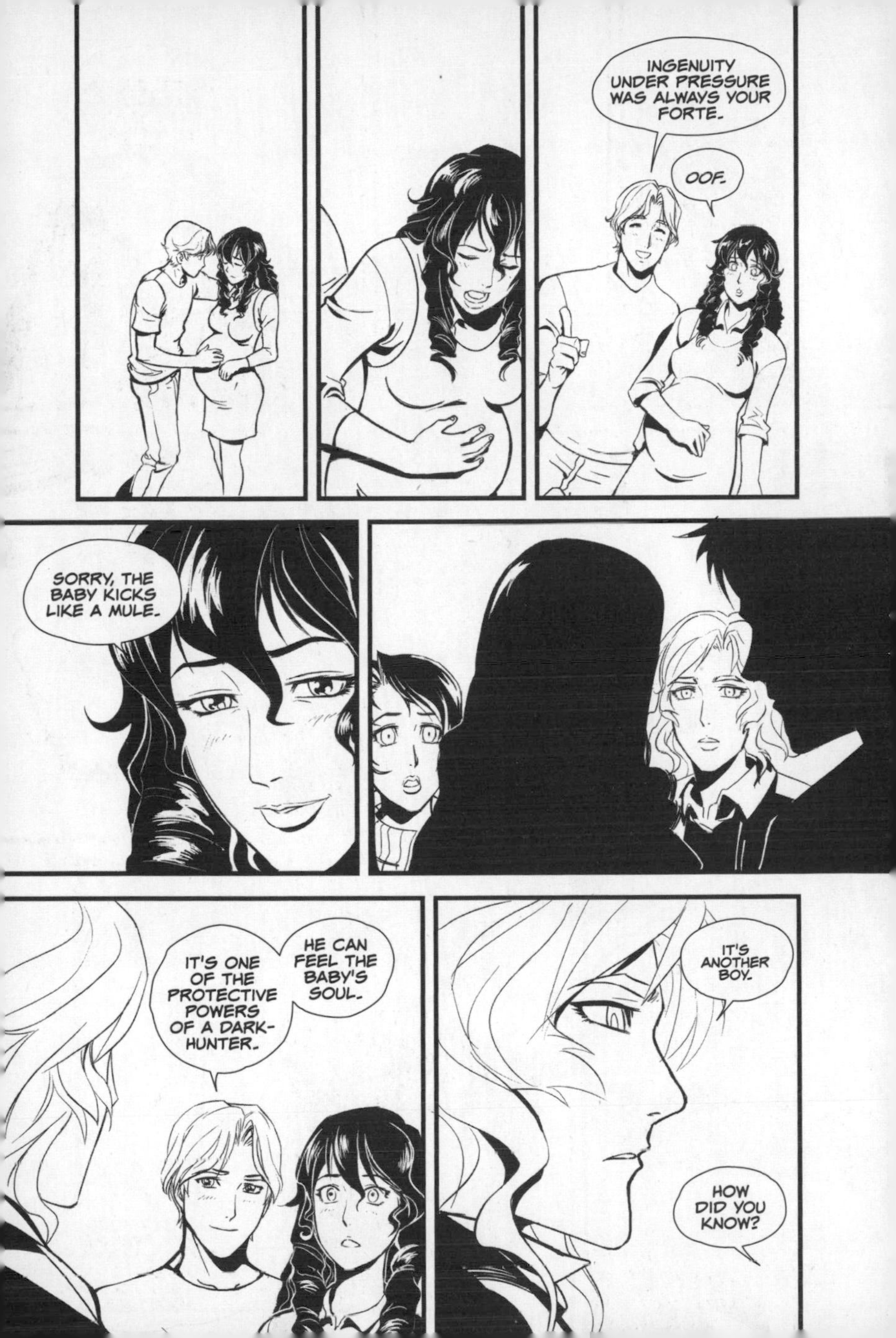
INGENUITY UNDER PRESSURE WAS ALWAYS YOUR FORTE.
OOF.
SORRY, THE BABY KICKS LIKE A MULE.
IT'S ANOTHER BOY.
HOW DID YOU KNOW?
HE CAN FEEL THE BABY'S SOUL.
IT'S ONE OF THE PROTECTIVE POWERS OF A DARK-HUNTER.

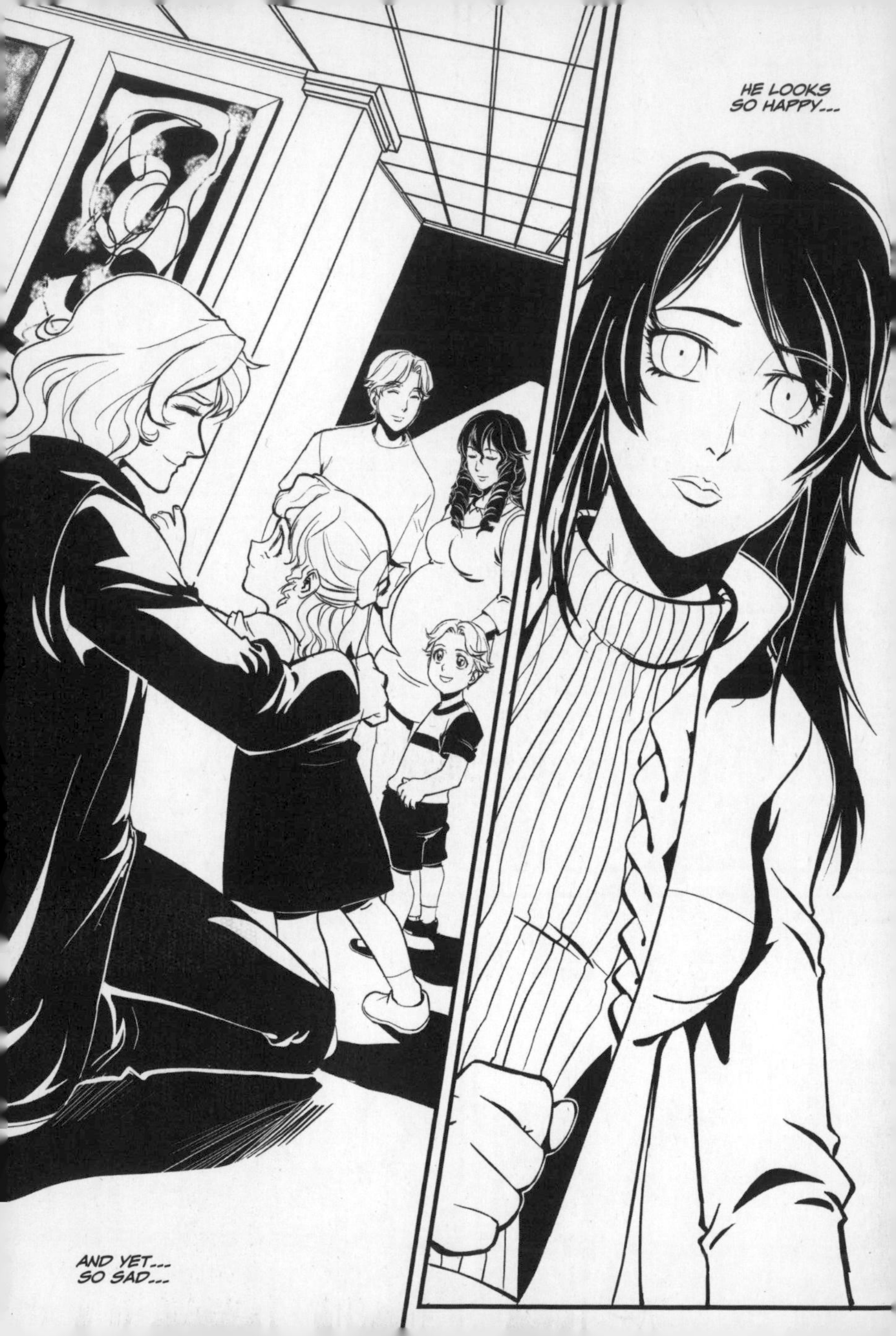
HE LOOKS SO HAPPY...
AND YET... SO SAD...

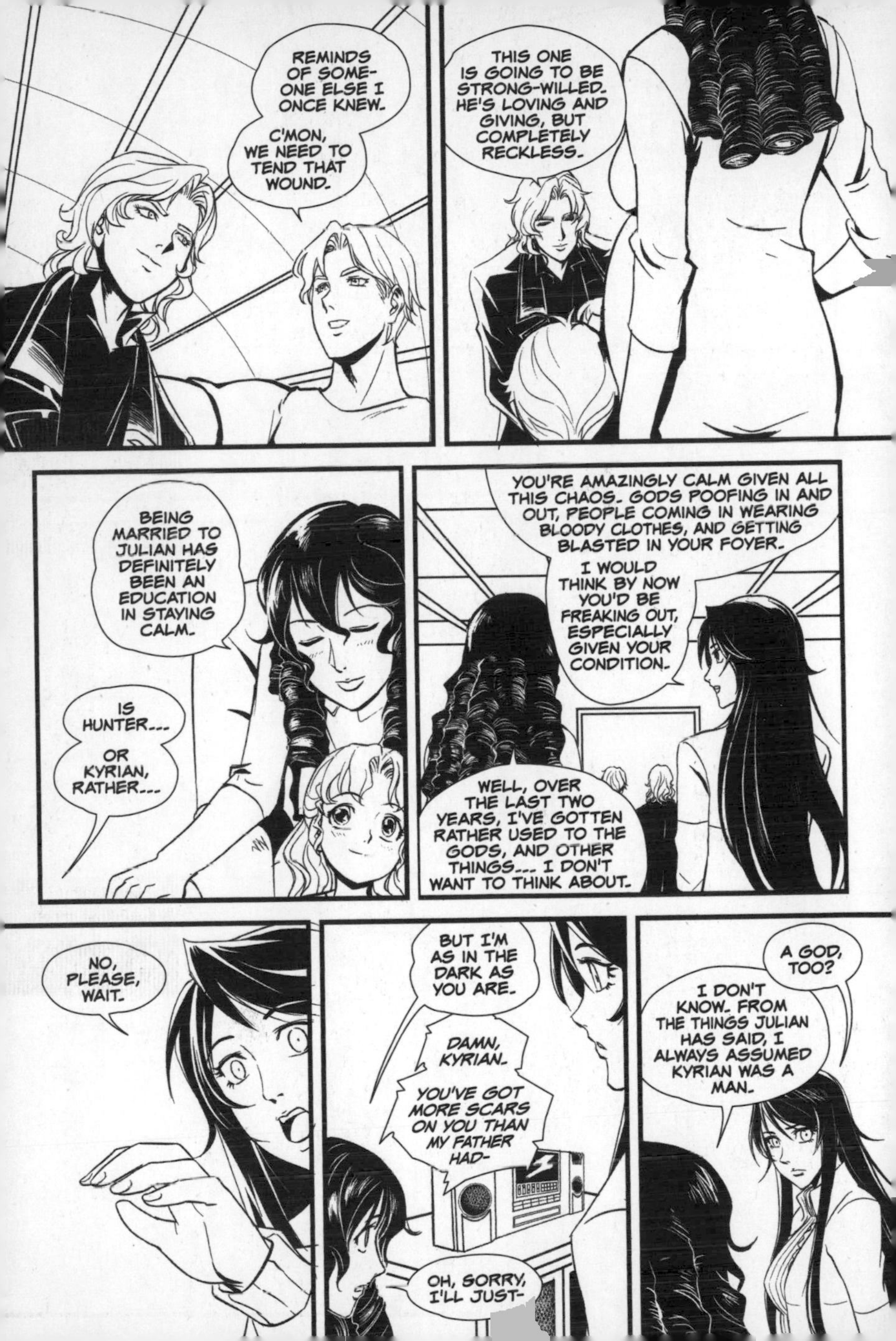
THIS ONE IS GOING TO BE STRONG-WILLED. HE'S LOVING AND GIVING, BUT COMPLETELY RECKLESS.
REMINDS OF SOME-ONE ELSE I ONCE KNEW.
C'MON, WE NEED TO TEND THAT WOUND.
YOU'RE AMAZINGLY CALM GIVEN ALL THIS CHAOS. GODS POOFING IN AND OUT, PEOPLE COMING IN WEARING BLOODY CLOTHES, AND GETTING BLASTED IN YOUR FOYER.
I WOULD THINK BY NOW YOU'D BE FREAKING OUT, ESPECIALLY GIVEN YOUR CONDITION.
WELL, OVER THE LAST TWO YEARS, I'VE GOTTEN RATHER USED TO THE GODS, AND OTHER THINGS... I DON'T WANT TO THINK ABOUT.
BEING MARRIED TO JULIAN HAS DEFINITELY BEEN AN EDUCATION IN STAYING CALM.
IS HUNTER...
OR KYRIAN, RATHER...
A GOD, TOO?
I DON'T KNOW. FROM THE THINGS JULIAN HAS SAID, I ALWAYS ASSUMED KYRIAN WAS A MAN.
BUT I'M AS IN THE DARK AS YOU ARE.
DAMN, KYRIAN.
YOU'VE GOT MORE SCARS ON YOU THAN MY FATHER HAD-
OH, SORRY, I'LL JUST-
NO, PLEASE, WAIT.

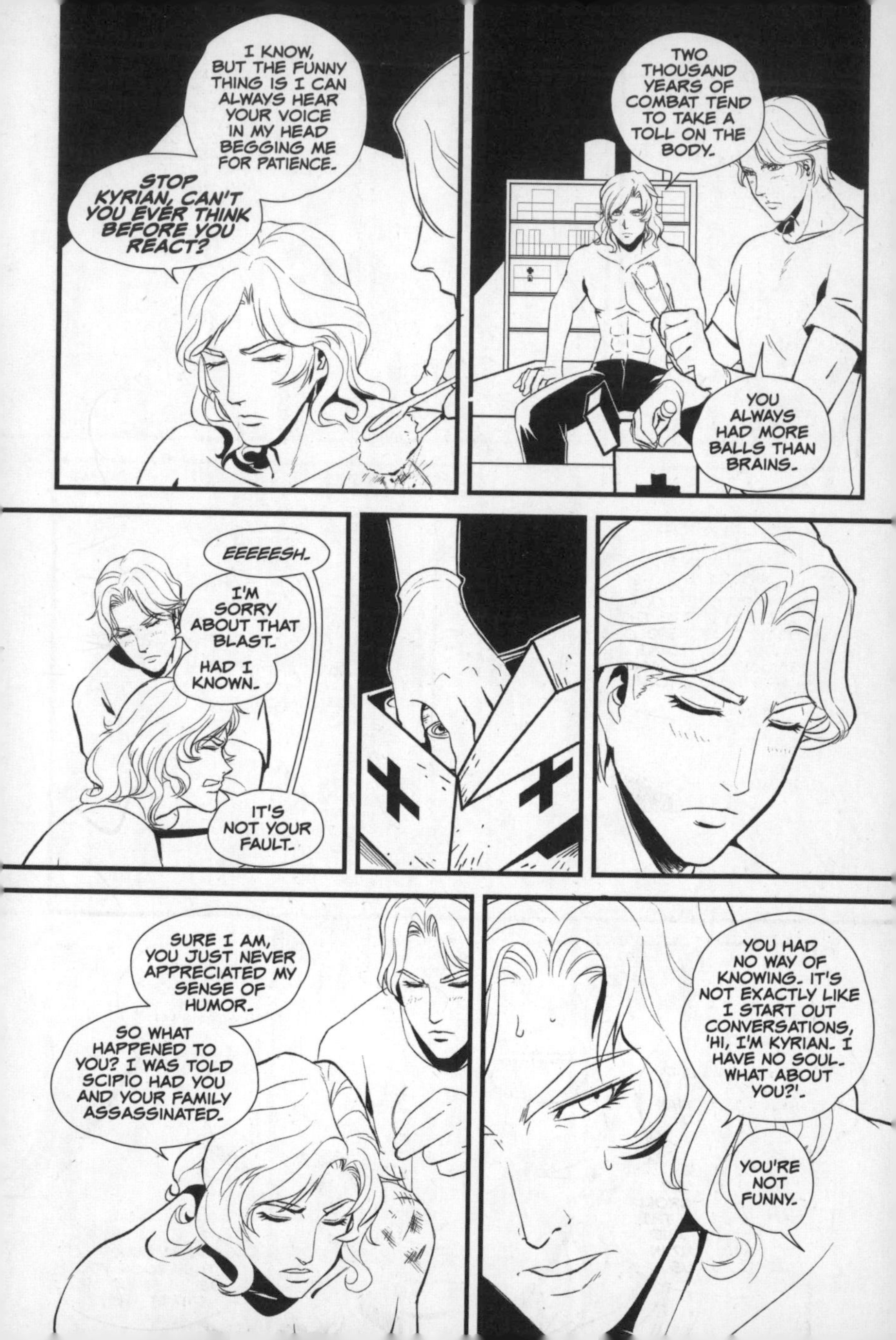
TWO THOUSAND YEARS OF COMBAT TEND TO TAKE A TOLL ON THE BODY.
YOU ALWAYS HAD MORE BALLS THAN BRAINS.
I KNOW, BUT THE FUNNY THING IS I CAN ALWAYS HEAR YOUR VOICE IN MY HEAD BEGGING ME FOR PATIENCE.
STOP KYRIAN, CAN'T YOU EVER THINK BEFORE YOU REACT?
EEEEESH.
I'M SORRY ABOUT THAT BLAST.
HAD I KNOWN.
IT'S NOT YOUR FAULT.
YOU HAD NO WAY OF KNOWING. IT'S NOT EXACTLY LIKE I START OUT CONVERSATIONS, 'HI, I'M KYRIAN. I HAVE NO SOUL. WHAT ABOUT YOU?'.
YOU'RE NOT FUNNY.
SURE I AM, YOU JUST NEVER APPRECIATED MY SENSE OF HUMOR.
SO WHAT HAPPENED TO YOU? I WAS TOLD SCIPIO HAD YOU AND YOUR FAMILY ASSASSINATED.

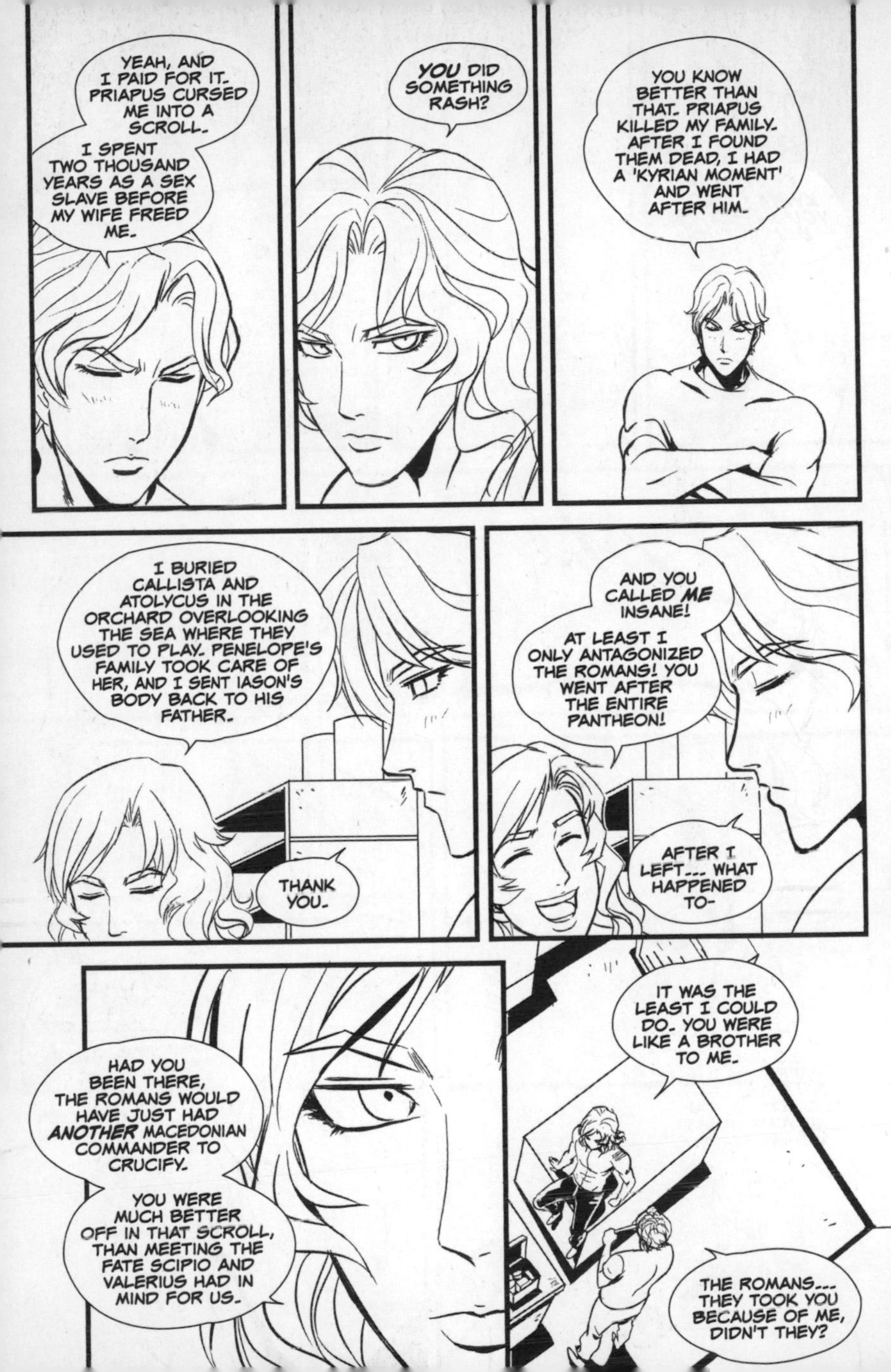
YOU KNOW BETTER THAN THAT. PRIAPUS KILLED MY FAMILY. AFTER I FOUND THEM DEAD, I HAD A 'KYRIAN MOMENT' AND WENT AFTER HIM.
YOU DID SOMETHING RASH?
YEAH, AND I PAID FOR IT. PRIAPUS CURSED ME INTO A SCROLL.
I SPENT TWO THOUSAND YEARS AS A SEX SLAVE BEFORE MY WIFE FREED ME.
AND YOU CALLED ME INSANE!
AT LEAST I ONLY ANTAGONIZED THE ROMANS! YOU WENT AFTER THE ENTIRE PANTHEON!
AFTER I LEFT... WHAT HAPPENED TO-
I BURIED CALLISTA AND ATOLYCUS IN THE ORCHARD OVERLOOKING THE SEA WHERE THEY USED TO PLAY. PENELOPE'S FAMILY TOOK CARE OF HER, AND I SENT IASON'S BODY BACK TO HIS FATHER.
THANK YOU.
IT WAS THE LEAST I COULD DO. YOU WERE LIKE A BROTHER TO ME.
THE ROMANS... THEY TOOK YOU BECAUSE OF ME, DIDN'T THEY?
HAD YOU BEEN THERE, THE ROMANS WOULD HAVE JUST HAD ANOTHER MACEDONIAN COMMANDER TO CRUCIFY.
YOU WERE MUCH BETTER OFF IN THAT SCROLL, THAN MEETING THE FATE SCIPIO AND VALERIUS HAD IN MIND FOR US.

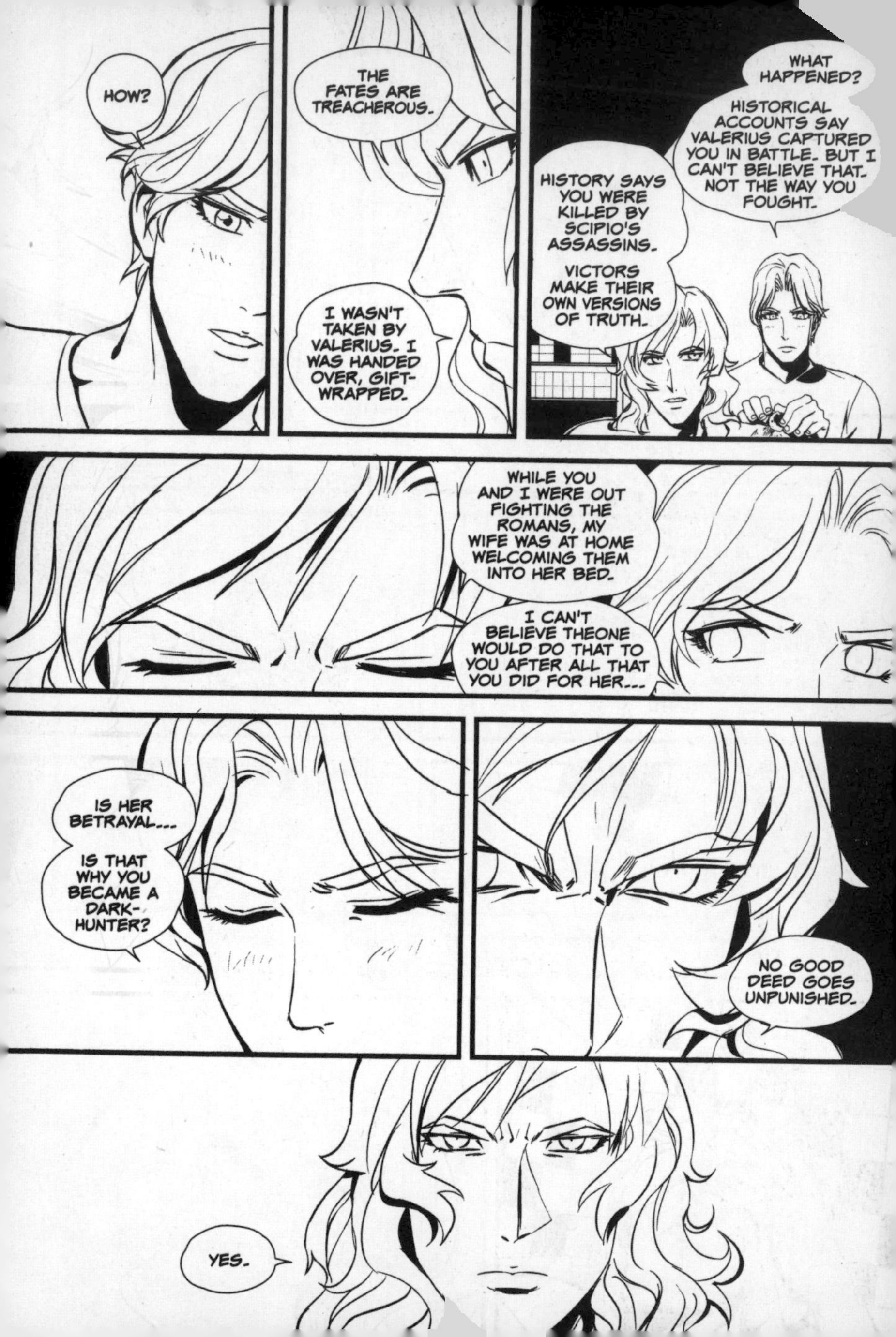

WHAT HAPPENED?
HISTORICAL ACCOUNTS SAY VALERIUS CAPTURED YOU IN BATTLE. BUT I CAN'T BELIEVE THAT. NOT THE WAY YOU FOUGHT.
HISTORY SAYS YOU WERE KILLED BY SCIPIO'S ASSASSINS.
VICTORS MAKE THEIR OWN VERSIONS OF TRUTH.
THE FATES ARE TREACHEROUS.
I WASN'T TAKEN BY VALERIUS. I WAS HANDED OVER, GIFT-WRAPPED.
HOW?
WHILE YOU AND I WERE OUT FIGHTING THE ROMANS, MY WIFE WAS AT HOME WELCOMING THEM INTO HER BED.
I CAN'T BELIEVE THEONE WOULD DO THAT TO YOU AFTER ALL THAT YOU DID FOR HER...
NO GOOD DEED GOES UNPUNISHED.
IS HER BETRAYAL...
IS THAT WHY YOU BECAME A DARK-HUNTER?
YES.

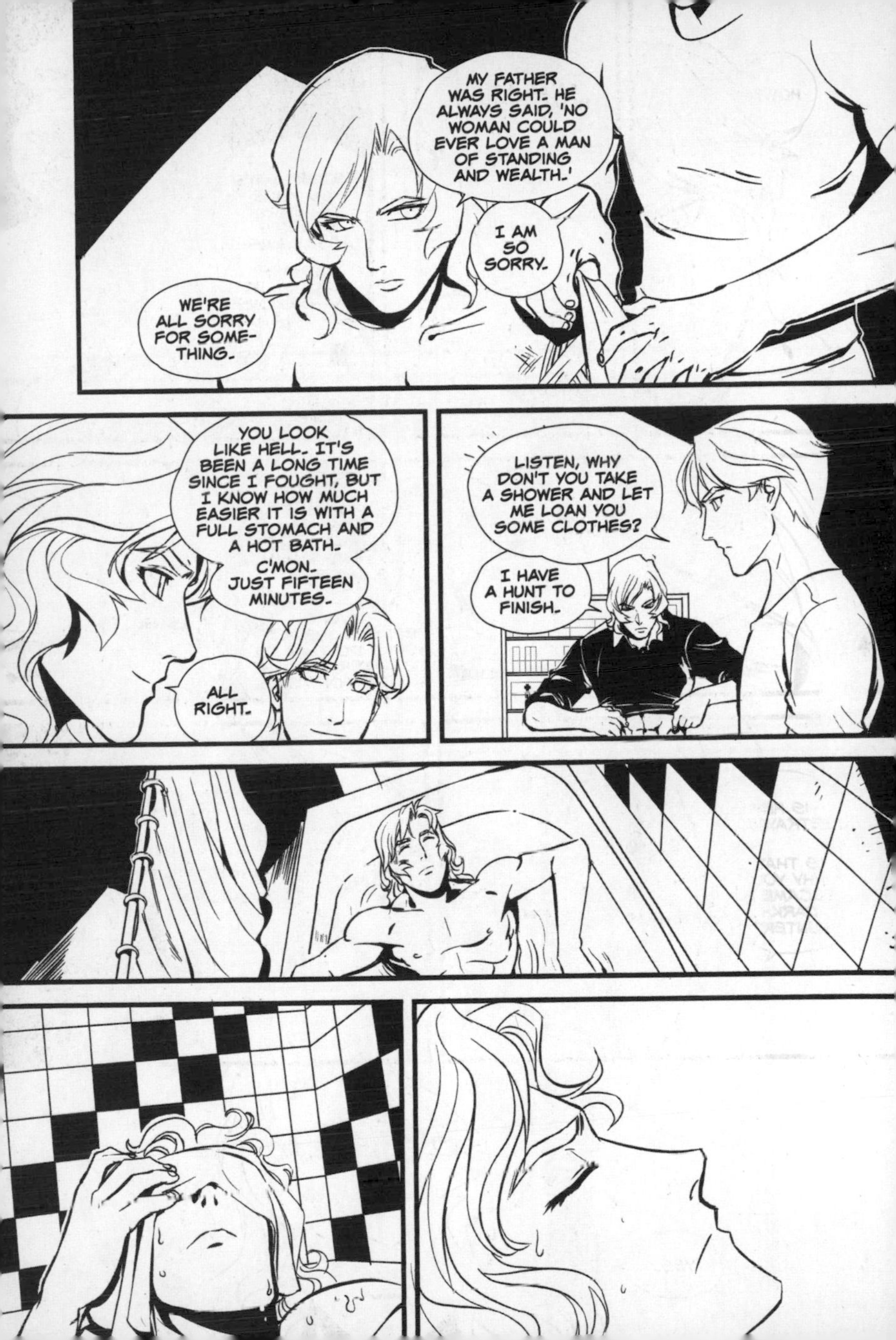
MY FATHER WAS RIGHT. HE ALWAYS SAID, 'NO WOMAN COULD EVER LOVE A MAN OF STANDING AND WEALTH.'
I AM SO SORRY.
WE'RE ALL SORRY FOR SOME-THING.
LISTEN, WHY DON'T YOU TAKE A SHOWER AND LET ME LOAN YOU SOME CLOTHES?
I HAVE A HUNT TO FINISH.
YOU LOOK LIKE HELL. IT'S BEEN A LONG TIME SINCE I FOUGHT, BUT I KNOW HOW MUCH EASIER IT IS WITH A FULL STOMACH AND A HOT BATH.
C'MON. JUST FIFTEEN MINUTES.
ALL RIGHT.

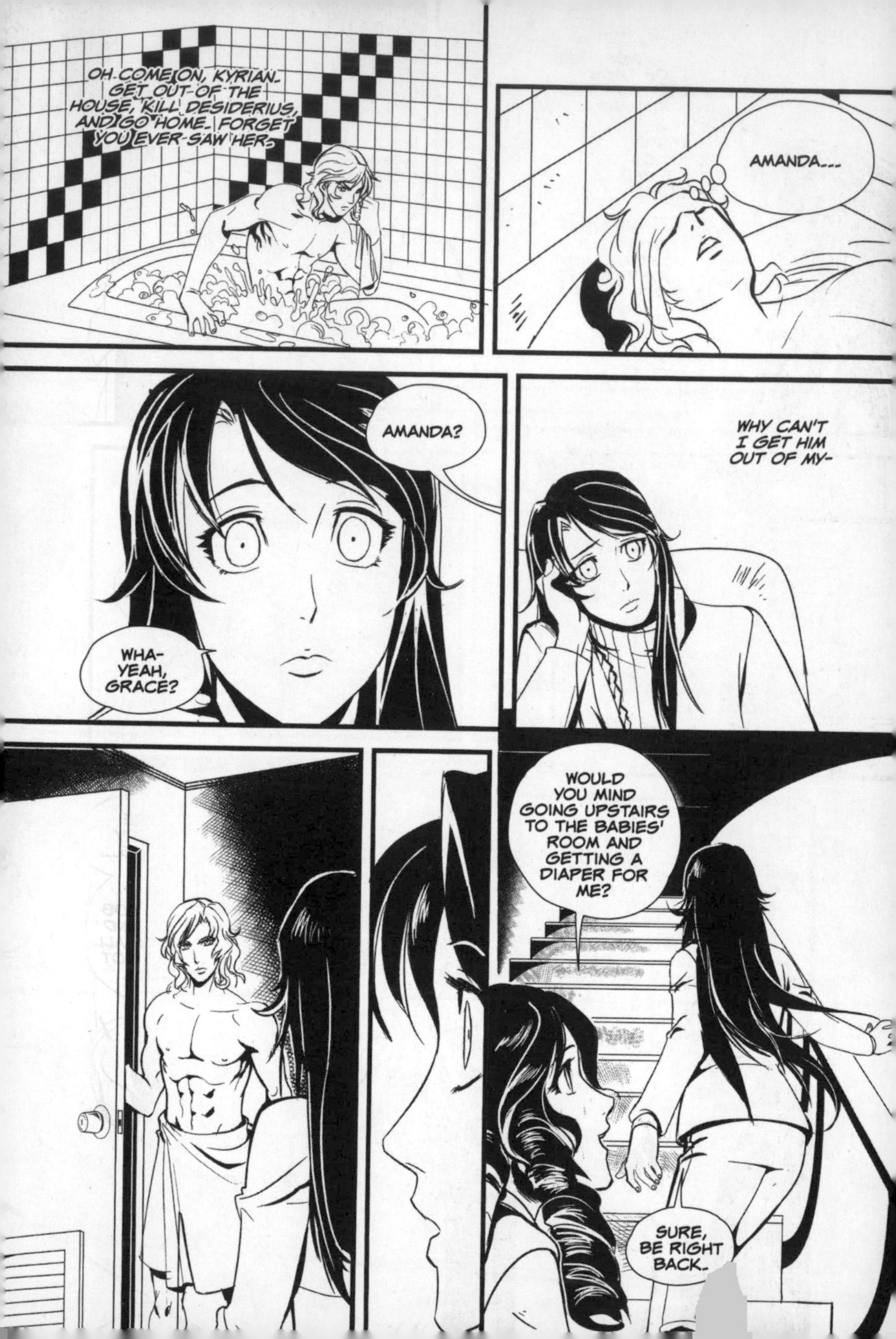
AMANDA...
OH, COME ON, KYRIAN. GET OUT OF THE HOUSE, KILL DESIDERIUS, AND GO HOME. FORGET YOU EVER SAW HER.
WHY CAN'T I GET HIM OUT OF MY-
AMANDA?
WHA- YEAH, GRACE?
WOULD YOU MIND GOING UPSTAIRS TO THE BABIES' ROOM AND GETTING A DIAPER FOR ME?
SURE, BE RIGHT BACK.

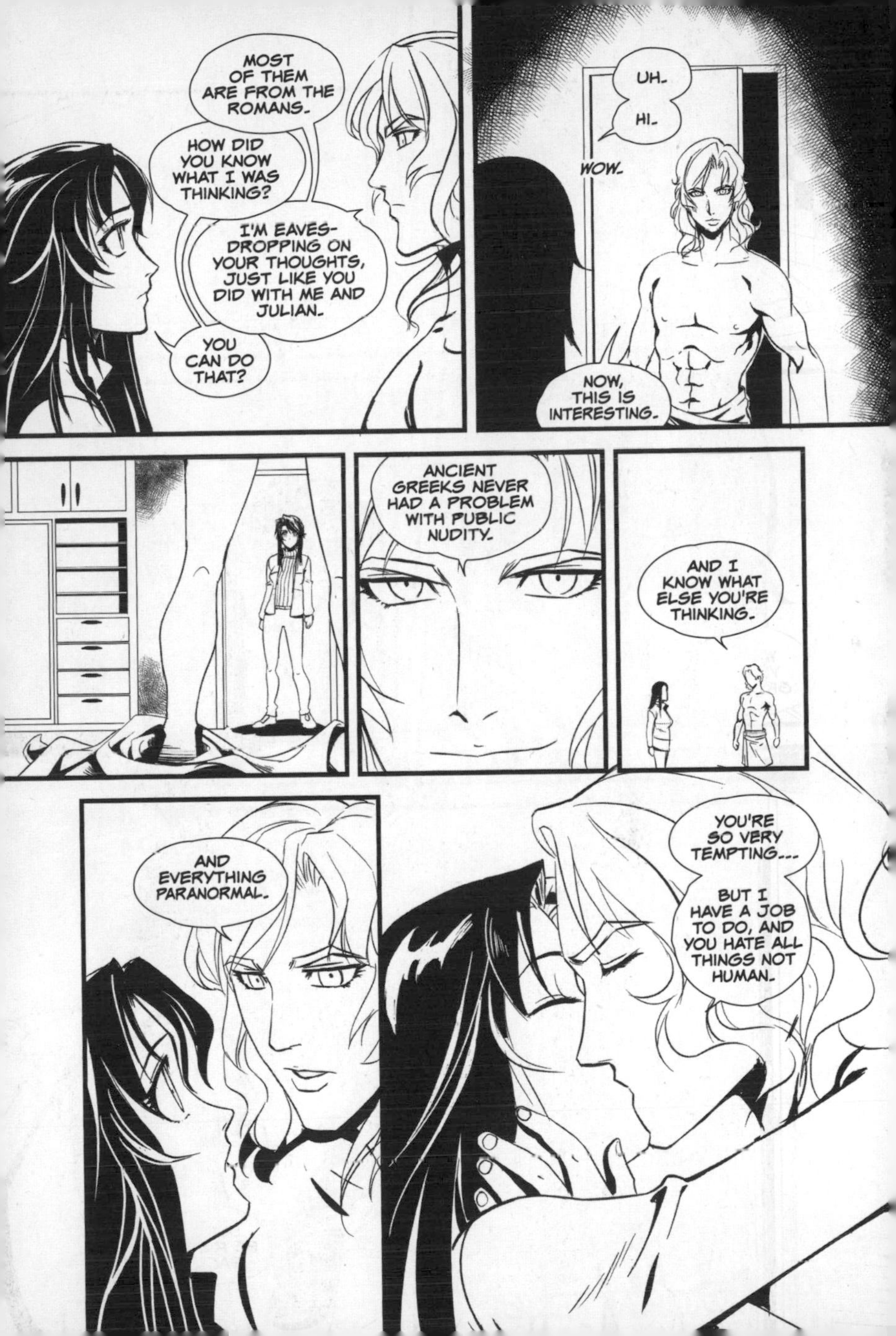
MOST OF THEM ARE FROM THE ROMANS.
HOW DID YOU KNOW WHAT I WAS THINKING?
I'M EAVES-DROPPING ON YOUR THOUGHTS, JUST LIKE YOU DID WITH ME AND JULIAN.
YOU CAN DO THAT?
UH.
HI.
WOW.
NOW, THIS IS INTERESTING.
ANCIENT GREEKS NEVER HAD A PROBLEM WITH PUBLIC NUDITY.
AND I KNOW WHAT ELSE YOU'RE THINKING.
AND EVERYTHING PARANORMAL.
YOU'RE SO VERY TEMPTING...
BUT I HAVE A JOB TO DO, AND YOU HATE ALL THINGS NOT HUMAN.

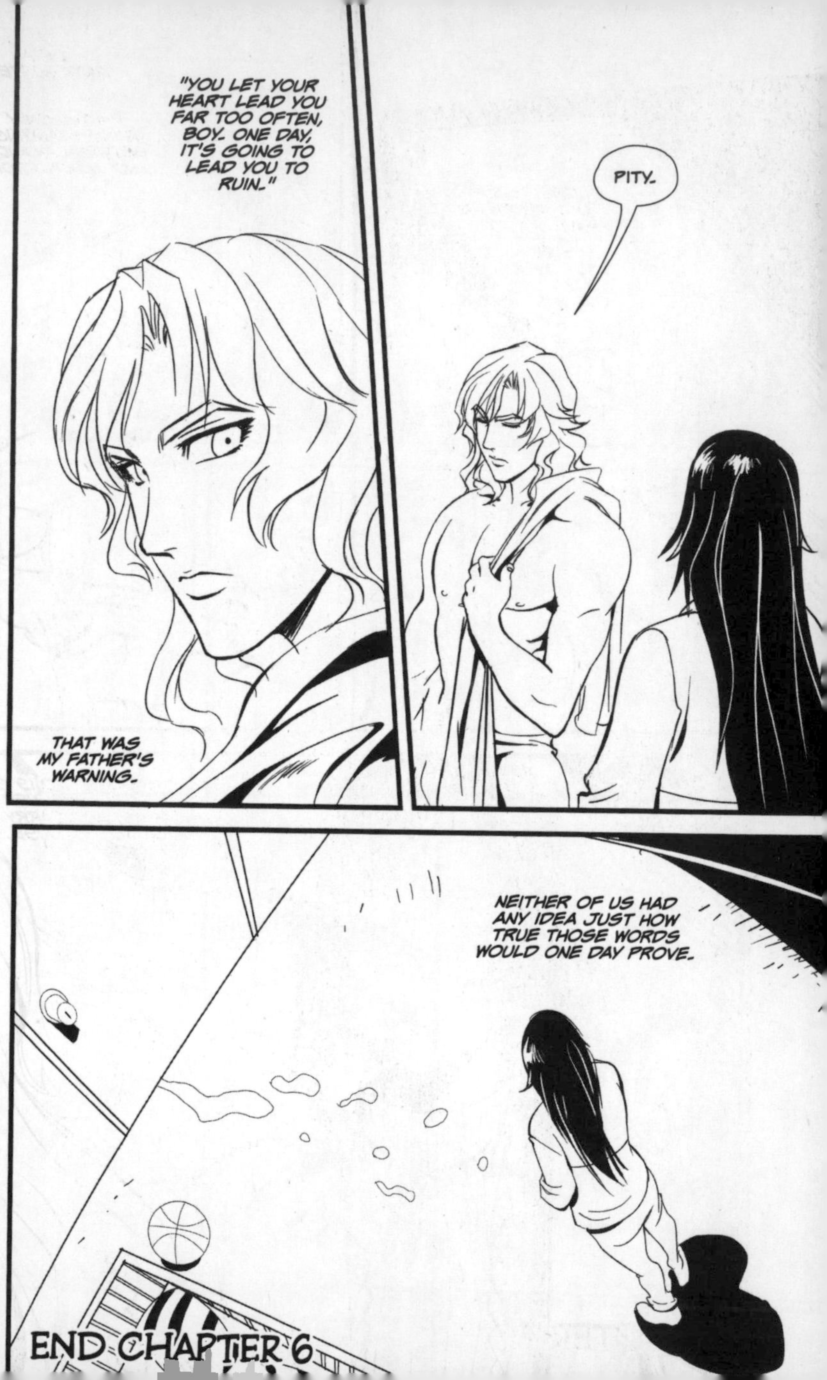
PITY.
"YOU LET YOUR HEART LEAD YOU FAR TOO OFTEN, BOY. ONE DAY, IT'S GOING TO LEAD YOU TO RUIN."
THAT WAS MY FATHER'S WARNING.
NEITHER OF US HAD ANY IDEA JUST HOW TRUE THOSE WORDS WOULD ONE DAY PROVE.
END CHAPTER 6

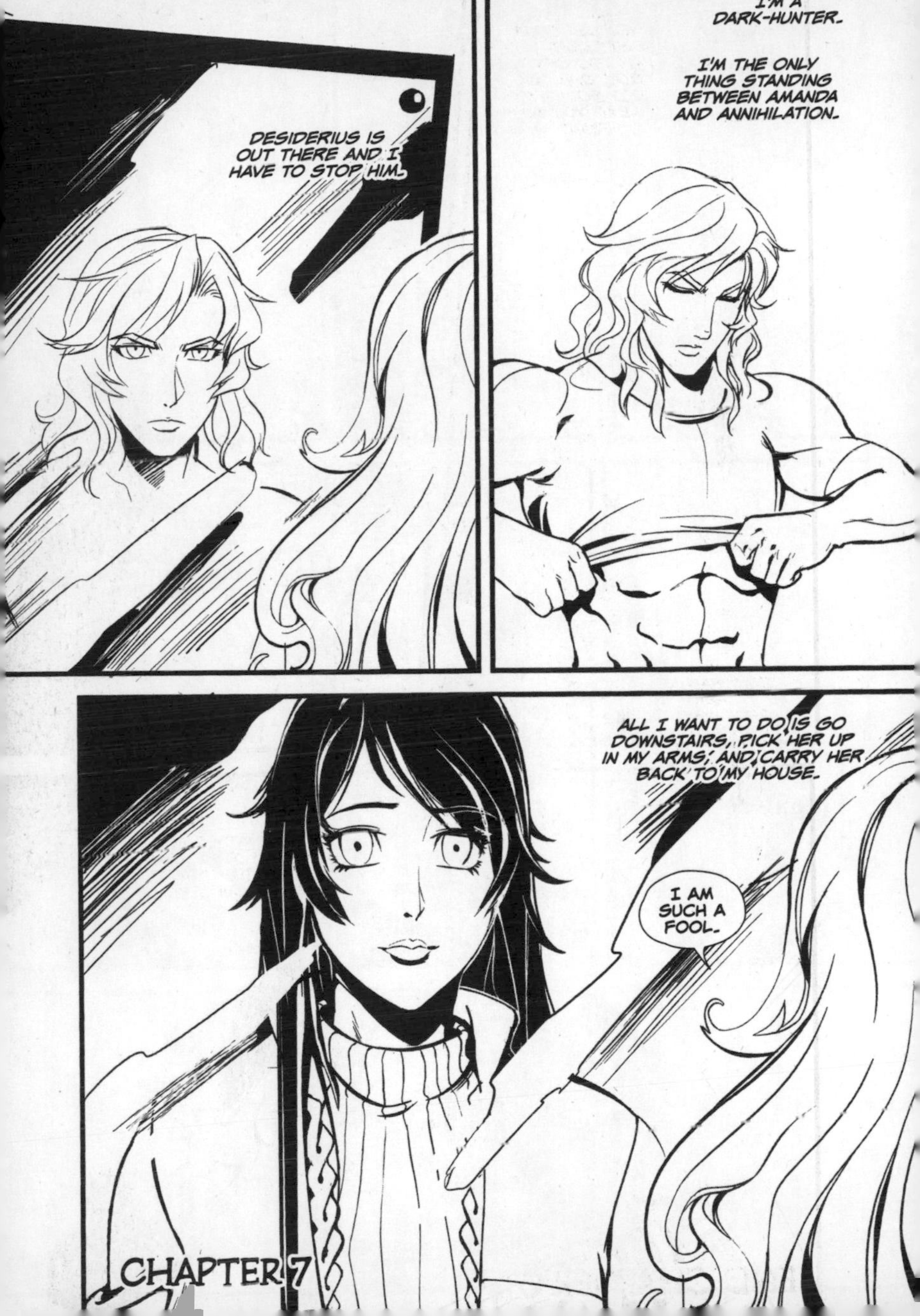
I'M A DARK-HUNTER.
I'M THE ONLY THING STANDING BETWEEN AMANDA AND ANNIHILATION.
DESIDERIUS IS OUT THERE AND I HAVE TO STOP HIM.
ALL I WANT TO DO IS GO DOWNSTAIRS, PICK HER UP IN MY ARMS, AND CARRY HER BACK TO MY HOUSE.
I AM SUCH A FOOL.
CHAPTER 7

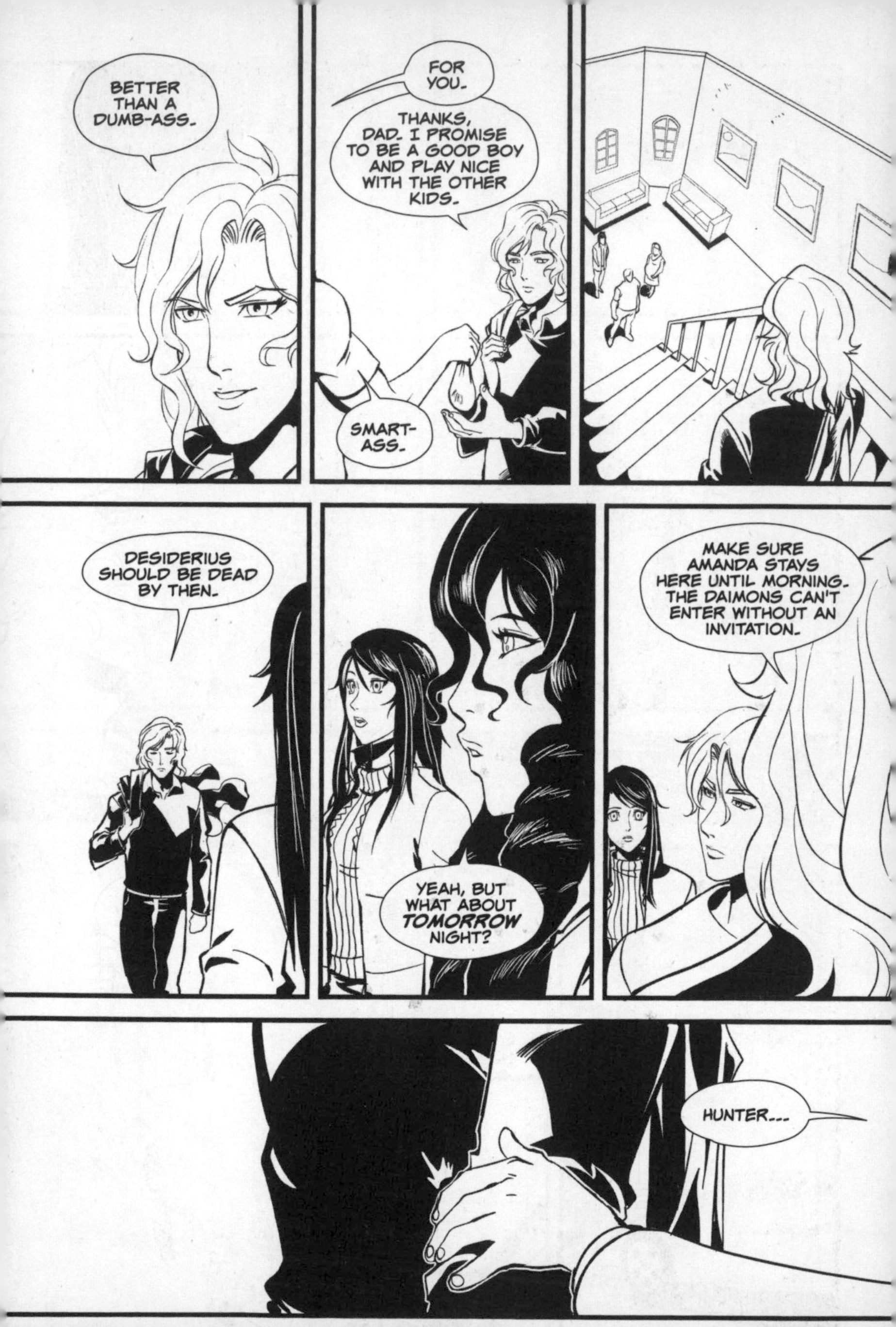
FOR YOU.
THANKS, DAD. I PROMISE TO BE A GOOD BOY AND PLAY NICE WITH THE OTHER KIDS.
SMART-ASS.
BETTER THAN A DUMB-ASS.
MAKE SURE AMANDA STAYS HERE UNTIL MORNING. THE DAIMONS CAN'T ENTER WITHOUT AN INVITATION.
YEAH, BUT WHAT ABOUT *TOMORROW* NIGHT?
DESIDERIUS SHOULD BE DEAD BY THEN.
HUNTER...

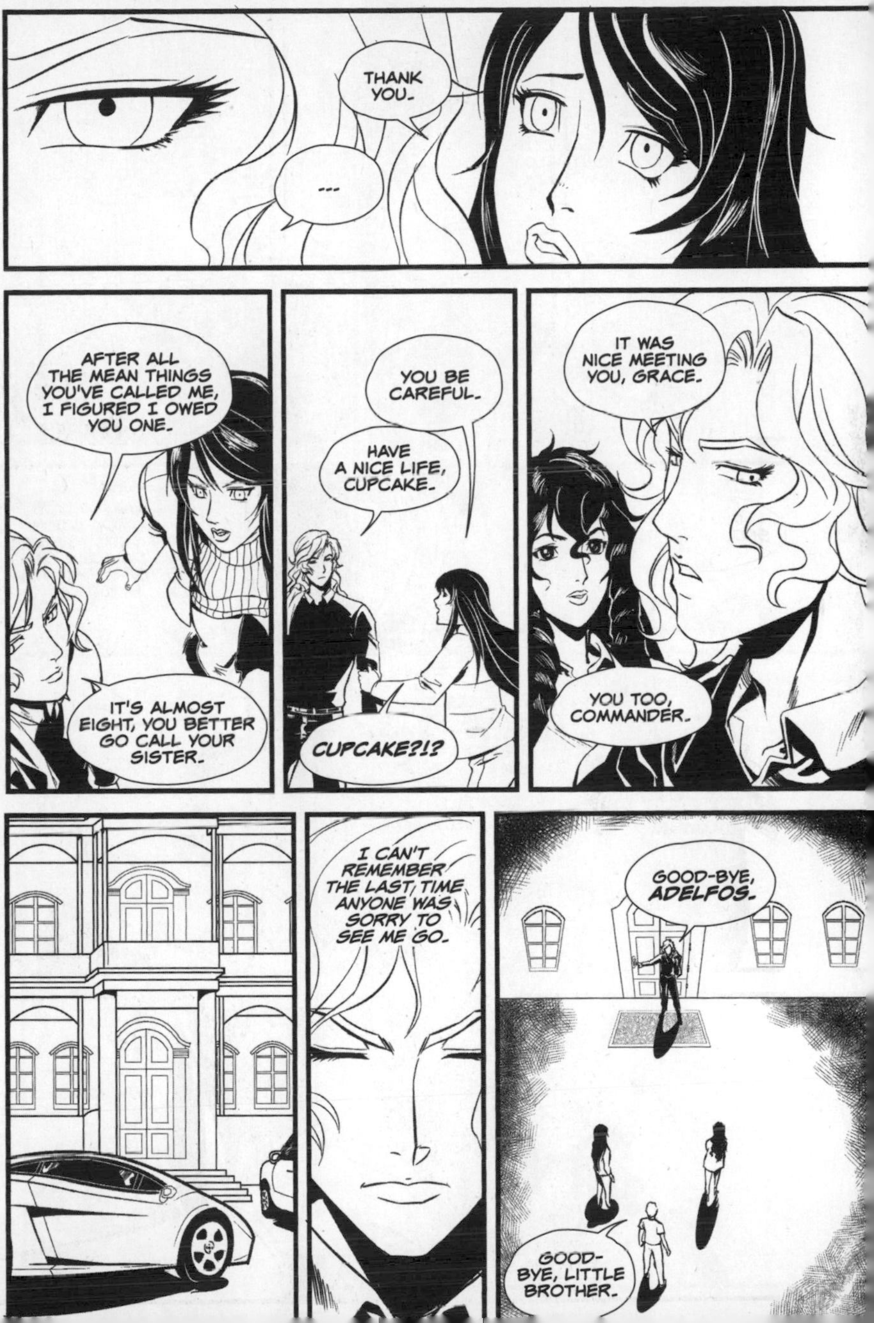
THANK YOU.
...
IT WAS NICE MEETING YOU, GRACE.
YOU TOO, COMMANDER.
YOU BE CAREFUL.
HAVE A NICE LIFE, CUPCAKE.
CUPCAKE?!?
AFTER ALL THE MEAN THINGS YOU'VE CALLED ME, I FIGURED I OWED YOU ONE.
IT'S ALMOST EIGHT, YOU BETTER GO CALL YOUR SISTER.
GOOD-BYE, **ADELFOS.**
GOOD-BYE, LITTLE BROTHER.
I CAN'T REMEMBER THE LAST TIME ANYONE WAS SORRY TO SEE ME GO.

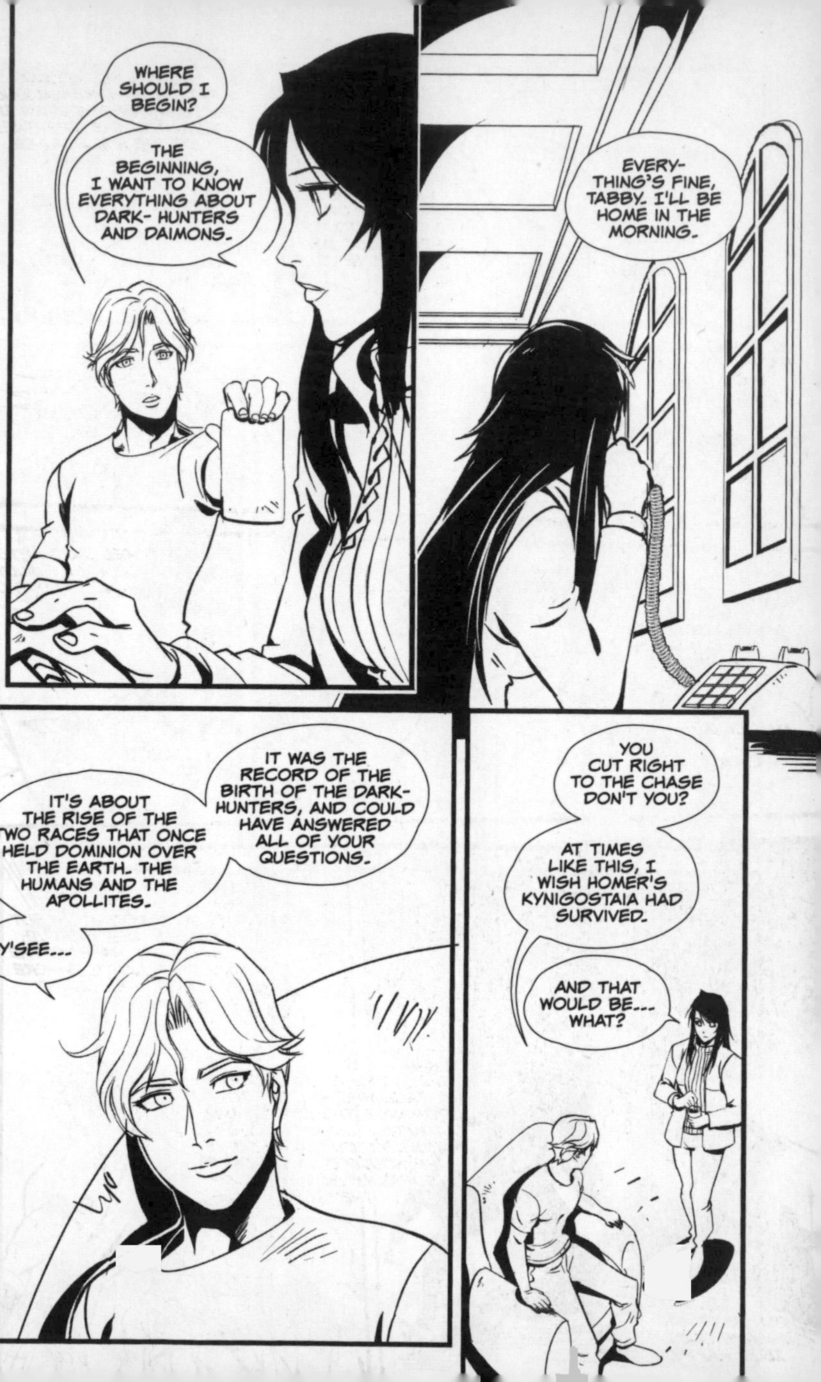
EVERY-THING'S FINE, TABBY. I'LL BE HOME IN THE MORNING.
WHERE SHOULD I BEGIN?
THE BEGINNING, I WANT TO KNOW EVERYTHING ABOUT DARK-HUNTERS AND DAIMONS.
YOU CUT RIGHT TO THE CHASE DON'T YOU?
AT TIMES LIKE THIS, I WISH HOMER'S KYNIGOSTAIA HAD SURVIVED.
AND THAT WOULD BE... WHAT?
IT WAS THE RECORD OF THE BIRTH OF THE DARK-HUNTERS, AND COULD HAVE ANSWERED ALL OF YOUR QUESTIONS.
IT'S ABOUT THE RISE OF THE TWO RACES THAT ONCE HELD DOMINION OVER THE EARTH. THE HUMANS AND THE APOLLITES.
Y'SEE...

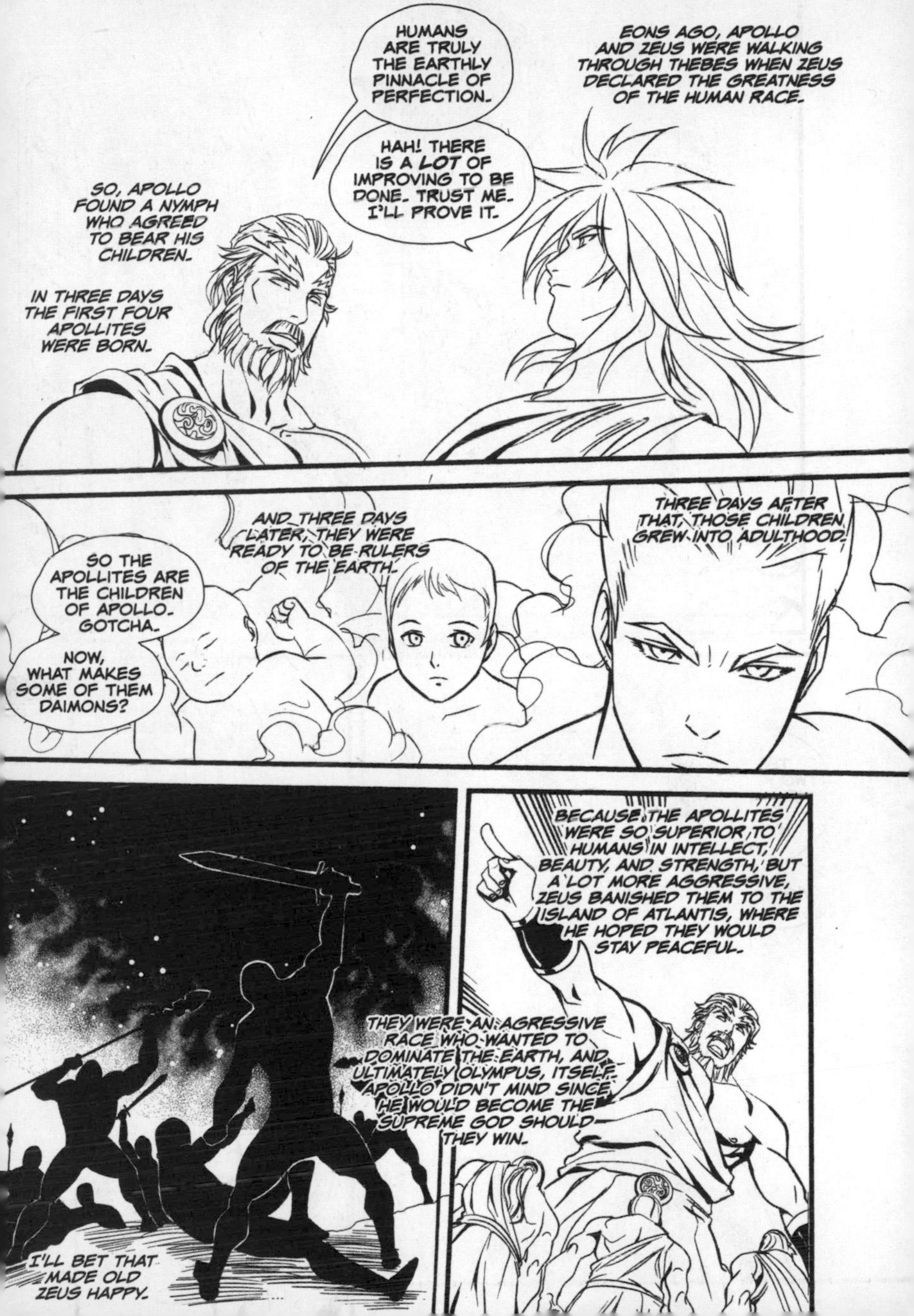
EONS AGO, APOLLO AND ZEUS WERE WALKING THROUGH THEBES WHEN ZEUS DECLARED THE GREATNESS OF THE HUMAN RACE.
HUMANS ARE TRULY THE EARTHLY PINNACLE OF PERFECTION.
HAH! THERE IS A *LOT* OF IMPROVING TO BE DONE. TRUST ME. I'LL PROVE IT.
SO, APOLLO FOUND A NYMPH WHO AGREED TO BEAR HIS CHILDREN.
IN THREE DAYS THE FIRST FOUR APOLLITES WERE BORN.
THREE DAYS AFTER THAT, THOSE CHILDREN GREW INTO ADULTHOOD.
AND THREE DAYS LATER, THEY WERE READY TO BE RULERS OF THE EARTH.
SO THE APOLLITES ARE THE CHILDREN OF APOLLO. GOTCHA.
NOW, WHAT MAKES SOME OF THEM DAIMONS?
BECAUSE THE APOLLITES WERE SO SUPERIOR TO HUMANS IN INTELLECT, BEAUTY, AND STRENGTH, BUT A LOT MORE AGGRESSIVE, ZEUS BANISHED THEM TO THE ISLAND OF ATLANTIS, WHERE HE HOPED THEY WOULD STAY PEACEFUL.
THEY WERE AN AGRESSIVE RACE WHO WANTED TO DOMINATE THE EARTH, AND ULTIMATELY OLYMPUS, ITSELF. APOLLO DIDN'T MIND SINCE HE WOULD BECOME THE SUPREME GOD SHOULD THEY WIN.
I'LL BET THAT MADE OLD ZEUS HAPPY.

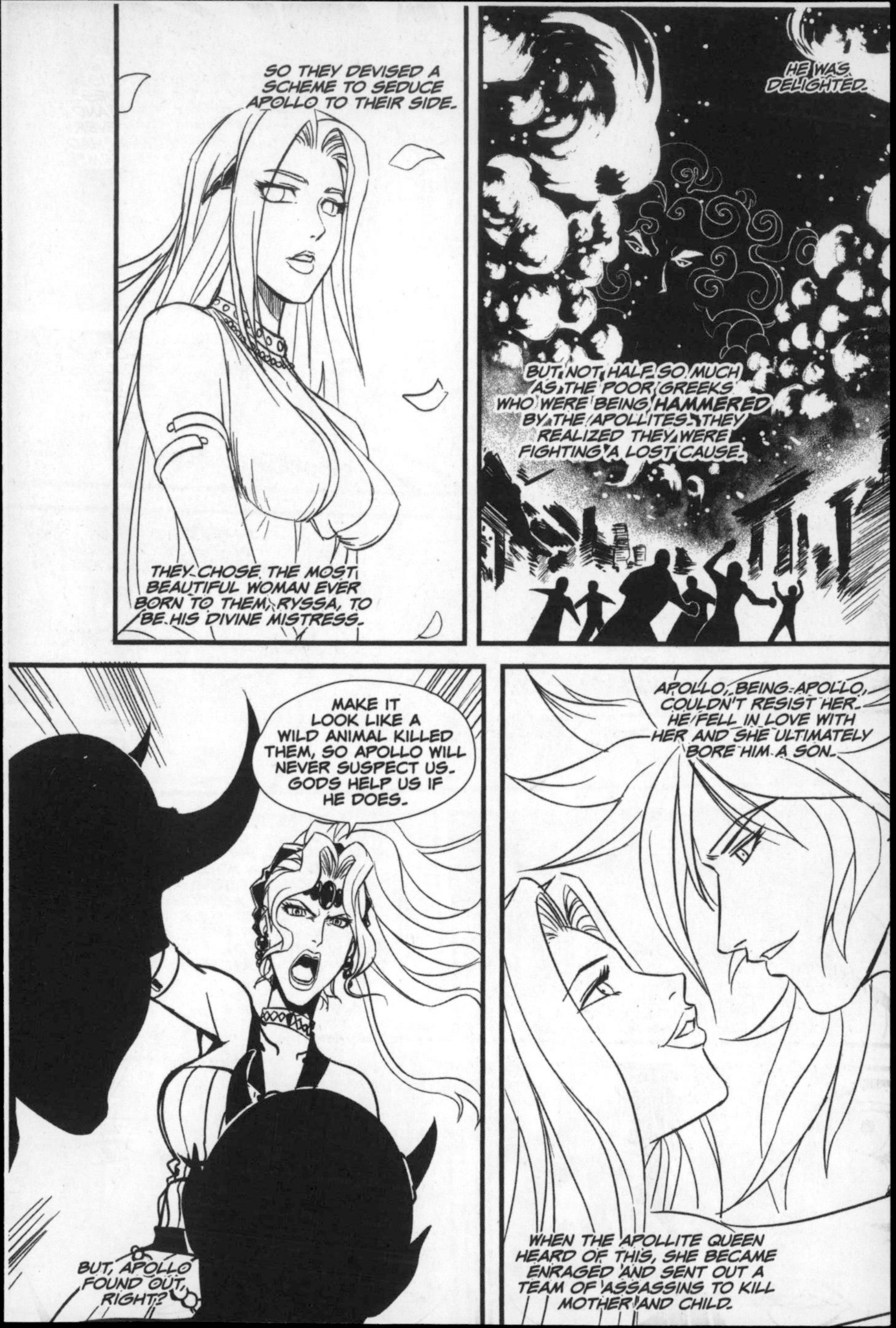
SO THEY DEVISED A SCHEME TO SEDUCE APOLLO TO THEIR SIDE.
THEY CHOSE THE MOST BEAUTIFUL WOMAN EVER BORN TO THEM, RYSSA, TO BE HIS DIVINE MISTRESS.
HE WAS DELIGHTED.
BUT NOT HALF SO MUCH AS THE POOR GREEKS WHO WERE BEING **HAMMERED** BY THE APOLLITES. THEY REALIZED THEY WERE FIGHTING A LOST CAUSE.
MAKE IT LOOK LIKE A WILD ANIMAL KILLED THEM, SO APOLLO WILL NEVER SUSPECT US. GODS HELP US IF HE DOES.
BUT, APOLLO FOUND OUT, RIGHT?
APOLLO, BEING APOLLO, COULDN'T RESIST HER. HE FELL IN LOVE WITH HER AND SHE ULTIMATELY BORE HIM A SON.
WHEN THE APOLLITE QUEEN HEARD OF THIS, SHE BECAME ENRAGED AND SENT OUT A TEAM OF ASSASSINS TO KILL MOTHER AND CHILD.

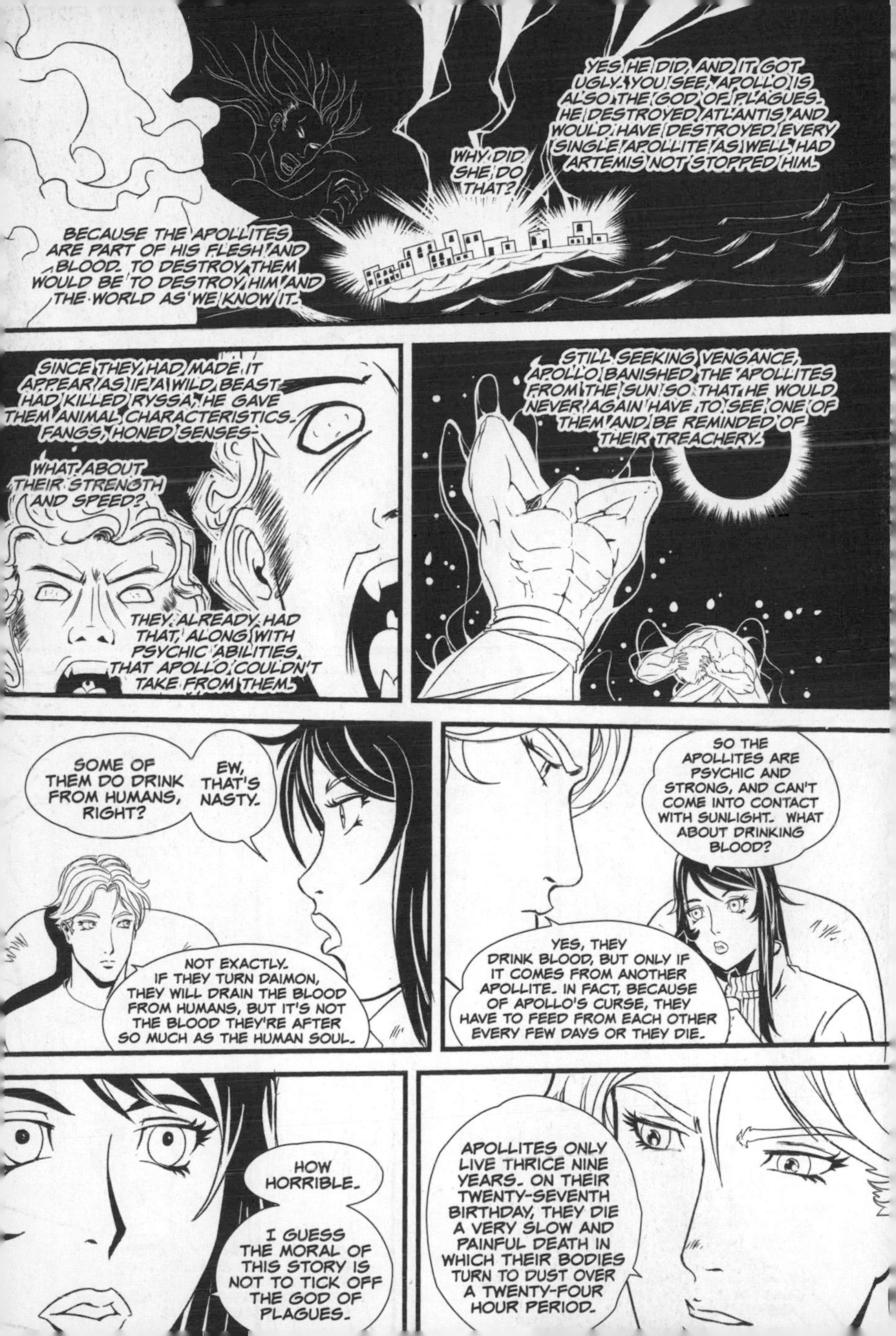

YES HE DID, AND IT GOT UGLY. YOU SEE, APOLLO IS ALSO THE GOD OF PLAGUES. HE DESTROYED ATLANTIS AND WOULD HAVE DESTROYED EVERY SINGLE APOLLITE AS WELL HAD ARTEMIS NOT STOPPED HIM.
WHY DID SHE DO THAT?
BECAUSE THE APOLLITES ARE PART OF HIS FLESH AND BLOOD. TO DESTROY THEM WOULD BE TO DESTROY HIM AND THE WORLD AS WE KNOW IT.
SINCE THEY HAD MADE IT APPEAR AS IF A WILD BEAST HAD KILLED RYSSA, HE GAVE THEM ANIMAL CHARACTERISTICS. FANGS, HONED SENSES-
WHAT ABOUT THEIR STRENGTH AND SPEED?
THEY ALREADY HAD THAT, ALONG WITH PSYCHIC ABILITIES, THAT APOLLO COULDN'T TAKE FROM THEM.
STILL SEEKING VENGANCE, APOLLO BANISHED THE APOLLITES FROM THE SUN SO THAT HE WOULD NEVER AGAIN HAVE TO SEE ONE OF THEM AND BE REMINDED OF THEIR TREACHERY.
SOME OF THEM DO DRINK FROM HUMANS, RIGHT?
EW, THAT'S NASTY.
NOT EXACTLY. IF THEY TURN DAIMON, THEY WILL DRAIN THE BLOOD FROM HUMANS, BUT IT'S NOT THE BLOOD THEY'RE AFTER SO MUCH AS THE HUMAN SOUL.
SO THE APOLLITES ARE PSYCHIC AND STRONG, AND CAN'T COME INTO CONTACT WITH SUNLIGHT. WHAT ABOUT DRINKING BLOOD?
YES, THEY DRINK BLOOD, BUT ONLY IF IT COMES FROM ANOTHER APOLLITE. IN FACT, BECAUSE OF APOLLO'S CURSE, THEY HAVE TO FEED FROM EACH OTHER EVERY FEW DAYS OR THEY DIE.
HOW HORRIBLE.
I GUESS THE MORAL OF THIS STORY IS NOT TO TICK OFF THE GOD OF PLAGUES.
APOLLITES ONLY LIVE THRICE NINE YEARS. ON THEIR TWENTY-SEVENTH BIRTHDAY, THEY DIE A VERY SLOW AND PAINFUL DEATH IN WHICH THEIR BODIES TURN TO DUST OVER A TWENTY-FOUR HOUR PERIOD.

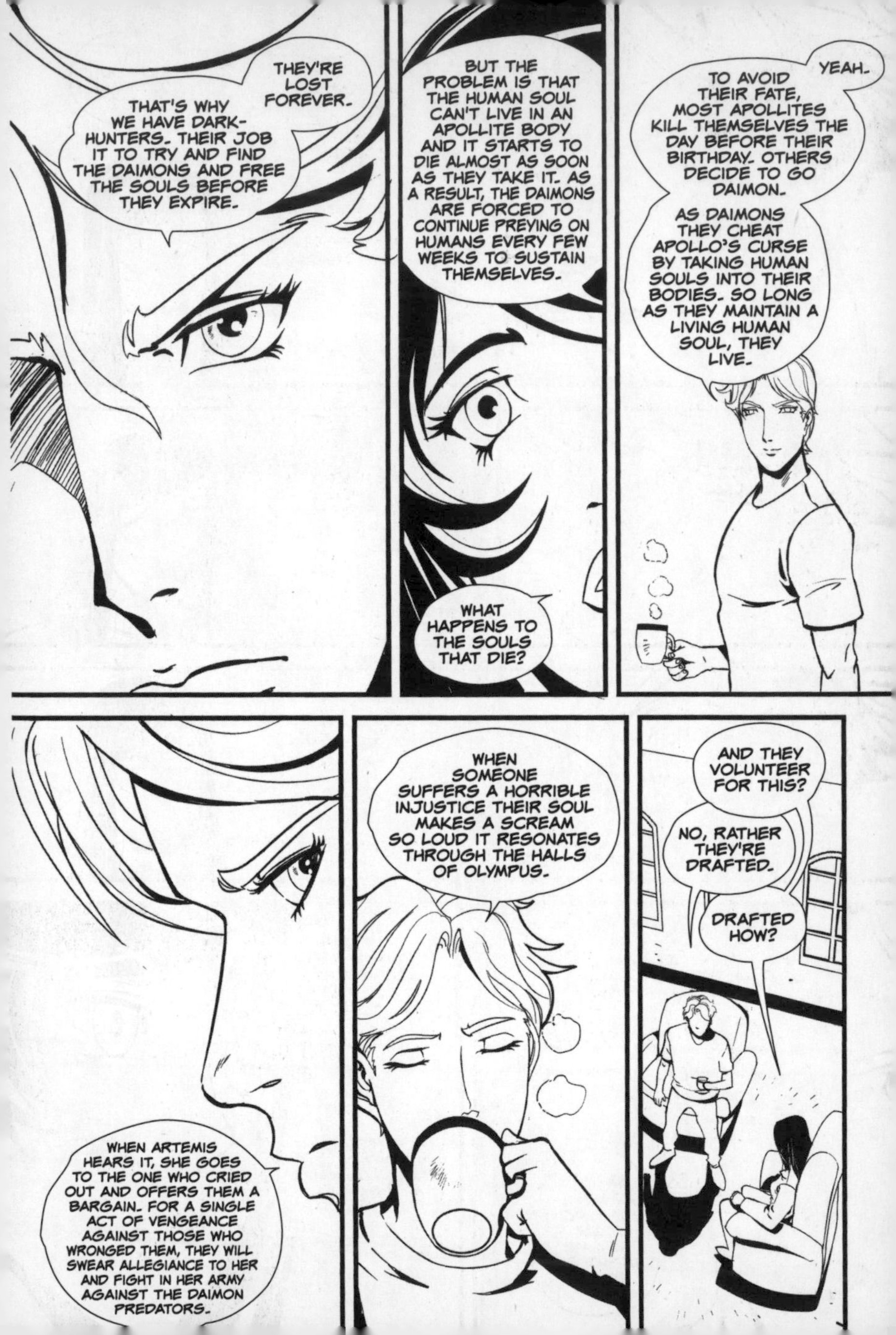
YEAH.
TO AVOID THEIR FATE, MOST APOLLITES KILL THEMSELVES THE DAY BEFORE THEIR BIRTHDAY. OTHERS DECIDE TO GO DAIMON.
AS DAIMONS THEY CHEAT APOLLO'S CURSE BY TAKING HUMAN SOULS INTO THEIR BODIES. SO LONG AS THEY MAINTAIN A LIVING HUMAN SOUL, THEY LIVE.
BUT THE PROBLEM IS THAT THE HUMAN SOUL CAN'T LIVE IN AN APOLLITE BODY AND IT STARTS TO DIE ALMOST AS SOON AS THEY TAKE IT. AS A RESULT, THE DAIMONS ARE FORCED TO CONTINUE PREYING ON HUMANS EVERY FEW WEEKS TO SUSTAIN THEMSELVES.
WHAT HAPPENS TO THE SOULS THAT DIE?
THEY'RE LOST FOREVER.
THAT'S WHY WE HAVE DARK-HUNTERS. THEIR JOB IT TO TRY AND FIND THE DAIMONS AND FREE THE SOULS BEFORE THEY EXPIRE.
AND THEY VOLUNTEER FOR THIS?
NO, RATHER THEY'RE DRAFTED.
DRAFTED HOW?
WHEN SOMEONE SUFFERS A HORRIBLE INJUSTICE THEIR SOUL MAKES A SCREAM SO LOUD IT RESONATES THROUGH THE HALLS OF OLYMPUS.
WHEN ARTEMIS HEARS IT, SHE GOES TO THE ONE WHO CRIED OUT AND OFFERS THEM A BARGAIN. FOR A SINGLE ACT OF VENGEANCE AGAINST THOSE WHO WRONGED THEM, THEY WILL SWEAR ALLEGIANCE TO HER AND FIGHT IN HER ARMY AGAINST THE DAIMON PREDATORS.

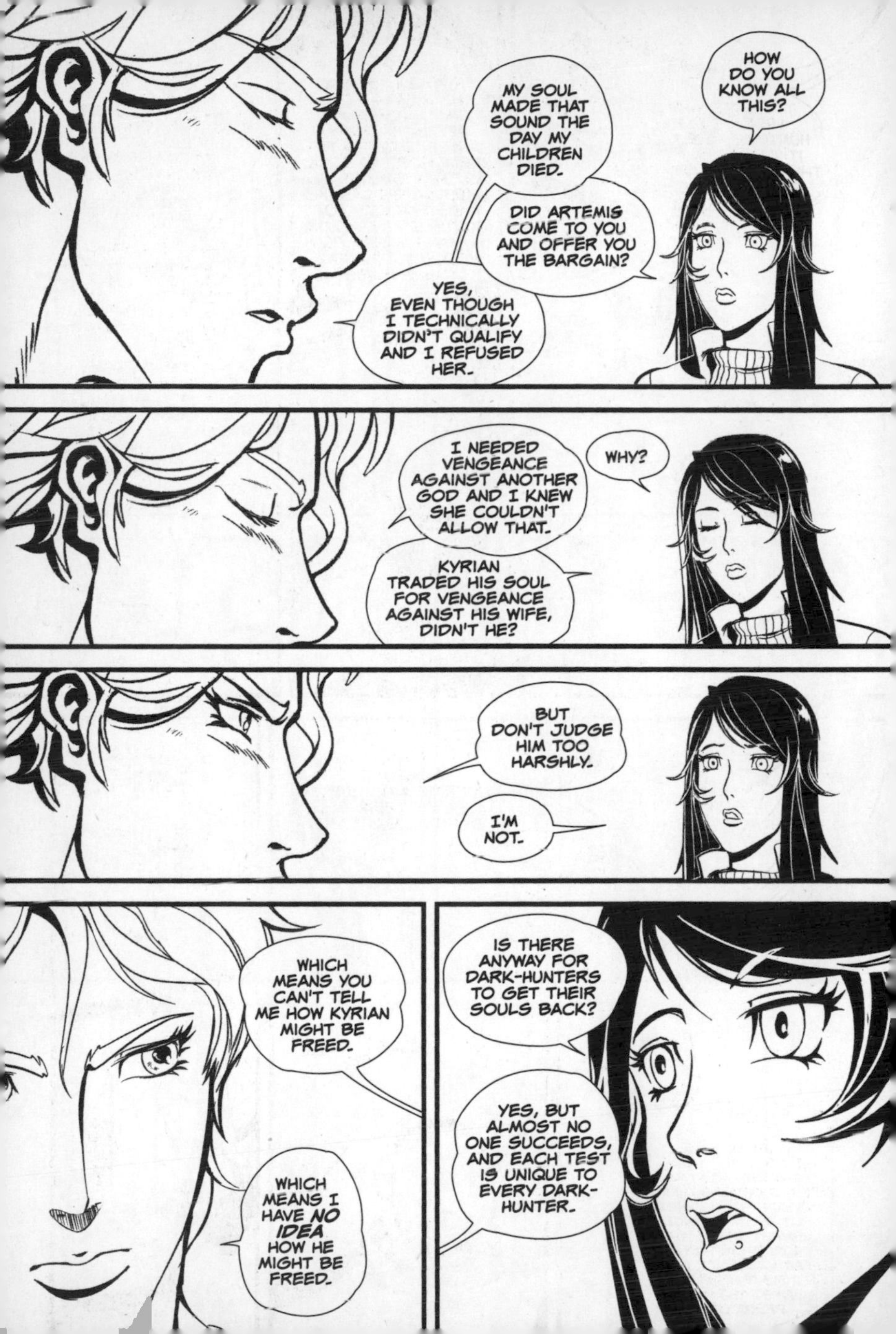
HOW DO YOU KNOW ALL THIS?
MY SOUL MADE THAT SOUND THE DAY MY CHILDREN DIED.
DID ARTEMIS COME TO YOU AND OFFER YOU THE BARGAIN?
YES, EVEN THOUGH I TECHNICALLY DIDN'T QUALIFY AND I REFUSED HER.
WHY?
I NEEDED VENGEANCE AGAINST ANOTHER GOD AND I KNEW SHE COULDN'T ALLOW THAT.
KYRIAN TRADED HIS SOUL FOR VENGEANCE AGAINST HIS WIFE, DIDN'T HE?
BUT DON'T JUDGE HIM TOO HARSHLY.
I'M NOT.
IS THERE ANYWAY FOR DARK-HUNTERS TO GET THEIR SOULS BACK?
YES, BUT ALMOST NO ONE SUCCEEDS, AND EACH TEST IS UNIQUE TO EVERY DARK-HUNTER.
WHICH MEANS YOU CAN'T TELL ME HOW KYRIAN MIGHT BE FREED.
WHICH MEANS I HAVE *NO IDEA* HOW HE MIGHT BE FREED.

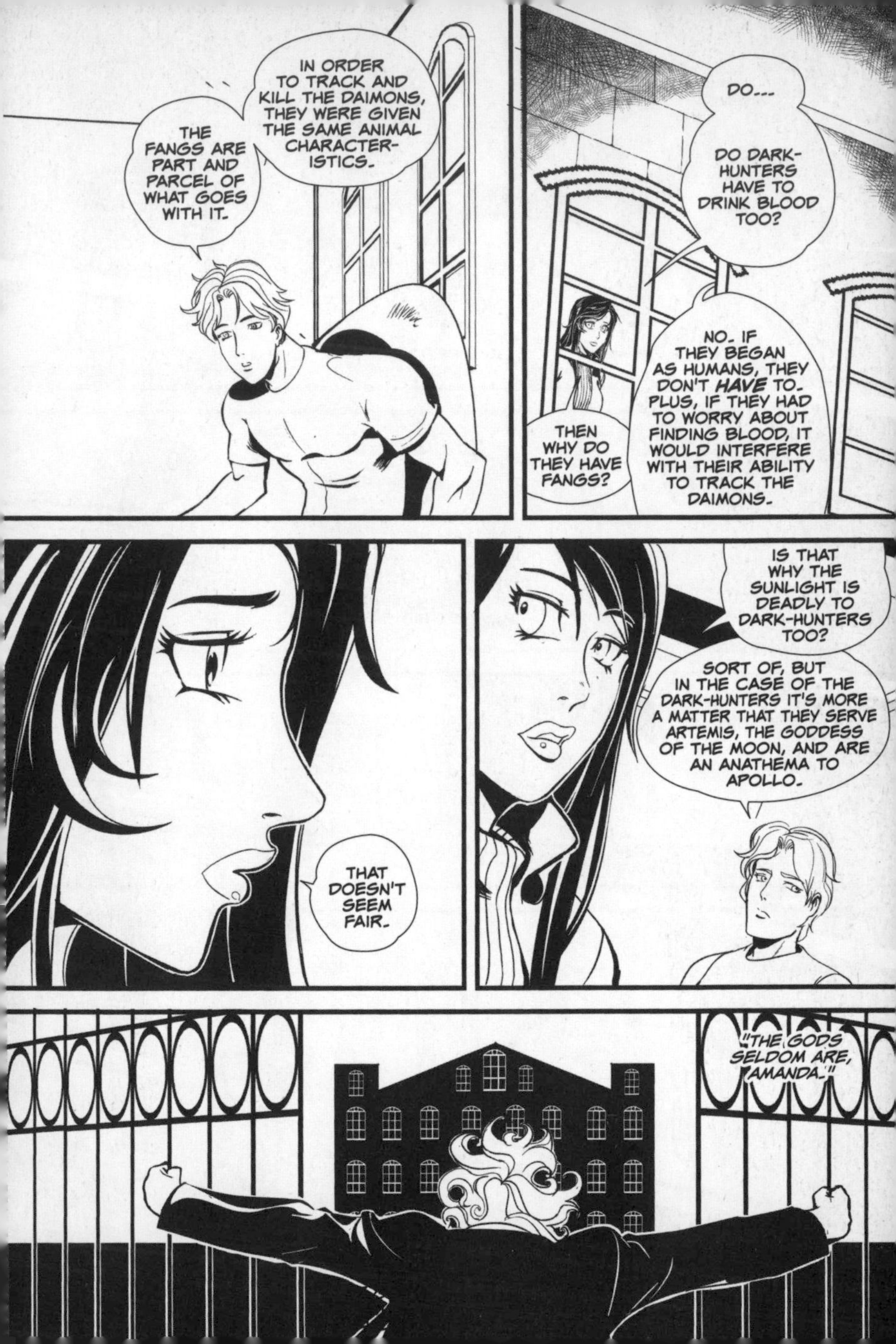
DO...
DO DARK-HUNTERS HAVE TO DRINK BLOOD TOO?
NO. IF THEY BEGAN AS HUMANS, THEY DON'T *HAVE* TO. PLUS, IF THEY HAD TO WORRY ABOUT FINDING BLOOD, IT WOULD INTERFERE WITH THEIR ABILITY TO TRACK THE DAIMONS.
THEN WHY DO THEY HAVE FANGS?
IN ORDER TO TRACK AND KILL THE DAIMONS, THEY WERE GIVEN THE SAME ANIMAL CHARACTERISTICS.
THE FANGS ARE PART AND PARCEL OF WHAT GOES WITH IT.
IS THAT WHY THE SUNLIGHT IS DEADLY TO DARK-HUNTERS TOO?
SORT OF, BUT IN THE CASE OF THE DARK-HUNTERS IT'S MORE A MATTER THAT THEY SERVE ARTEMIS, THE GODDESS OF THE MOON, AND ARE AN ANATHEMA TO APOLLO.
THAT DOESN'T SEEM FAIR.
"THE GODS SELDOM ARE, AMANDA."

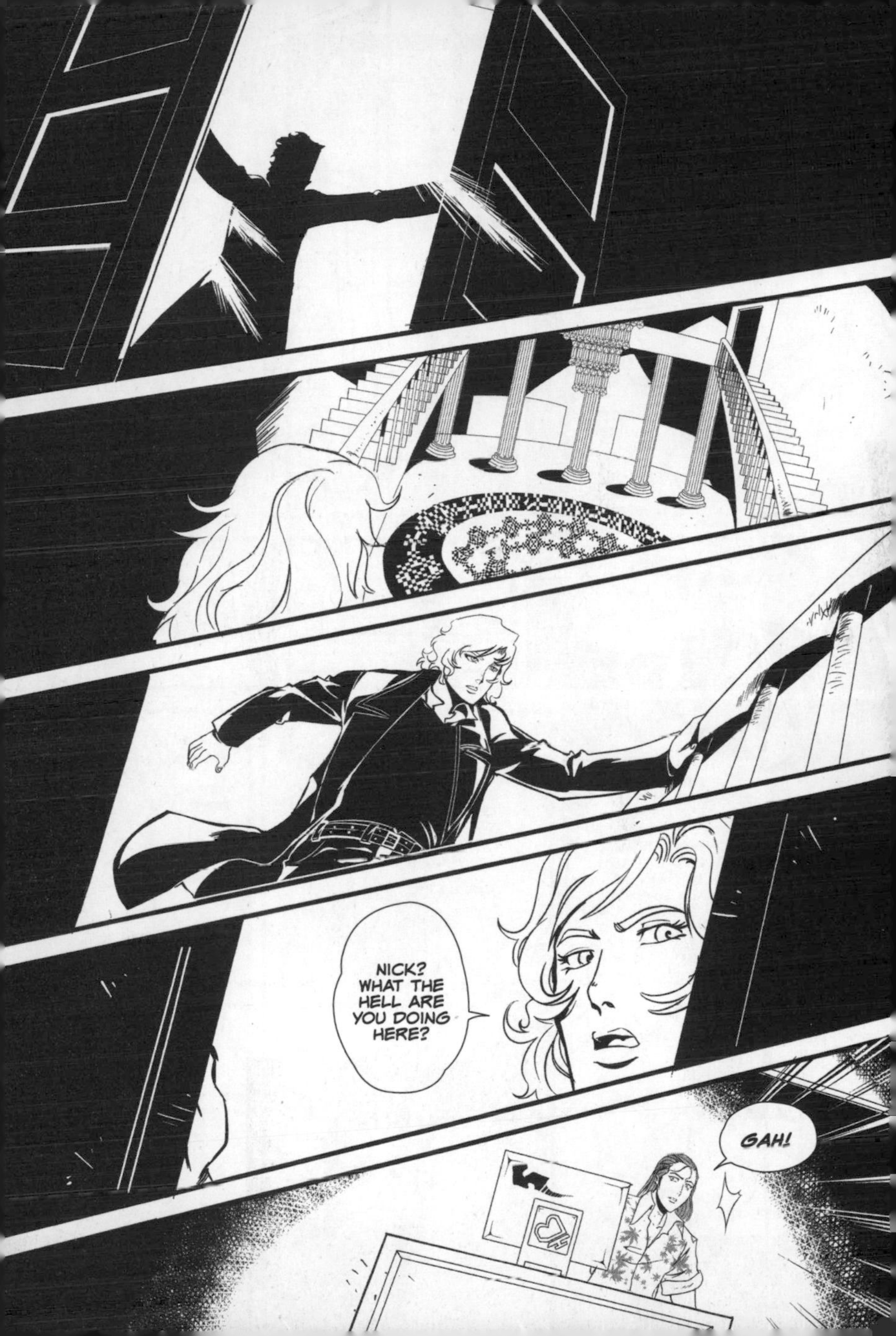
NICK? WHAT THE HELL ARE YOU DOING HERE?
GAH!

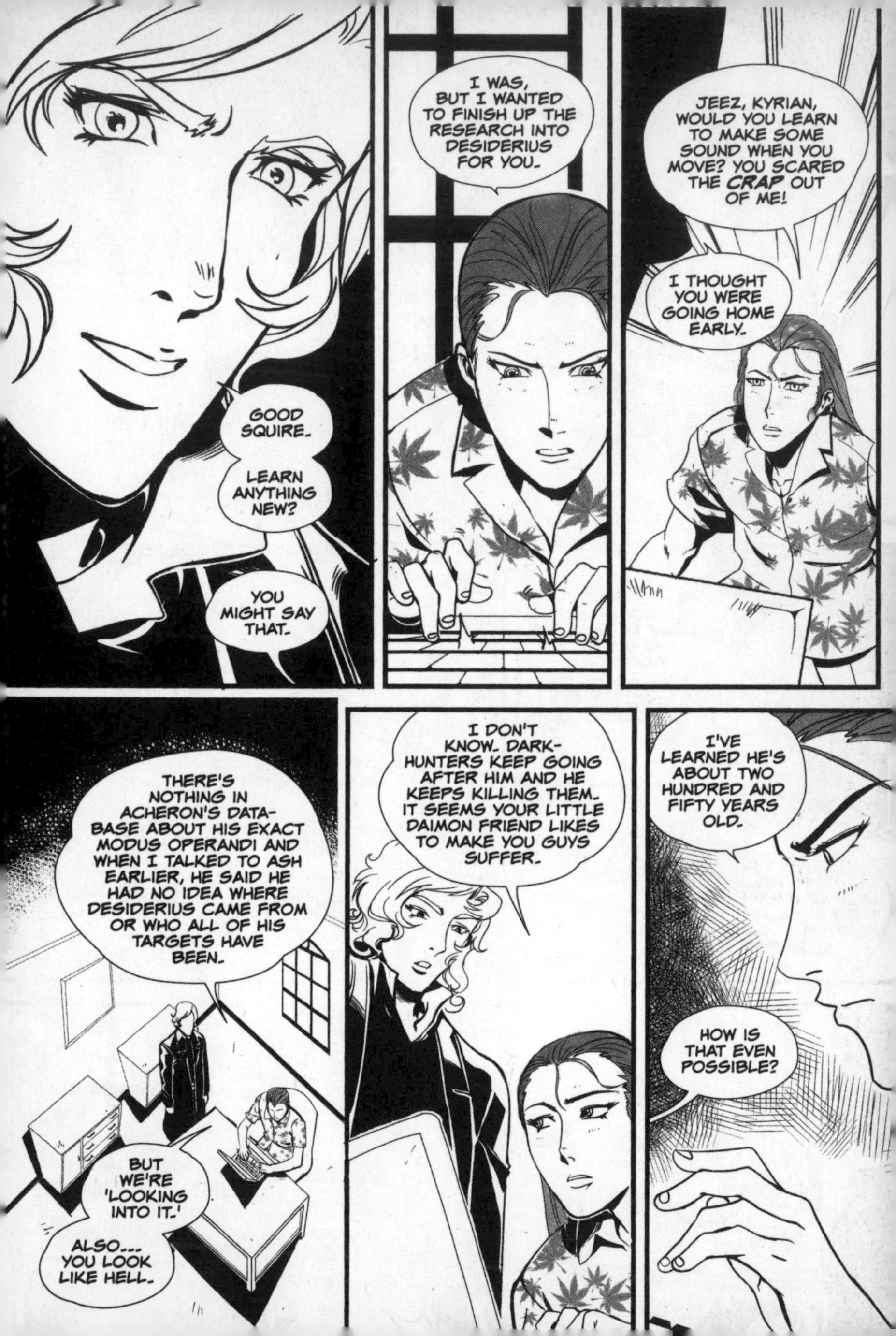
JEEZ, KYRIAN, WOULD YOU LEARN TO MAKE SOME SOUND WHEN YOU MOVE? YOU SCARED THE *CRAP* OUT OF ME!
I THOUGHT YOU WERE GOING HOME EARLY.
I WAS, BUT I WANTED TO FINISH UP THE RESEARCH INTO DESIDERIUS FOR YOU.
GOOD SQUIRE.
LEARN ANYTHING NEW?
YOU MIGHT SAY THAT.
I'VE LEARNED HE'S ABOUT TWO HUNDRED AND FIFTY YEARS OLD.
HOW IS THAT EVEN POSSIBLE?
I DON'T KNOW. DARK-HUNTERS KEEP GOING AFTER HIM AND HE KEEPS KILLING THEM. IT SEEMS YOUR LITTLE DAIMON FRIEND LIKES TO MAKE YOU GUYS SUFFER.
THERE'S NOTHING IN ACHERON'S DATABASE ABOUT HIS EXACT MODUS OPERANDI AND WHEN I TALKED TO ASH EARLIER, HE SAID HE HAD NO IDEA WHERE DESIDERIUS CAME FROM OR WHO ALL OF HIS TARGETS HAVE BEEN.
BUT WE'RE 'LOOKING INTO IT.'
ALSO... YOU LOOK LIKE HELL.

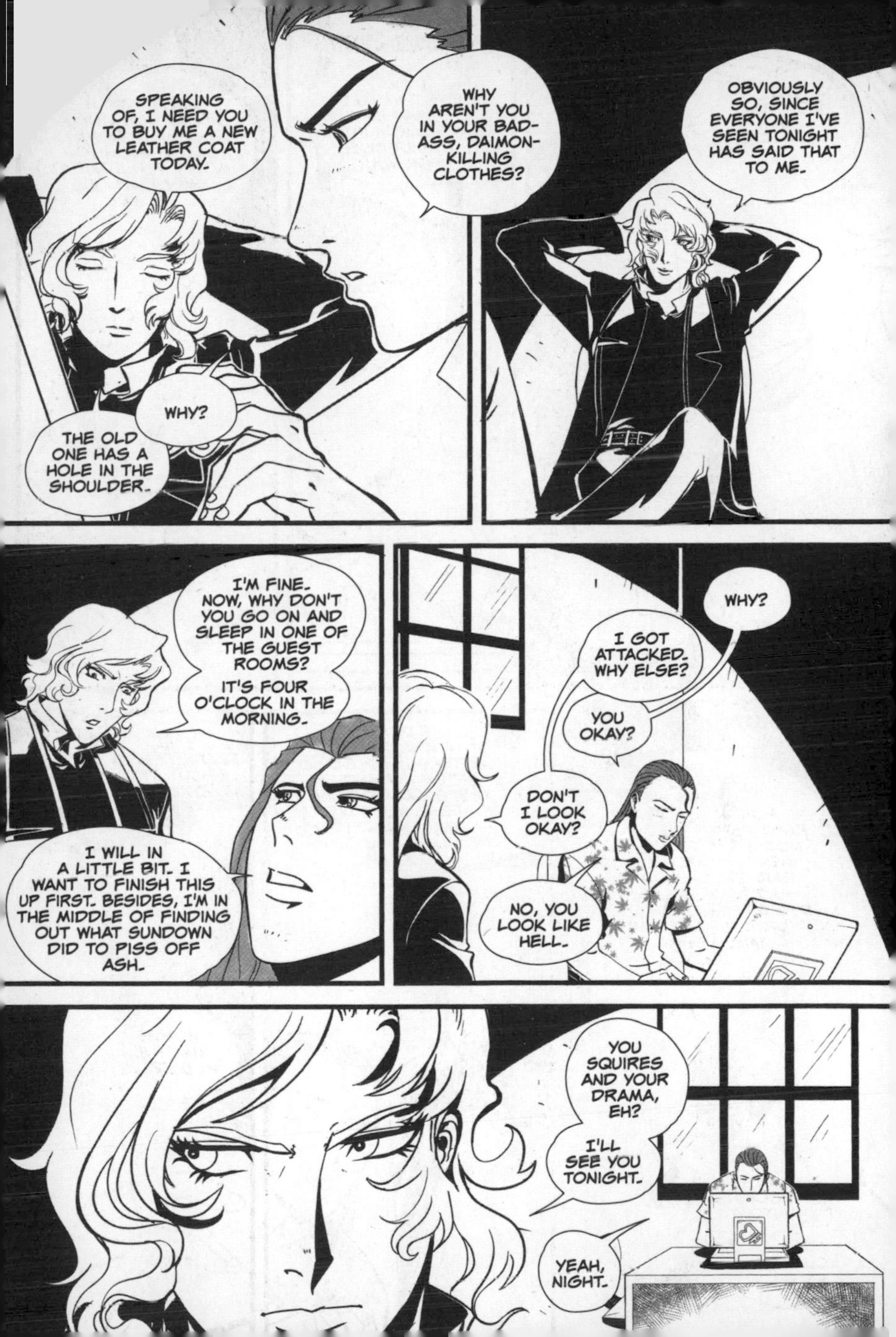
OBVIOUSLY SO, SINCE EVERYONE I'VE SEEN TONIGHT HAS SAID THAT TO ME.
WHY AREN'T YOU IN YOUR BAD-ASS, DAIMON-KILLING CLOTHES?
SPEAKING OF, I NEED YOU TO BUY ME A NEW LEATHER COAT TODAY.
WHY?
THE OLD ONE HAS A HOLE IN THE SHOULDER.
WHY?
I GOT ATTACKED. WHY ELSE?
YOU OKAY?
DON'T I LOOK OKAY?
NO, YOU LOOK LIKE HELL.
I'M FINE. NOW, WHY DON'T YOU GO ON AND SLEEP IN ONE OF THE GUEST ROOMS?
IT'S FOUR O'CLOCK IN THE MORNING.
I WILL IN A LITTLE BIT. I WANT TO FINISH THIS UP FIRST. BESIDES, I'M IN THE MIDDLE OF FINDING OUT WHAT SUNDOWN DID TO PISS OFF ASH.
YOU SQUIRES AND YOUR DRAMA, EH?
I'LL SEE YOU TONIGHT.
YEAH, NIGHT.

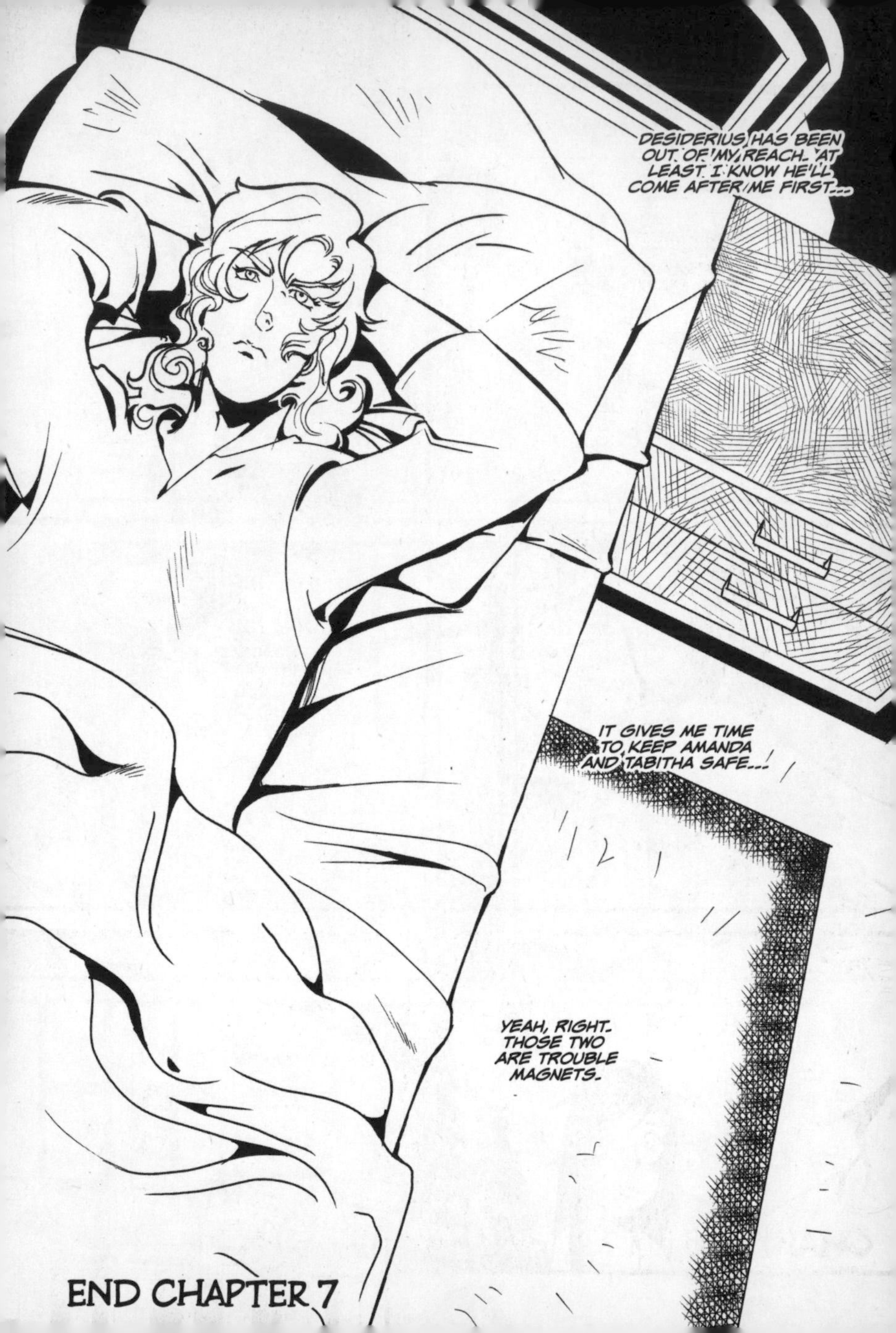
DESIDERIUS HAS BEEN OUT OF MY REACH. AT LEAST I KNOW HE'LL COME AFTER ME FIRST...
IT GIVES ME TIME TO KEEP AMANDA AND TABITHA SAFE...!
YEAH, RIGHT. THOSE TWO ARE TROUBLE MAGNETS.
END CHAPTER 7

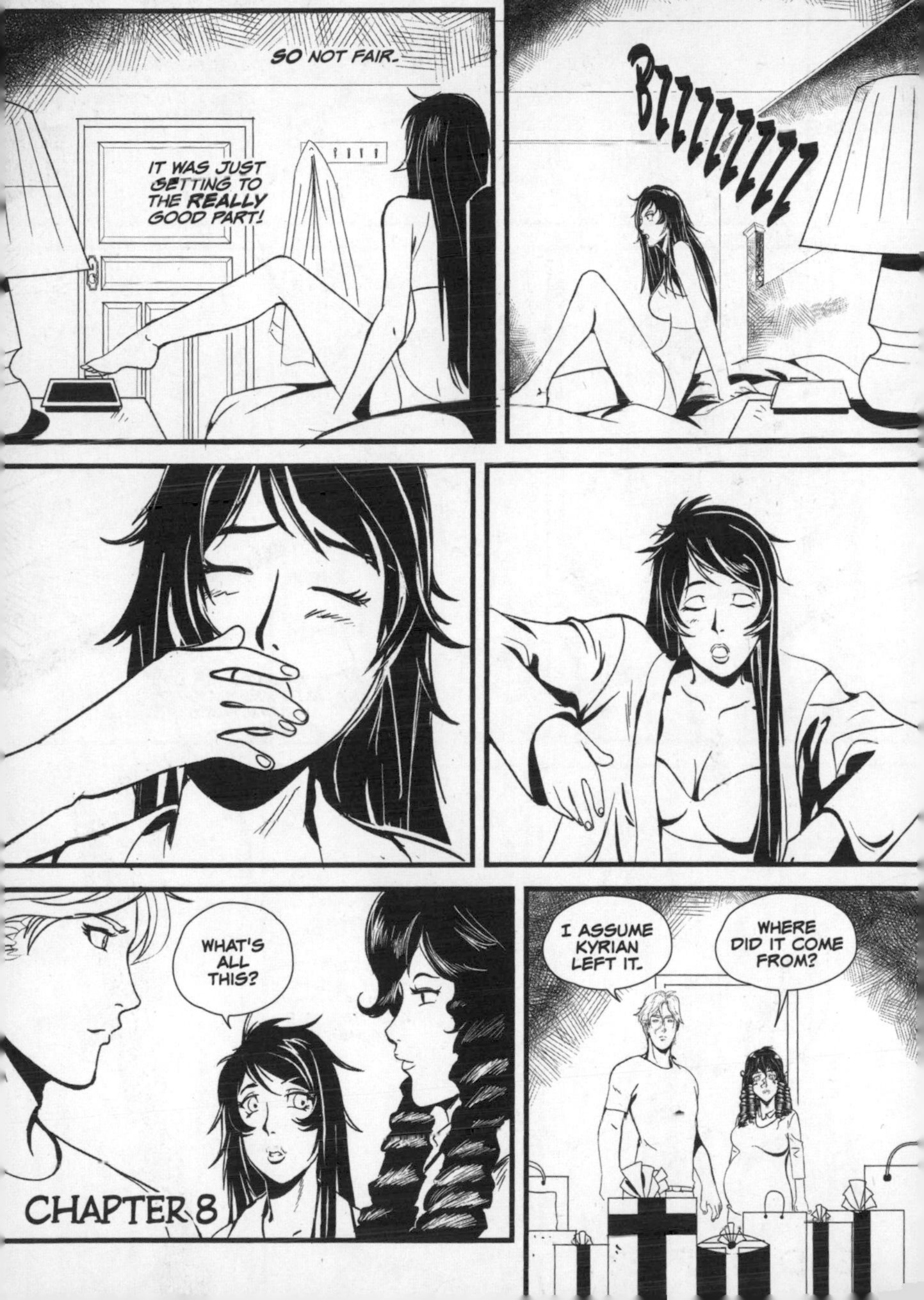
BZZZZZZZZZZ
SO NOT FAIR.
IT WAS JUST GETTING TO THE REALLY GOOD PART!
WHERE DID IT COME FROM?
I ASSUME KYRIAN LEFT IT.
WHAT'S ALL THIS?
CHAPTER 8

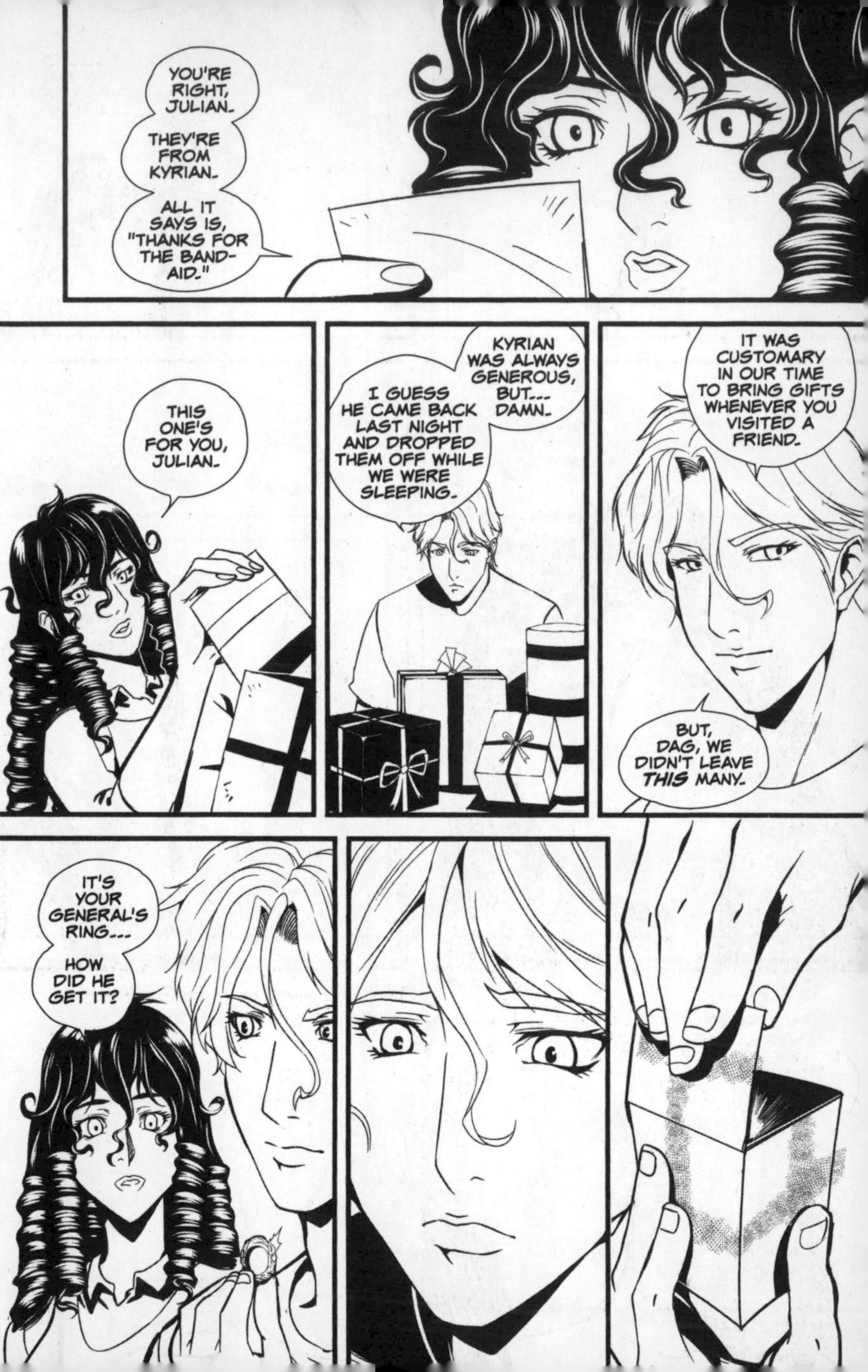
YOU'RE RIGHT, JULIAN.
THEY'RE FROM KYRIAN.
ALL IT SAYS IS, "THANKS FOR THE BAND-AID."
IT WAS CUSTOMARY IN OUR TIME TO BRING GIFTS WHENEVER YOU VISITED A FRIEND.
BUT, DAG, WE DIDN'T LEAVE *THIS* MANY.
KYRIAN WAS ALWAYS GENEROUS, BUT... DAMN.
I GUESS HE CAME BACK LAST NIGHT AND DROPPED THEM OFF WHILE WE WERE SLEEPING.
THIS ONE'S FOR YOU, JULIAN.
IT'S YOUR GENERAL'S RING...
HOW DID HE GET IT?

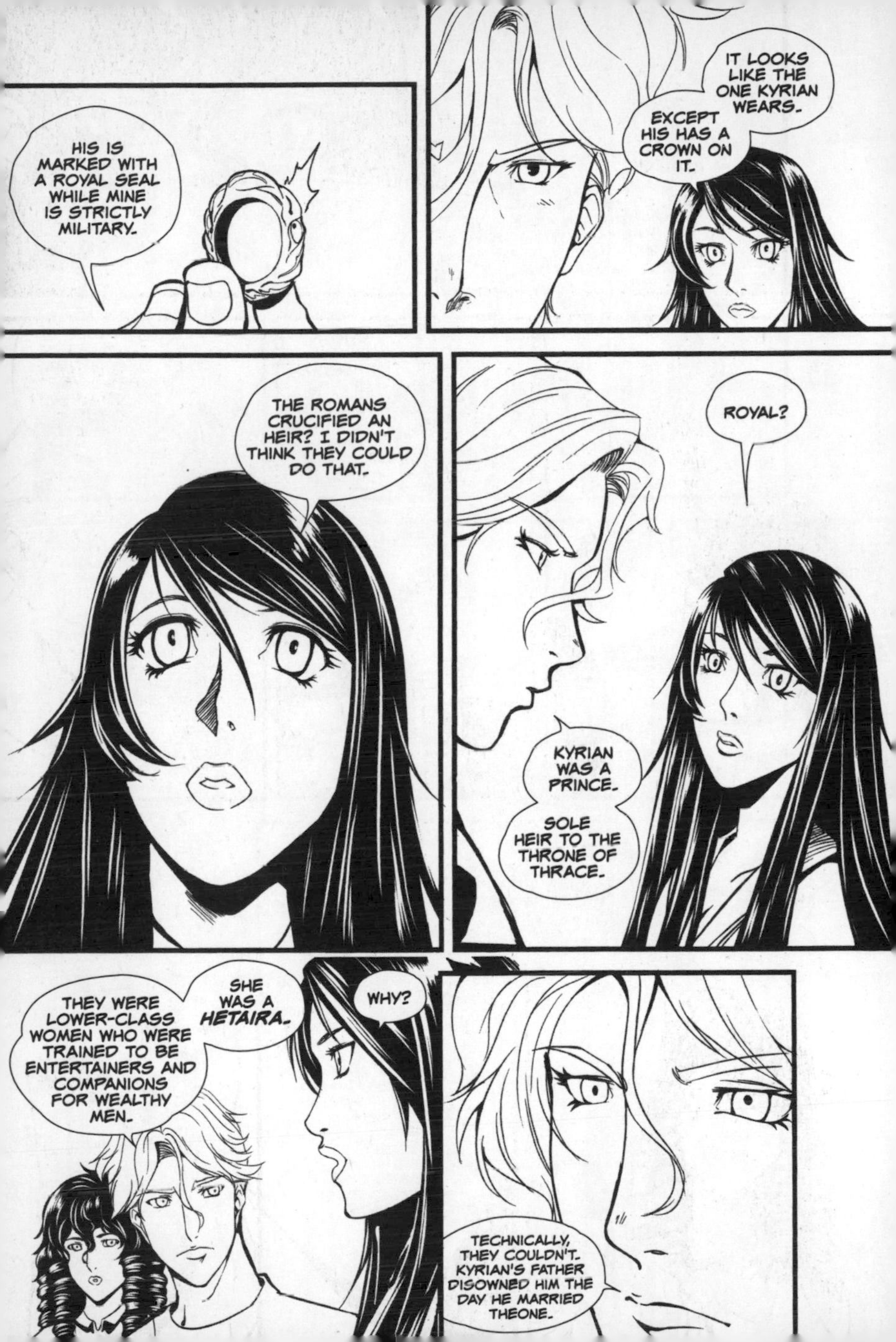
IT LOOKS LIKE THE ONE KYRIAN WEARS.
EXCEPT HIS HAS A CROWN ON IT.
HIS IS MARKED WITH A ROYAL SEAL WHILE MINE IS STRICTLY MILITARY.
ROYAL?
KYRIAN WAS A PRINCE.
SOLE HEIR TO THE THRONE OF THRACE.
THE ROMANS CRUCIFIED AN HEIR? I DIDN'T THINK THEY COULD DO THAT.
TECHNICALLY, THEY COULDN'T. KYRIAN'S FATHER DISOWNED HIM THE DAY HE MARRIED THEONE.
WHY?
SHE WAS A *HETAIRA*.
THEY WERE LOWER-CLASS WOMEN WHO WERE TRAINED TO BE ENTERTAINERS AND COMPANIONS FOR WEALTHY MEN.

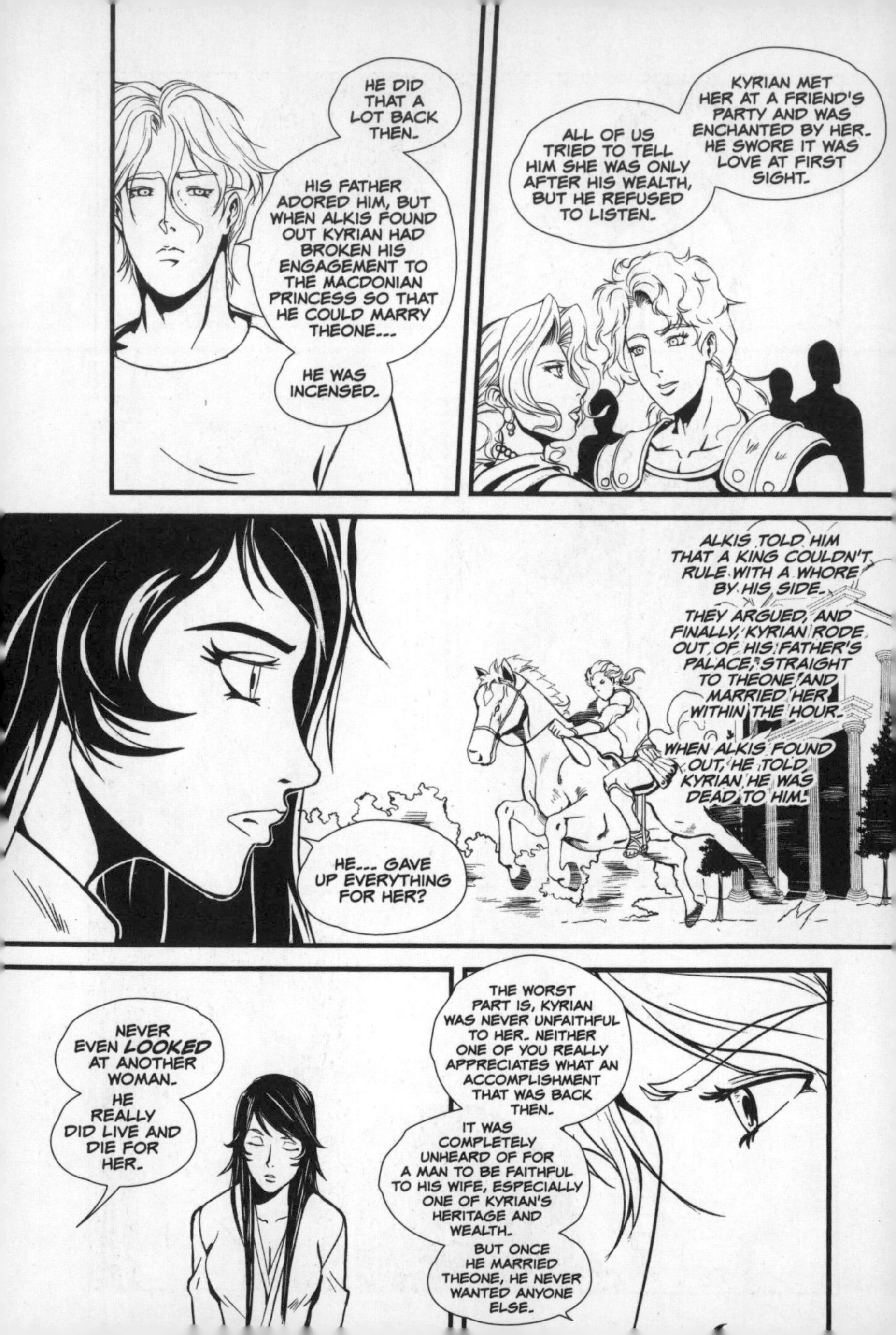
KYRIAN MET HER AT A FRIEND'S PARTY AND WAS ENCHANTED BY HER. HE SWORE IT WAS LOVE AT FIRST SIGHT.
ALL OF US TRIED TO TELL HIM SHE WAS ONLY AFTER HIS WEALTH, BUT HE REFUSED TO LISTEN.
HE DID THAT A LOT BACK THEN.
HIS FATHER ADORED HIM, BUT WHEN ALKIS FOUND OUT KYRIAN HAD BROKEN HIS ENGAGEMENT TO THE MACDONIAN PRINCESS SO THAT HE COULD MARRY THEONE...
HE WAS INCENSED.
ALKIS TOLD HIM THAT A KING COULDN'T RULE WITH A WHORE BY HIS SIDE.
THEY ARGUED, AND FINALLY, KYRIAN RODE OUT OF HIS FATHER'S PALACE, STRAIGHT TO THEONE AND MARRIED HER WITHIN THE HOUR.
WHEN ALKIS FOUND OUT, HE TOLD KYRIAN HE WAS DEAD TO HIM.
HE... GAVE UP EVERYTHING FOR HER?
THE WORST PART IS, KYRIAN WAS NEVER UNFAITHFUL TO HER. NEITHER ONE OF YOU REALLY APPRECIATES WHAT AN ACCOMPLISHMENT THAT WAS BACK THEN.
IT WAS COMPLETELY UNHEARD OF FOR A MAN TO BE FAITHFUL TO HIS WIFE, ESPECIALLY ONE OF KYRIAN'S HERITAGE AND WEALTH.
BUT ONCE HE MARRIED THEONE, HE NEVER WANTED ANYONE ELSE.
NEVER EVEN *LOOKED* AT ANOTHER WOMAN.
HE REALLY DID LIVE AND DIE FOR HER.

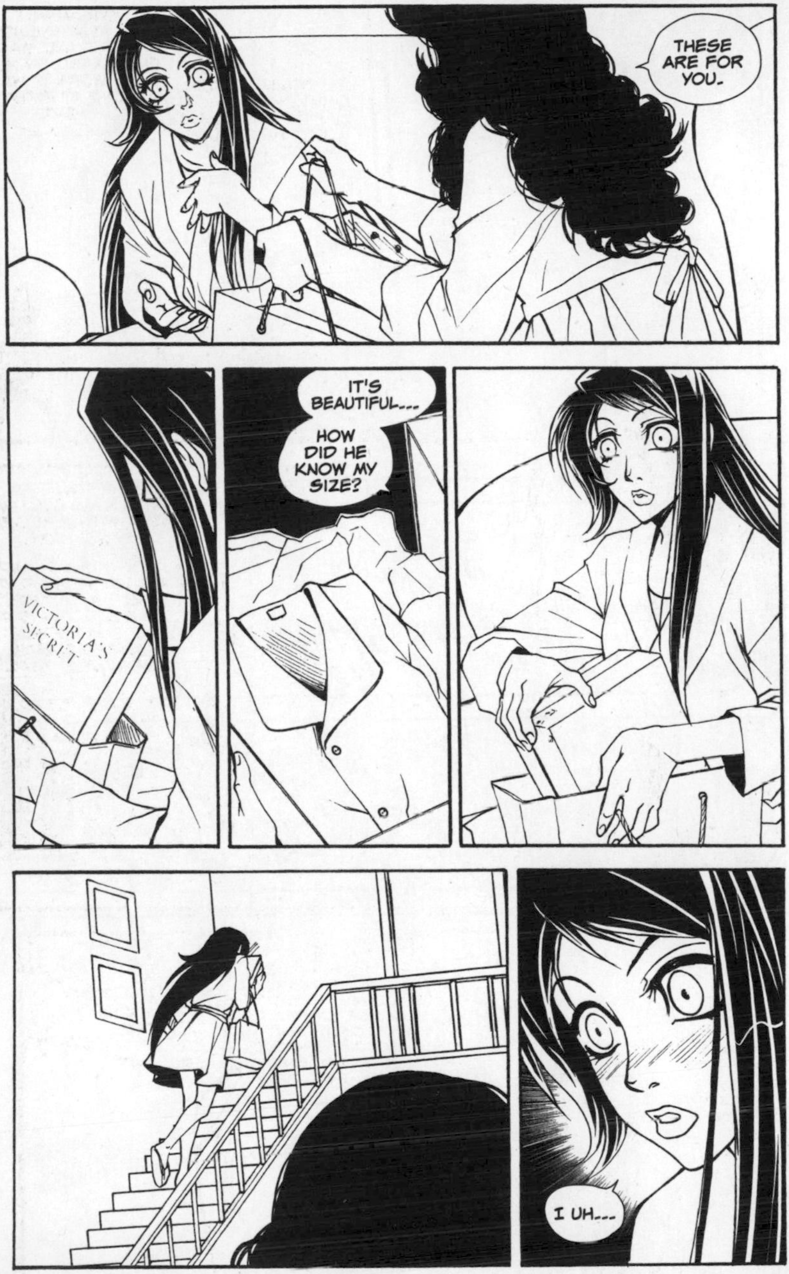
THESE ARE FOR YOU.
IT'S BEAUTIFUL...
HOW DID HE KNOW MY SIZE?
VICTORIA'S SECRET
I UH...

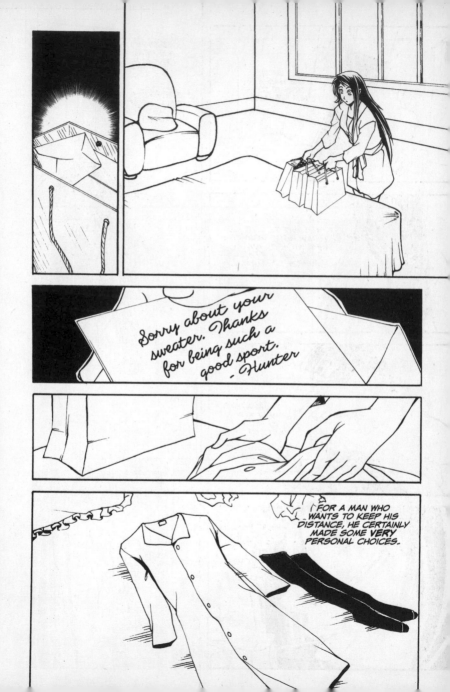

Sorry about your sweater. Thanks for being such a good sport.
- Hunter

FOR A MAN WHO WANTS TO KEEP HIS DISTANCE, HE CERTAINLY MADE SOME **VERY** PERSONAL CHOICES.

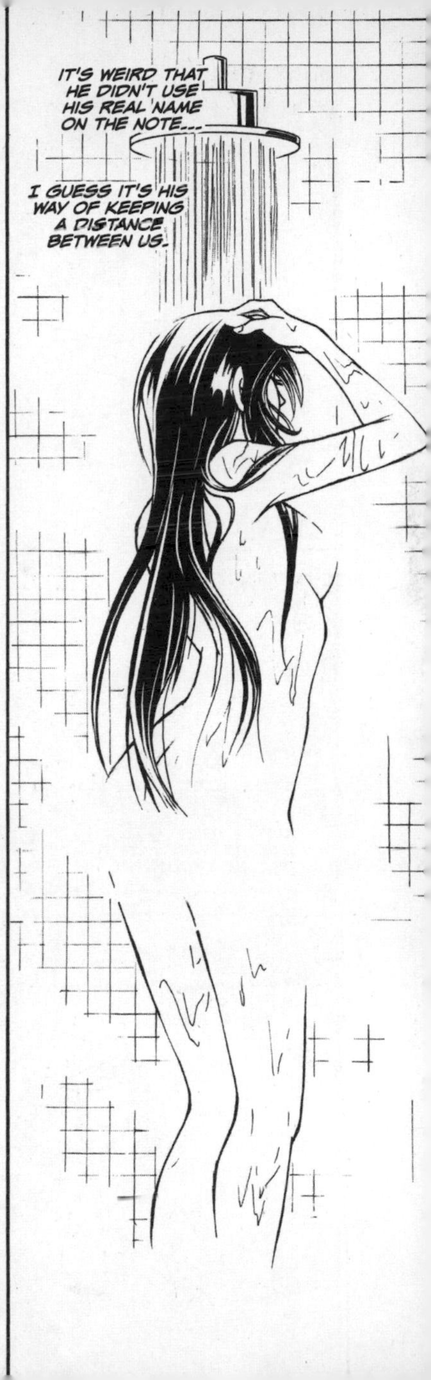
IT'S WEIRD THAT HE DIDN'T USE HIS REAL NAME ON THE NOTE...
I GUESS IT'S HIS WAY OF KEEPING A DISTANCE BETWEEN US.

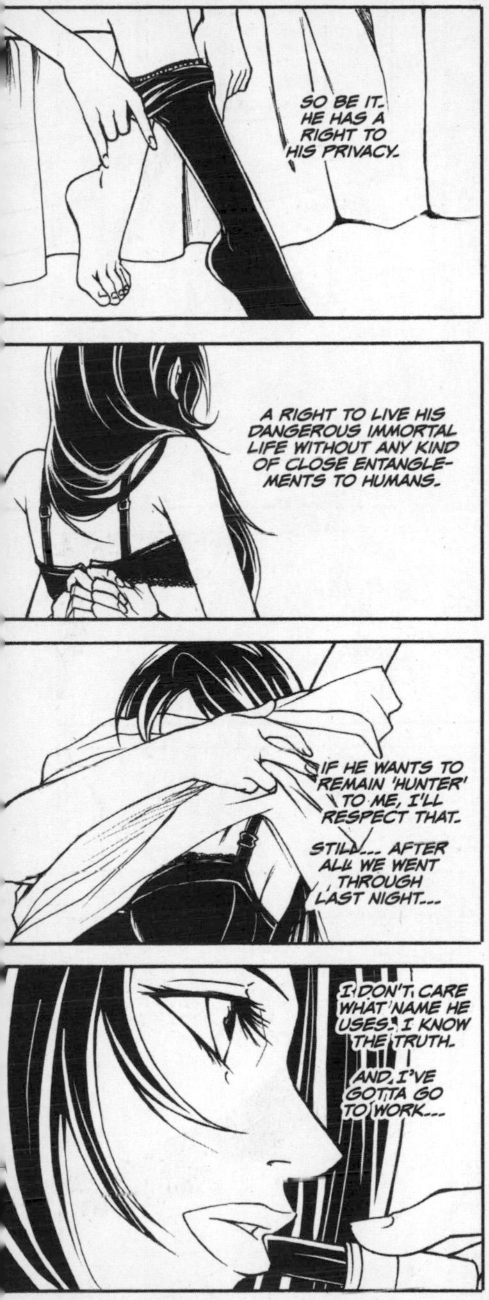
SO BE IT. HE HAS A RIGHT TO HIS PRIVACY.
A RIGHT TO LIVE HIS DANGEROUS IMMORTAL LIFE WITHOUT ANY KIND OF CLOSE ENTANGLE-MENTS TO HUMANS.
IF HE WANTS TO REMAIN 'HUNTER' TO ME, I'LL RESPECT THAT.
STILL... AFTER ALL WE WENT THROUGH LAST NIGHT...
I DON'T CARE WHAT NAME HE USES. I KNOW THE TRUTH.
AND I'VE GOTTA GO TO WORK...

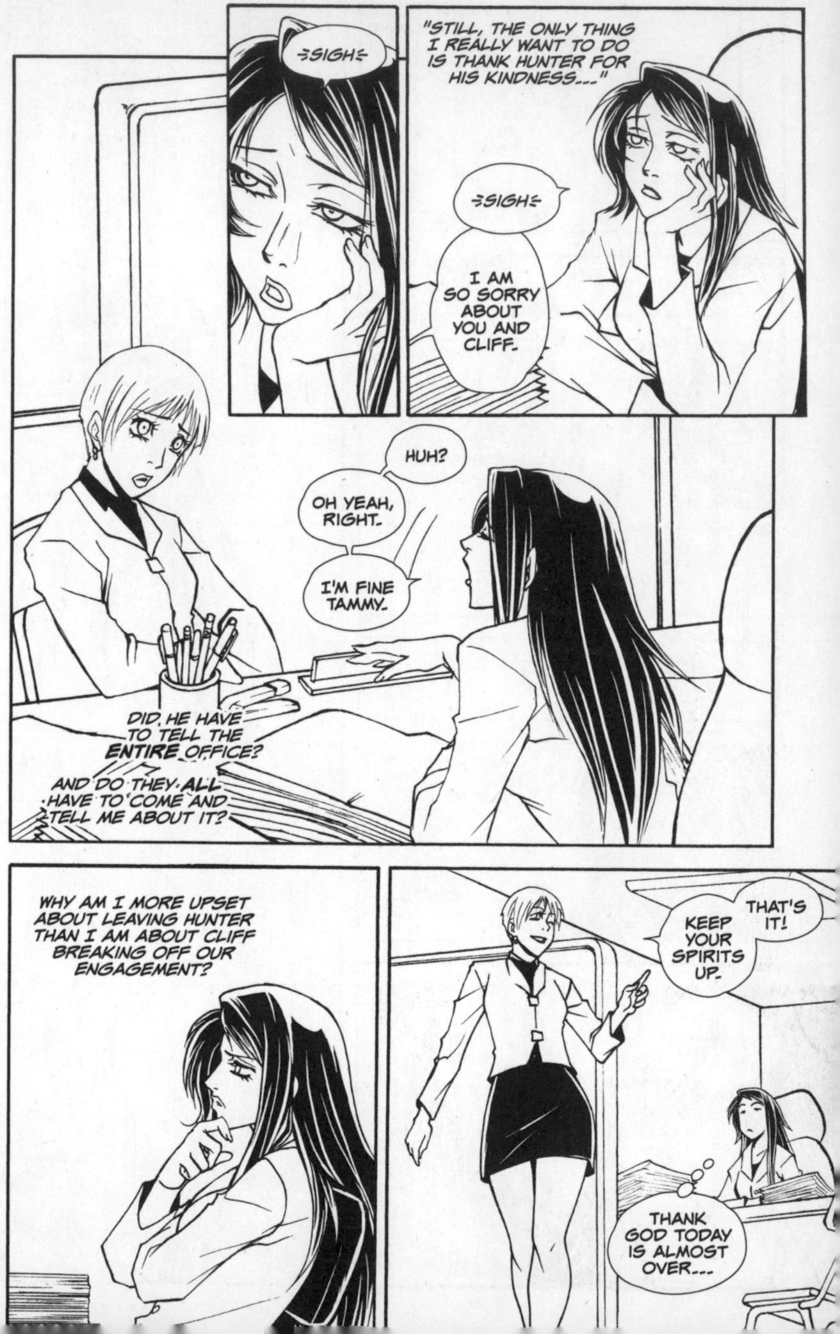
"STILL, THE ONLY THING I REALLY WANT TO DO IS THANK HUNTER FOR HIS KINDNESS..."
⇉SIGH⇇
I AM SO SORRY ABOUT YOU AND CLIFF.
⇉SIGH⇇
HUH?
OH YEAH, RIGHT.
I'M FINE TAMMY.
DID HE HAVE TO TELL THE ENTIRE OFFICE?
AND DO THEY ALL HAVE TO COME AND TELL ME ABOUT IT?
THAT'S IT!
KEEP YOUR SPIRITS UP.
THANK GOD TODAY IS ALMOST OVER...
WHY AM I MORE UPSET ABOUT LEAVING HUNTER THAN I AM ABOUT CLIFF BREAKING OFF OUR ENGAGEMENT?

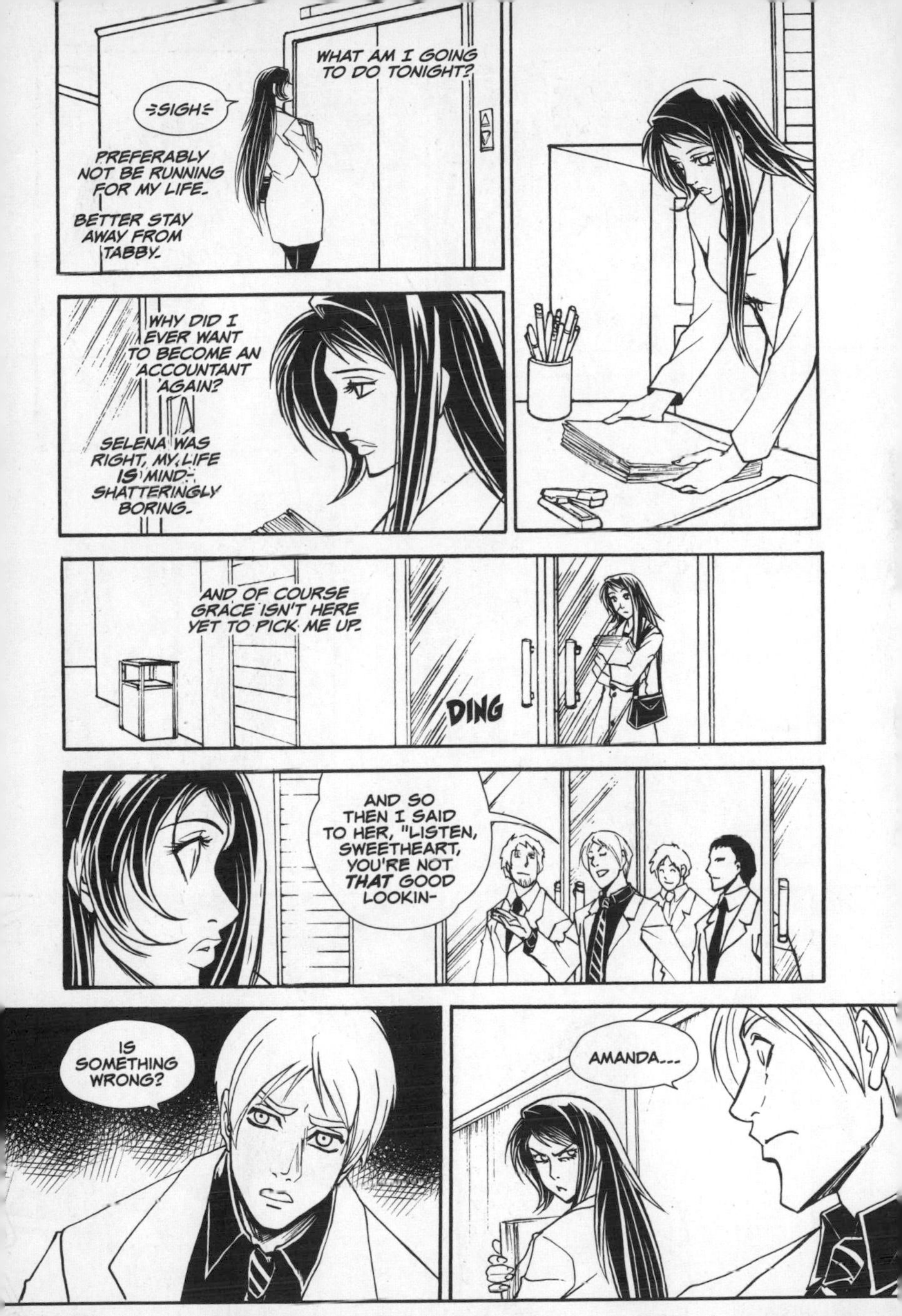
WHAT AM I GOING TO DO TONIGHT?
=SIGH=
PREFERABLY NOT BE RUNNING FOR MY LIFE.
BETTER STAY AWAY FROM TABBY.
WHY DID I EVER WANT TO BECOME AN ACCOUNTANT AGAIN?
SELENA WAS RIGHT, MY LIFE IS MIND-SHATTERINGLY BORING.
AND OF COURSE GRACE ISN'T HERE YET TO PICK ME UP.
DING
AND SO THEN I SAID TO HER, "LISTEN, SWEETHEART, YOU'RE NOT THAT GOOD LOOKIN-
AMANDA...
IS SOMETHING WRONG?

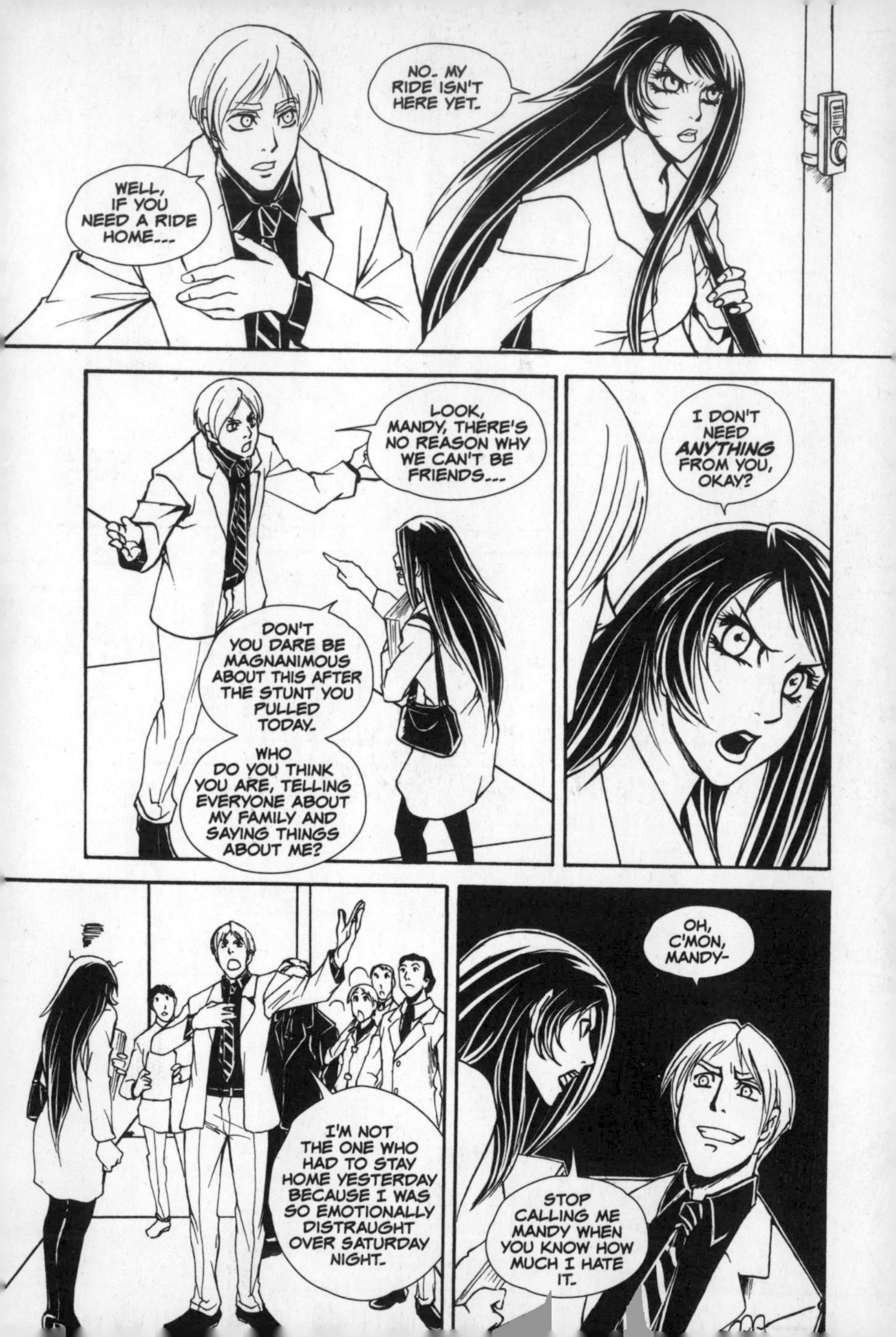
NO. MY RIDE ISN'T HERE YET.
WELL, IF YOU NEED A RIDE HOME...
I DON'T NEED ANYTHING FROM YOU, OKAY?
LOOK, MANDY, THERE'S NO REASON WHY WE CAN'T BE FRIENDS...
DON'T YOU DARE BE MAGNANIMOUS ABOUT THIS AFTER THE STUNT YOU PULLED TODAY.
WHO DO YOU THINK YOU ARE, TELLING EVERYONE ABOUT MY FAMILY AND SAYING THINGS ABOUT ME?
OH, C'MON, MANDY-
STOP CALLING ME MANDY WHEN YOU KNOW HOW MUCH I HATE IT.
I'M NOT THE ONE WHO HAD TO STAY HOME YESTERDAY BECAUSE I WAS SO EMOTIONALLY DISTRAUGHT OVER SATURDAY NIGHT.

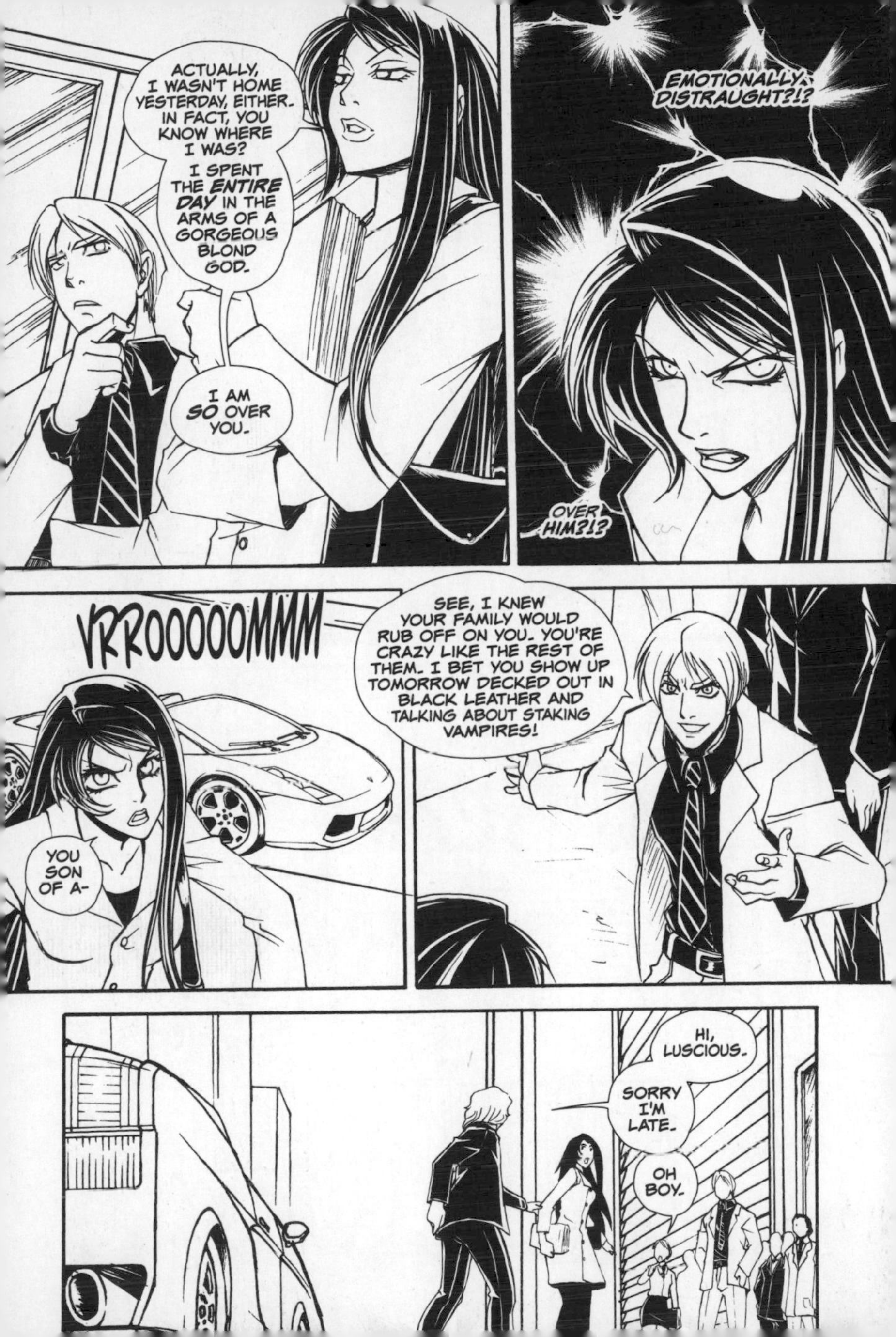
EMOTIONALLY DISTRAUGHT?!?
OVER HIM?!?
ACTUALLY, I WASN'T HOME YESTERDAY, EITHER. IN FACT, YOU KNOW WHERE I WAS?
I SPENT THE **ENTIRE DAY** IN THE ARMS OF A GORGEOUS BLOND GOD.
I AM **SO** OVER YOU.
SEE, I KNEW YOUR FAMILY WOULD RUB OFF ON YOU. YOU'RE CRAZY LIKE THE REST OF THEM. I BET YOU SHOW UP TOMORROW DECKED OUT IN BLACK LEATHER AND TALKING ABOUT STAKING VAMPIRES!
VRROOOOOMMM
YOU SON OF A-
HI, LUSCIOUS.
SORRY I'M LATE.
OH BOY.

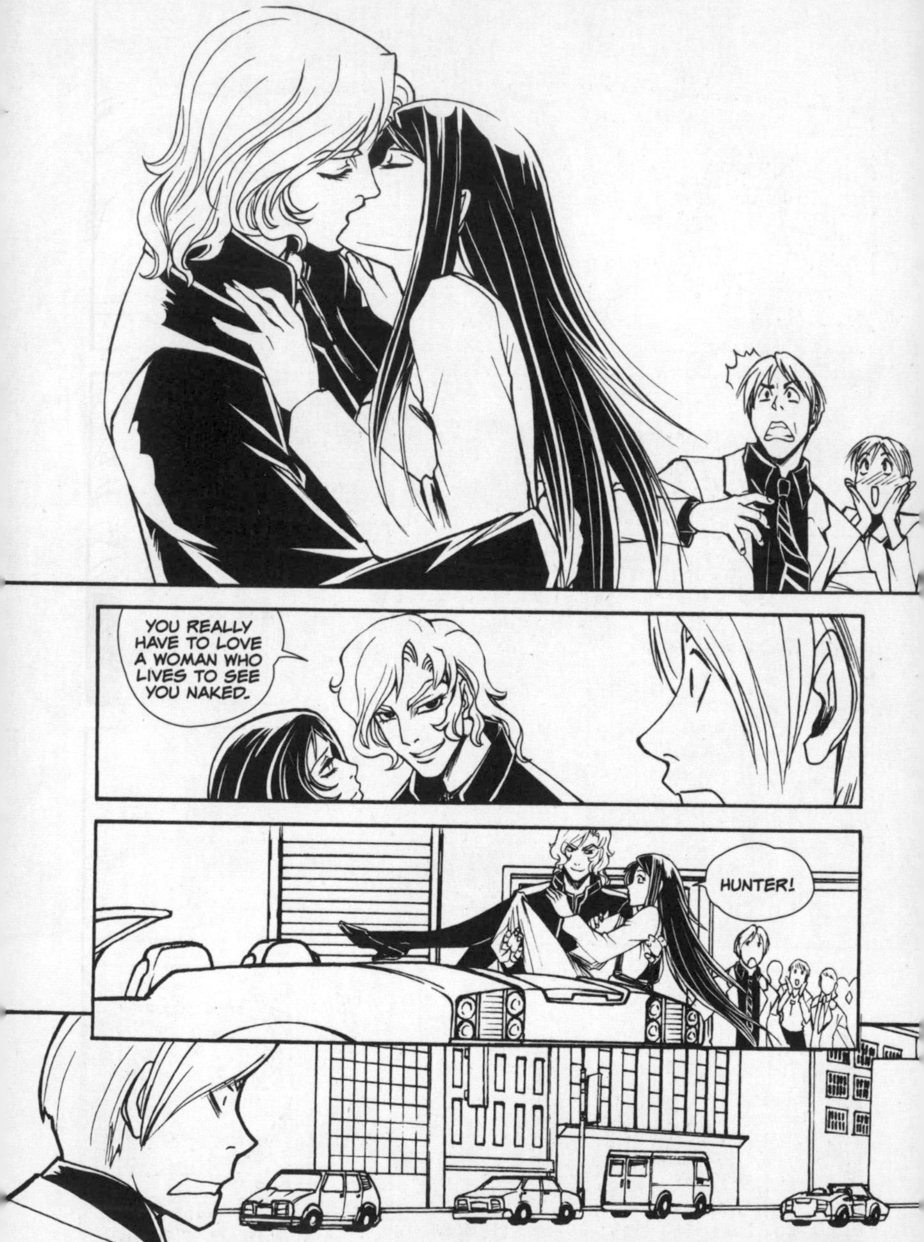
YOU REALLY HAVE TO LOVE A WOMAN WHO LIVES TO SEE YOU NAKED.
HUNTER!

END CHAPTER 8

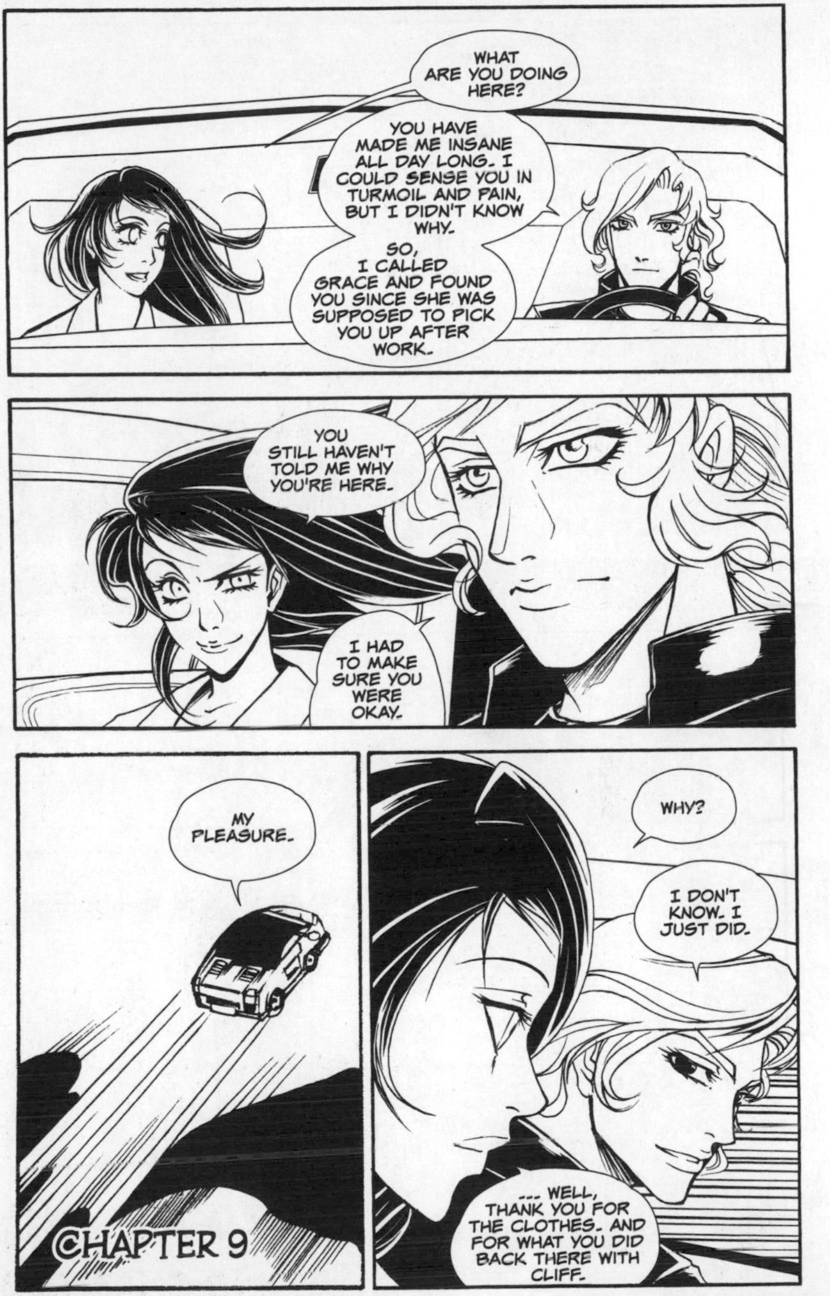
WHAT ARE YOU DOING HERE?
YOU HAVE MADE ME INSANE ALL DAY LONG. I COULD SENSE YOU IN TURMOIL AND PAIN, BUT I DIDN'T KNOW WHY.
SO, I CALLED GRACE AND FOUND YOU SINCE SHE WAS SUPPOSED TO PICK YOU UP AFTER WORK.
YOU STILL HAVEN'T TOLD ME WHY YOU'RE HERE.
I HAD TO MAKE SURE YOU WERE OKAY.
WHY?
I DON'T KNOW. I JUST DID.
... WELL, THANK YOU FOR THE CLOTHES. AND FOR WHAT YOU DID BACK THERE WITH CLIFF.
MY PLEASURE.
CHAPTER 9

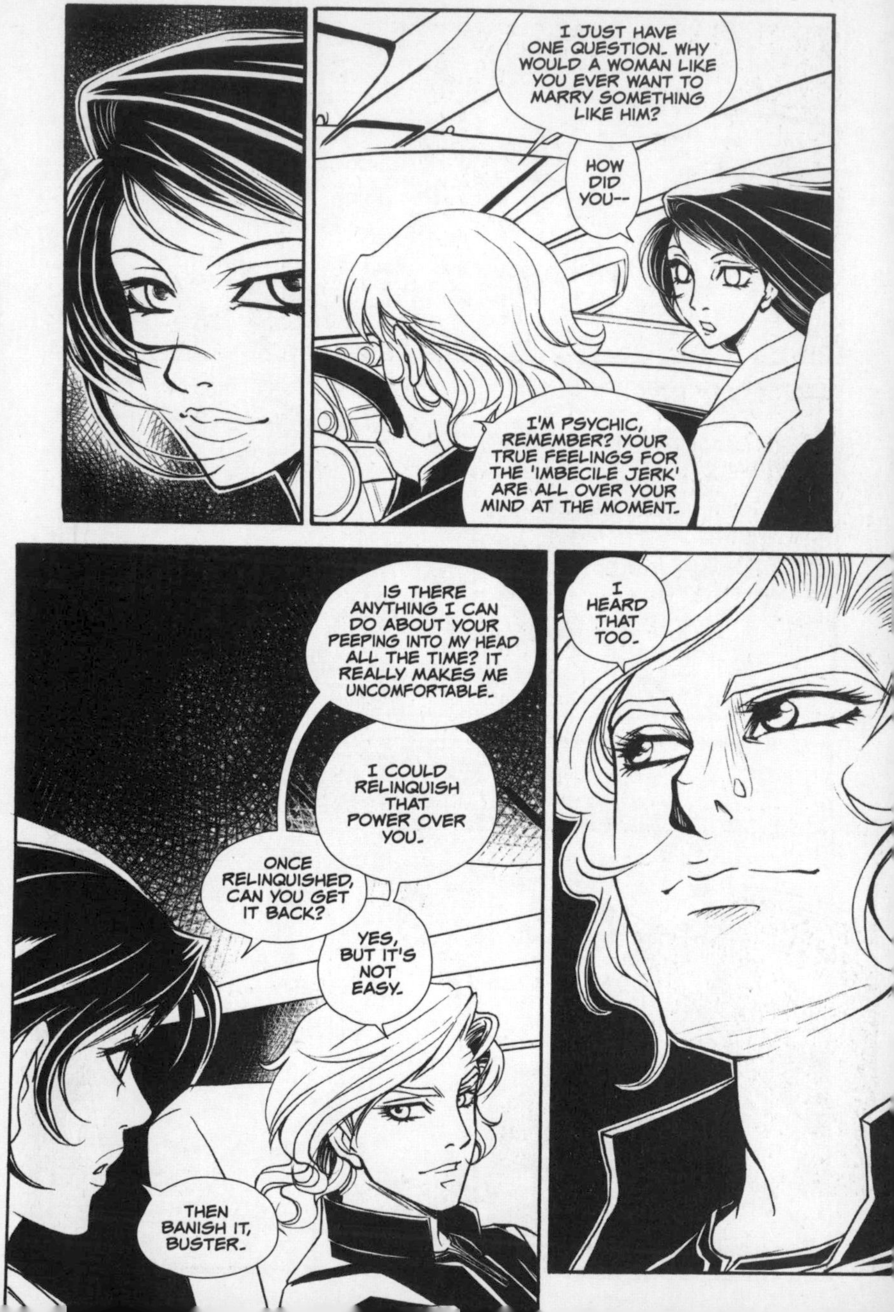
I JUST HAVE ONE QUESTION. WHY WOULD A WOMAN LIKE YOU EVER WANT TO MARRY SOMETHING LIKE HIM?
HOW DID YOU--
I'M PSYCHIC, REMEMBER? YOUR TRUE FEELINGS FOR THE 'IMBECILE JERK' ARE ALL OVER YOUR MIND AT THE MOMENT.
IS THERE ANYTHING I CAN DO ABOUT YOUR PEEPING INTO MY HEAD ALL THE TIME? IT REALLY MAKES ME UNCOMFORTABLE.
I COULD RELINQUISH THAT POWER OVER YOU.
ONCE RELINQUISHED, CAN YOU GET IT BACK?
YES, BUT IT'S NOT EASY.
THEN BANISH IT, BUSTER.
I HEARD THAT TOO.

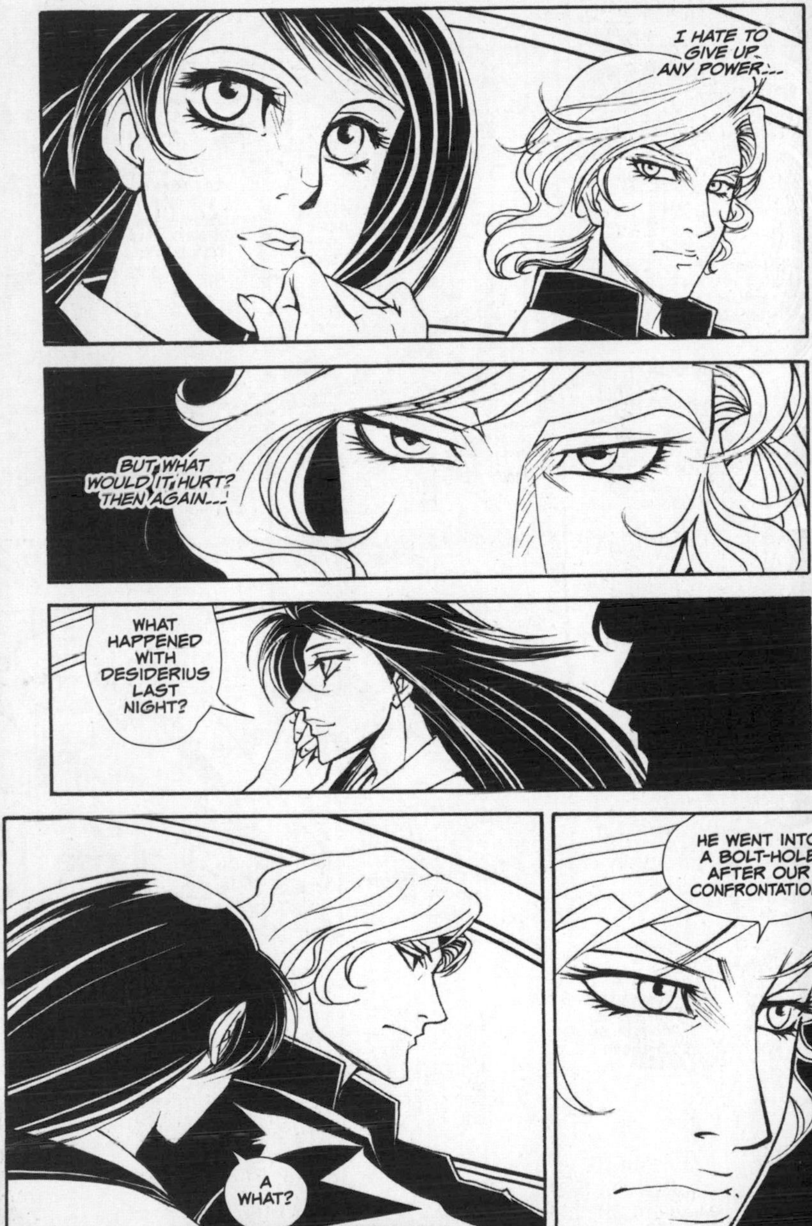
I HATE TO GIVE UP ANY POWER...
BUT WHAT WOULD IT HURT? THEN AGAIN...
WHAT HAPPENED WITH DESIDERIUS LAST NIGHT?
HE WENT INTO A BOLT-HOLE AFTER OUR CONFRONTATION.
A WHAT?

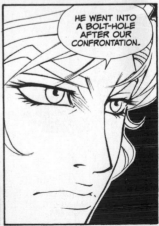

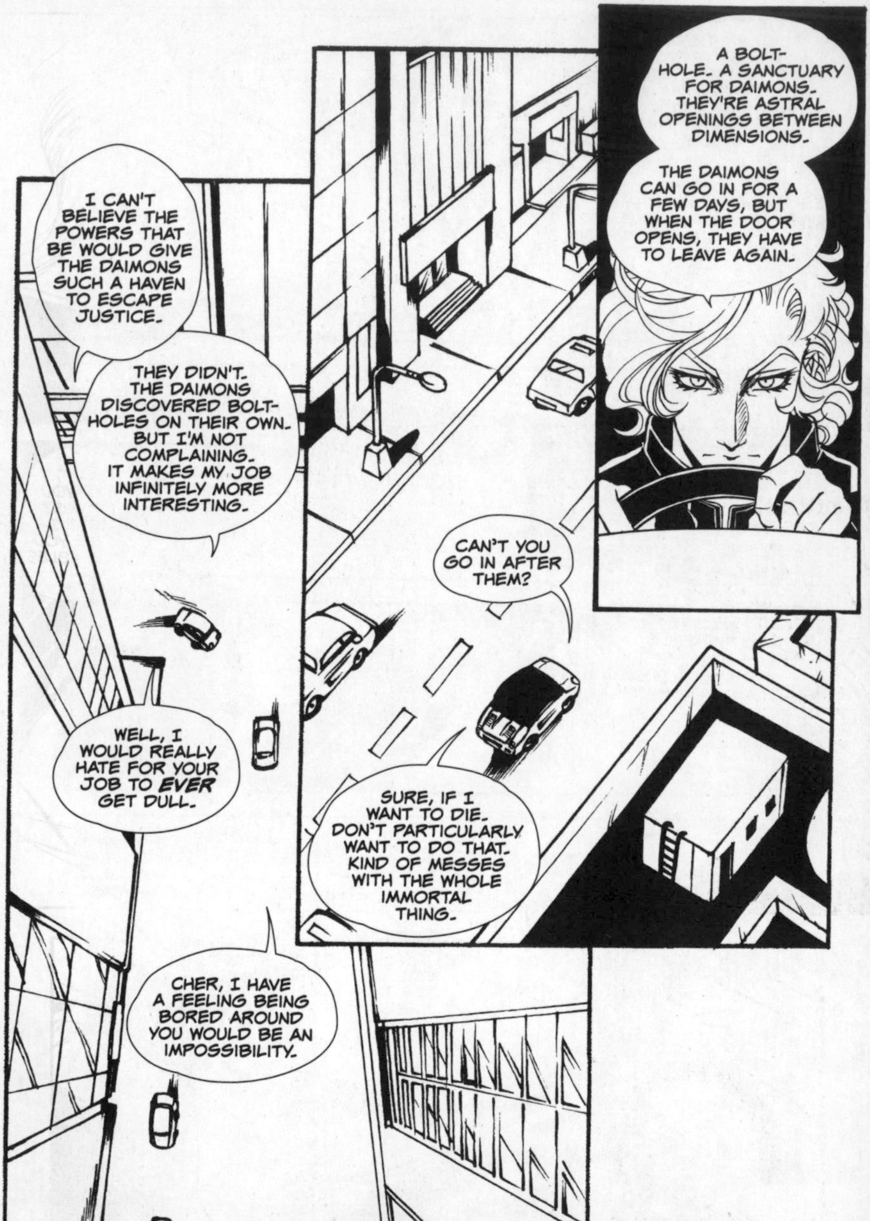
A BOLT-HOLE. A SANCTUARY FOR DAIMONS. THEY'RE ASTRAL OPENINGS BETWEEN DIMENSIONS.
THE DAIMONS CAN GO IN FOR A FEW DAYS, BUT WHEN THE DOOR OPENS, THEY HAVE TO LEAVE AGAIN.
CAN'T YOU GO IN AFTER THEM?
SURE, IF I WANT TO DIE. DON'T PARTICULARLY WANT TO DO THAT. KIND OF MESSES WITH THE WHOLE IMMORTAL THING.
I CAN'T BELIEVE THE POWERS THAT BE WOULD GIVE THE DAIMONS SUCH A HAVEN TO ESCAPE JUSTICE.
THEY DIDN'T. THE DAIMONS DISCOVERED BOLT-HOLES ON THEIR OWN. BUT I'M NOT COMPLAINING. IT MAKES MY JOB INFINITELY MORE INTERESTING.
WELL, I WOULD REALLY HATE FOR YOUR JOB TO *EVER* GET DULL.
CHER, I HAVE A FEELING BEING BORED AROUND YOU WOULD BE AN IMPOSSIBILITY.

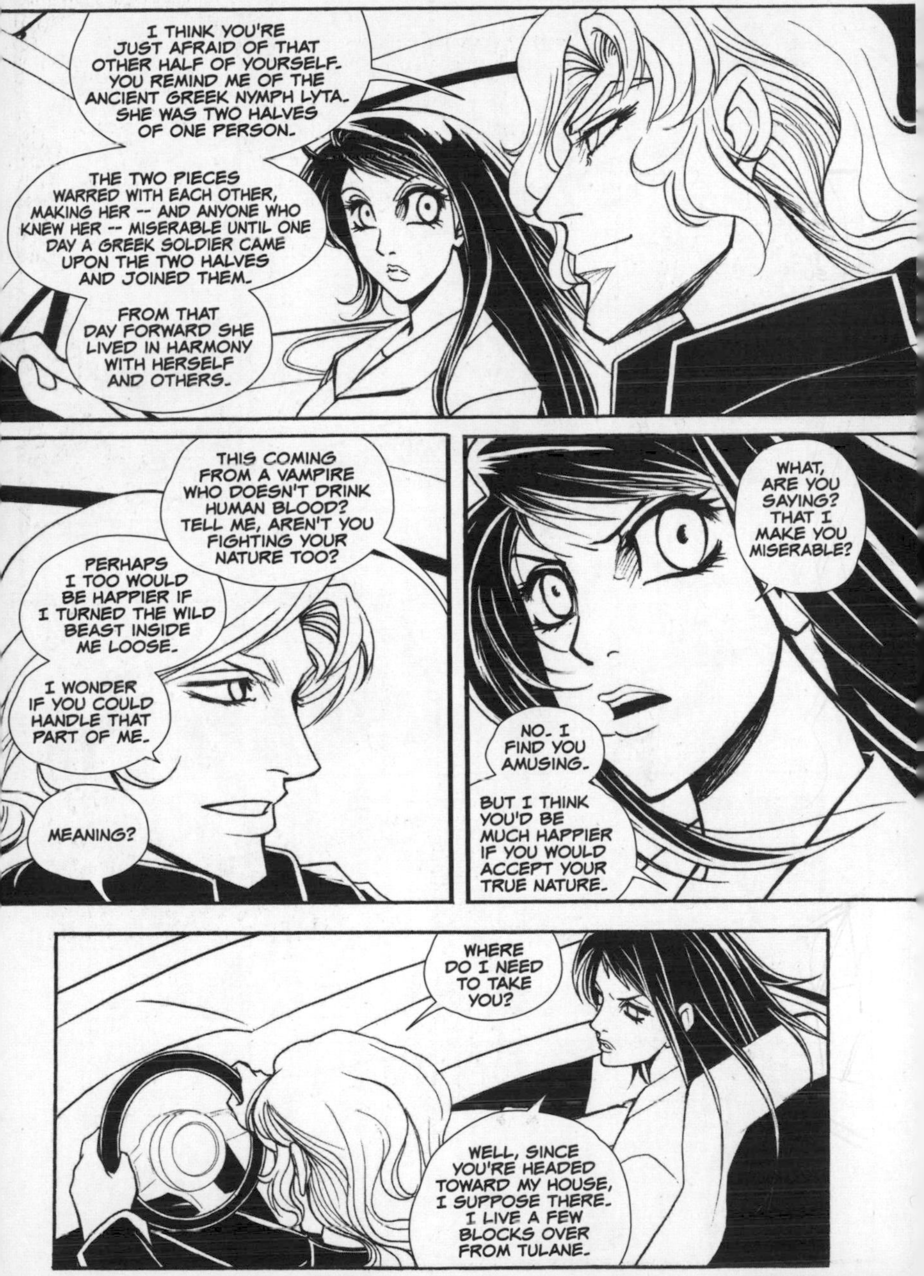
I THINK YOU'RE JUST AFRAID OF THAT OTHER HALF OF YOURSELF. YOU REMIND ME OF THE ANCIENT GREEK NYMPH LYTA. SHE WAS TWO HALVES OF ONE PERSON.
THE TWO PIECES WARRED WITH EACH OTHER, MAKING HER -- AND ANYONE WHO KNEW HER -- MISERABLE UNTIL ONE DAY A GREEK SOLDIER CAME UPON THE TWO HALVES AND JOINED THEM.
FROM THAT DAY FORWARD SHE LIVED IN HARMONY WITH HERSELF AND OTHERS.
WHAT, ARE YOU SAYING? THAT I MAKE YOU MISERABLE?
NO. I FIND YOU AMUSING.
BUT I THINK YOU'D BE MUCH HAPPIER IF YOU WOULD ACCEPT YOUR TRUE NATURE.
THIS COMING FROM A VAMPIRE WHO DOESN'T DRINK HUMAN BLOOD? TELL ME, AREN'T YOU FIGHTING YOUR NATURE TOO?
PERHAPS I TOO WOULD BE HAPPIER IF I TURNED THE WILD BEAST INSIDE ME LOOSE.
I WONDER IF YOU COULD HANDLE THAT PART OF ME.
MEANING?
WHERE DO I NEED TO TAKE YOU?
WELL, SINCE YOU'RE HEADED TOWARD MY HOUSE, I SUPPOSE THERE. I LIVE A FEW BLOCKS OVER FROM TULANE.

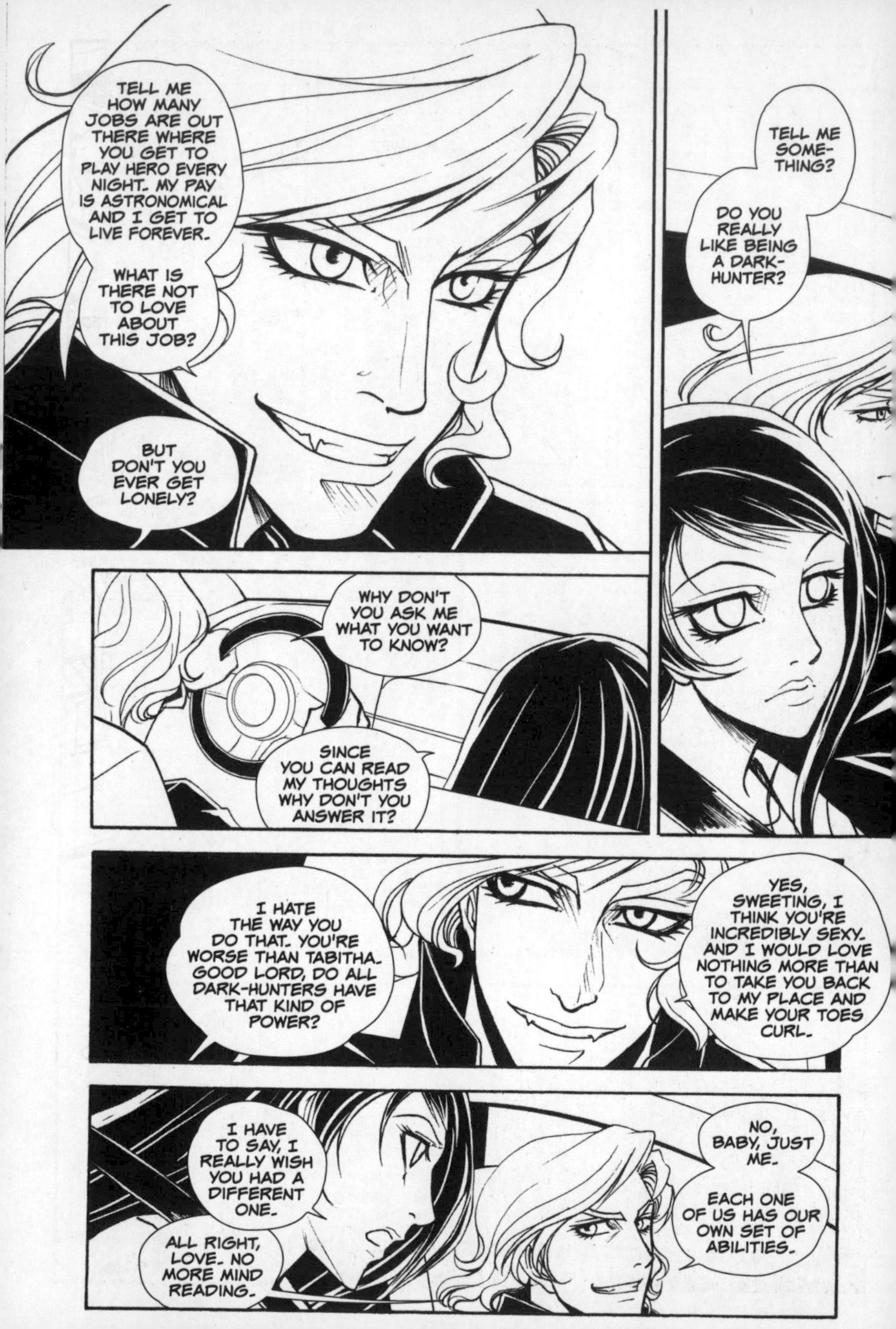
TELL ME SOME-THING?
DO YOU REALLY LIKE BEING A DARK-HUNTER?
TELL ME HOW MANY JOBS ARE OUT THERE WHERE YOU GET TO PLAY HERO EVERY NIGHT. MY PAY IS ASTRONOMICAL AND I GET TO LIVE FOREVER.
WHAT IS THERE NOT TO LOVE ABOUT THIS JOB?
BUT DON'T YOU EVER GET LONELY?
WHY DON'T YOU ASK ME WHAT YOU WANT TO KNOW?
SINCE YOU CAN READ MY THOUGHTS WHY DON'T YOU ANSWER IT?
YES, SWEETING, I THINK YOU'RE INCREDIBLY SEXY. AND I WOULD LOVE NOTHING MORE THAN TO TAKE YOU BACK TO MY PLACE AND MAKE YOUR TOES CURL.
I HATE THE WAY YOU DO THAT. YOU'RE WORSE THAN TABITHA. GOOD LORD, DO ALL DARK-HUNTERS HAVE THAT KIND OF POWER?
NO, BABY, JUST ME.
EACH ONE OF US HAS OUR OWN SET OF ABILITIES.
I HAVE TO SAY, I REALLY WISH YOU HAD A DIFFERENT ONE.
ALL RIGHT, LOVE. NO MORE MIND READING.

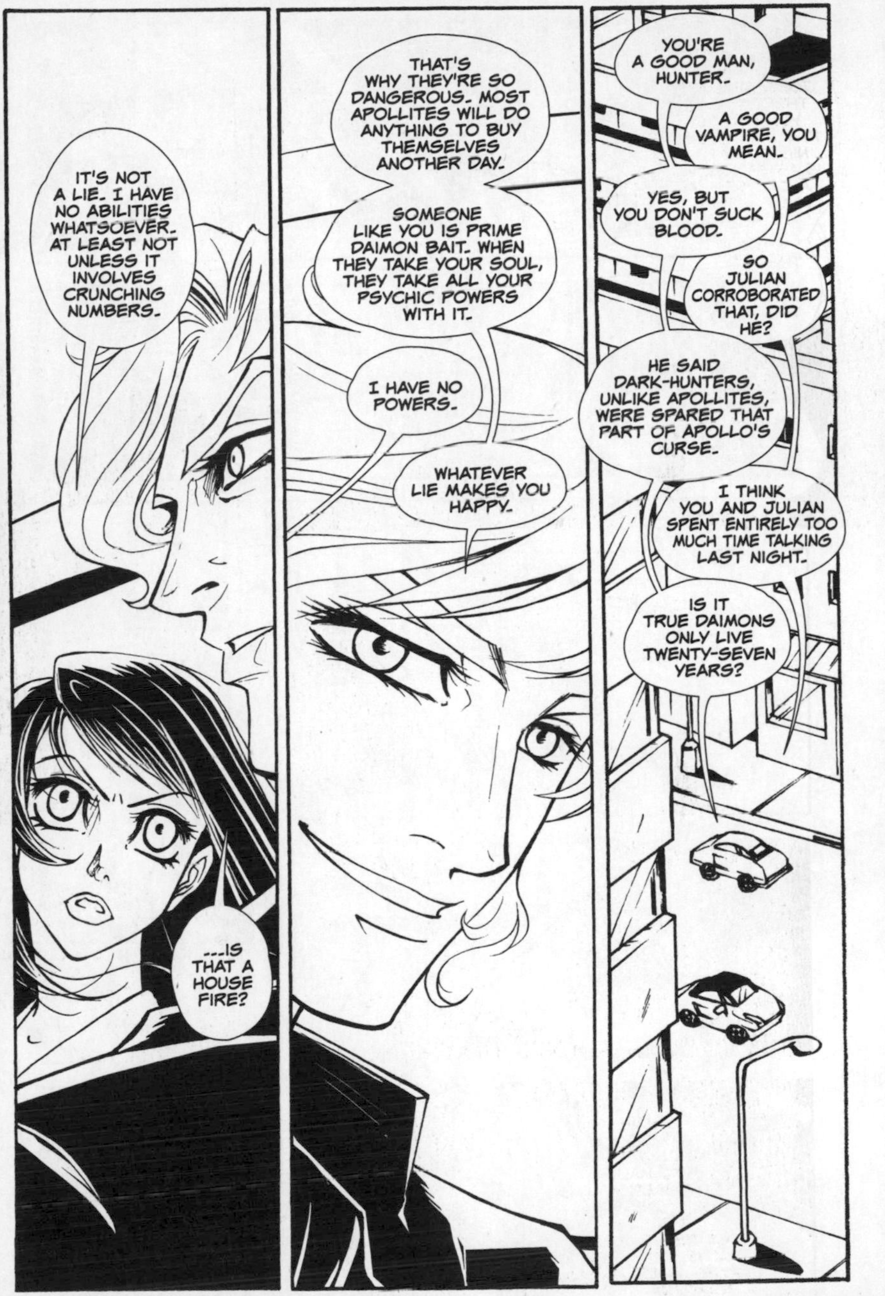
YOU'RE A GOOD MAN, HUNTER.
A GOOD VAMPIRE, YOU MEAN.
YES, BUT YOU DON'T SUCK BLOOD.
SO JULIAN CORROBORATED THAT, DID HE?
HE SAID DARK-HUNTERS, UNLIKE APOLLITES, WERE SPARED THAT PART OF APOLLO'S CURSE.
I THINK YOU AND JULIAN SPENT ENTIRELY TOO MUCH TIME TALKING LAST NIGHT.
IS IT TRUE DAIMONS ONLY LIVE TWENTY-SEVEN YEARS?
THAT'S WHY THEY'RE SO DANGEROUS. MOST APOLLITES WILL DO ANYTHING TO BUY THEMSELVES ANOTHER DAY.
SOMEONE LIKE YOU IS PRIME DAIMON BAIT. WHEN THEY TAKE YOUR SOUL, THEY TAKE ALL YOUR PSYCHIC POWERS WITH IT.
I HAVE NO POWERS.
WHATEVER LIE MAKES YOU HAPPY.
IT'S NOT A LIE. I HAVE NO ABILITIES WHATSOEVER. AT LEAST NOT UNLESS IT INVOLVES CRUNCHING NUMBERS.
...IS THAT A HOUSE FIRE?

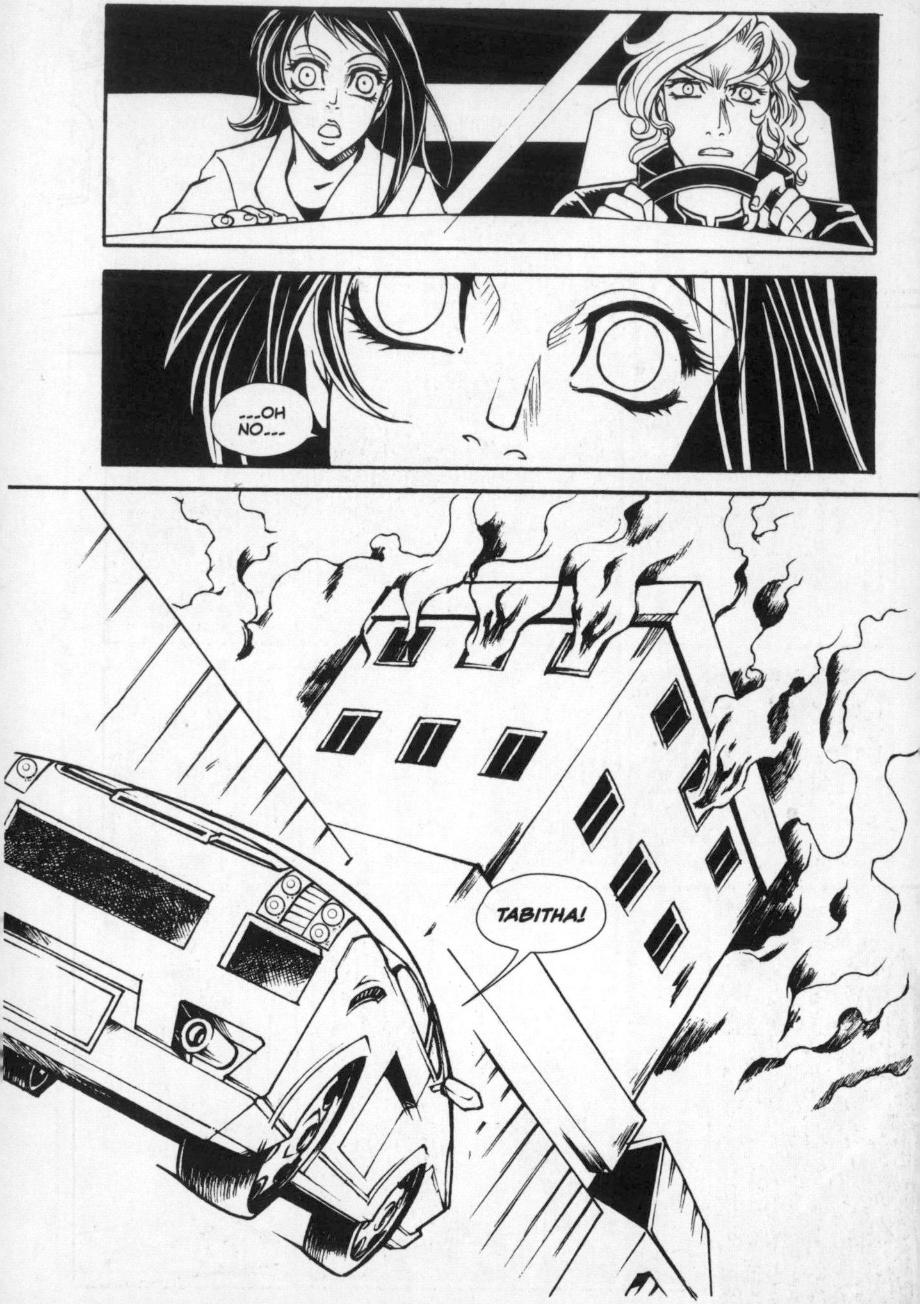
---OH NO---
TABITHA!

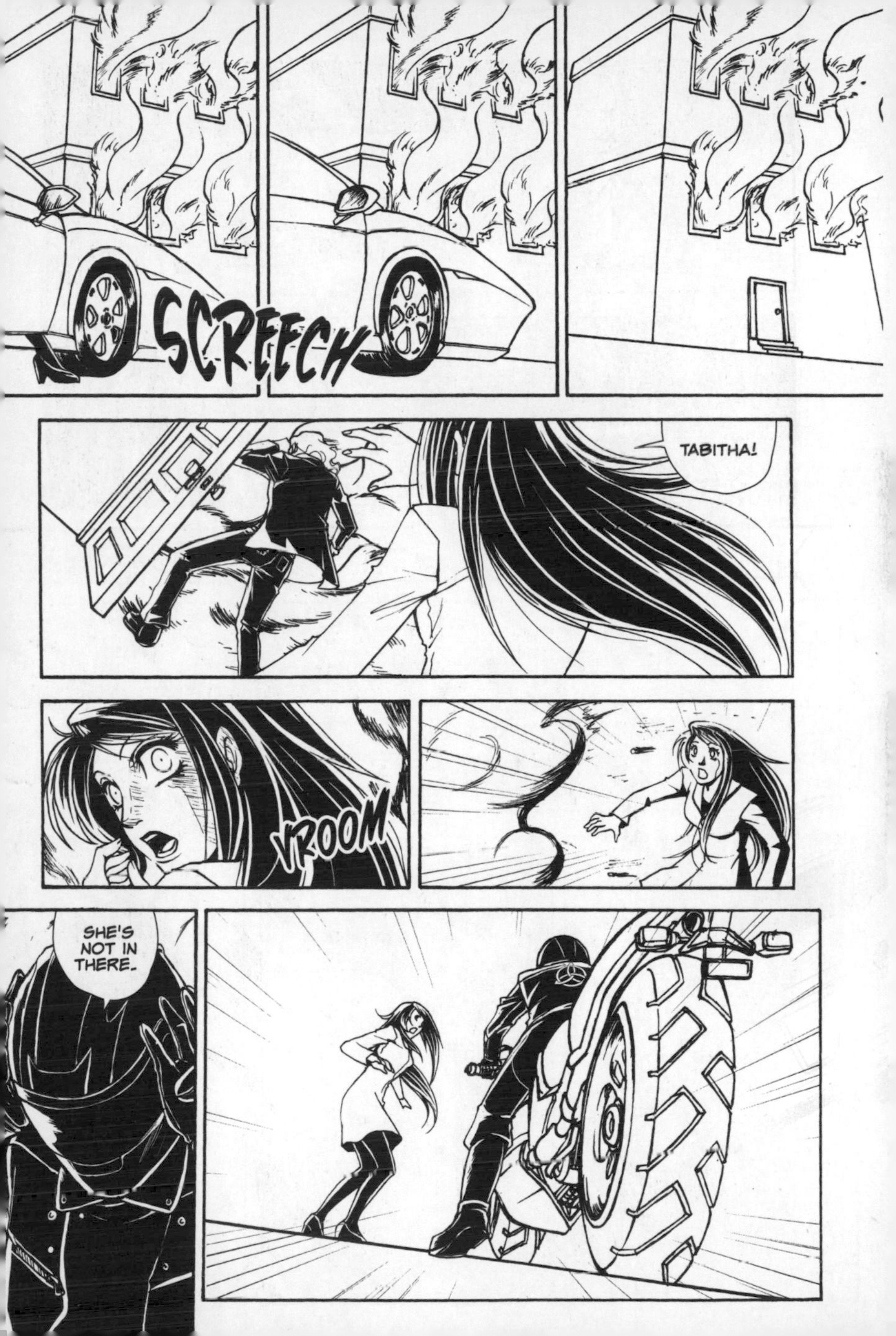
SCREECH
TABITHA!
VROOM
SHE'S NOT IN THERE.

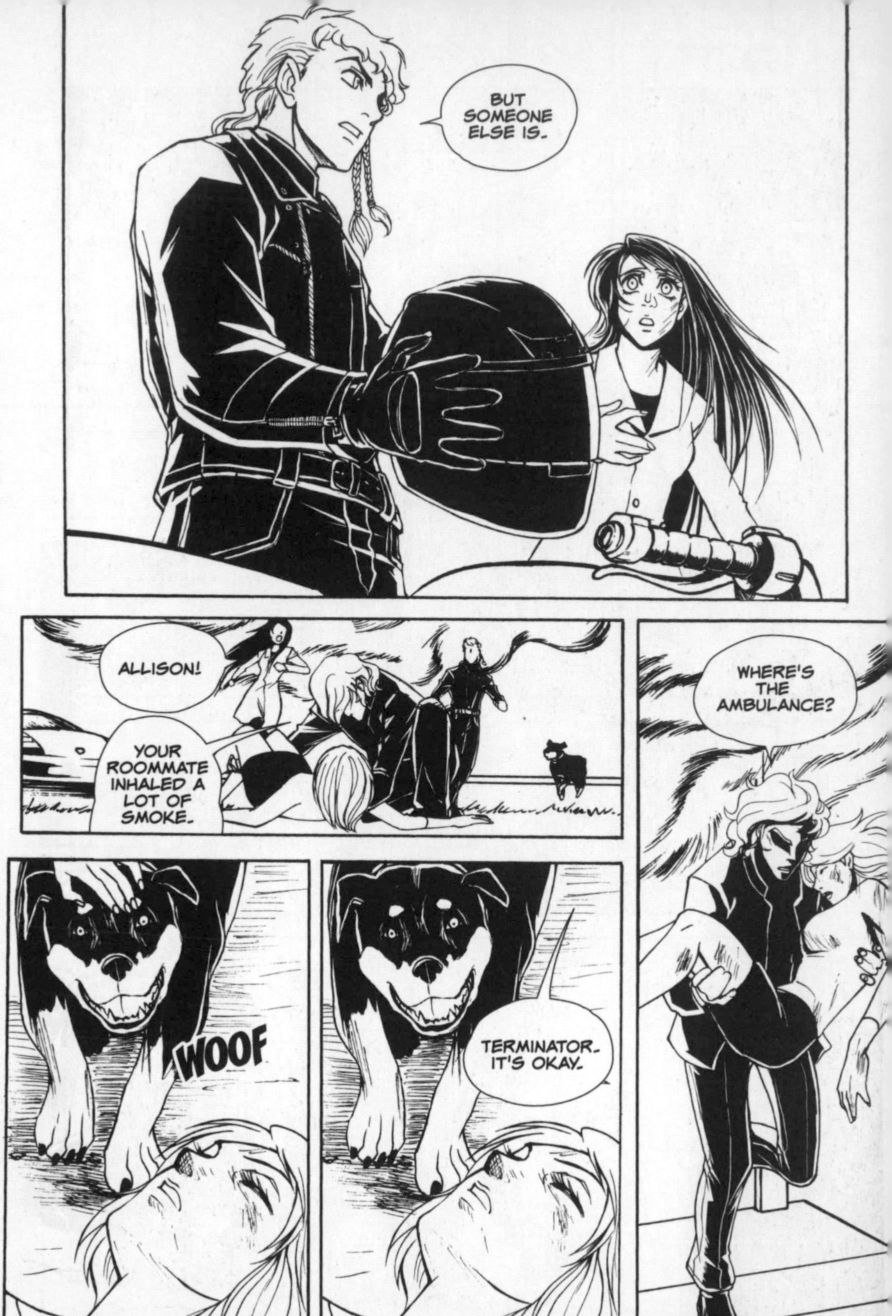
BUT SOMEONE ELSE IS.
WHERE'S THE AMBULANCE?
ALLISON!
YOUR ROOMMATE INHALED A LOT OF SMOKE.
TERMINATOR. IT'S OKAY.
WOOF

HER LUNGS ARE SINGED.

CAN YOU HELP HER, TALON?

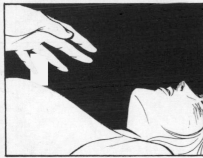

YES.

YOU'RE A DARK-HUNTER TOO?

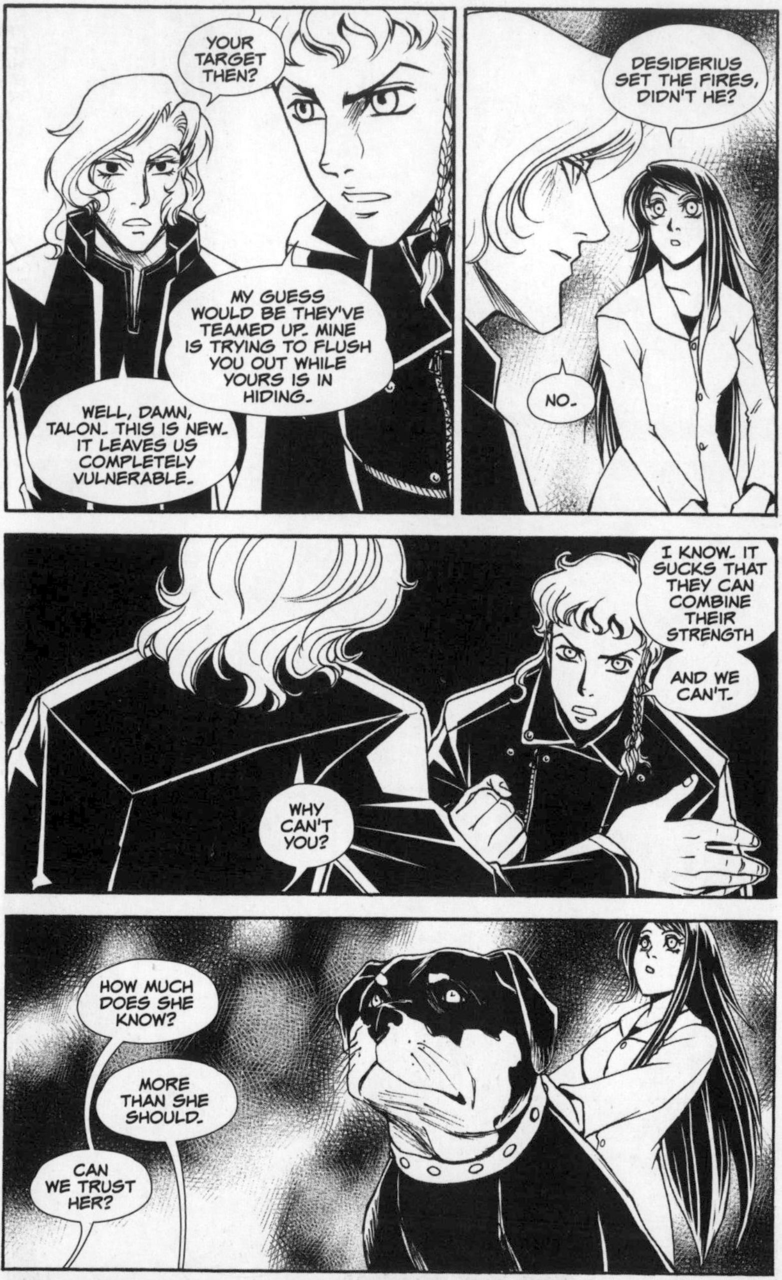
DESIDERIUS SET THE FIRES, DIDN'T HE?
NO.
YOUR TARGET THEN?
MY GUESS WOULD BE THEY'VE TEAMED UP. MINE IS TRYING TO FLUSH YOU OUT WHILE YOURS IS IN HIDING.
WELL, DAMN, TALON. THIS IS NEW. IT LEAVES US COMPLETELY VULNERABLE.
I KNOW. IT SUCKS THAT THEY CAN COMBINE THEIR STRENGTH
AND WE CAN'T.
WHY CAN'T YOU?
HOW MUCH DOES SHE KNOW?
MORE THAN SHE SHOULD.
CAN WE TRUST HER?

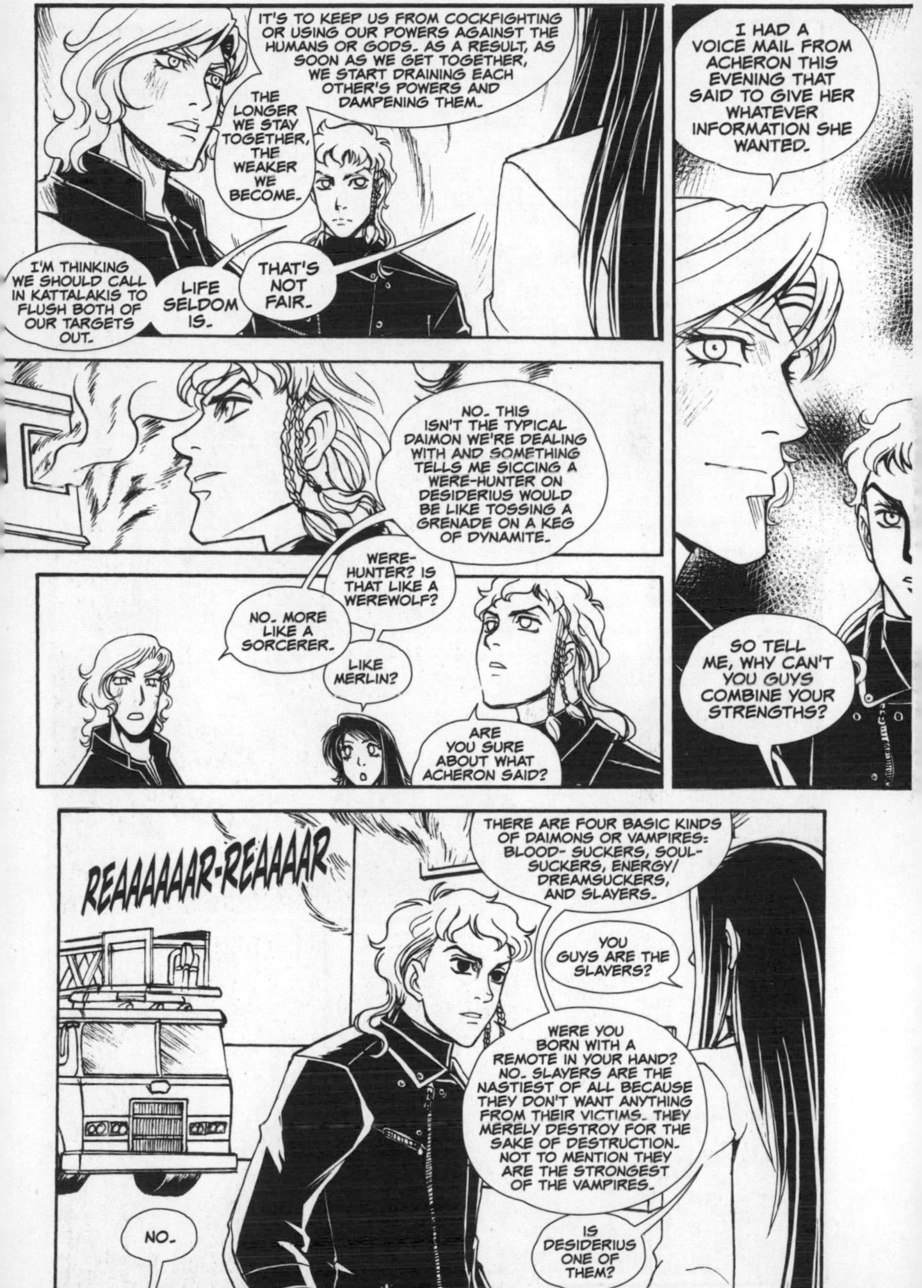
I HAD A VOICE MAIL FROM ACHERON THIS EVENING THAT SAID TO GIVE HER WHATEVER INFORMATION SHE WANTED.
SO TELL ME, WHY CAN'T YOU GUYS COMBINE YOUR STRENGTHS?
IT'S TO KEEP US FROM COCKFIGHTING OR USING OUR POWERS AGAINST THE HUMANS OR GODS. AS A RESULT, AS SOON AS WE GET TOGETHER, WE START DRAINING EACH OTHER'S POWERS AND DAMPENING THEM.
THE LONGER WE STAY TOGETHER, THE WEAKER WE BECOME.
THAT'S NOT FAIR.
LIFE SELDOM IS.
I'M THINKING WE SHOULD CALL IN KATTALAKIS TO FLUSH BOTH OF OUR TARGETS OUT.
NO. THIS ISN'T THE TYPICAL DAIMON WE'RE DEALING WITH AND SOMETHING TELLS ME SICCING A WERE-HUNTER ON DESIDERIUS WOULD BE LIKE TOSSING A GRENADE ON A KEG OF DYNAMITE.
WERE-HUNTER? IS THAT LIKE A WEREWOLF?
NO. MORE LIKE A SORCERER.
LIKE MERLIN?
ARE YOU SURE ABOUT WHAT ACHERON SAID?
THERE ARE FOUR BASIC KINDS OF DAIMONS OR VAMPIRES: BLOOD- SUCKERS, SOUL-SUCKERS, ENERGY/ DREAMSUCKERS, AND SLAYERS.
REAAAAAAR-REAAAAR
YOU GUYS ARE THE SLAYERS?
WERE YOU BORN WITH A REMOTE IN YOUR HAND? NO. SLAYERS ARE THE NASTIEST OF ALL BECAUSE THEY DON'T WANT ANYTHING FROM THEIR VICTIMS. THEY MERELY DESTROY FOR THE SAKE OF DESTRUCTION. NOT TO MENTION THEY ARE THE STRONGEST OF THE VAMPIRES.
IS DESIDERIUS ONE OF THEM?
NO.

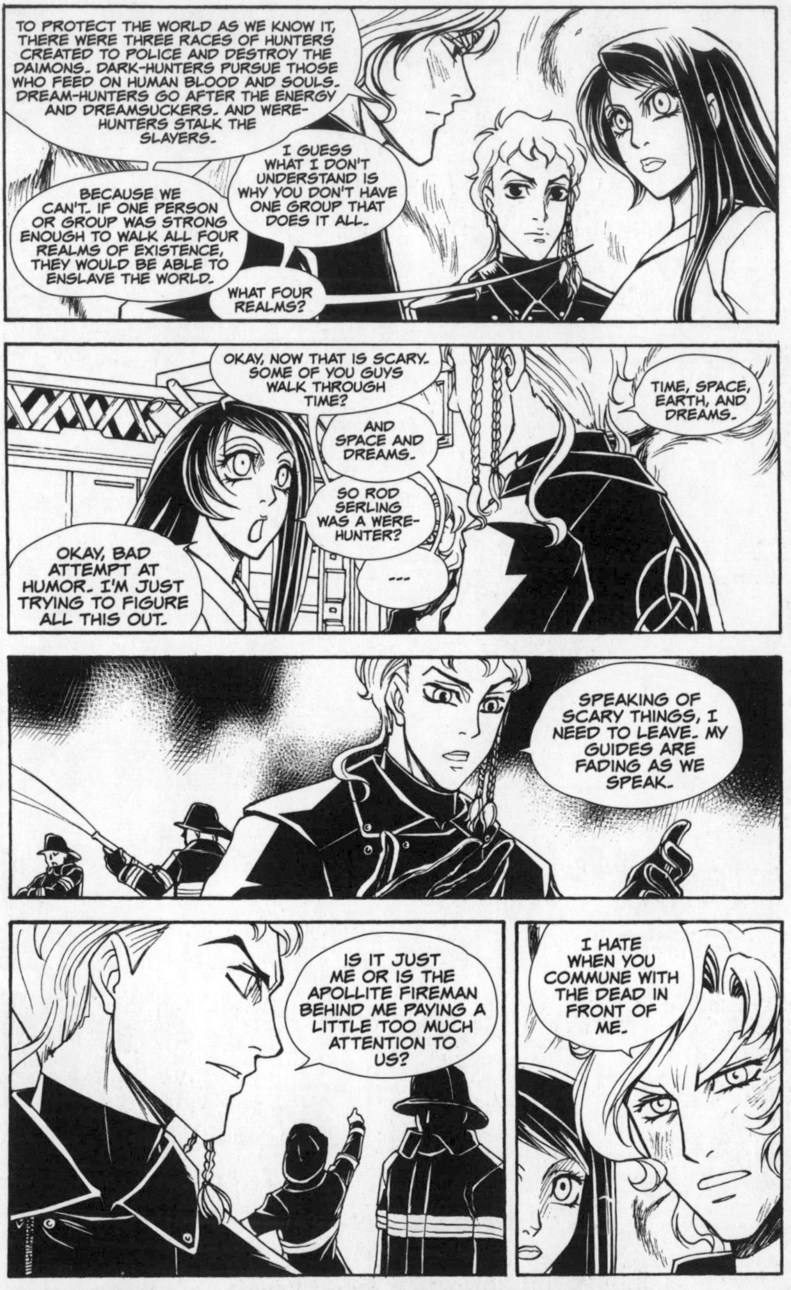
TO PROTECT THE WORLD AS WE KNOW IT, THERE WERE THREE RACES OF HUNTERS CREATED TO POLICE AND DESTROY THE DAIMONS. DARK-HUNTERS PURSUE THOSE WHO FEED ON HUMAN BLOOD AND SOULS. DREAM-HUNTERS GO AFTER THE ENERGY AND DREAMSUCKERS. AND WERE-HUNTERS STALK THE SLAYERS.
I GUESS WHAT I DON'T UNDERSTAND IS WHY YOU DON'T HAVE ONE GROUP THAT DOES IT ALL.
BECAUSE WE CAN'T. IF ONE PERSON OR GROUP WAS STRONG ENOUGH TO WALK ALL FOUR REALMS OF EXISTENCE, THEY WOULD BE ABLE TO ENSLAVE THE WORLD.
WHAT FOUR REALMS?
TIME, SPACE, EARTH, AND DREAMS.
OKAY, NOW THAT IS SCARY. SOME OF YOU GUYS WALK THROUGH TIME?
AND SPACE AND DREAMS.
SO ROD SERLING WAS A WERE-HUNTER?
...
OKAY, BAD ATTEMPT AT HUMOR. I'M JUST TRYING TO FIGURE ALL THIS OUT.
SPEAKING OF SCARY THINGS, I NEED TO LEAVE. MY GUIDES ARE FADING AS WE SPEAK.
I HATE WHEN YOU COMMUNE WITH THE DEAD IN FRONT OF ME.
IS IT JUST ME OR IS THE APOLLITE FIREMAN BEHIND ME PAYING A LITTLE TOO MUCH ATTENTION TO US?

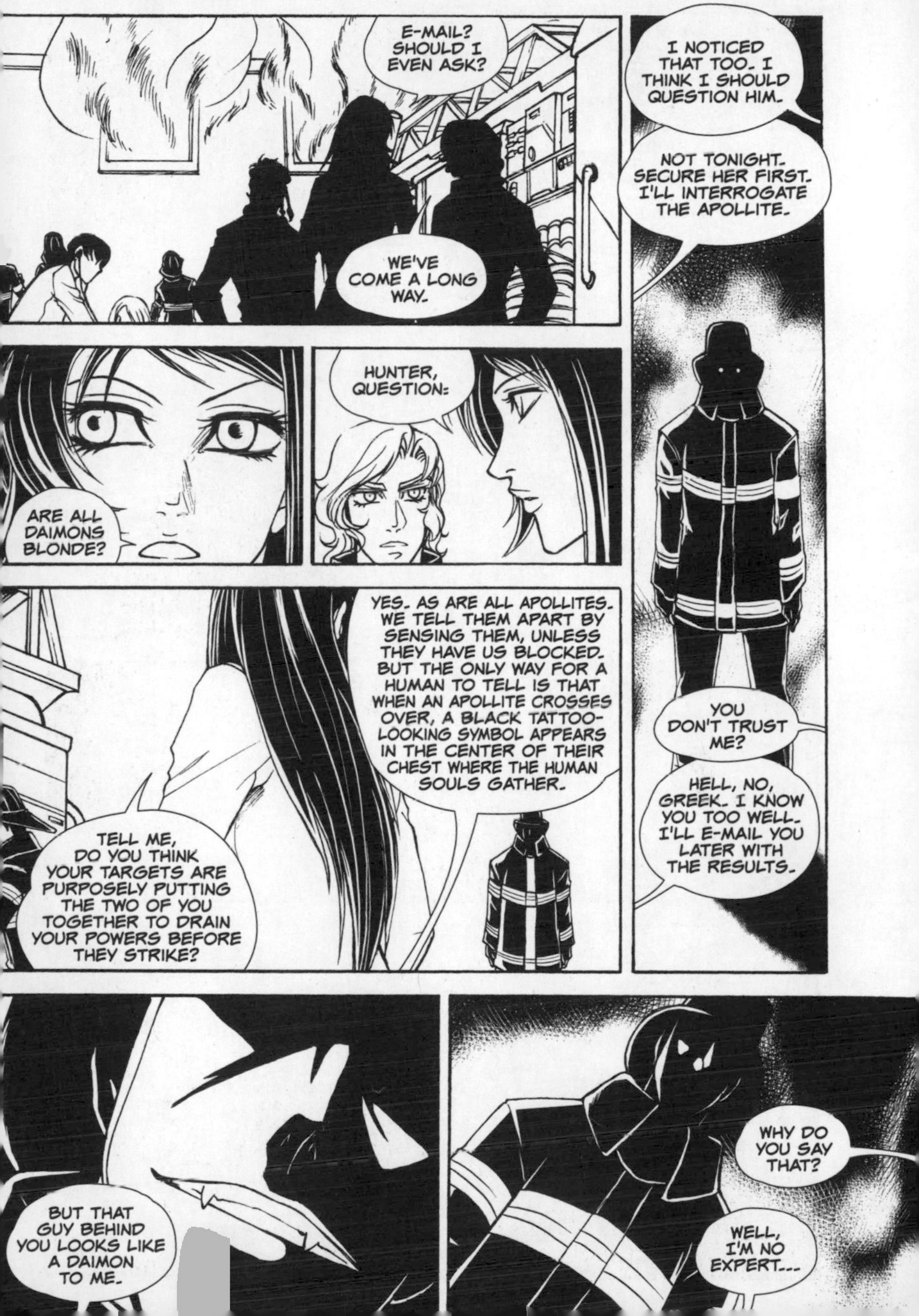
I NOTICED THAT TOO. I THINK I SHOULD QUESTION HIM.
NOT TONIGHT. SECURE HER FIRST. I'LL INTERROGATE THE APOLLITE.
YOU DON'T TRUST ME?
HELL, NO, GREEK. I KNOW YOU TOO WELL. I'LL E-MAIL YOU LATER WITH THE RESULTS.
E-MAIL? SHOULD I EVEN ASK?
WE'VE COME A LONG WAY.
HUNTER, QUESTION:
ARE ALL DAIMONS BLONDE?
YES. AS ARE ALL APOLLITES. WE TELL THEM APART BY SENSING THEM, UNLESS THEY HAVE US BLOCKED. BUT THE ONLY WAY FOR A HUMAN TO TELL IS THAT WHEN AN APOLLITE CROSSES OVER, A BLACK TATTOO-LOOKING SYMBOL APPEARS IN THE CENTER OF THEIR CHEST WHERE THE HUMAN SOULS GATHER.
TELL ME, DO YOU THINK YOUR TARGETS ARE PURPOSELY PUTTING THE TWO OF YOU TOGETHER TO DRAIN YOUR POWERS BEFORE THEY STRIKE?
WHY DO YOU SAY THAT?
WELL, I'M NO EXPERT...
BUT THAT GUY BEHIND YOU LOOKS LIKE A DAIMON TO ME.

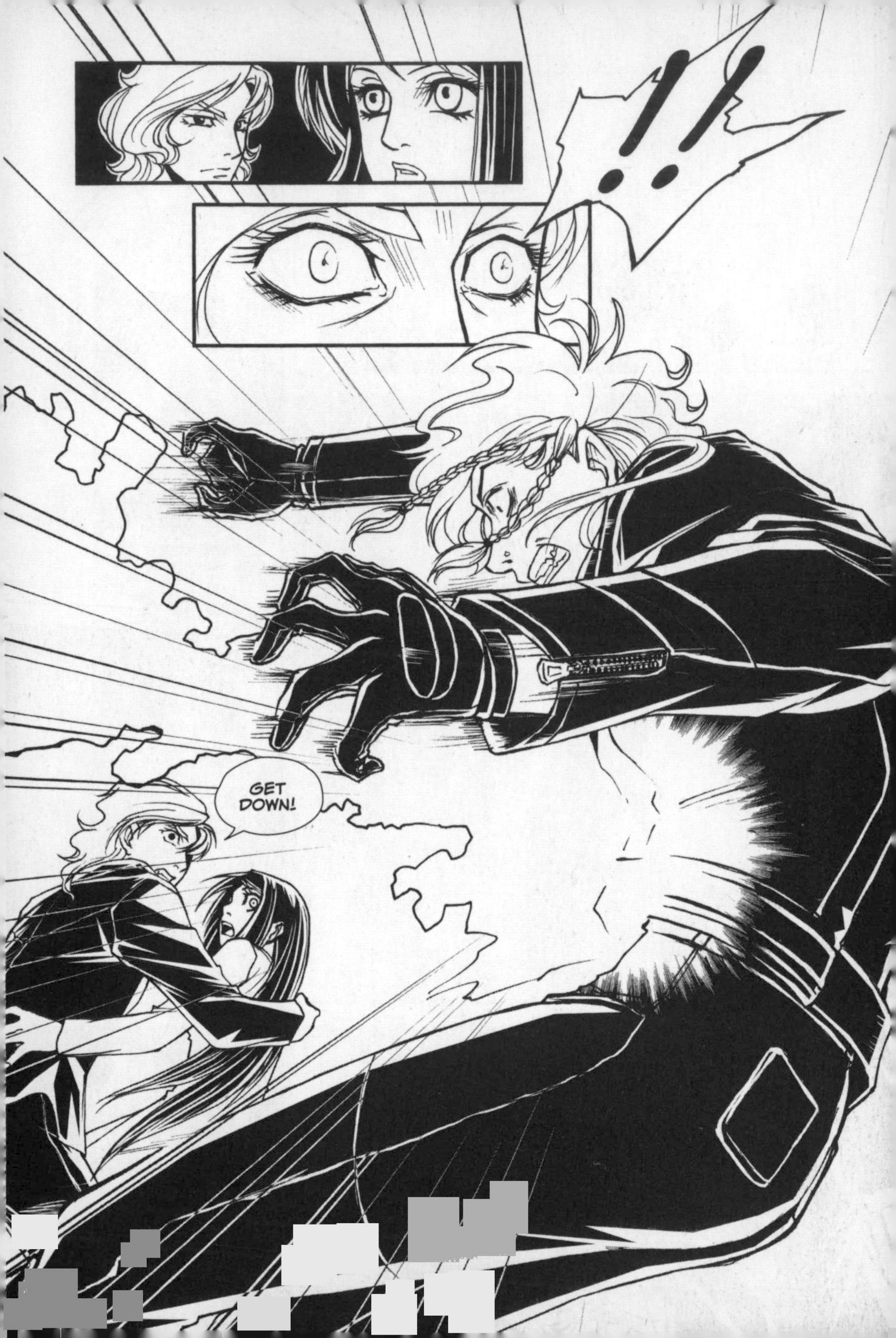
!!
GET DOWN!

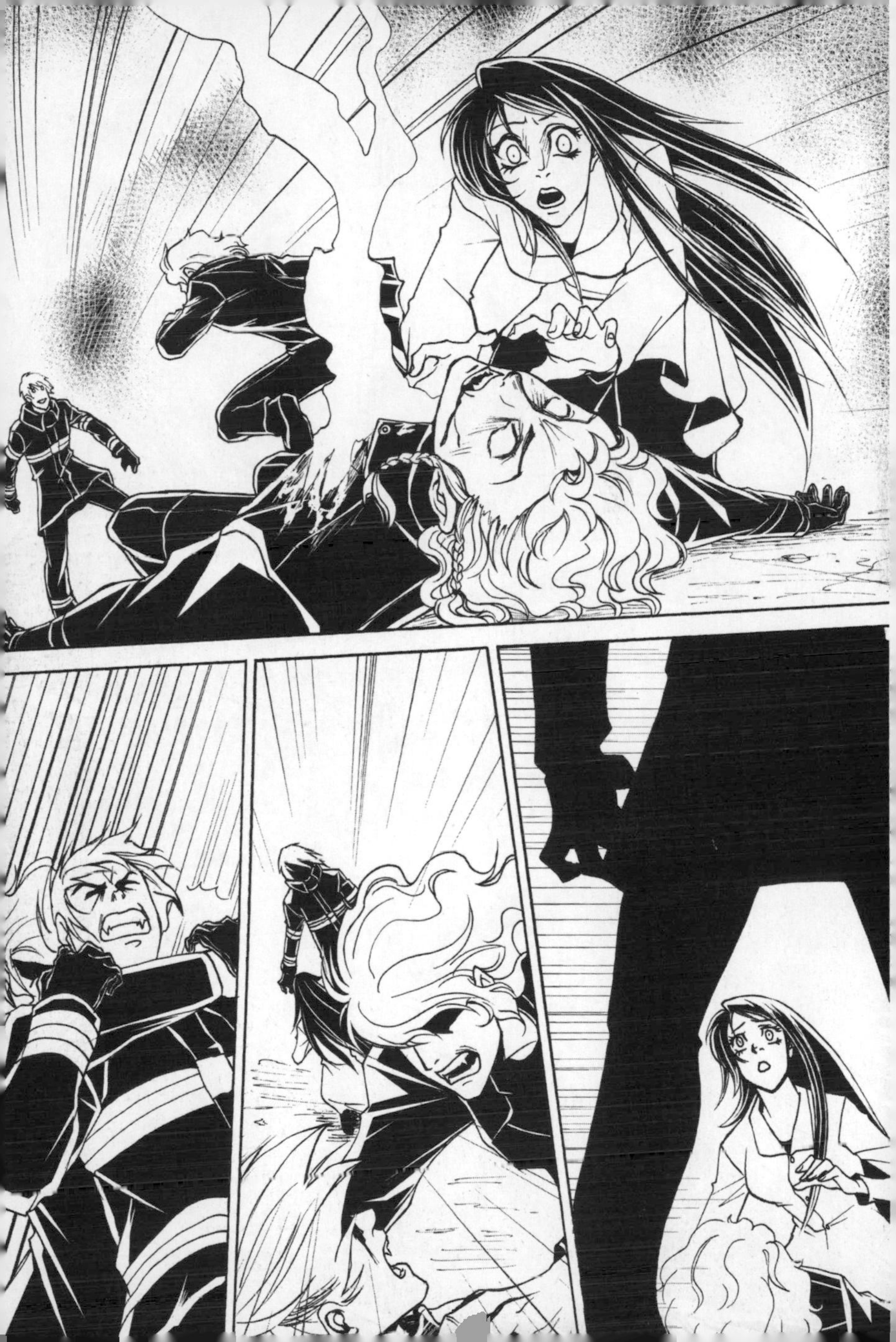

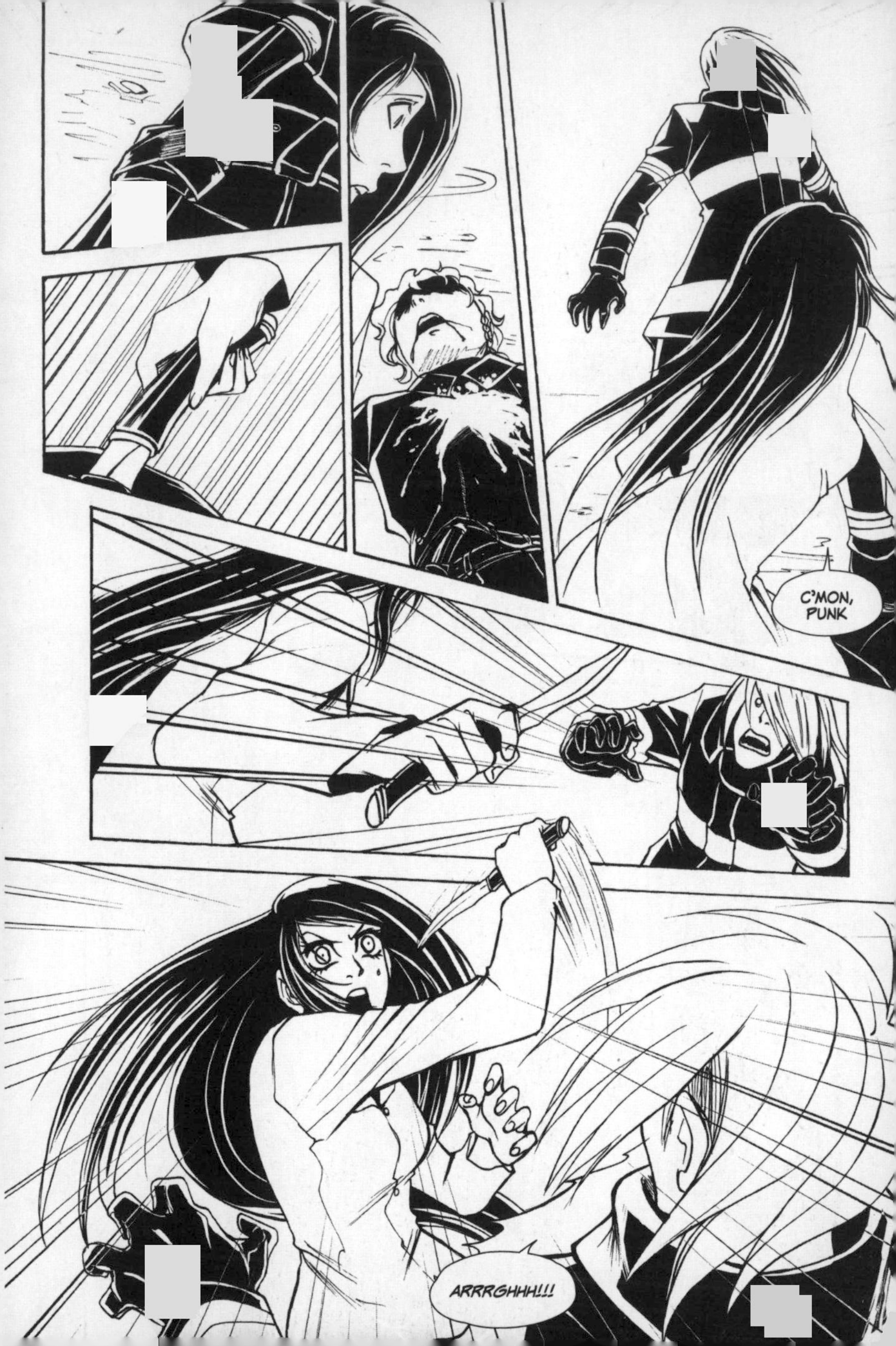
C'MON, PUNK
ARRRGHHH!!!

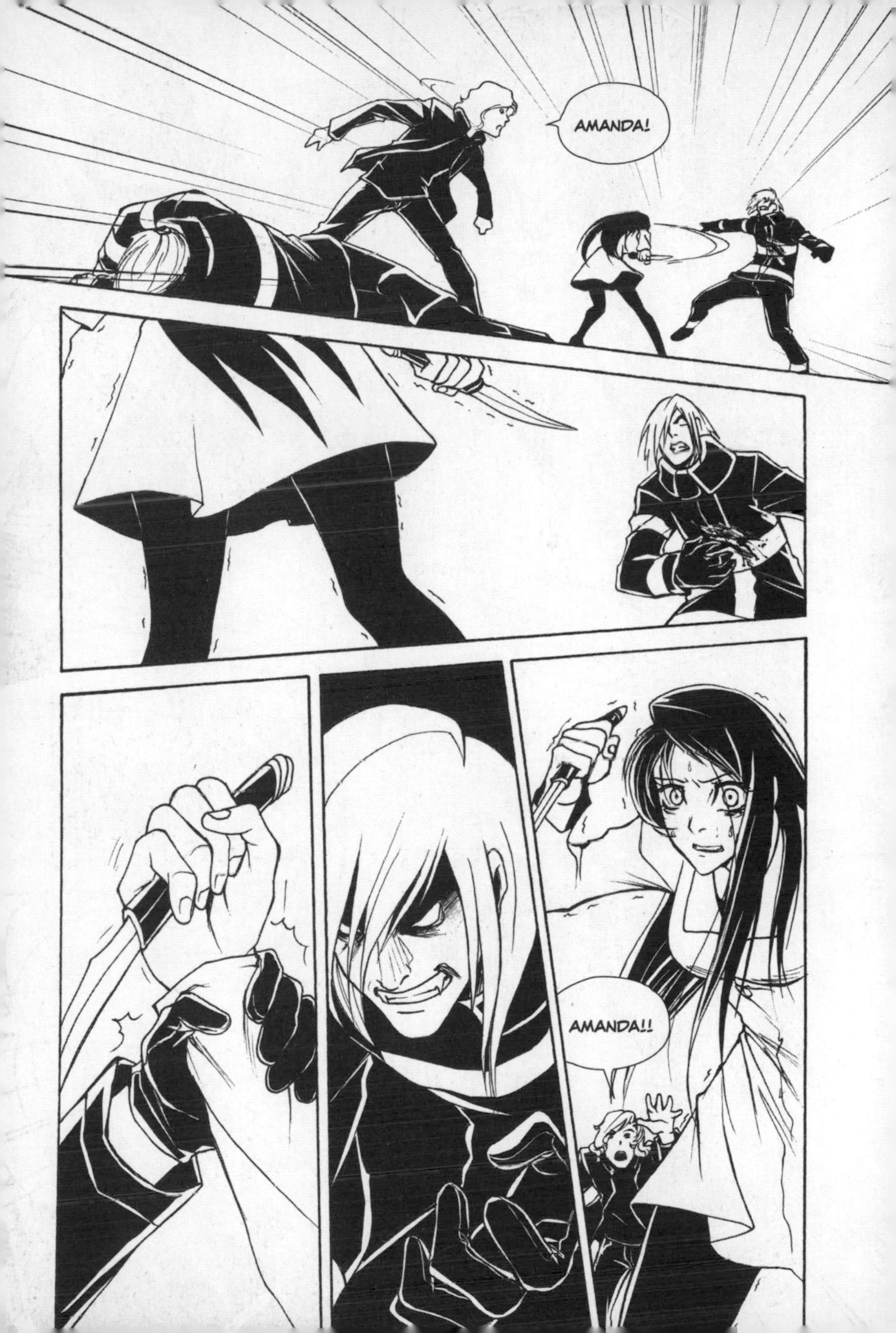
AMANDA!
AMANDA!!

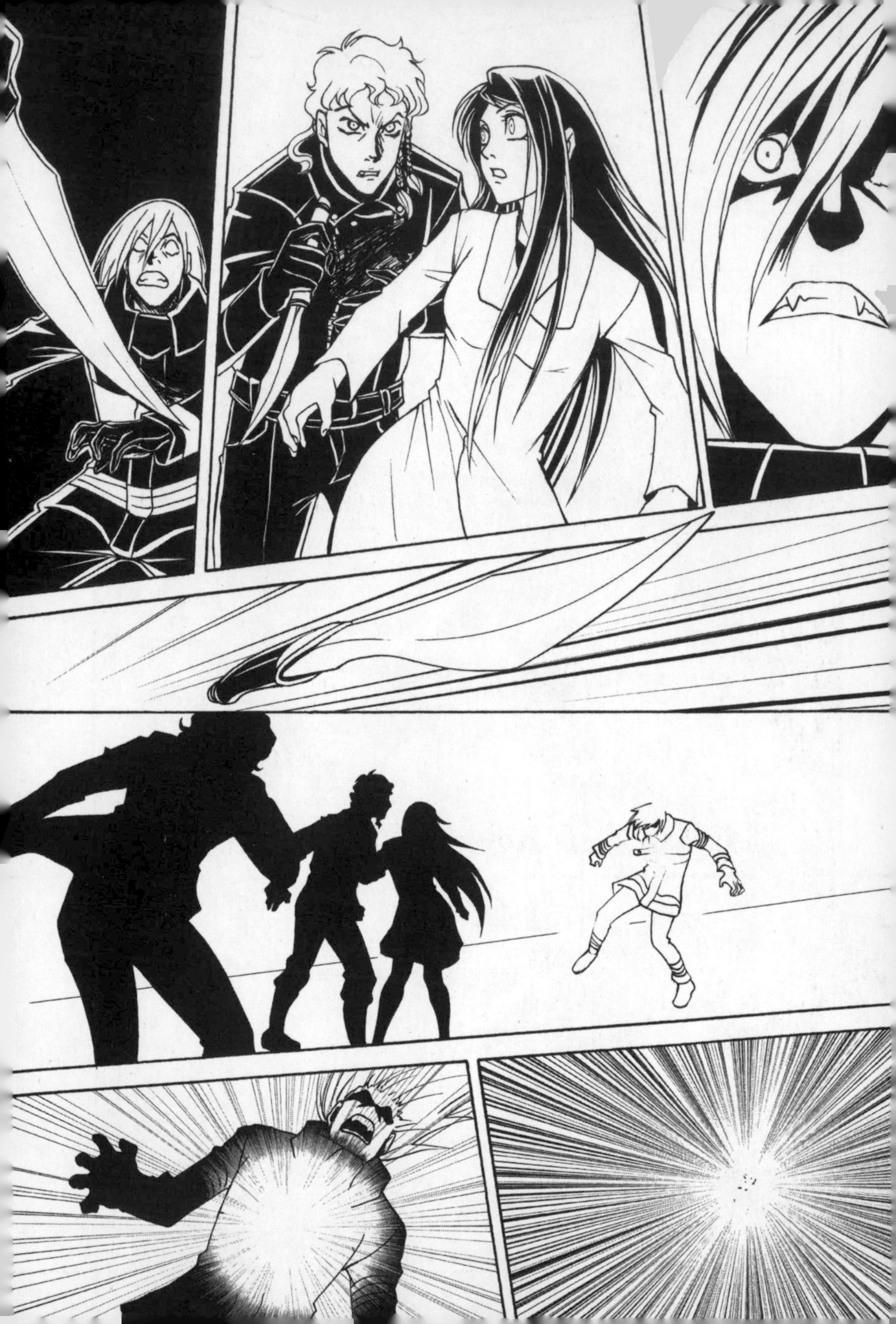

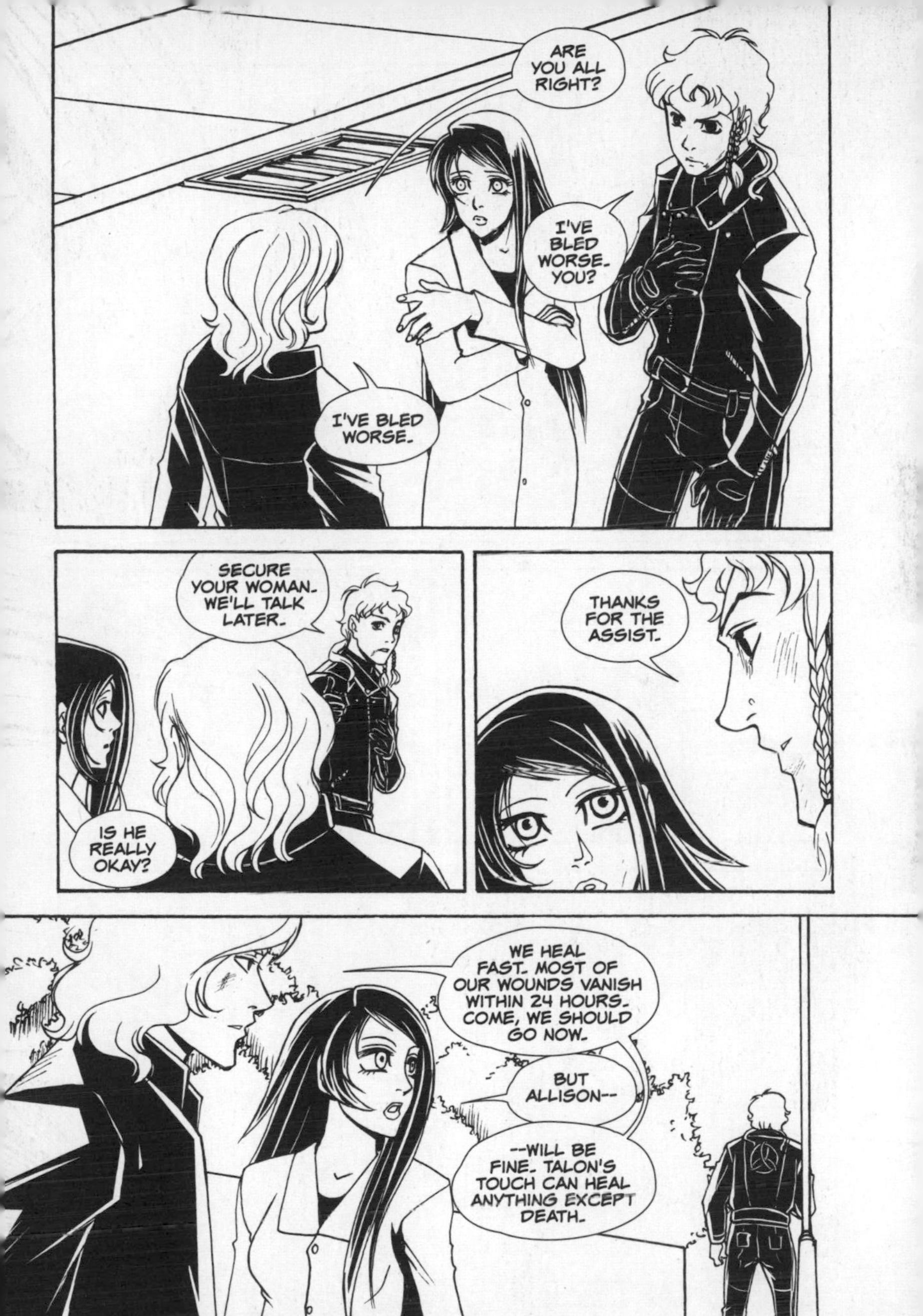
ARE YOU ALL RIGHT?
I'VE BLED WORSE. YOU?
I'VE BLED WORSE.
THANKS FOR THE ASSIST.
SECURE YOUR WOMAN. WE'LL TALK LATER.
IS HE REALLY OKAY?
WE HEAL FAST. MOST OF OUR WOUNDS VANISH WITHIN 24 HOURS. COME, WE SHOULD GO NOW.
BUT ALLISON--
--WILL BE FINE. TALON'S TOUCH CAN HEAL ANYTHING EXCEPT DEATH.

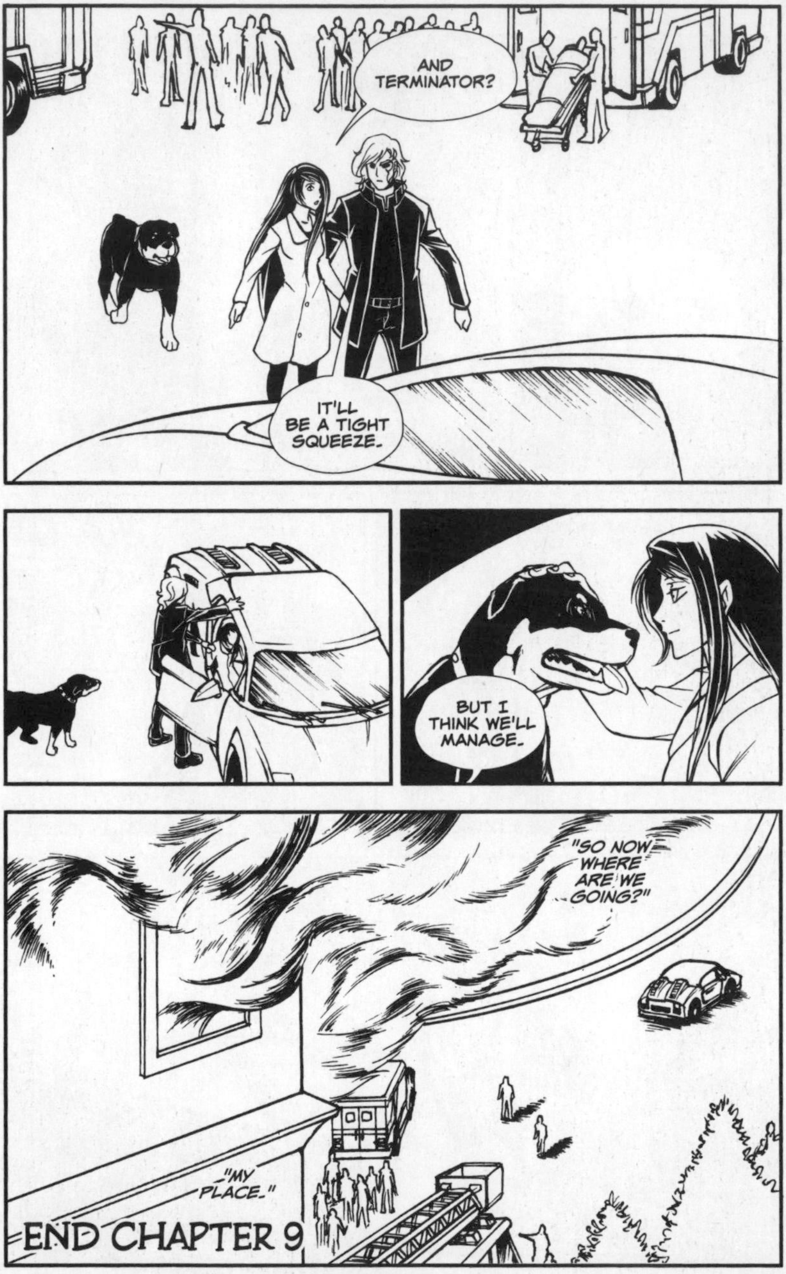
AND TERMINATOR?
IT'LL BE A TIGHT SQUEEZE.
BUT I THINK WE'LL MANAGE.
"SO NOW WHERE ARE WE GOING?"
"MY PLACE."
END CHAPTER 9

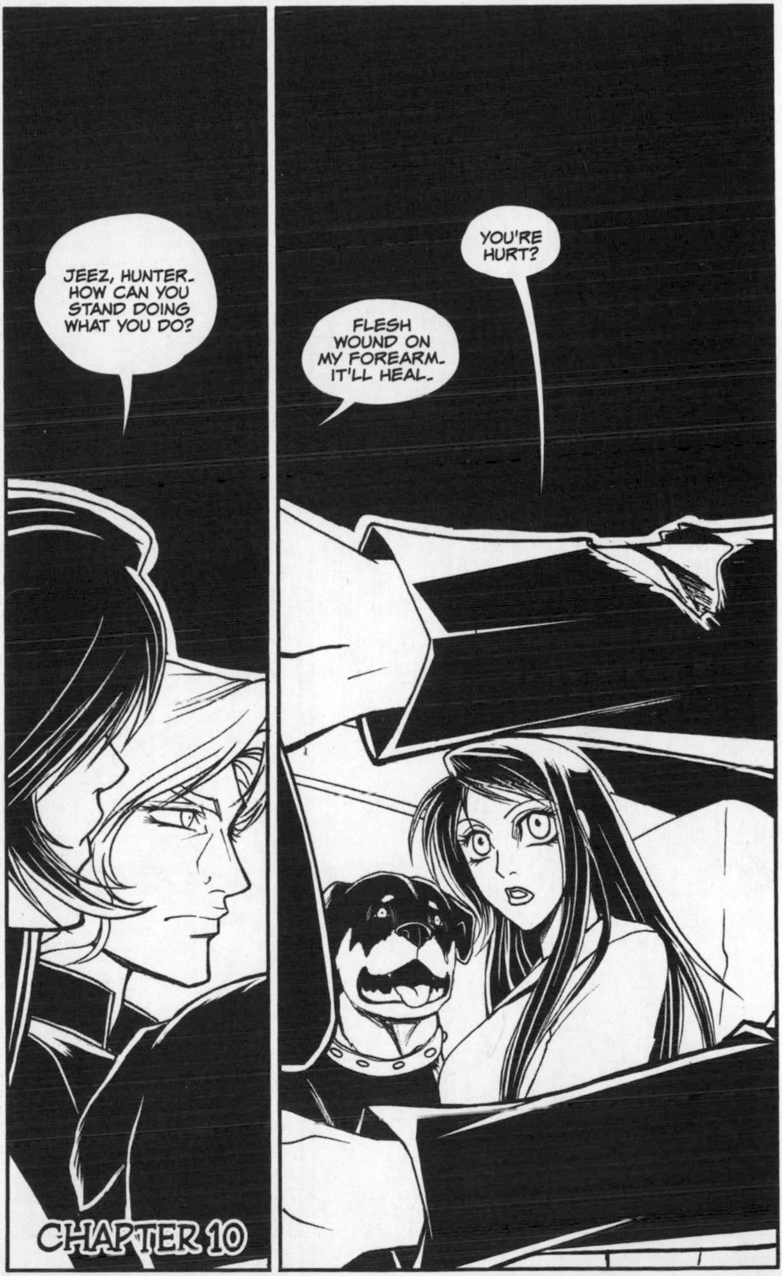
YOU'RE HURT?
FLESH WOUND ON MY FOREARM. IT'LL HEAL.
JEEZ, HUNTER. HOW CAN YOU STAND DOING WHAT YOU DO?
CHAPTER 10

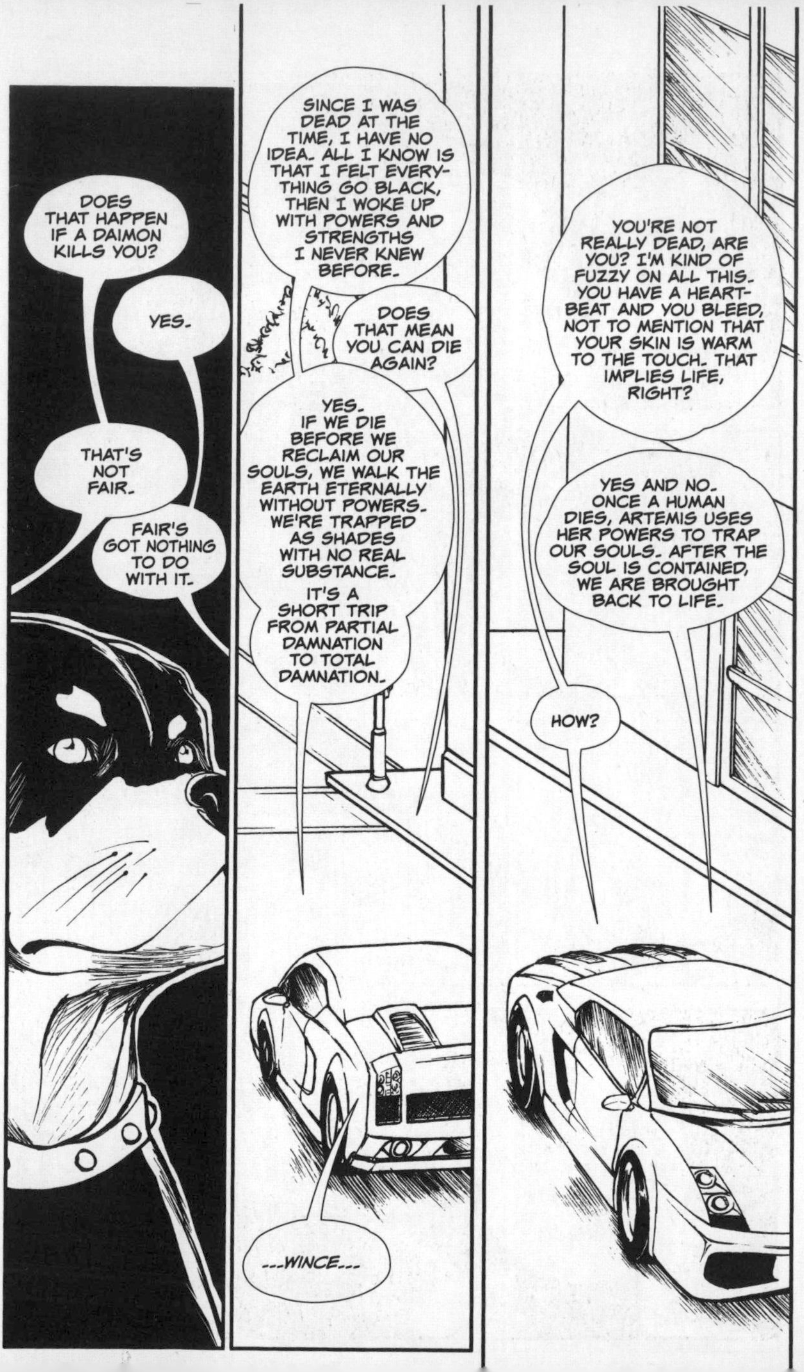
YOU'RE NOT REALLY DEAD, ARE YOU? I'M KIND OF FUZZY ON ALL THIS. YOU HAVE A HEART-BEAT AND YOU BLEED, NOT TO MENTION THAT YOUR SKIN IS WARM TO THE TOUCH. THAT IMPLIES LIFE, RIGHT?
YES AND NO. ONCE A HUMAN DIES, ARTEMIS USES HER POWERS TO TRAP OUR SOULS. AFTER THE SOUL IS CONTAINED, WE ARE BROUGHT BACK TO LIFE.
HOW?
SINCE I WAS DEAD AT THE TIME, I HAVE NO IDEA. ALL I KNOW IS THAT I FELT EVERY-THING GO BLACK, THEN I WOKE UP WITH POWERS AND STRENGTHS I NEVER KNEW BEFORE.
DOES THAT MEAN YOU CAN DIE AGAIN?
YES. IF WE DIE BEFORE WE RECLAIM OUR SOULS, WE WALK THE EARTH ETERNALLY WITHOUT POWERS. WE'RE TRAPPED AS SHADES WITH NO REAL SUBSTANCE.
IT'S A SHORT TRIP FROM PARTIAL DAMNATION TO TOTAL DAMNATION.
...WINCE...
DOES THAT HAPPEN IF A DAIMON KILLS YOU?
YES.
THAT'S NOT FAIR.
FAIR'S GOT NOTHING TO DO WITH IT.

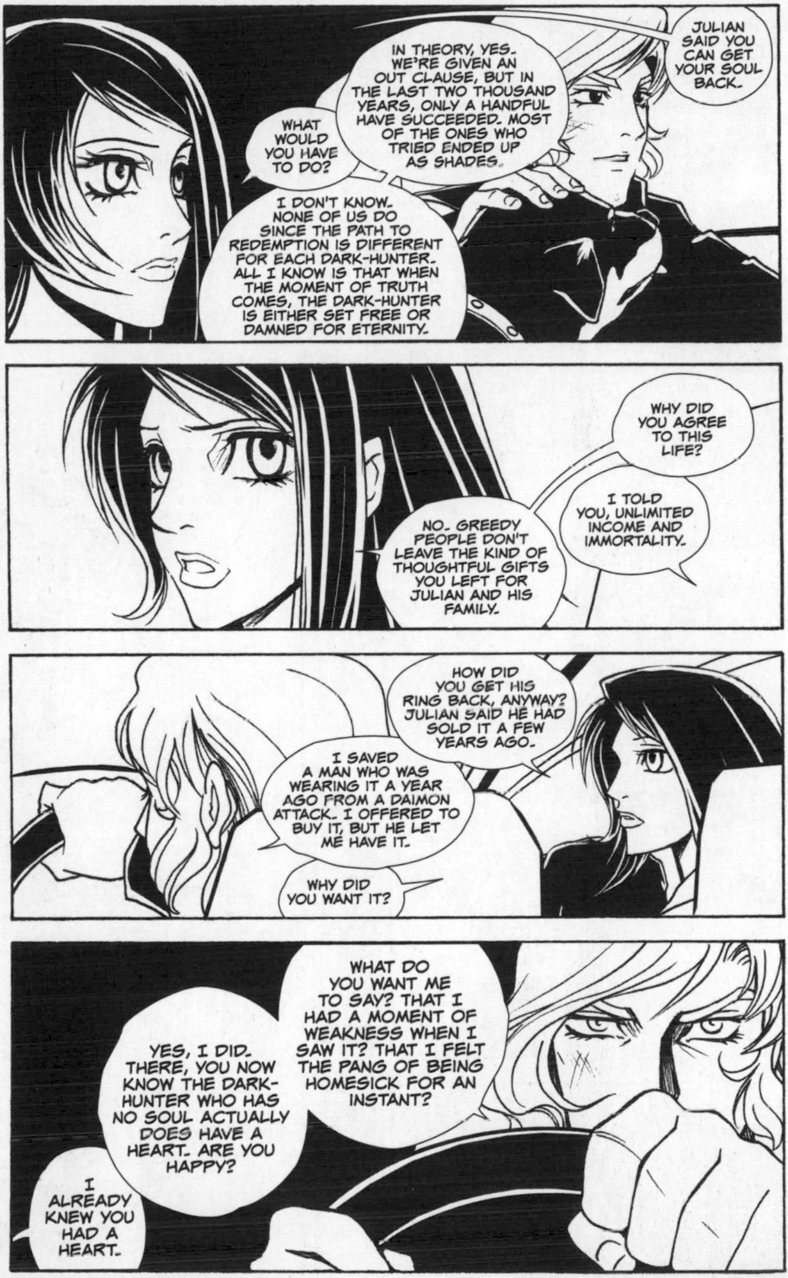
JULIAN SAID YOU CAN GET YOUR SOUL BACK.
IN THEORY, YES. WE'RE GIVEN AN OUT CLAUSE, BUT IN THE LAST TWO THOUSAND YEARS, ONLY A HANDFUL HAVE SUCCEEDED. MOST OF THE ONES WHO TRIED ENDED UP AS SHADES.
WHAT WOULD YOU HAVE TO DO?
I DON'T KNOW. NONE OF US DO SINCE THE PATH TO REDEMPTION IS DIFFERENT FOR EACH DARK-HUNTER. ALL I KNOW IS THAT WHEN THE MOMENT OF TRUTH COMES, THE DARK-HUNTER IS EITHER SET FREE OR DAMNED FOR ETERNITY.
WHY DID YOU AGREE TO THIS LIFE?
I TOLD YOU, UNLIMITED INCOME AND IMMORTALITY.
NO. GREEDY PEOPLE DON'T LEAVE THE KIND OF THOUGHTFUL GIFTS YOU LEFT FOR JULIAN AND HIS FAMILY.
HOW DID YOU GET HIS RING BACK, ANYWAY? JULIAN SAID HE HAD SOLD IT A FEW YEARS AGO.
I SAVED A MAN WHO WAS WEARING IT A YEAR AGO FROM A DAIMON ATTACK. I OFFERED TO BUY IT, BUT HE LET ME HAVE IT.
WHY DID YOU WANT IT?
WHAT DO YOU WANT ME TO SAY? THAT I HAD A MOMENT OF WEAKNESS WHEN I SAW IT? THAT I FELT THE PANG OF BEING HOMESICK FOR AN INSTANT?
YES, I DID. THERE, YOU NOW KNOW THE DARK-HUNTER WHO HAS NO SOUL ACTUALLY DOES HAVE A HEART. ARE YOU HAPPY?
I ALREADY KNEW YOU HAD A HEART.

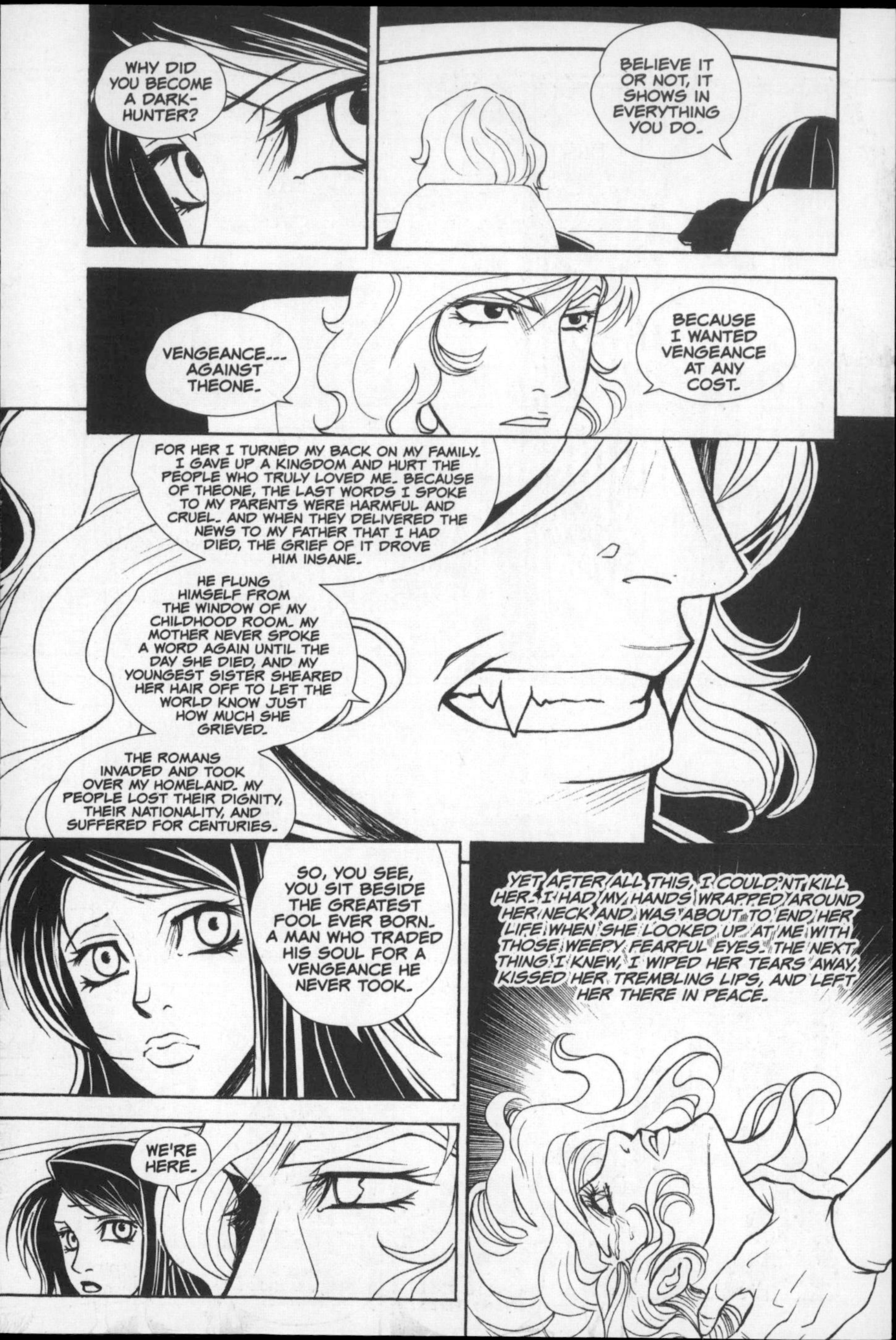
BELIEVE IT OR NOT, IT SHOWS IN EVERYTHING YOU DO.
WHY DID YOU BECOME A DARK-HUNTER?
BECAUSE I WANTED VENGEANCE AT ANY COST.
VENGEANCE... AGAINST THEONE.
FOR HER I TURNED MY BACK ON MY FAMILY. I GAVE UP A KINGDOM AND HURT THE PEOPLE WHO TRULY LOVED ME. BECAUSE OF THEONE, THE LAST WORDS I SPOKE TO MY PARENTS WERE HARMFUL AND CRUEL. AND WHEN THEY DELIVERED THE NEWS TO MY FATHER THAT I HAD DIED, THE GRIEF OF IT DROVE HIM INSANE.
HE FLUNG HIMSELF FROM THE WINDOW OF MY CHILDHOOD ROOM. MY MOTHER NEVER SPOKE A WORD AGAIN UNTIL THE DAY SHE DIED, AND MY YOUNGEST SISTER SHEARED HER HAIR OFF TO LET THE WORLD KNOW JUST HOW MUCH SHE GRIEVED.
THE ROMANS INVADED AND TOOK OVER MY HOMELAND. MY PEOPLE LOST THEIR DIGNITY, THEIR NATIONALITY, AND SUFFERED FOR CENTURIES.
YET AFTER ALL THIS, I COULD'NT KILL HER. I HAD MY HANDS WRAPPED AROUND HER NECK AND WAS ABOUT TO END HER LIFE WHEN SHE LOOKED UP AT ME WITH THOSE WEEPY FEARFUL EYES. THE NEXT THING I KNEW, I WIPED HER TEARS AWAY, KISSED HER TREMBLING LIPS, AND LEFT HER THERE IN PEACE.
SO, YOU SEE, YOU SIT BESIDE THE GREATEST FOOL EVER BORN. A MAN WHO TRADED HIS SOUL FOR A VENGEANCE HE NEVER TOOK.
WE'RE HERE.

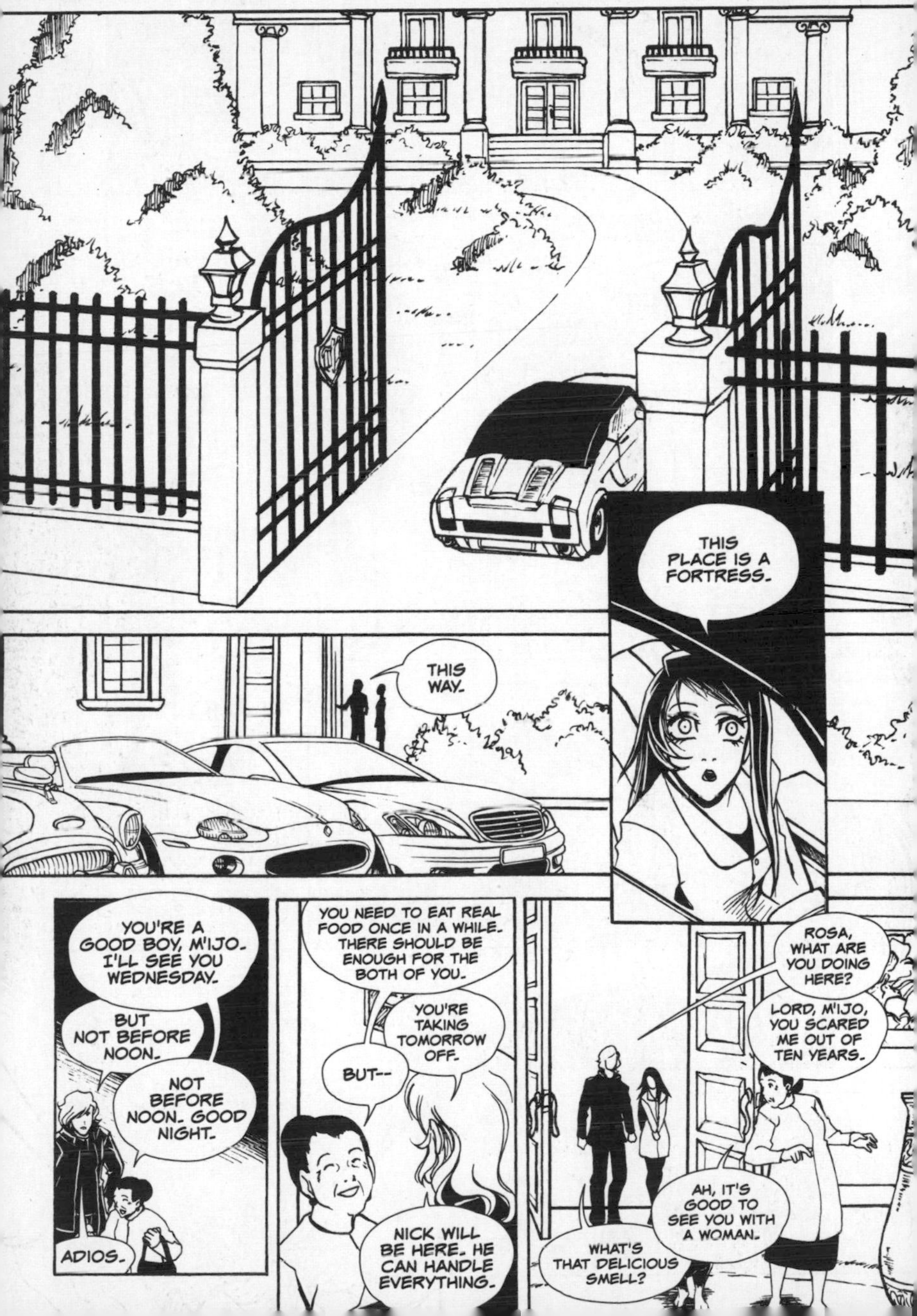
THIS PLACE IS A FORTRESS.
THIS WAY.
ROSA, WHAT ARE YOU DOING HERE?
LORD, M'IJO, YOU SCARED ME OUT OF TEN YEARS.
AH, IT'S GOOD TO SEE YOU WITH A WOMAN.
WHAT'S THAT DELICIOUS SMELL?
YOU NEED TO EAT REAL FOOD ONCE IN A WHILE. THERE SHOULD BE ENOUGH FOR THE BOTH OF YOU.
YOU'RE TAKING TOMORROW OFF.
BUT--
NICK WILL BE HERE. HE CAN HANDLE EVERYTHING.
YOU'RE A GOOD BOY, M'IJO. I'LL SEE YOU WEDNESDAY.
BUT NOT BEFORE NOON.
NOT BEFORE NOON. GOOD NIGHT.
ADIOS.

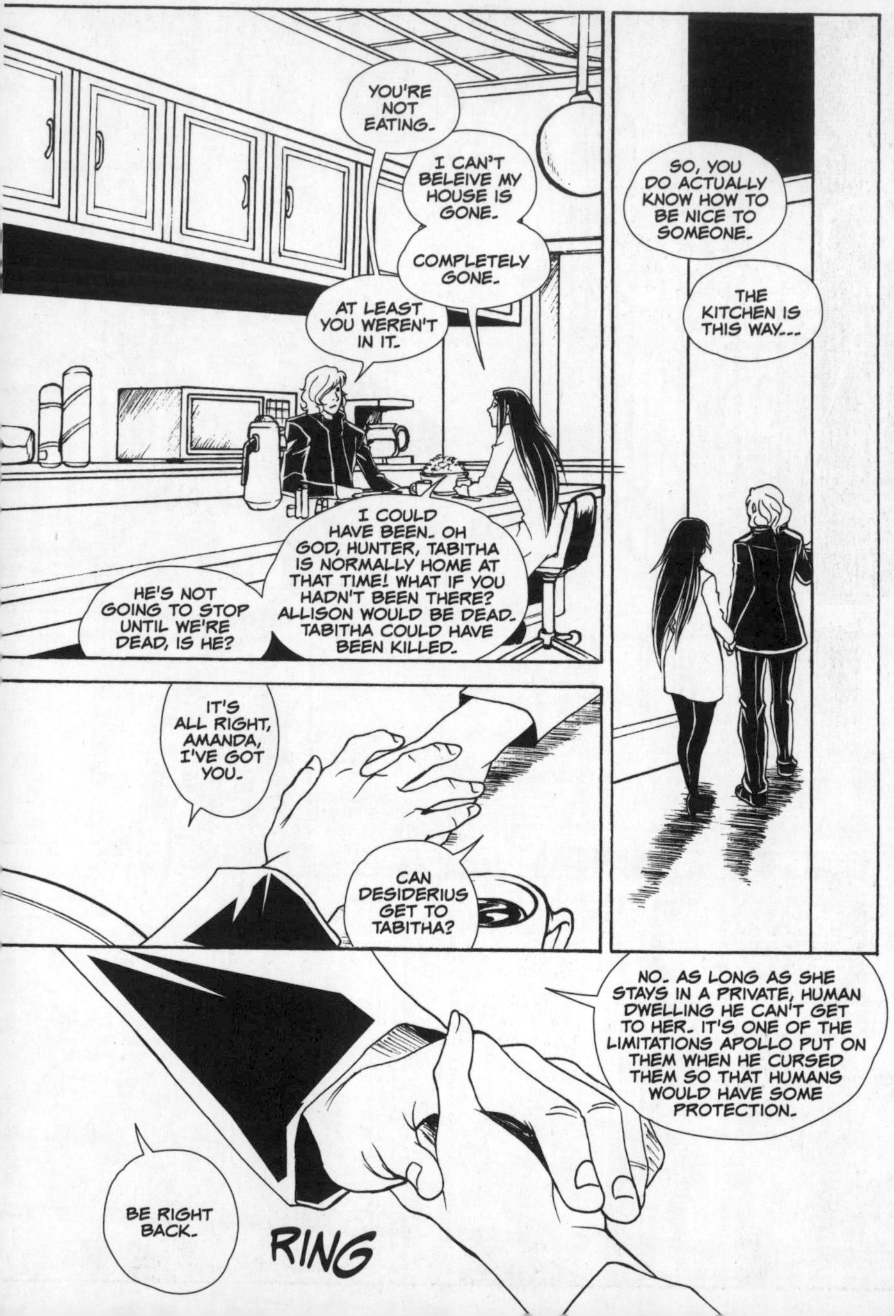
SO, YOU DO ACTUALLY KNOW HOW TO BE NICE TO SOMEONE.
THE KITCHEN IS THIS WAY...
YOU'RE NOT EATING.
I CAN'T BELEIVE MY HOUSE IS GONE.
COMPLETELY GONE.
AT LEAST YOU WEREN'T IN IT.
I COULD HAVE BEEN. OH GOD, HUNTER, TABITHA IS NORMALLY HOME AT THAT TIME! WHAT IF YOU HADN'T BEEN THERE? ALLISON WOULD BE DEAD. TABITHA COULD HAVE BEEN KILLED.
HE'S NOT GOING TO STOP UNTIL WE'RE DEAD, IS HE?
IT'S ALL RIGHT, AMANDA, I'VE GOT YOU.
CAN DESIDERIUS GET TO TABITHA?
NO. AS LONG AS SHE STAYS IN A PRIVATE, HUMAN DWELLING HE CAN'T GET TO HER. IT'S ONE OF THE LIMITATIONS APOLLO PUT ON THEM WHEN HE CURSED THEM SO THAT HUMANS WOULD HAVE SOME PROTECTION.
RING
BE RIGHT BACK.

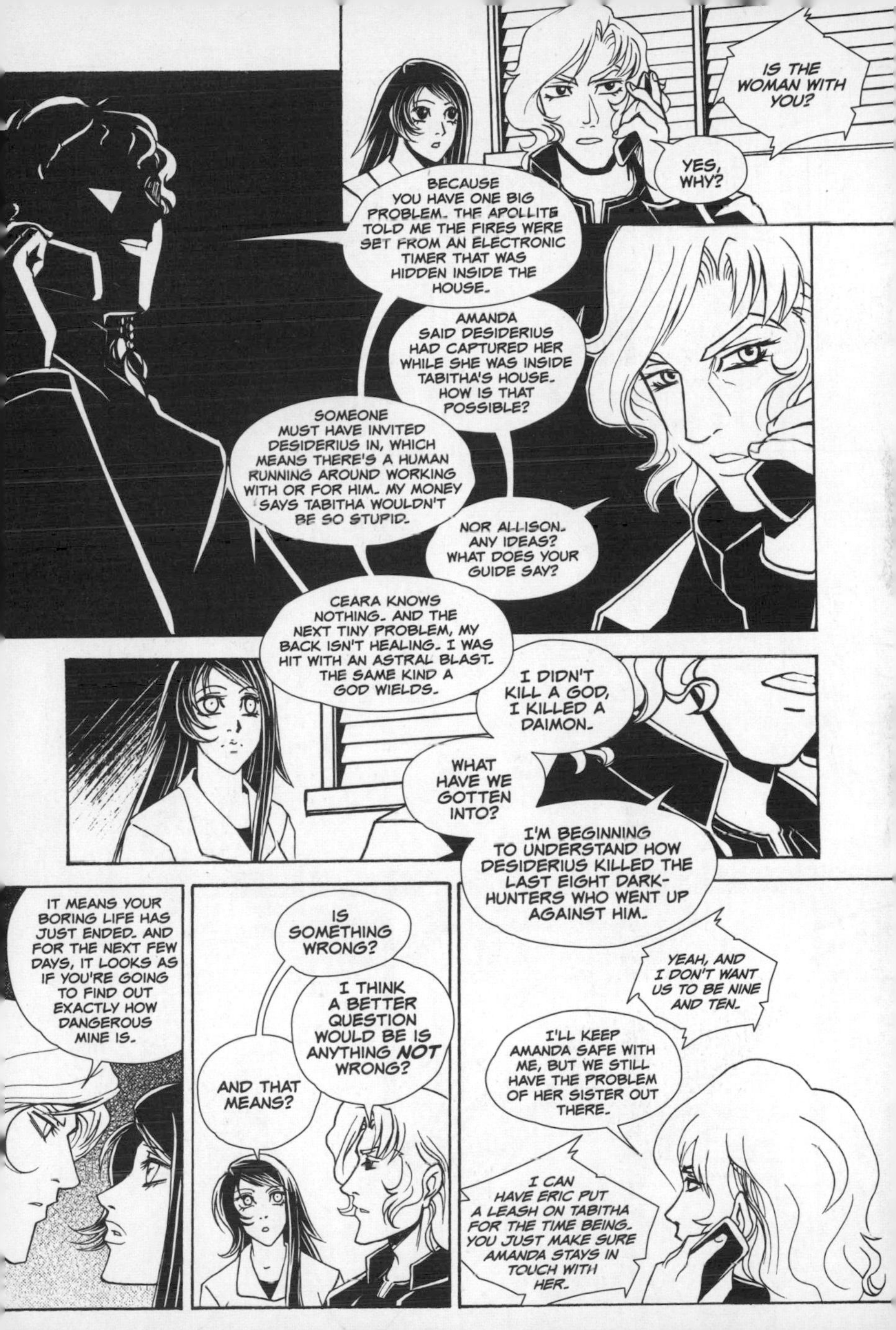
IS THE WOMAN WITH YOU?
YES, WHY?
BECAUSE YOU HAVE ONE BIG PROBLEM. THE APOLLITE TOLD ME THE FIRES WERE SET FROM AN ELECTRONIC TIMER THAT WAS HIDDEN INSIDE THE HOUSE.
AMANDA SAID DESIDERIUS HAD CAPTURED HER WHILE SHE WAS INSIDE TABITHA'S HOUSE. HOW IS THAT POSSIBLE?
SOMEONE MUST HAVE INVITED DESIDERIUS IN, WHICH MEANS THERE'S A HUMAN RUNNING AROUND WORKING WITH OR FOR HIM. MY MONEY SAYS TABITHA WOULDN'T BE SO STUPID.
NOR ALLISON. ANY IDEAS? WHAT DOES YOUR GUIDE SAY?
CEARA KNOWS NOTHING. AND THE NEXT TINY PROBLEM, MY BACK ISN'T HEALING. I WAS HIT WITH AN ASTRAL BLAST. THE SAME KIND A GOD WIELDS.
I DIDN'T KILL A GOD, I KILLED A DAIMON.
WHAT HAVE WE GOTTEN INTO?
I'M BEGINNING TO UNDERSTAND HOW DESIDERIUS KILLED THE LAST EIGHT DARK-HUNTERS WHO WENT UP AGAINST HIM.
YEAH, AND I DON'T WANT US TO BE NINE AND TEN.
I'LL KEEP AMANDA SAFE WITH ME, BUT WE STILL HAVE THE PROBLEM OF HER SISTER OUT THERE.
I CAN HAVE ERIC PUT A LEASH ON TABITHA FOR THE TIME BEING. YOU JUST MAKE SURE AMANDA STAYS IN TOUCH WITH HER.
IS SOMETHING WRONG?
I THINK A BETTER QUESTION WOULD BE IS ANYTHING NOT WRONG?
AND THAT MEANS?
IT MEANS YOUR BORING LIFE HAS JUST ENDED. AND FOR THE NEXT FEW DAYS, IT LOOKS AS IF YOU'RE GOING TO FIND OUT EXACTLY HOW DANGEROUS MINE IS.

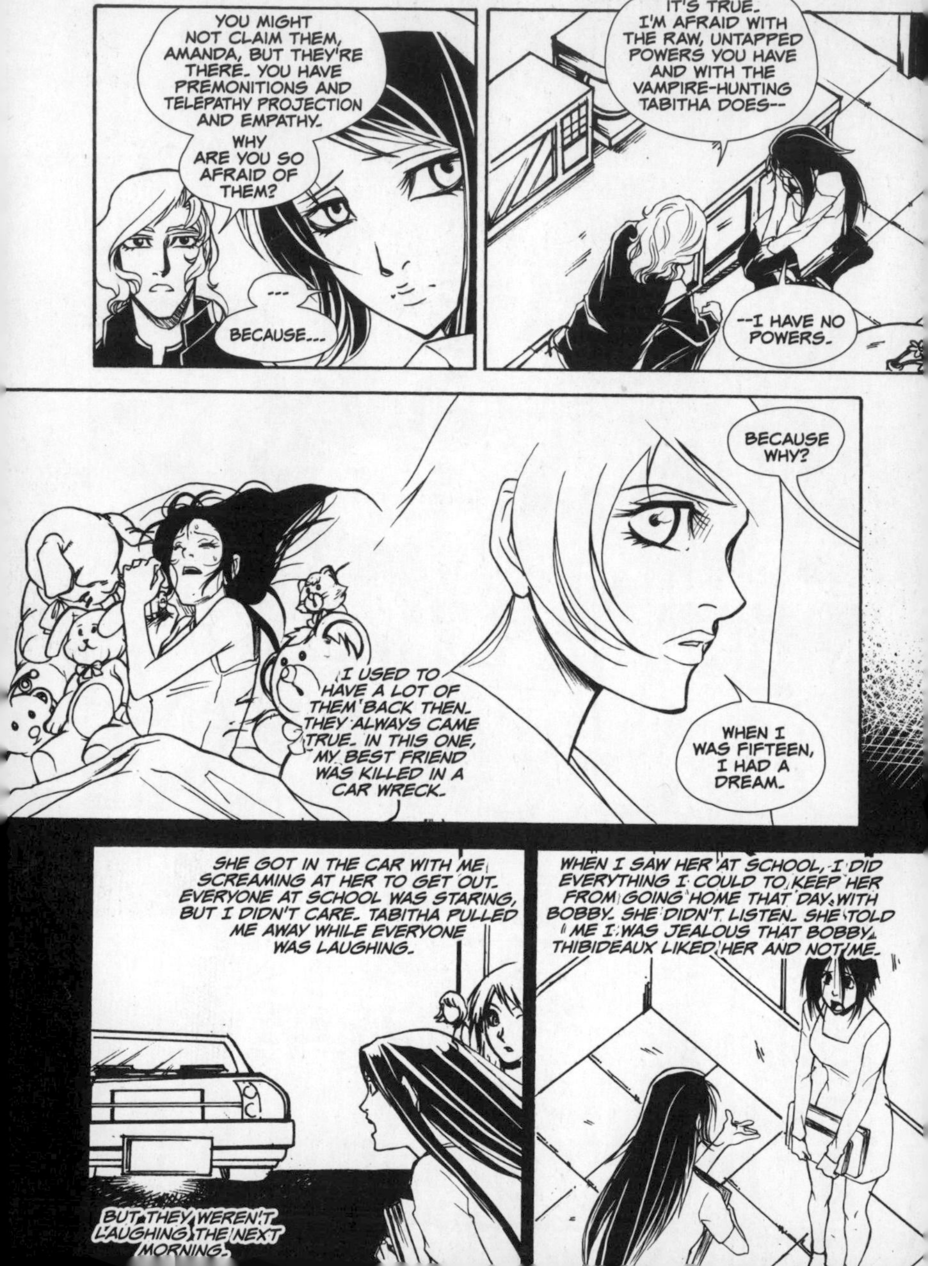
IT'S TRUE. I'M AFRAID WITH THE RAW, UNTAPPED POWERS YOU HAVE AND WITH THE VAMPIRE-HUNTING TABITHA DOES--
--I HAVE NO POWERS.
YOU MIGHT NOT CLAIM THEM, AMANDA, BUT THEY'RE THERE. YOU HAVE PREMONITIONS AND TELEPATHY PROJECTION AND EMPATHY.
WHY ARE YOU SO AFRAID OF THEM?

BECAUSE...
BECAUSE WHY?
WHEN I WAS FIFTEEN, I HAD A DREAM.
I USED TO HAVE A LOT OF THEM BACK THEN. THEY ALWAYS CAME TRUE. IN THIS ONE, MY BEST FRIEND WAS KILLED IN A CAR WRECK.
WHEN I SAW HER AT SCHOOL, I DID EVERYTHING I COULD TO KEEP HER FROM GOING HOME THAT DAY WITH BOBBY. SHE DIDN'T LISTEN. SHE TOLD ME I WAS JEALOUS THAT BOBBY THIBIDEAUX LIKED HER AND NOT ME.
SHE GOT IN THE CAR WITH ME SCREAMING AT HER TO GET OUT. EVERYONE AT SCHOOL WAS STARING, BUT I DIDN'T CARE. TABITHA PULLED ME AWAY WHILE EVERYONE WAS LAUGHING.
BUT THEY WEREN'T LAUGHING THE NEXT MORNING.

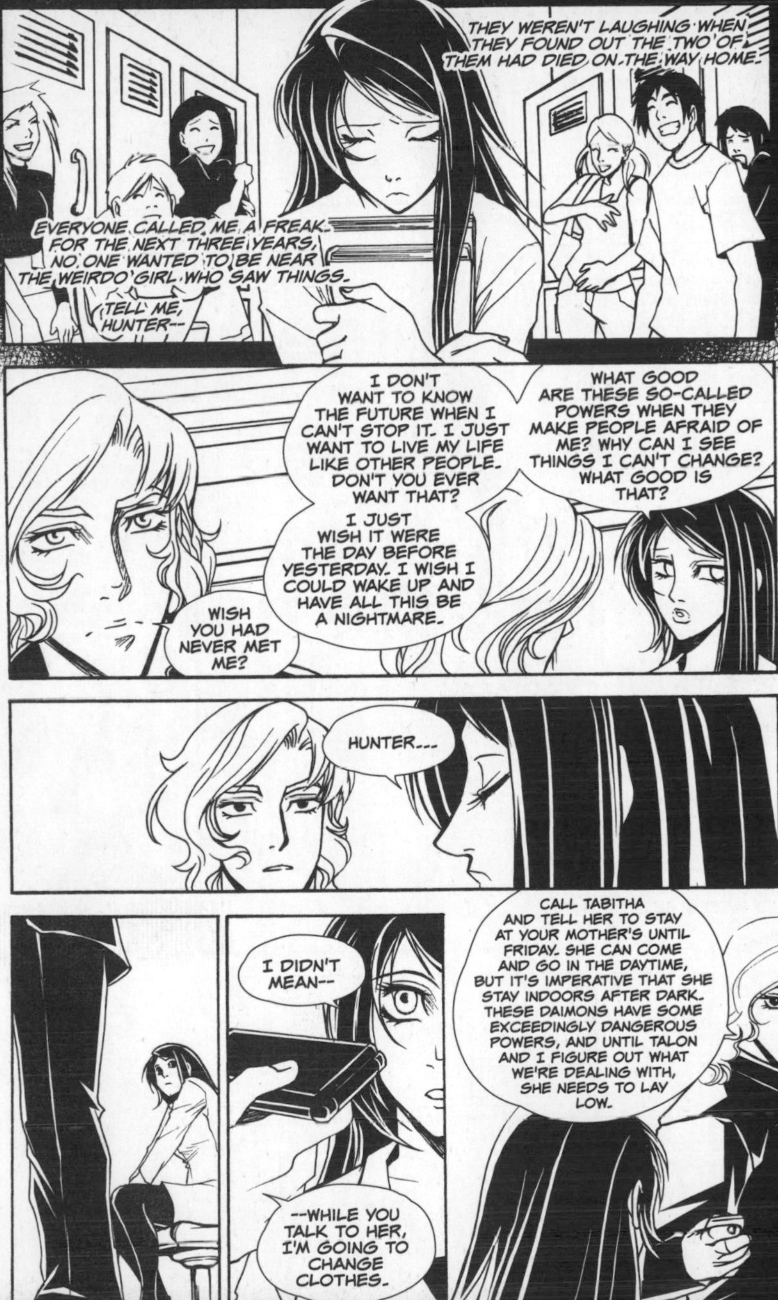
THEY WEREN'T LAUGHING WHEN THEY FOUND OUT THE TWO OF THEM HAD DIED ON THE WAY HOME.
EVERYONE CALLED ME A FREAK FOR THE NEXT THREE YEARS. NO ONE WANTED TO BE NEAR THE WEIRDO GIRL WHO SAW THINGS.
TELL ME, HUNTER--
WHAT GOOD ARE THESE SO-CALLED POWERS WHEN THEY MAKE PEOPLE AFRAID OF ME? WHY CAN I SEE THINGS I CAN'T CHANGE? WHAT GOOD IS THAT?
I DON'T WANT TO KNOW THE FUTURE WHEN I CAN'T STOP IT. I JUST WANT TO LIVE MY LIFE LIKE OTHER PEOPLE. DON'T YOU EVER WANT THAT?
I JUST WISH IT WERE THE DAY BEFORE YESTERDAY. I WISH I COULD WAKE UP AND HAVE ALL THIS BE A NIGHTMARE.
WISH YOU HAD NEVER MET ME?
HUNTER...
CALL TABITHA AND TELL HER TO STAY AT YOUR MOTHER'S UNTIL FRIDAY. SHE CAN COME AND GO IN THE DAYTIME, BUT IT'S IMPERATIVE THAT SHE STAY INDOORS AFTER DARK. THESE DAIMONS HAVE SOME EXCEEDINGLY DANGEROUS POWERS, AND UNTIL TALON AND I FIGURE OUT WHAT WE'RE DEALING WITH, SHE NEEDS TO LAY LOW.
I DIDN'T MEAN--
--WHILE YOU TALK TO HER, I'M GOING TO CHANGE CLOTHES.

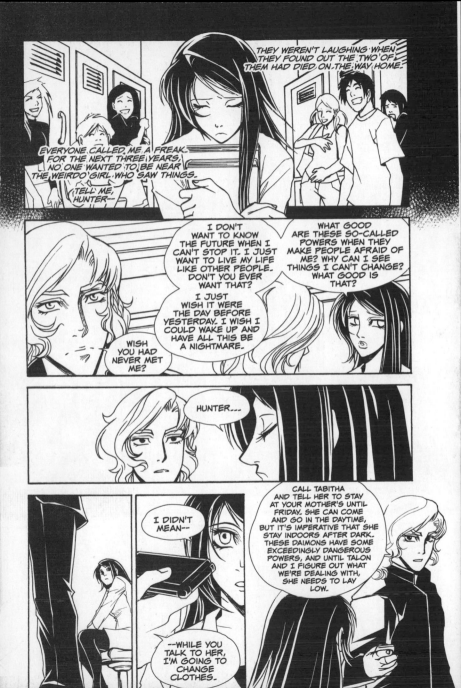

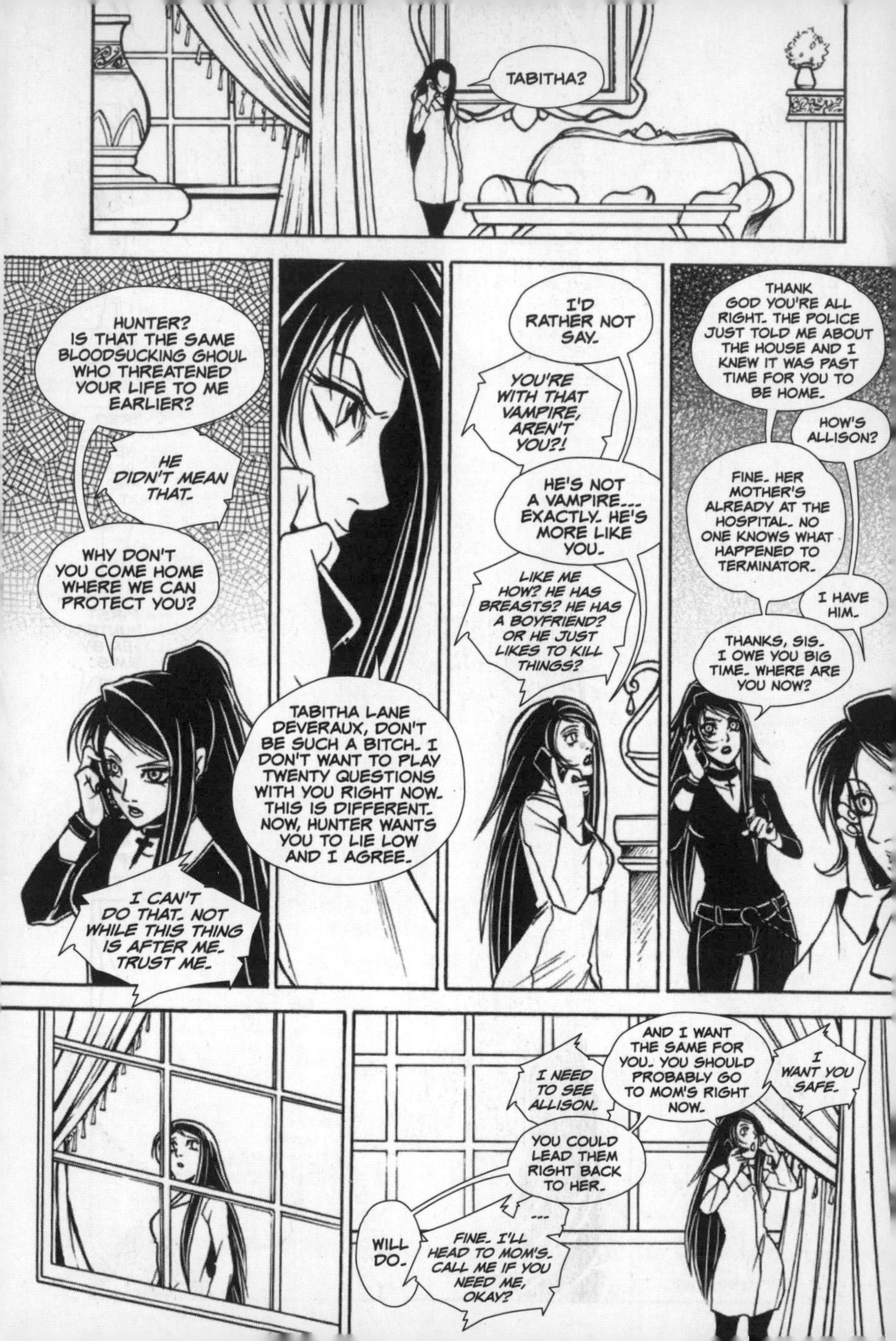
TABITHA?
THANK GOD YOU'RE ALL RIGHT. THE POLICE JUST TOLD ME ABOUT THE HOUSE AND I KNEW IT WAS PAST TIME FOR YOU TO BE HOME.
HOW'S ALLISON?
FINE. HER MOTHER'S ALREADY AT THE HOSPITAL. NO ONE KNOWS WHAT HAPPENED TO TERMINATOR.
I HAVE HIM.
THANKS, SIS. I OWE YOU BIG TIME. WHERE ARE YOU NOW?
I'D RATHER NOT SAY.
YOU'RE WITH THAT VAMPIRE, AREN'T YOU?!
HE'S NOT A VAMPIRE... EXACTLY. HE'S MORE LIKE YOU.
LIKE ME HOW? HE HAS BREASTS? HE HAS A BOYFRIEND? OR HE JUST LIKES TO KILL THINGS?
TABITHA LANE DEVERAUX, DON'T BE SUCH A BITCH. I DON'T WANT TO PLAY TWENTY QUESTIONS WITH YOU RIGHT NOW. THIS IS DIFFERENT. NOW, HUNTER WANTS YOU TO LIE LOW AND I AGREE.
HUNTER? IS THAT THE SAME BLOODSUCKING GHOUL WHO THREATENED YOUR LIFE TO ME EARLIER?
HE DIDN'T MEAN THAT.
WHY DON'T YOU COME HOME WHERE WE CAN PROTECT YOU?
I CAN'T DO THAT. NOT WHILE THIS THING IS AFTER ME. TRUST ME.
I WANT YOU SAFE.
AND I WANT THE SAME FOR YOU. YOU SHOULD PROBABLY GO TO MOM'S RIGHT NOW.
I NEED TO SEE ALLISON.
YOU COULD LEAD THEM RIGHT BACK TO HER.
...
FINE. I'LL HEAD TO MOM'S. CALL ME IF YOU NEED ME, OKAY?
WILL DO.

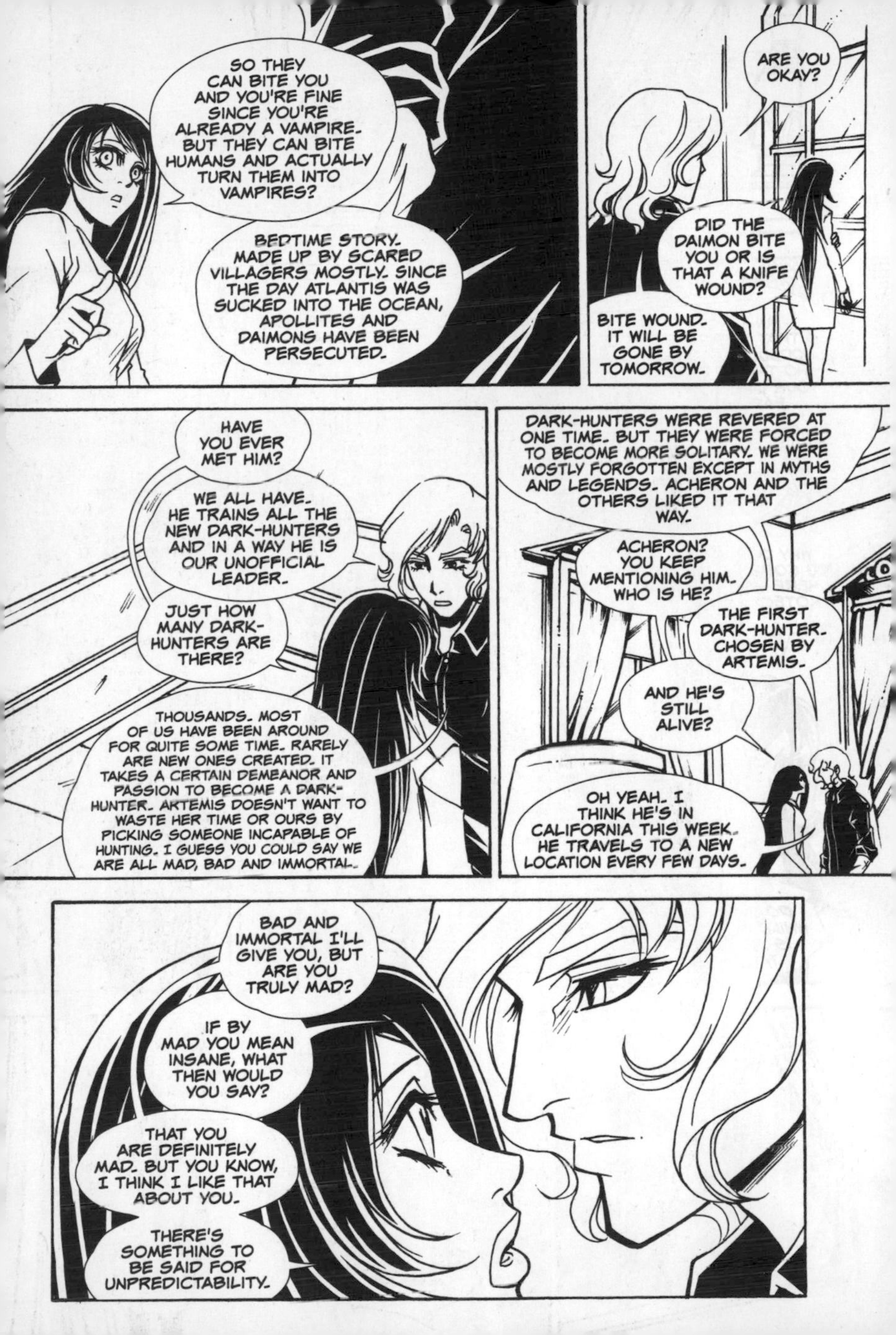
ARE YOU OKAY?
DID THE DAIMON BITE YOU OR IS THAT A KNIFE WOUND?
BITE WOUND. IT WILL BE GONE BY TOMORROW.
SO THEY CAN BITE YOU AND YOU'RE FINE SINCE YOU'RE ALREADY A VAMPIRE. BUT THEY CAN BITE HUMANS AND ACTUALLY TURN THEM INTO VAMPIRES?
BEDTIME STORY. MADE UP BY SCARED VILLAGERS MOSTLY. SINCE THE DAY ATLANTIS WAS SUCKED INTO THE OCEAN, APOLLITES AND DAIMONS HAVE BEEN PERSECUTED.
DARK-HUNTERS WERE REVERED AT ONE TIME. BUT THEY WERE FORCED TO BECOME MORE SOLITARY. WE WERE MOSTLY FORGOTTEN EXCEPT IN MYTHS AND LEGENDS. ACHERON AND THE OTHERS LIKED IT THAT WAY.
ACHERON? YOU KEEP MENTIONING HIM. WHO IS HE?
THE FIRST DARK-HUNTER. CHOSEN BY ARTEMIS.
AND HE'S STILL ALIVE?
OH YEAH. I THINK HE'S IN CALIFORNIA THIS WEEK. HE TRAVELS TO A NEW LOCATION EVERY FEW DAYS.
HAVE YOU EVER MET HIM?
WE ALL HAVE. HE TRAINS ALL THE NEW DARK-HUNTERS AND IN A WAY HE IS OUR UNOFFICIAL LEADER.
JUST HOW MANY DARK-HUNTERS ARE THERE?
THOUSANDS. MOST OF US HAVE BEEN AROUND FOR QUITE SOME TIME. RARELY ARE NEW ONES CREATED. IT TAKES A CERTAIN DEMEANOR AND PASSION TO BECOME A DARK-HUNTER. ARTEMIS DOESN'T WANT TO WASTE HER TIME OR OURS BY PICKING SOMEONE INCAPABLE OF HUNTING. I GUESS YOU COULD SAY WE ARE ALL MAD, BAD AND IMMORTAL.
BAD AND IMMORTAL I'LL GIVE YOU, BUT ARE YOU TRULY MAD?
IF BY MAD YOU MEAN INSANE, WHAT THEN WOULD YOU SAY?
THAT YOU ARE DEFINITELY MAD. BUT YOU KNOW, I THINK I LIKE THAT ABOUT YOU.
THERE'S SOMETHING TO BE SAID FOR UNPREDICTABILITY.

YOU KNOW, THIS IS A BIG HOUSE FOR ONE PERSON. HOW LONG HAVE YOU LIVED HERE?

A LITTLE OVER A HUNDRED YEARS.

YOU KNOW, YOU STILL HAVEN'T TOLD ME HOW YOU KNEW SO MUCH ABOUT MY SISTER THE NIGHT WE MET.

TALON AND TABITHA HAVE A MUTUAL FRIEND.

ONE OF TABITHA'S ZOO CREW? I'LL BE IT'S GARY.

SINCE THIS PERSON SPIES FOR US, I'M GIVING AWAY NOTHING.

THAT WAS A REALLY NOSY QUESTION. I'M SORRY.

IT SOUNDS REALLY LONELY.

WHAT ABOUT YOU? HAVE YOU LIVED HERE ALL YOUR LIFE.

BORN AND RAISED. MY MOTHER'S PARENTS IMMIGRATED FROM ROMANIA DURING THE DEPRESSION AND MY FATHER'S PEOPLE WERE BACKWOODS CAJUNS.

HAVE YOU EVER HAD ANY CHILDREN?

NO, DARK-HUNTERS ARE STERILE.

SO YOU ARE IMPOTENT.

HARDLY. I CAN HAVE SEX. I JUST CAN'T PROCREATE.

ARE YOU SERIOUS?

I'VE LIVED IN GENEVA, LONDON, BARCELONA, HAMBURG, ATHENS. BEFORE THAT I WANDERED AROUND. NOW THERE'S NO NEED FOR ME TO MOVE. I LIKE NEW ORLEANS.

IT'S ALL RIGHT.

WOULD YOU LIKE A TOUR OF THE HOUSE?

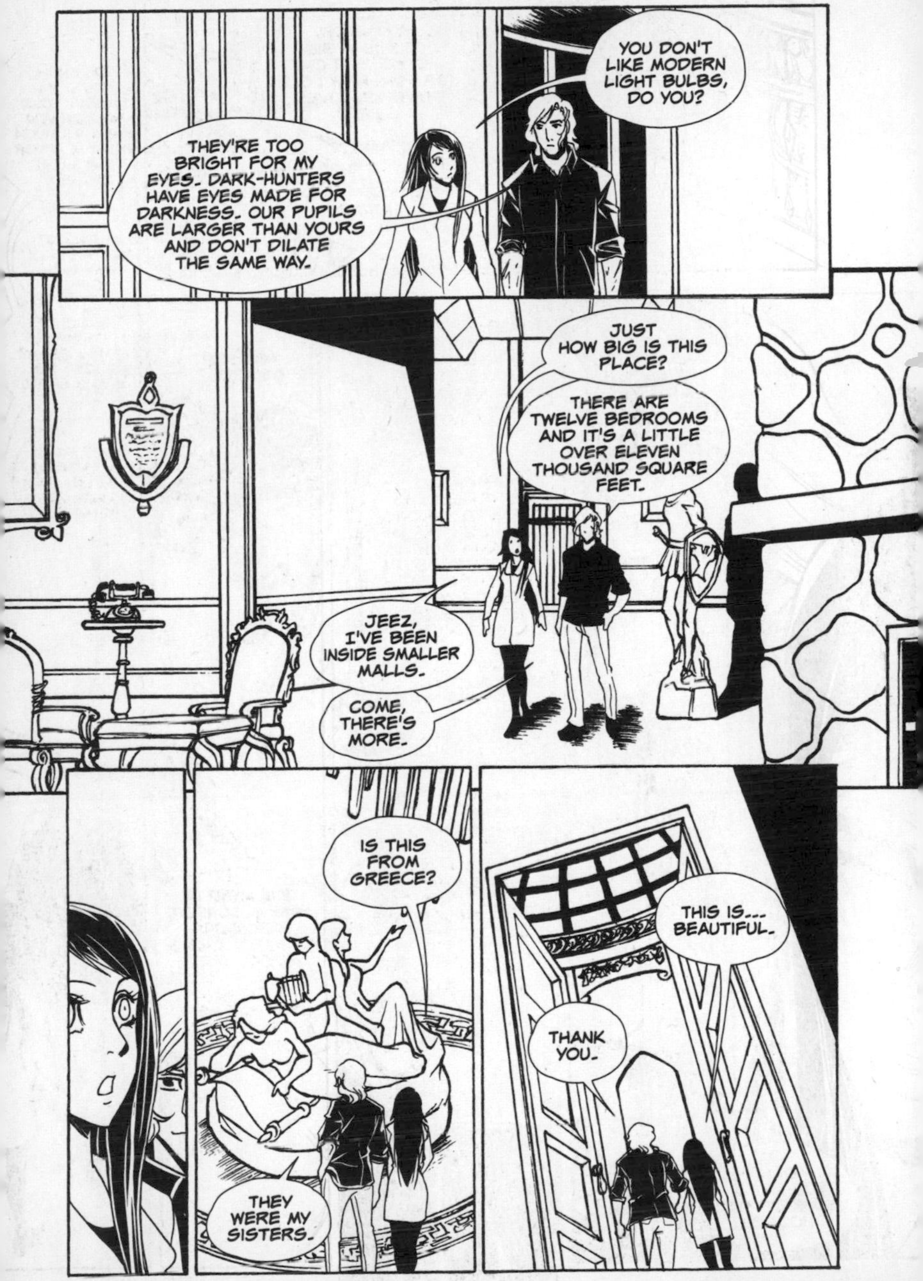
YOU DON'T LIKE MODERN LIGHT BULBS, DO YOU?
THEY'RE TOO BRIGHT FOR MY EYES. DARK-HUNTERS HAVE EYES MADE FOR DARKNESS. OUR PUPILS ARE LARGER THAN YOURS AND DON'T DILATE THE SAME WAY.
JUST HOW BIG IS THIS PLACE?
THERE ARE TWELVE BEDROOMS AND IT'S A LITTLE OVER ELEVEN THOUSAND SQUARE FEET.
JEEZ, I'VE BEEN INSIDE SMALLER MALLS.
COME, THERE'S MORE.
THIS IS... BEAUTIFUL.
THANK YOU.
IS THIS FROM GREECE?
THEY WERE MY SISTERS.

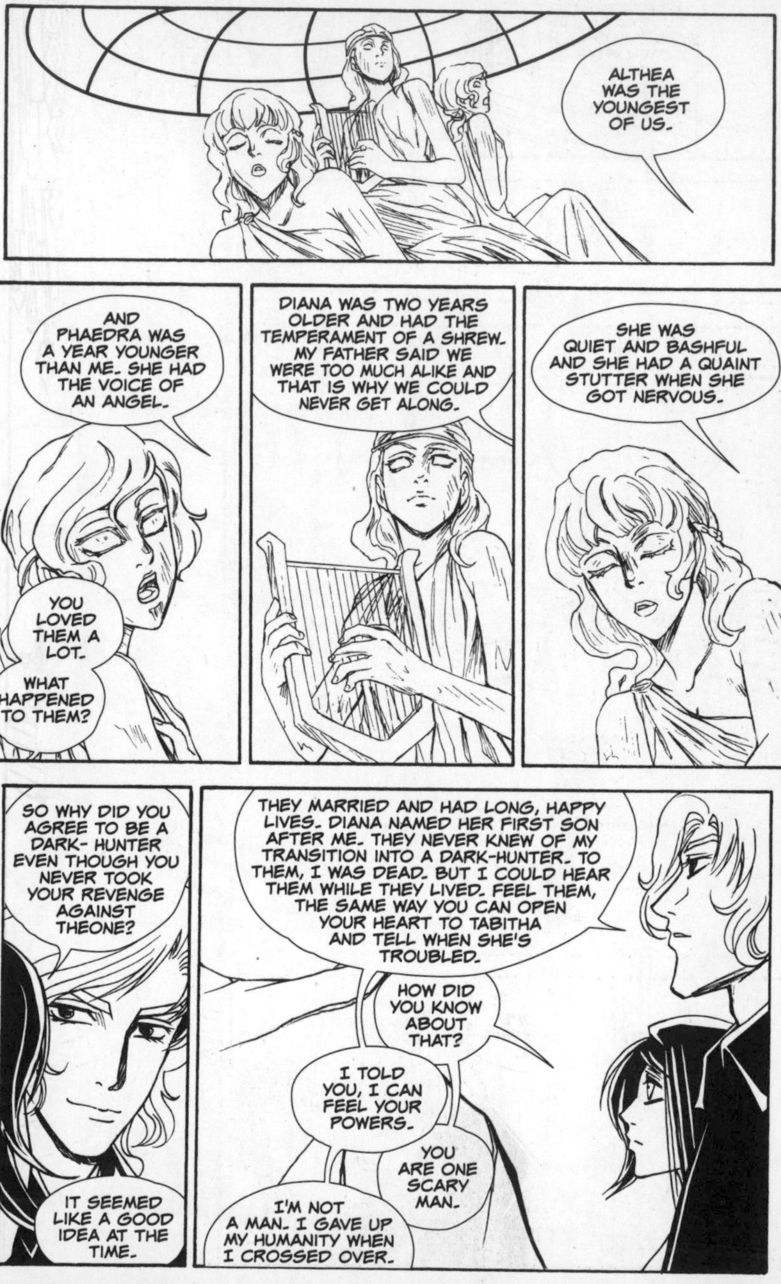
ALTHEA WAS THE YOUNGEST OF US.
SHE WAS QUIET AND BASHFUL AND SHE HAD A QUAINT STUTTER WHEN SHE GOT NERVOUS.
DIANA WAS TWO YEARS OLDER AND HAD THE TEMPERAMENT OF A SHREW. MY FATHER SAID WE WERE TOO MUCH ALIKE AND THAT IS WHY WE COULD NEVER GET ALONG.
AND PHAEDRA WAS A YEAR YOUNGER THAN ME. SHE HAD THE VOICE OF AN ANGEL.
YOU LOVED THEM A LOT.
WHAT HAPPENED TO THEM?
THEY MARRIED AND HAD LONG, HAPPY LIVES. DIANA NAMED HER FIRST SON AFTER ME. THEY NEVER KNEW OF MY TRANSITION INTO A DARK-HUNTER. TO THEM, I WAS DEAD. BUT I COULD HEAR THEM WHILE THEY LIVED. FEEL THEM, THE SAME WAY YOU CAN OPEN YOUR HEART TO TABITHA AND TELL WHEN SHE'S TROUBLED.
HOW DID YOU KNOW ABOUT THAT?
I TOLD YOU, I CAN FEEL YOUR POWERS.
YOU ARE ONE SCARY MAN.
I'M NOT A MAN. I GAVE UP MY HUMANITY WHEN I CROSSED OVER.
SO WHY DID YOU AGREE TO BE A DARK-HUNTER EVEN THOUGH YOU NEVER TOOK YOUR REVENGE AGAINST THEONE?
IT SEEMED LIKE A GOOD IDEA AT THE TIME.

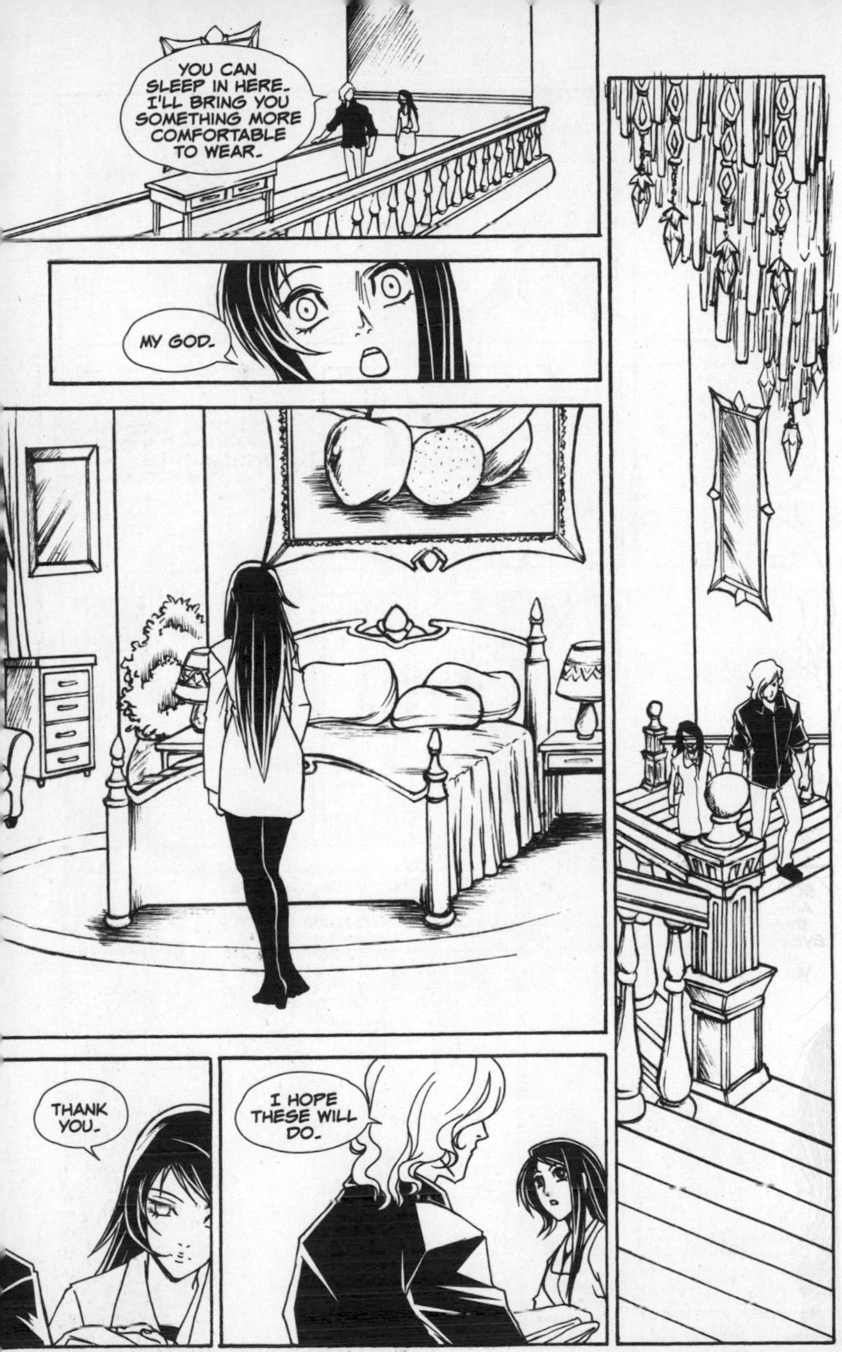
YOU CAN SLEEP IN HERE. I'LL BRING YOU SOMETHING MORE COMFORTABLE TO WEAR.
MY GOD.
I HOPE THESE WILL DO.
THANK YOU.

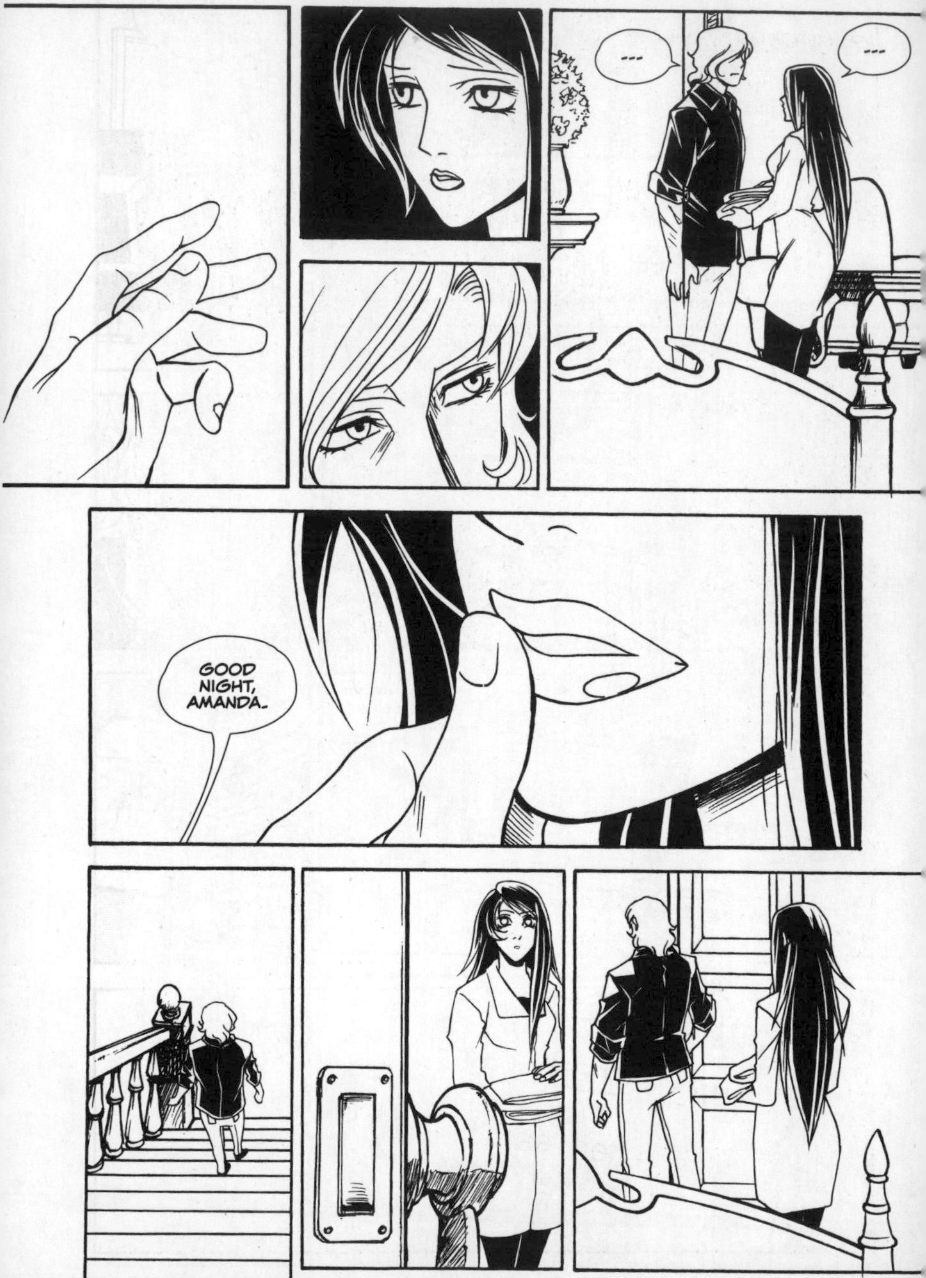

GOOD NIGHT, AMANDA_

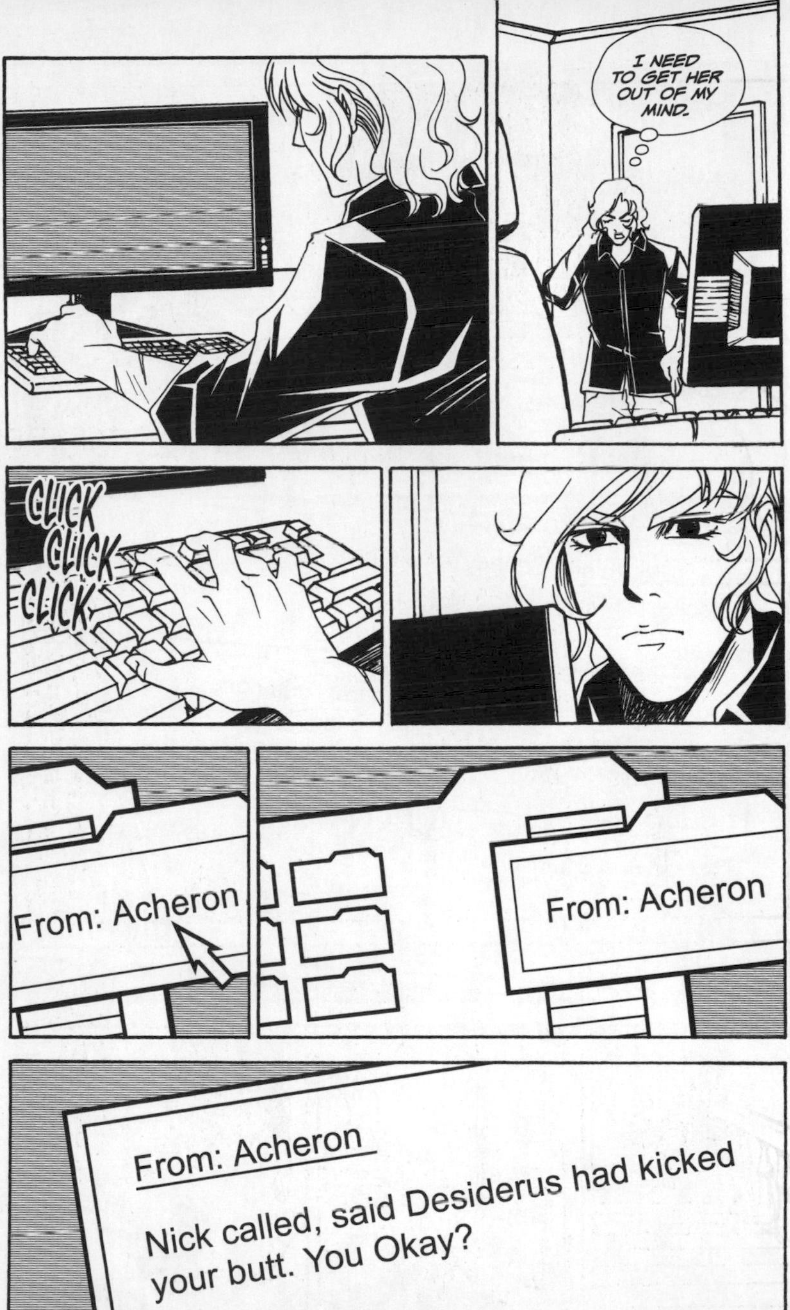
I NEED TO GET HER OUT OF MY MIND.
CLICK CLICK CLICK
From: Acheron
From: Acheron
From: Acheron
Nick called, said Desiderus had kicked your butt. You Okay?

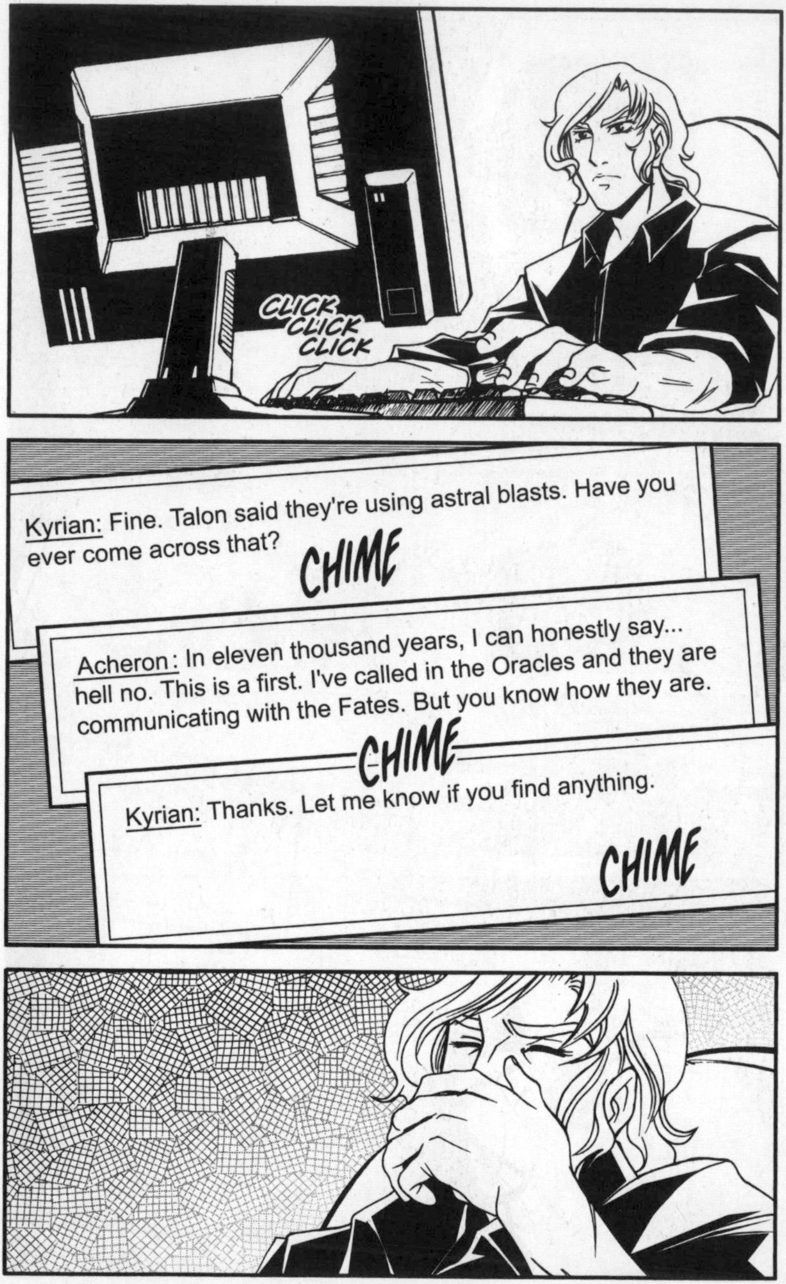
CLICK CLICK CLICK
Kyrian: Fine. Talon said they're using astral blasts. Have you ever come across that?
CHIME
Acheron: In eleven thousand years, I can honestly say... hell no. This is a first. I've called in the Oracles and they are communicating with the Fates. But you know how they are.
CHIME
Kyrian: Thanks. Let me know if you find anything.
CHIME

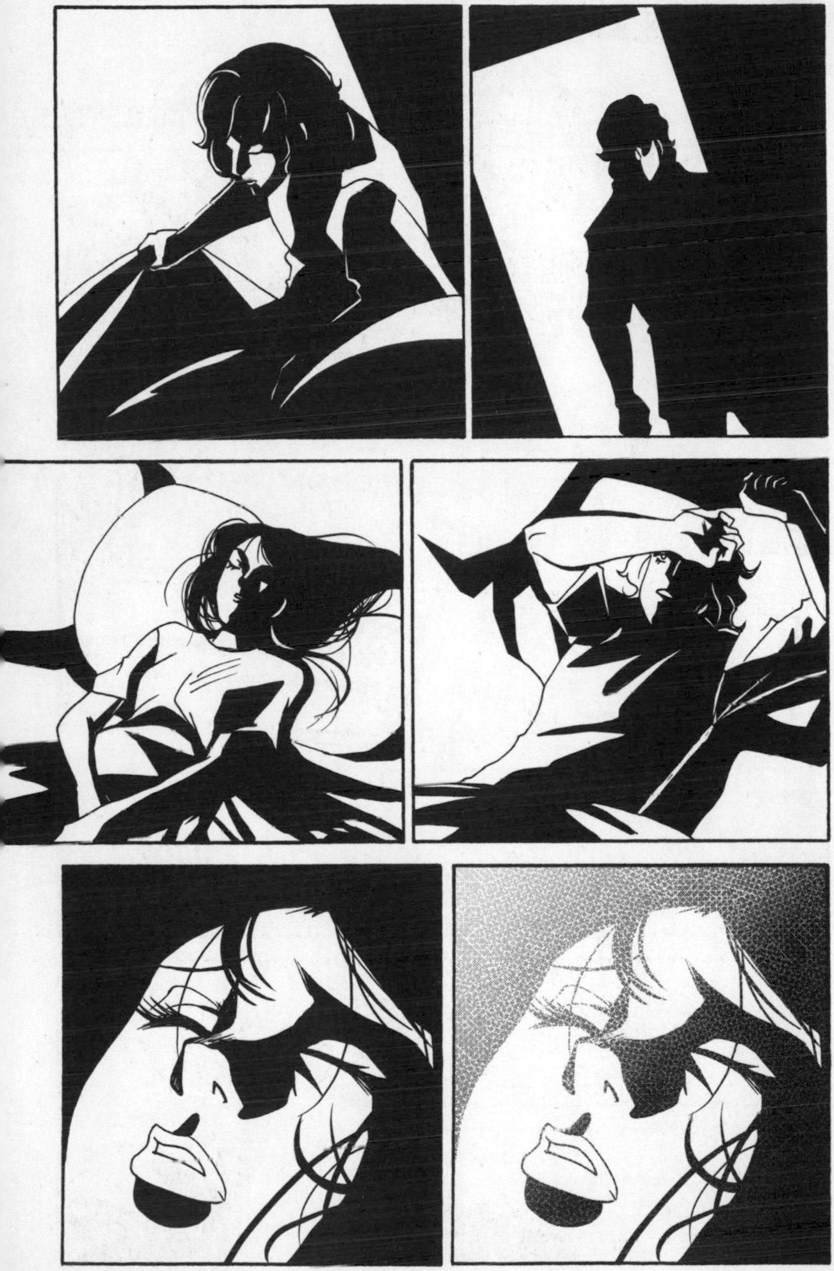

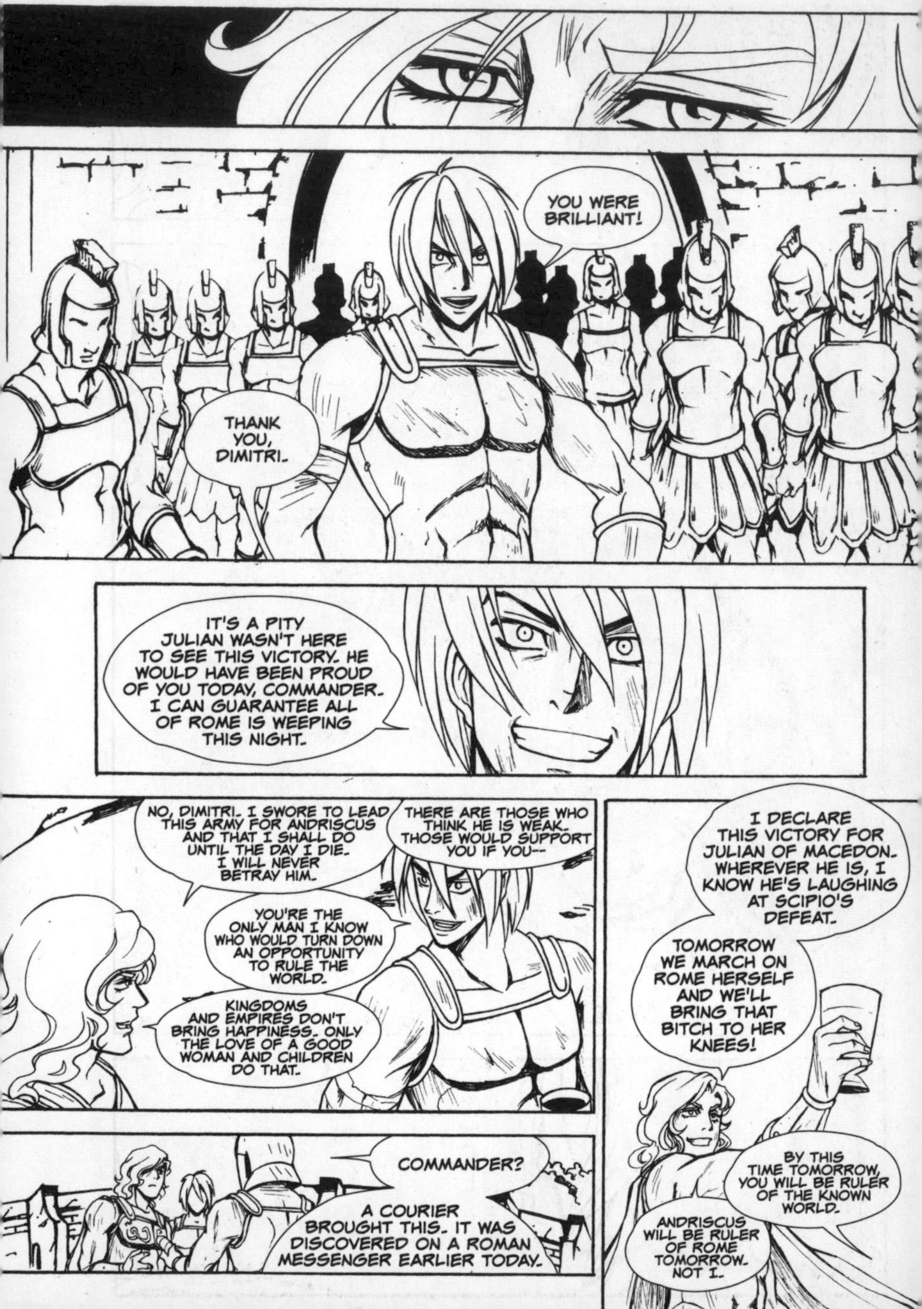
YOU WERE BRILLIANT!
THANK YOU, DIMITRI.
IT'S A PITY JULIAN WASN'T HERE TO SEE THIS VICTORY. HE WOULD HAVE BEEN PROUD OF YOU TODAY, COMMANDER. I CAN GUARANTEE ALL OF ROME IS WEEPING THIS NIGHT.
I DECLARE THIS VICTORY FOR JULIAN OF MACEDON. WHEREVER HE IS, I KNOW HE'S LAUGHING AT SCIPIO'S DEFEAT.
TOMORROW WE MARCH ON ROME HERSELF AND WE'LL BRING THAT BITCH TO HER KNEES!
BY THIS TIME TOMORROW, YOU WILL BE RULER OF THE KNOWN WORLD.
ANDRISCUS WILL BE RULER OF ROME TOMORROW. NOT I.
THERE ARE THOSE WHO THINK HE IS WEAK. THOSE WOULD SUPPORT YOU IF YOU--
NO, DIMITRI. I SWORE TO LEAD THIS ARMY FOR ANDRISCUS AND THAT I SHALL DO UNTIL THE DAY I DIE. I WILL NEVER BETRAY HIM.
YOU'RE THE ONLY MAN I KNOW WHO WOULD TURN DOWN AN OPPORTUNITY TO RULE THE WORLD.
KINGDOMS AND EMPIRES DON'T BRING HAPPINESS. ONLY THE LOVE OF A GOOD WOMAN AND CHILDREN DO THAT.
COMMANDER?
A COURIER BROUGHT THIS. IT WAS DISCOVERED ON A ROMAN MESSENGER EARLIER TODAY.

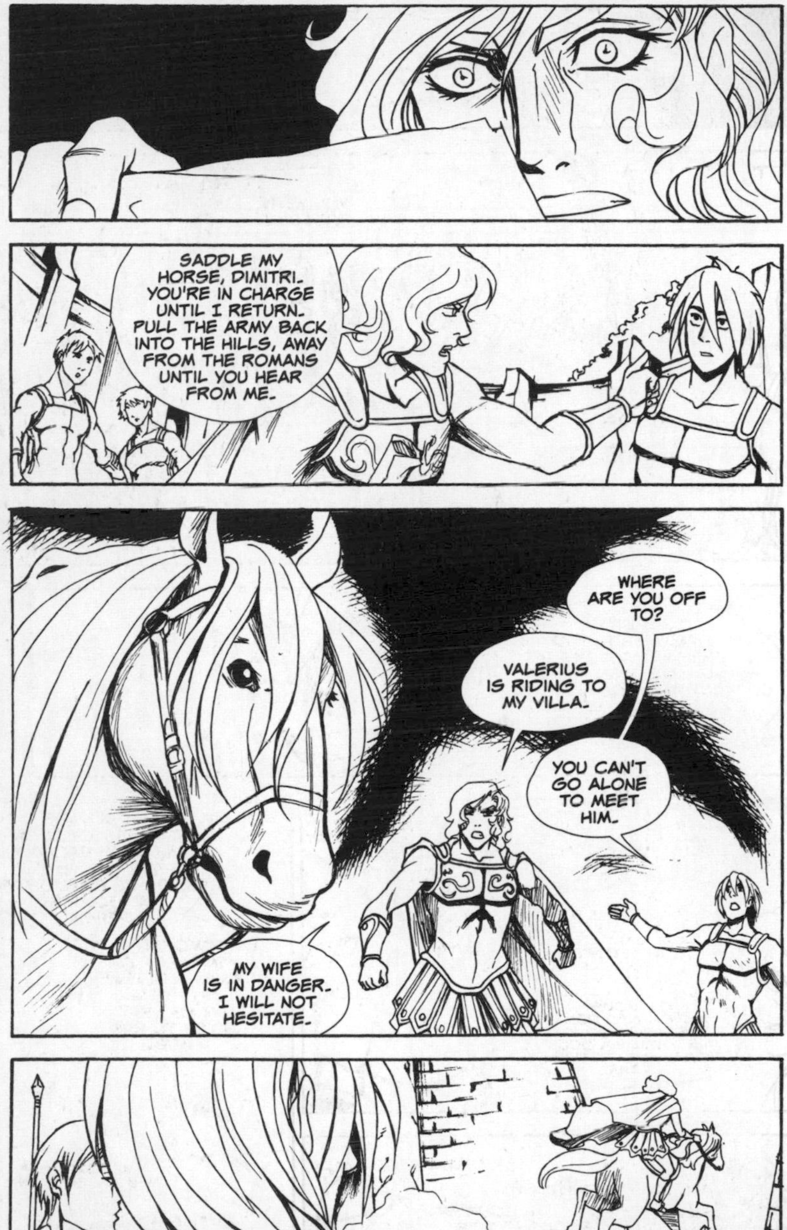
SADDLE MY HORSE, DIMITRI. YOU'RE IN CHARGE UNTIL I RETURN. PULL THE ARMY BACK INTO THE HILLS, AWAY FROM THE ROMANS UNTIL YOU HEAR FROM ME.
WHERE ARE YOU OFF TO?
VALERIUS IS RIDING TO MY VILLA.
YOU CAN'T GO ALONE TO MEET HIM.
MY WIFE IS IN DANGER. I WILL NOT HESITATE.

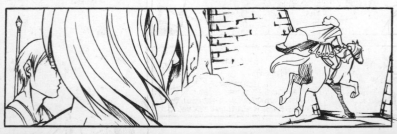

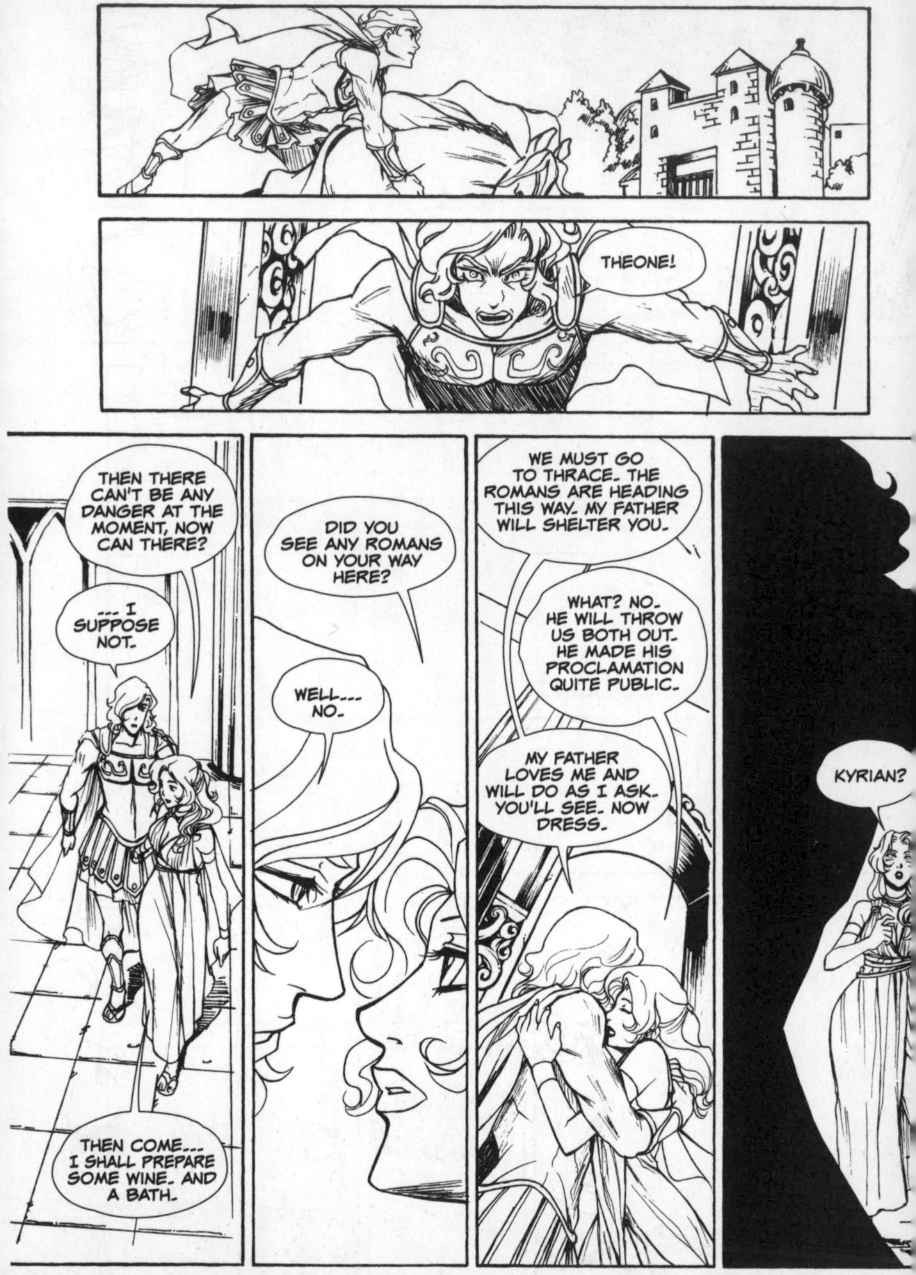
THEONE!
KYRIAN?
WE MUST GO TO THRACE. THE ROMANS ARE HEADING THIS WAY. MY FATHER WILL SHELTER YOU.
WHAT? NO. HE WILL THROW US BOTH OUT. HE MADE HIS PROCLAMATION QUITE PUBLIC.
MY FATHER LOVES ME AND WILL DO AS I ASK. YOU'LL SEE. NOW DRESS.
DID YOU SEE ANY ROMANS ON YOUR WAY HERE?
WELL... NO.
THEN THERE CAN'T BE ANY DANGER AT THE MOMENT, NOW CAN THERE?
... I SUPPOSE NOT.
THEN COME... I SHALL PREPARE SOME WINE. AND A BATH.

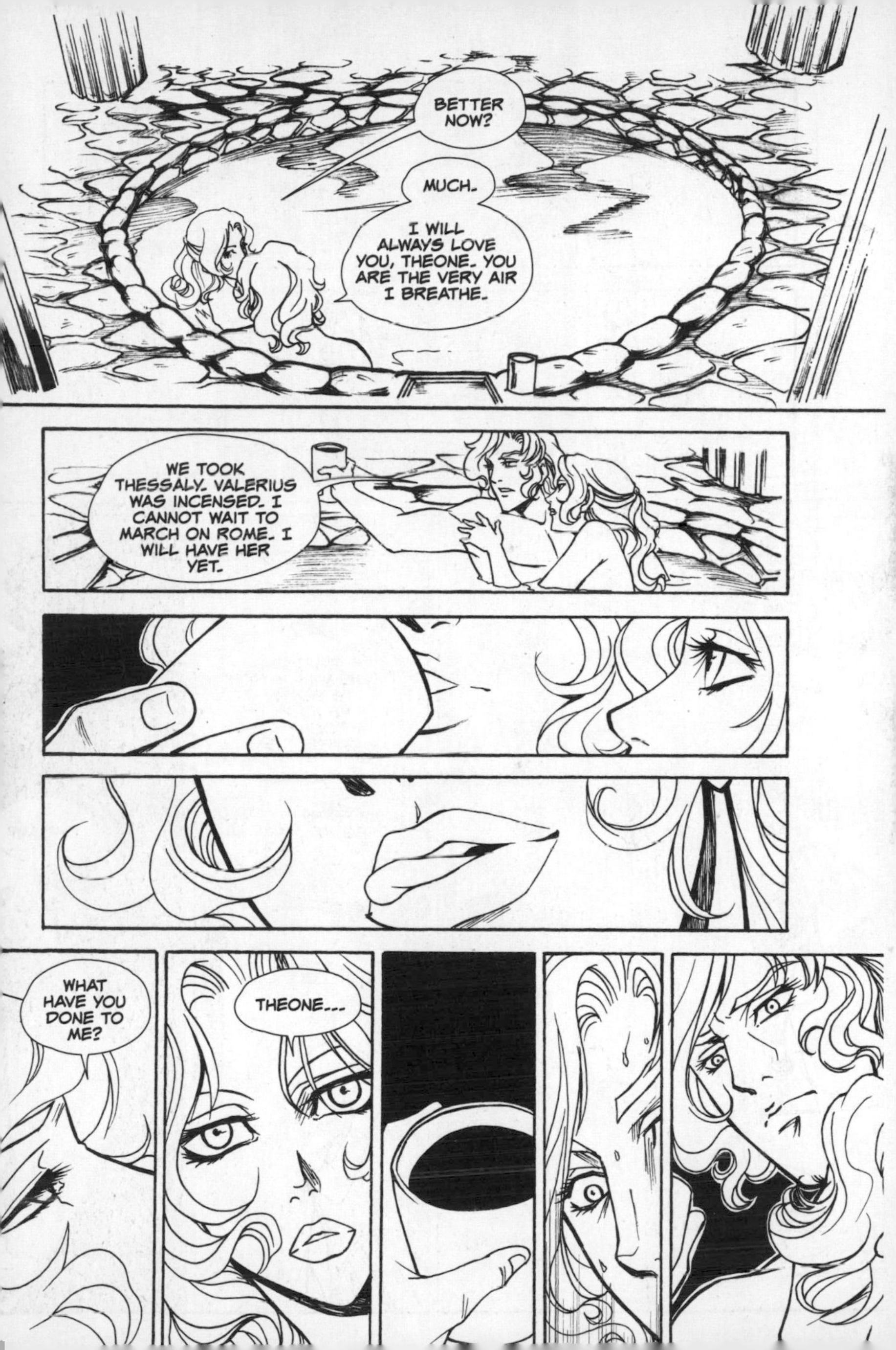
BETTER NOW?
MUCH.
I WILL ALWAYS LOVE YOU, THEONE. YOU ARE THE VERY AIR I BREATHE.
WE TOOK THESSALY. VALERIUS WAS INCENSED. I CANNOT WAIT TO MARCH ON ROME. I WILL HAVE HER YET.
THEONE...
WHAT HAVE YOU DONE TO ME?

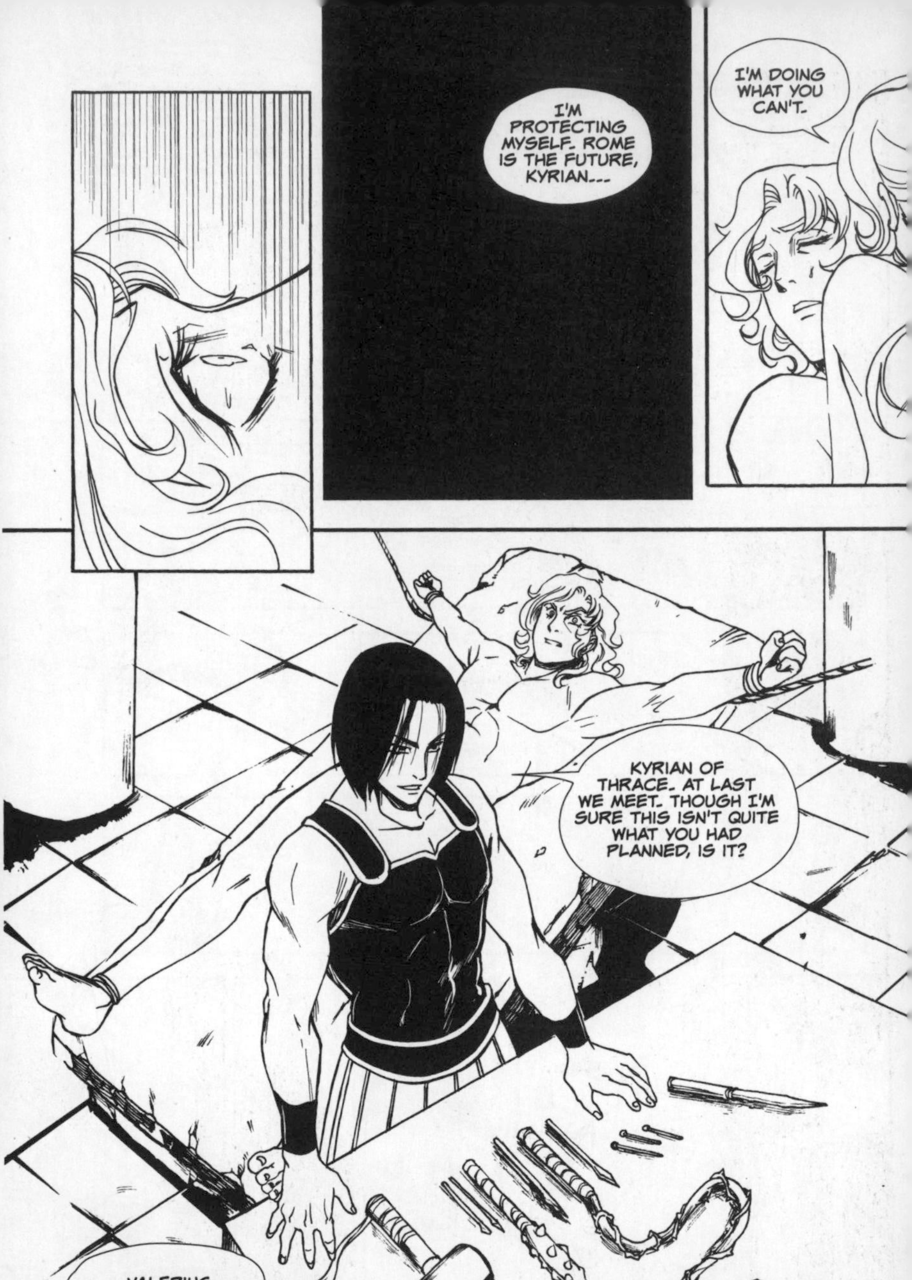
I'M DOING WHAT YOU CAN'T.
I'M PROTECTING MYSELF. ROME IS THE FUTURE, KYRIAN...
KYRIAN OF THRACE. AT LAST WE MEET. THOUGH I'M SURE THIS ISN'T QUITE WHAT YOU HAD PLANNED, IS IT?
... VALERIUS...

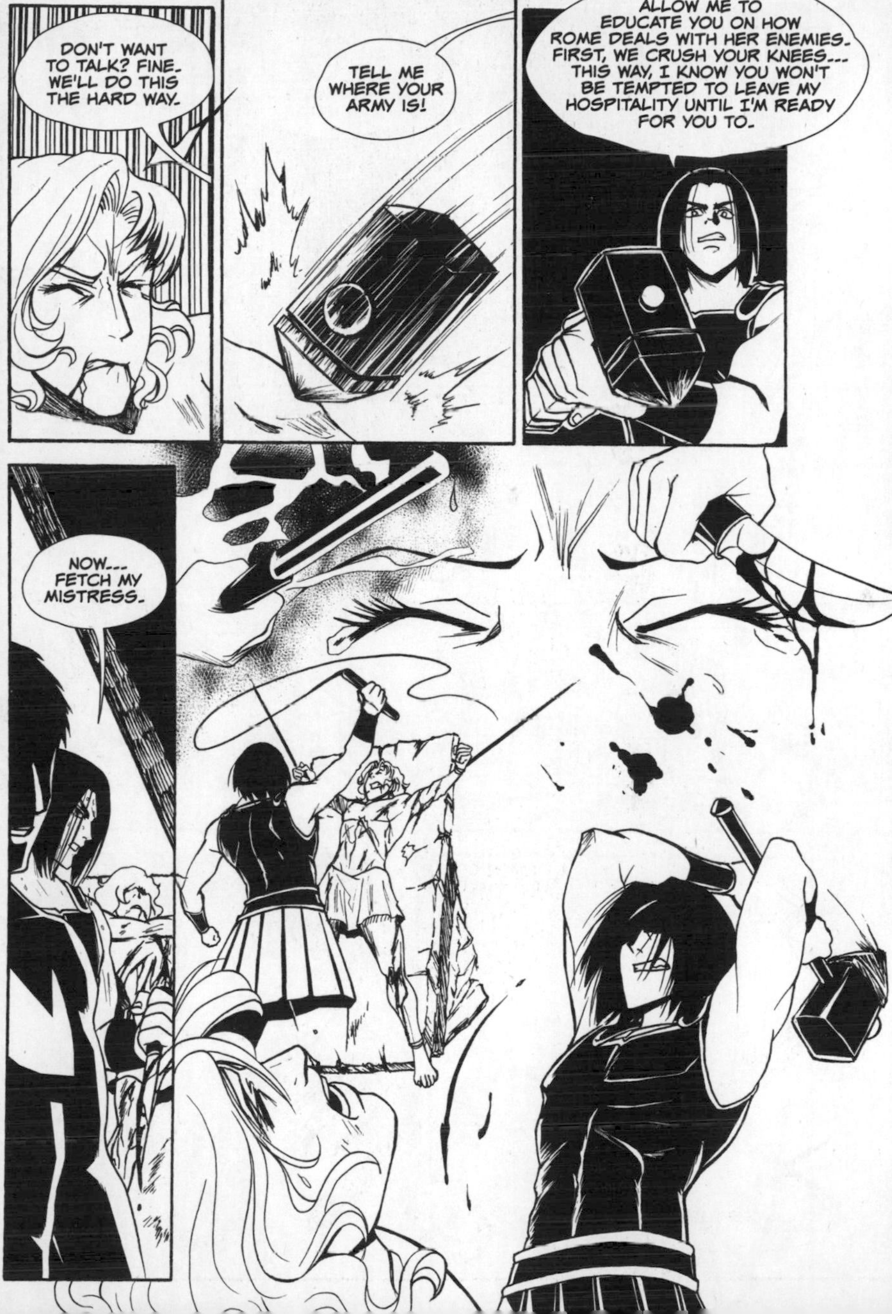
ALLOW ME TO EDUCATE YOU ON HOW ROME DEALS WITH HER ENEMIES. FIRST, WE CRUSH YOUR KNEES... THIS WAY, I KNOW YOU WON'T BE TEMPTED TO LEAVE MY HOSPITALITY UNTIL I'M READY FOR YOU TO.
TELL ME WHERE YOUR ARMY IS!
DON'T WANT TO TALK? FINE. WE'LL DO THIS THE HARD WAY.
NOW... FETCH MY MISTRESS.

--- WHY?

TELL ME, THEONE, HOW SHOULD I KILL YOUR HUSBAND? SHOULD I BEHEAD HIM AS BEFITTING A PRINCE?

NO.. YOU CAN'T AFFORD TO MAKE HIM A MARTYR. WERE I YOU, I'D CRUCIFY HIM LIKE A COMMON THIEF. LET HIM STAND AS AN EXAMPLE TO ROME'S ENEMIES, TO KNOW THERE IS NO HONOR OR GLORY IN ASSAULTING ROME.

VERY WELL.. YOU MAY SAY GOODBYE WHILE I MAKE THE ARRANGEMENTS.

NO---

BECAUSE I WAS THE NAMELESS DAUGHTER OF A PROSTITUTE. BECAUSE I WANT MY SECURITY AND I WILL DO ANYTHING TO PROTECT IT.

I BETRAYED MY FAMILY.... MY COUNTRY.... FOR YOU!

THEONE.... DID YOU EVER LOVE ME?

I AM A FOOL....

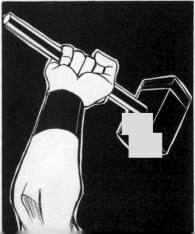

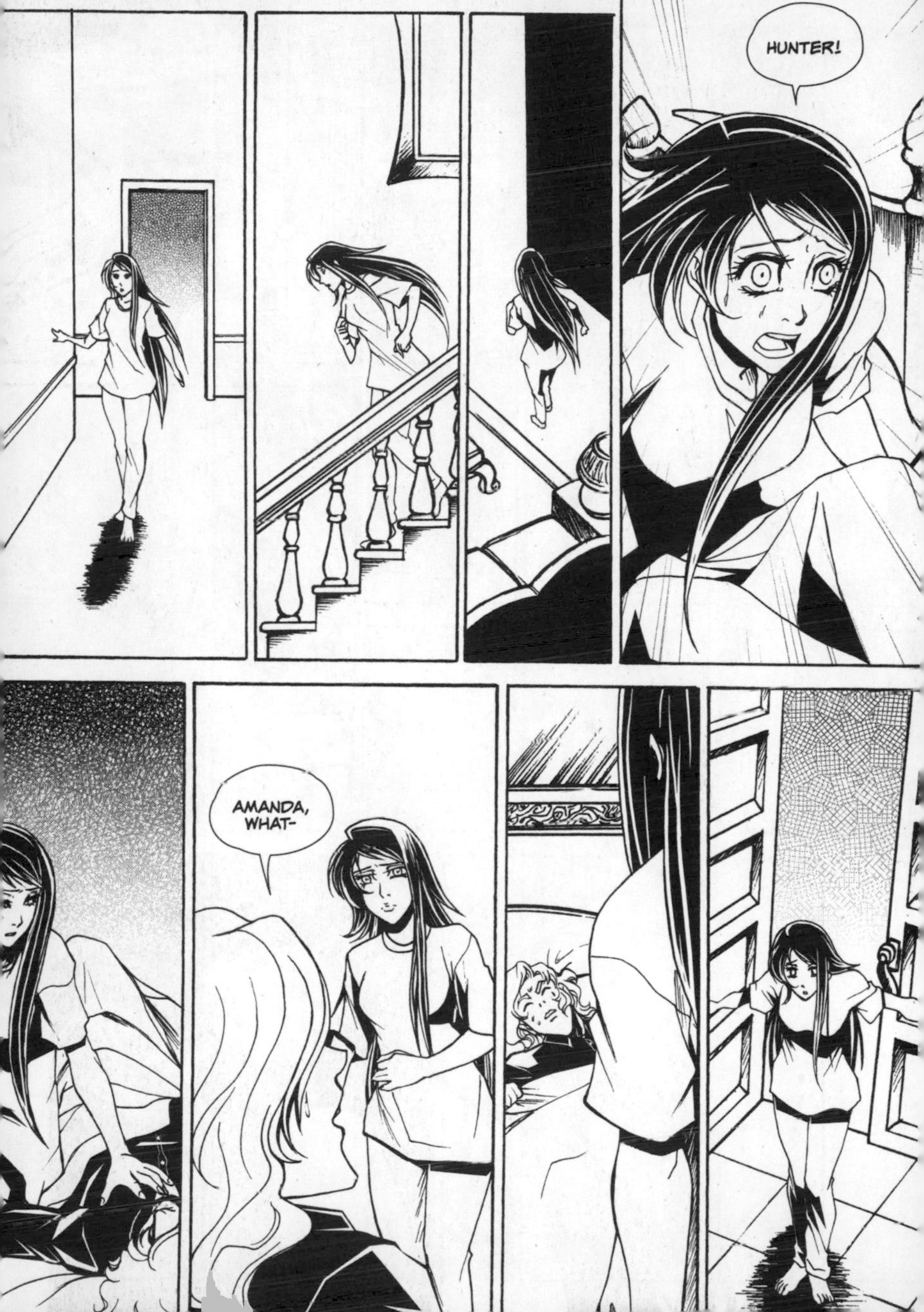
HUNTER!
AMANDA, WHAT-

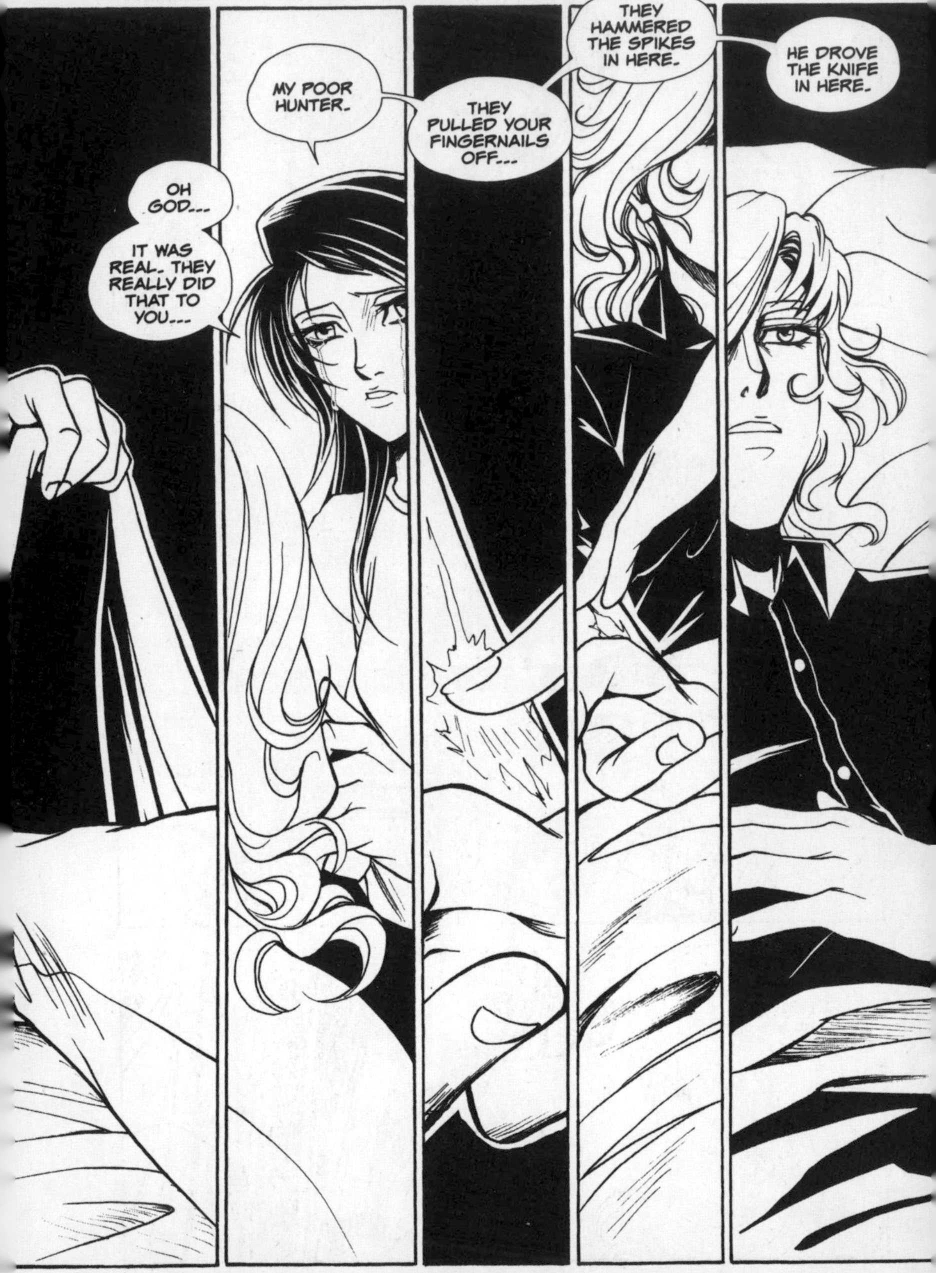
HE DROVE THE KNIFE IN HERE.
THEY HAMMERED THE SPIKES IN HERE.
THEY PULLED YOUR FINGERNAILS OFF...
MY POOR HUNTER.
OH GOD...
IT WAS REAL. THEY REALLY DID THAT TO YOU...

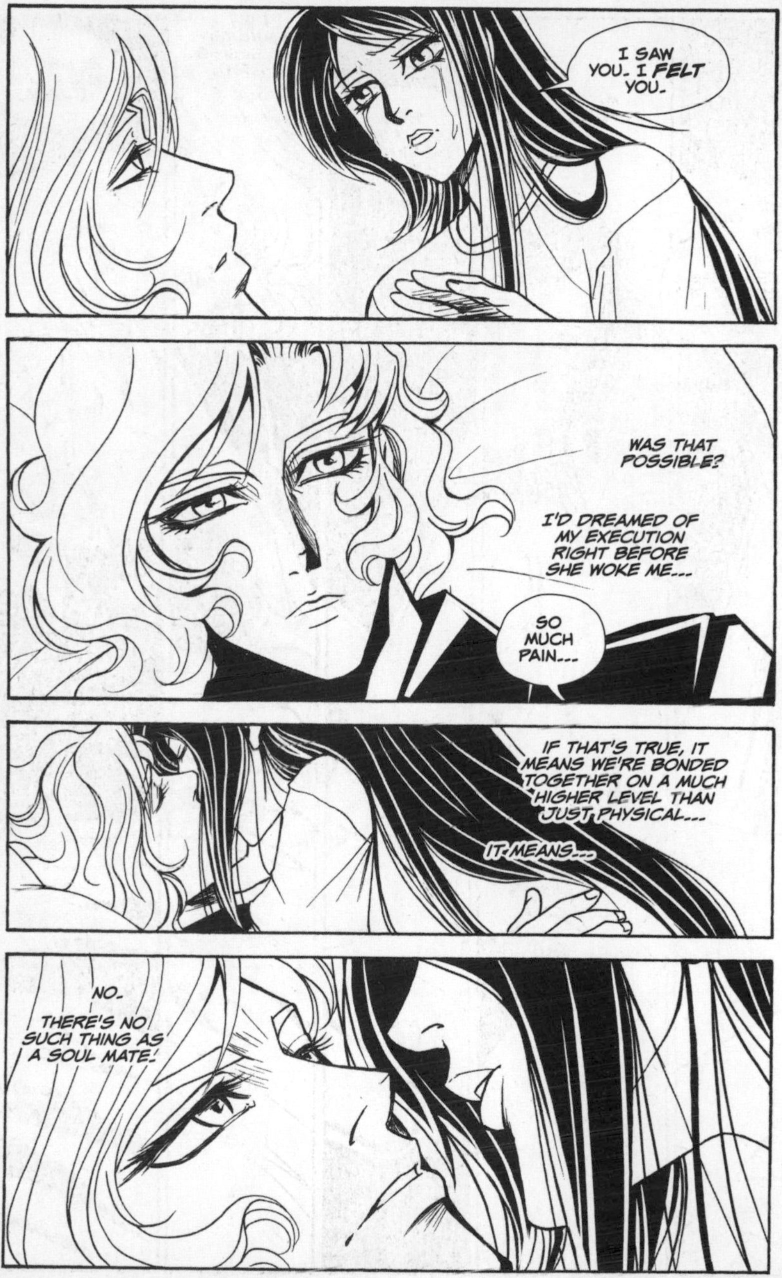
I SAW YOU. I FELT YOU.
WAS THAT POSSIBLE?
I'D DREAMED OF MY EXECUTION RIGHT BEFORE SHE WOKE ME...
SO MUCH PAIN...
IF THAT'S TRUE, IT MEANS WE'RE BONDED TOGETHER ON A MUCH HIGHER LEVEL THAN JUST PHYSICAL...
IT MEANS...
NO.
THERE'S NO SUCH THING AS A SOUL MATE!

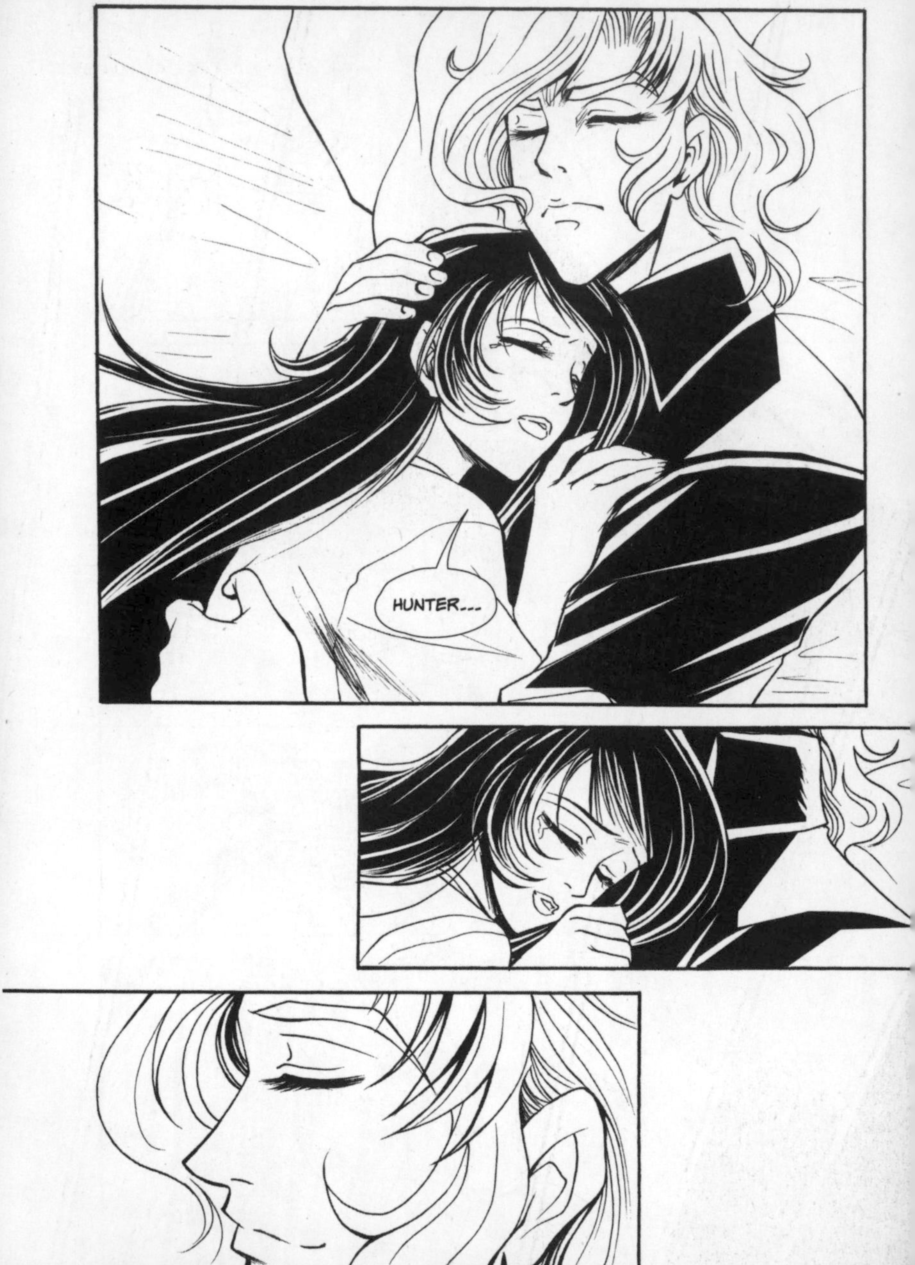
HUNTER...

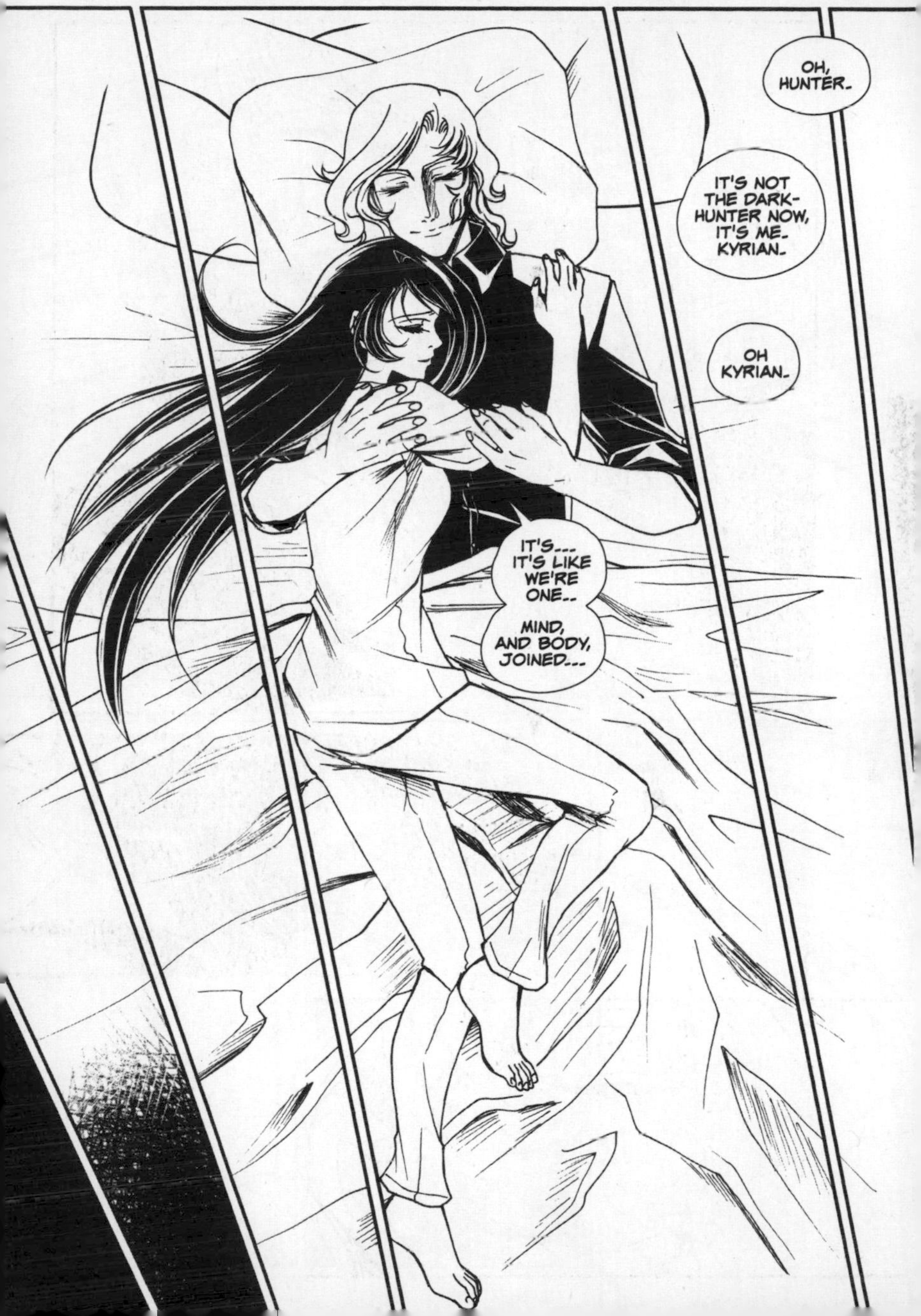
OH, HUNTER-
IT'S NOT THE DARK-HUNTER NOW, IT'S ME- KYRIAN-
OH KYRIAN-
IT'S... IT'S LIKE WE'RE ONE--
MIND, AND BODY, JOINED...

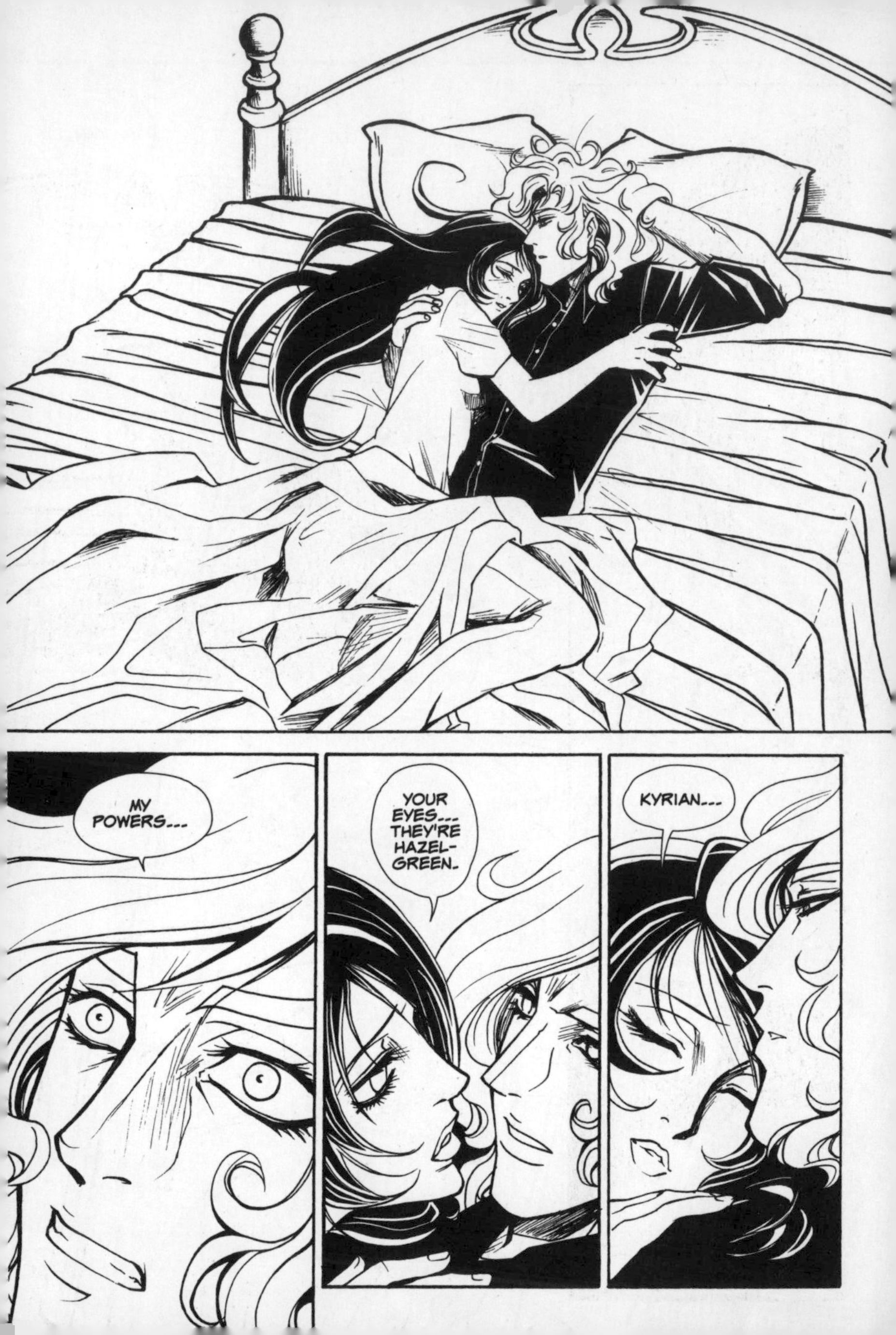
KYRIAN...
YOUR EYES... THEY'RE HAZEL-GREEN.
MY POWERS...

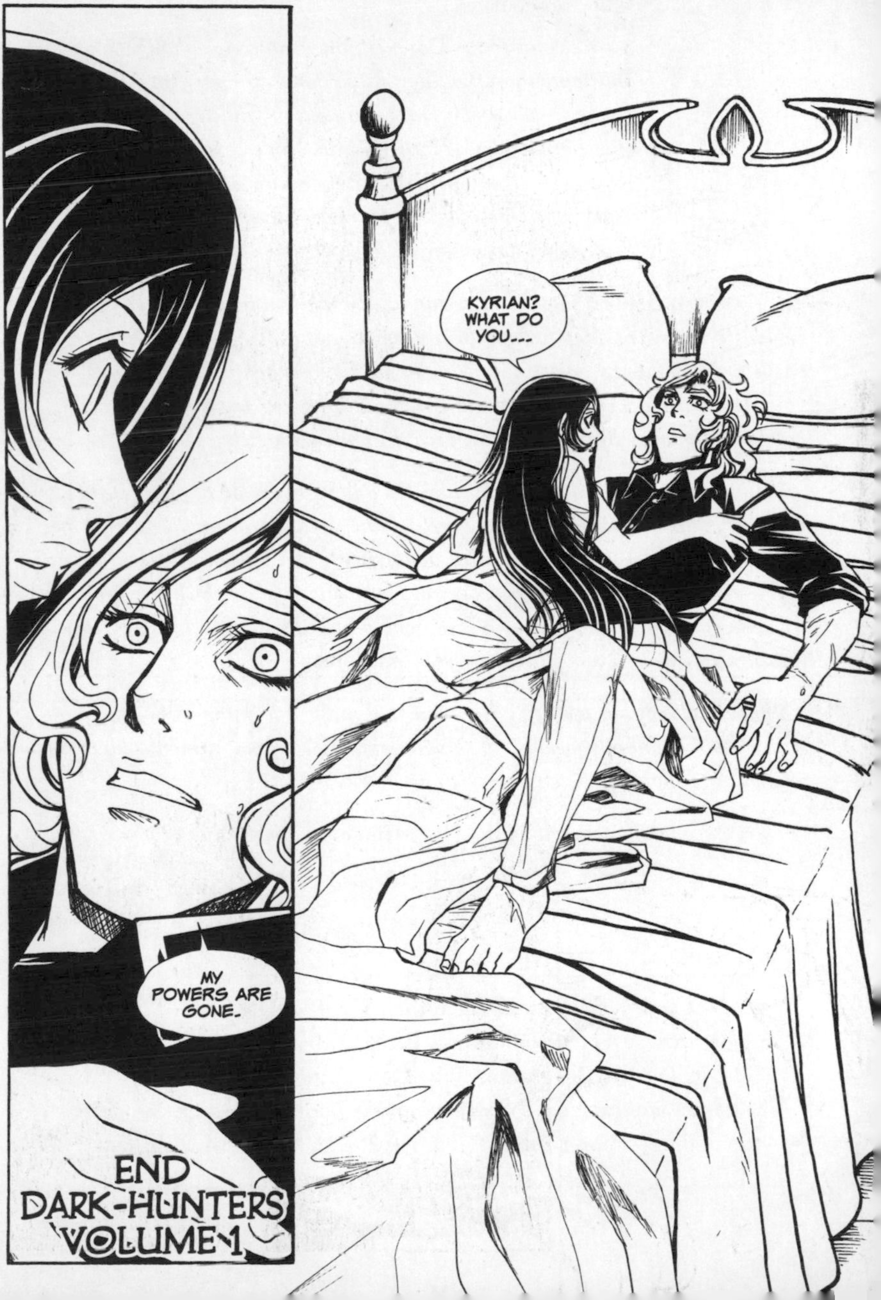
KYRIAN? WHAT DO YOU...
MY POWERS ARE GONE.
END DARK-HUNTERS VOLUME 1

*W*elcome to the Dark-Hunter realm. If you'd like to join the more than a million fans from over forty-five countries online, please visit Dark-Hunter.com and set up your own page in the Dark-Hunter world. You can interact with the characters from the books and declare your allegiance to either the Daimons, the Dark-Hunters, or one of the other groups we have waiting to greet you.

For years, I've been a huge manga and anime fan and have collected them zealously—in true Otaku fashion (and I mean that in the American sense of the word). Since I was a kid running home from school to catch anime episodes on cable, I've wanted nothing more than to one day see my own creation in manga style. Anime is a dream I have yet to achieve.

What you hold right now in your hand is a lifelong dream of mine. I can't thank my publisher, agent, or the Dabel Brothers enough for making this come true. It's with pride and deepest gratitude that I have Claudia's Dark-Hunter art framed and hanging next to works of Heise and Feimo, which I've been collecting for years. And of course Josh, who adapted the books into a script that I then edited. Thank you all for your hard work.

I hope you'll join us again in volume 2 and in the upcoming editions, where you'll eventually meet Simi, shown here. She's a great demon companion who loves to shop and listen to really bad music.

Thanks for taking this trip in the Dark-Hunter realm with us.

—Sherrilyn Kenyon
Cabal Kenyon, artist

#1 *New York Times* bestselling author, SHERRILYN KENYON has more than seventeen million copies of her books in print, in over thirty countries. The author of the Dark-Hunter novels and others, she has an international following and her books always appear at the top of the *New York Times*, *Publishers Weekly*, and *USA Today* lists.

 St. Martin's Griffin

CHECK OUT VOLUME 2, COMING SOON

Things are tightening up on Kyrian and Amanda. As they face a new kind of Daimon that appears to be on massive steroids, Kyrian's powers become unsteady. Amanda's powers are moving to the forefront, but she still wants to deny them. If they don't find a way to stabilize and unite their powers soon, more than their lives will be over—ours will be too.

Some days it really sucks to be human... and immortal.

They are Darkness. They are Shadow.
They are the Rulers of the Night.
THEY ARE THE DARK-HUNTERS.®

Don't miss a single title from
the world of the Dark-Hunters!

Fantasy Lover

Night Pleasures

Night Embrace

Dance with the Devil

Kiss of the Night

Night Play

Seize the Night

Sins of the Night

Unleash the Night

Dark Side of the Moon

Devil May Cry

The Dream-Hunter

Upon the Midnight Clear

Dream Chaser

One Silent Night

Acheron

Dream Warrior

St. Martin's Paperbacks

HE IS A LEGEND AMONG LEGENDS...
ACHERON

**THE LEADER OF THE
DARK-HUNTERS®
LIVES ON**

Eleven thousand years ago
a god was born. Cursed
into the body of a human,
Acheron spent a lifetime
of shame. His human
death unleashed an
unspeakable horror that
almost destroyed the earth.
Brought back against his
will, he became the sole
defender of mankind.

For centuries, he has
fought for our survival
and hidden a past he
never wants revealed.
Until a lone woman who
refuses to be intimidated
by him threatens his
very existence.

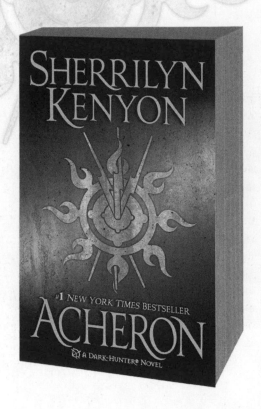

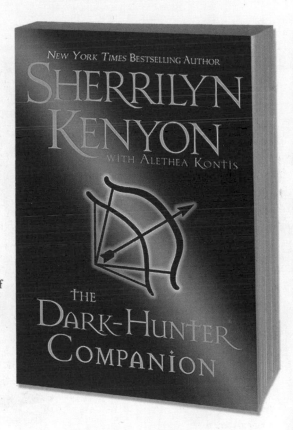

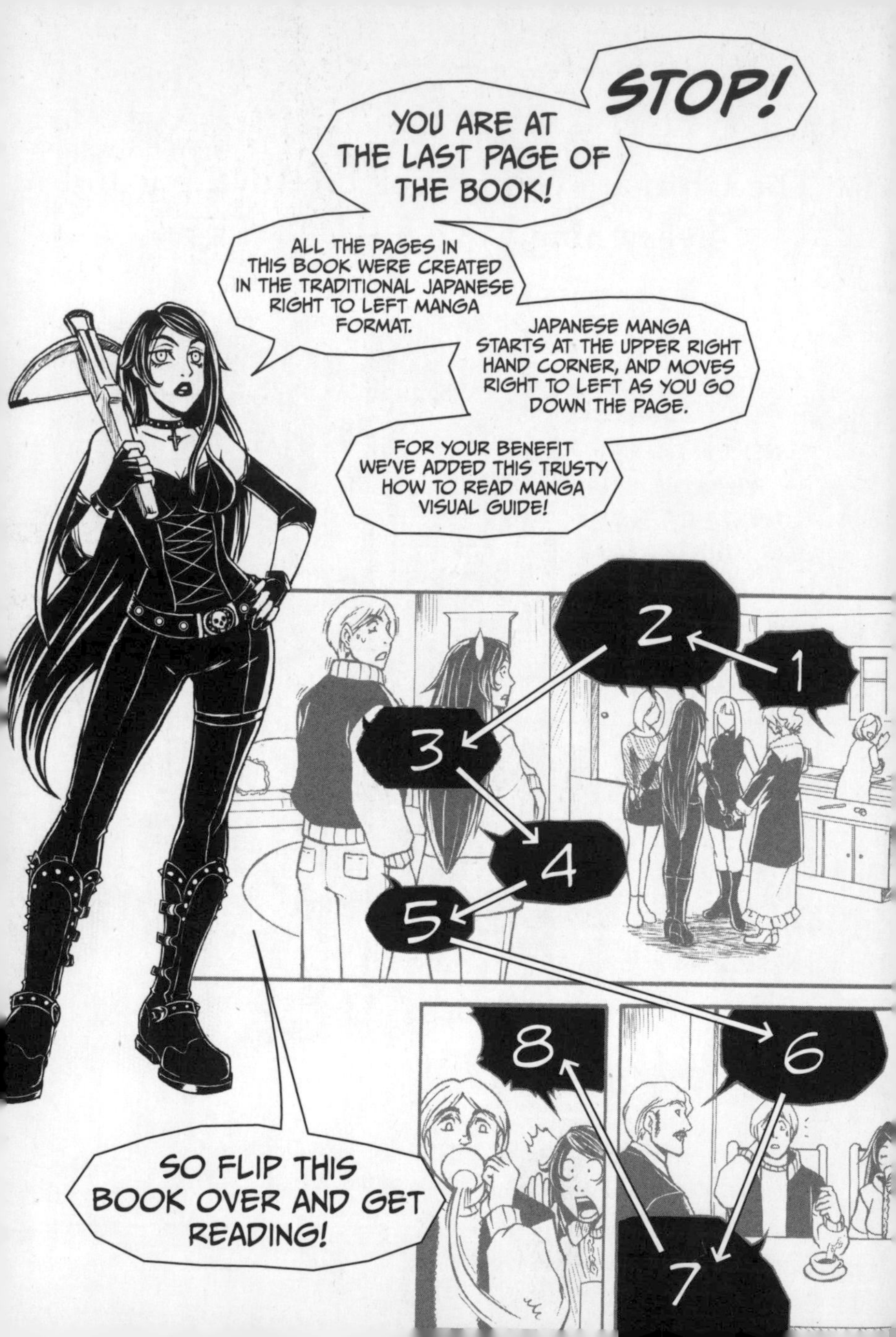
STOP!
YOU ARE AT THE LAST PAGE OF THE BOOK!
ALL THE PAGES IN THIS BOOK WERE CREATED IN THE TRADITIONAL JAPANESE RIGHT TO LEFT MANGA FORMAT.
JAPANESE MANGA STARTS AT THE UPPER RIGHT HAND CORNER, AND MOVES RIGHT TO LEFT AS YOU GO DOWN THE PAGE.
FOR YOUR BENEFIT WE'VE ADDED THIS TRUSTY HOW TO READ MANGA VISUAL GUIDE!
SO FLIP THIS BOOK OVER AND GET READING!
1
2
3
4
5
6
7
8